WHO OWNS ENGLAND?

GUY SHRUBSOLE

WHO OWNS ENGLAND?

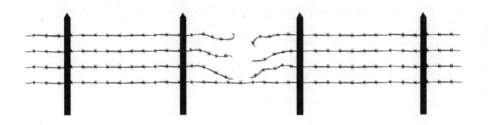

How We Lost
Our Green & Pleasant Land
& How to Take It Back

WILLIAM
COLLINS

William Collins
An imprint of HarperCollins*Publishers*
1 London Bridge Street
London SE1 9GF

WilliamCollinsBooks.com

First published in Great Britain in 2019 by William Collins

1

A catalogue record for this book is available from the British Library

ISBN 978-0-00-832167-3 (hardback)

Typeset in Freight Text by
Palimpsest Book Production Ltd, Falkirk, Stirlingshire

Printed and bound by CPI Group (UK) Ltd, Croydon CRO 4YY

MIX
Paper from
responsible sources
FSC **C007454**

Who possesses this landscape?
The man who bought it or I who am possessed by it?

– Norman MacCaig

CONTENTS

INTRODUCTION

It's often very difficult to find out who owns land in England. Land ownership remains our oldest, darkest, best-kept secret.

There's a reason for that: concealing wealth is part and parcel of preserving it. It's why big estates have high walls, why the law of trespass exists to keep prying commoners like you and me from seeing what the lord of the manor owns – and why the Government's Land Registry, the official record of land ownership in England and Wales, remains a largely closed book. The geographer Doreen Massey once observed that the secrecy surrounding land ownership was 'an indication of its political sensitivity'.

Owning land has unique benefits. The inherent scarcity of land means it's almost always a solid bet for investment. 'Buy land,' quipped Mark Twain, 'they're not making it anymore.' Own some land, particularly in a valuable location, and you're pretty much guaranteed a steady stream of rental income from it – whether by leasing it out for farming, or building flats on it and charging tenants rent.

In fact, a landowner need not do anything to make a profit from their land. 'Land ... is by far the greatest of monopolies,' raged Winston Churchill in a blistering polemic penned in 1909. Consider, wrote Churchill, 'the enrichment which comes to the landlord who happens to own a plot of land on the outskirts or at the centre of one of our great cities'. The landowner need only wait while other people work and pay taxes to make the city grow more prosperous: building businesses, installing roads and railways, paying for schools and hospitals and public amenities. 'All the while,' Churchill growled, 'the land monopolist has only to sit still and watch complacently his property multiplying in value, sometimes manifold, without either effort or contribution on his part; and that is justice!'

And that's why land – and who owns it – lies at the heart of the housing crisis. It's not because bricks and mortar have suddenly become incredibly expensive. It's because the value of the land itself has gone through the roof. According to the Office for National Statistics, the value of land in the UK has increased *fivefold* since 1995. Landowners are laughing all the way to the bank: over half of the UK's wealth is now locked up in land, dwarfing the amounts vested in savings.

Who owns land matters. How landowners use their land has implications for almost everything: where we build our homes, how we grow our food, how much space we leave for nature. After all, we're not just facing a housing crisis. We're also in the throes of an epoch-making environmental crisis, with our land scoured of species and natural habitats after decades of intensive farming. Our unsustainable food system is not only contributing to poor health; it also faces the biggest upheaval in generations thanks to Brexit. And all the while, our society has grown obscenely unequal, with wealth concentrated in the hands of a tiny few – including the ownership of land.

Politicians used to understand this. A century ago, the Liberal Chancellor of the Exchequer, Lloyd George, declared: 'The land enters into everything . . . the food the people eat, the water they drink, the houses they dwell in, the industries upon which their livelihood depends. Yet most of the land is in the hands of the few.' But today hardly any politicians even mention land in their speeches, let alone lift a finger to do anything about it.

Talking about land ownership has been taboo for far too long. Raise it in public debate, and sooner or later you're accused of 'the politics of envy'. But it's not a sign of envy to ask questions about how we might best use and share out our most scarce common resource. It should just be common sense. Questioning why the Duke of Westminster, for example, has come to own so much land isn't meant as an attack on him as a person. As Churchill said of land monopolists: 'It is not the individual I attack, it is the system.'

I first got interested in land because of the fact we're destroying the living world around us. Landowners like to portray themselves as wise stewards of the earth, but all too many of them abuse their property for short-term profit – despoiling habitats and wiping out wildlife in exchange for such things as coal mines, quarries and new roads. Later, after moving to London and paying stupid amounts of rent to land-lords for a roof over my head, I started to see how land isn't simply a rural issue, 'out there' in the countryside, but one that underpins how we all live. Homes have become assets, rather than places to live. Something's gone badly wrong when a country tolerates thousands sleeping rough on our streets every night at the same time as allowing thousands of homes to lie empty. Who owned those empty properties, I wondered. Who owned the vast tracts of countryside from which our birds and insects had been carelessly eliminated? I wanted to find out.

When I started investigating who owns England, however, I was astonished by how difficult it was to answer such a simple question. The pervasive secrecy around land ownership made me suspicious; what was there to hide? Why were large landowners so coy about revealing what they owned, and public authorities so reluctant to make the information available?

As I dug into the issue, I decided to start a blog to share what I found, whoownsengland.org. The response was overwhelming. Almost immediately I was inundated with offers of help – from people offering snippets of information about landowners near where they lived, to data experts offering hours of their spare time to help crunch the numbers. Indeed, this book was only made possible thanks to a growing movement of data journalists, coders and campaigners, determined to set information free and put land back onto the political agenda: I try to pay tribute to many of them in the acknowledgements section.

In particular, early on I started collaborating with the computer programmer and data journalist Anna Powell-Smith, who became the Technical Lead on whoownsengland.org. She's helped unlock the complex Land Registry datasets needed to investigate ownership, built many of the maps on the site, and advised extensively throughout. I'm extremely grateful to Anna for the coding wizardry and deep knowledge of data that she's brought to the project.

This book is about who owns England, how they got it, and what that means for the rest of us. It's part detective story, part history book, and part trespass through England's green and pleasant land. The book's subject, as its title states, is England, rather than Britain or the UK as a whole. Sometimes, in order to tell the story of England's landowning elite, I've strayed into the other nations that make up the UK – for example, to touch upon the huge Highland estates that many English lords have acquired over the centuries. At times, the nature of the available information has also made it hard to disaggregate figures on land ownership by nation: the Land Registry, for instance, covers both England and Wales, and the data it provides remains frustratingly opaque. Wherever possible, however, I've broken down the statistics by country to concentrate on England alone, or else sought to make clear where the numbers refer to other nations too.

But my focus is on England, for three reasons. First, the question of who owns Scotland has already been comprehensively answered by the Scottish land reformer and MSP Andy Wightman, whose books on the subject – and maps at whoownsscotland.org.uk – I thoroughly recommend. Kevin Cahill's *Who Owns Britain*, published in 2001, was another pioneering work that took a broader view, and on which I've sought to build. Second, I've lived most of my life in England, and feel qualified to write about it in a way that I don't about the other nations that make up the UK. Since I started writing my blog, I've been delighted to be contacted by various individuals and groups keen to uncover who owns

Wales and Northern Ireland; I hope their investigations bear fruit. Third, devolution, Scotland's independence movement and Brexit have all thrown into question not only the unity of the UK, but also what it means to be English. Is it possible to construct a progressive English identity that isn't based on xenophobia, nostalgia and grabbing land off Wales, Scotland, Ireland and the rest of the world? I'd argue that it is, but that land reform in England is a central part of doing so.

Uncovering the extraordinary story of how England has come to be owned by so few has, at times, made my blood boil. I hope it does the same for you, too. But I also hope that it inspires you to take action to make things better. In an old, conservative country like England it can often feel like things never change. But the example of successful land reform programmes in other countries, like Scotland, should give us hope – as should our own, forgotten history of land reform movements. Get land reform right, and we can go a long way towards ending the housing crisis, restoring nature and making our society more equal.

When discussing the size of estates, I've opted throughout to use acres as the unit of measurement. That might seem old-fashioned – why not talk of hectares? – but the reason is simply one of convenience. The UK as a whole is some 60 million acres, so if it were shared out equally among the current population, we'd have almost an acre each. To help visualise what that means, it's worth bearing in mind that Parliament Square covers roughly an acre.

'It is far easier to cling to privileges if few are privy to their extent,' wrote the land rights campaigner Marion Shoard, in a book published not long after I was born. Three decades on, most people remain unaware of quite how much land is owned by so few. Enough is enough. It's time to draw back the curtain, and uncover who owns England.

1

THIS LAND IS NOT MY LAND

Nearly half the county I grew up in is owned by just thirty landowners.

I was raised in Newbury in West Berkshire, a leafy part of the Home Counties. I always knew it was a well-off area; but only later in life did I discover just how much some of its inhabitants owned. Sixty-six thousand people – 40 per cent of the county's population – live in settlements that cover a mere 2.4 per cent of the land. Yet 44 per cent of the county is owned by just thirty individuals and organisations. And the ways in which those landowners have chosen to use their land have impacted profoundly on the lives of everyone else living nearby. To appreciate what that means, let me take you on a tour of the place I called home.

I spent much of my childhood outdoors, exploring. My parents were teachers at the local comprehensive, and I was lucky enough to grow up in a detached house with a big garden – one that was wild and rambling, full of trees and brambles and corners to hide in. Like Calvin in the comic strip *Calvin and Hobbes*, whose imagination often gets the better of him, I'd often find myself imagining my treehouse to be a fortress and that our backyard was an entire country.

The earth in our garden also seemed to have magical properties. It was both a source of new life, alive with green shoots and shiny beetles, and a window onto the distant past. Once, I found a medieval silver penny in our vegetable patch, glistening in the dark soil. Something about that childhood experience of being close to the earth, of having a patch of ground to which I feel a sense of belonging, has stayed with me all my life.

I was ten years old when they decided to drive a bypass through nine miles of countryside to the west of Newbury. In the late 1980s, Margaret Thatcher had spoken of her admiration for the 'great car economy' and boasted of delivering 'the largest road-building programme since the Romans'. In pursuit of this goal, the government gouged a motorway cutting through the ancient chalk downland of Twyford Down, and bull-dozed hundreds of homes in East London for the M11 link road. Now the woods and water-meadows of West Berkshire were in the road lobby's sights. To shave a few minutes off motorists' journeys, it was deemed necessary to put a bypass through four Sites of Special Scientific Interest.

The government had reckoned without a huge outpouring of oppo-sition from local residents and activists from across the country, who flocked to Newbury and staged one of the largest environmental protests ever seen in the UK. My parents took me on the 8,000-strong march organised by Friends of the Earth along the route of the proposed bypass, snaking past beautiful heathland and through a civil war battlefield. I remember looking longingly at the protesters' tree-houses perched high in the great oaks that were destined to be felled, and pleading with Dad to let me go and join them. 'Maybe when you're older,' he'd said.

Jim Hindle, one of the protesters who *was* old enough at the time to go and climb trees, later recounted: 'The land to be lost to the road was meant to be compensated by the gift of other land elsewhere. But once it was gone, that was that.' A new plantation would take years to grow and could never make up for the loss of ancient woodland, or the history that the road would obliterate. Where Hindle camped, 'the rest of the Snelsmore reserve backed away over the Lambourn Downs in a primor-dial soup of ferns and birches and moss. It seemed like another country, stretching away further than we could rightfully imagine; half wild and ancient and vast.'

Perhaps the potential to halt the road lay in gaining control over the land. A previous plan to put a motorway through Otmoor in Oxfordshire had been thwarted by the cunning of local Friends of the Earth members. They had bought a field along the route of the road called 'Alice's Meadow' – a reference to *Alice in Wonderland*, whose author Lewis Carroll had been inspired by the landscape of Otmoor. Dividing the field into 3,500 separate parcels, they had sold each one to a different person. This made compulsory purchase by the authorities virtually impossible, since they would have had to do deals with every single one of the landowners. Instead, an alternative route for the road was chosen, and Otmoor was saved.

Could opponents of the Newbury bypass count on the support of local landowners in halting the scheme? A young environmentalist, George Monbiot, initially hoped so. A huge swathe of land in the path of the bypass lay in the ownership of Sir Richard Sutton, a wealthy baronet who claims a lineage dating back to the Norman conquest. As Monbiot later recounted, 'The Sutton Estate, just to the west of Newbury, covers some of the most exalted watermeadows in southern England. In 1983, when I was waterkeeper there, the manager told me not to cut too much of the bankside vegetation. The estate was the guardian of the countryside. As such it had a duty to preserve its ancestral character.'

Hoping that this sense of *noblesse oblige* would make Sir Richard an ally against the bypass, Monbiot approached him to make common cause. But then the estate manager published his plans. 'Claiming that he was powerless to stop the road, he requested that he be allowed to supply the hardcore: he would dig out a further 100 acres of the meadows for gravel. Beside the road, he proposed building 1,600 houses, a hotel and an 18-hole golf course. As the new bypass was likely to fill up within a few years, he suggested that a second road should also pass through the estate.'

Other landowners along the route of the road were similarly craven. The Earl of Carnarvon, owner of Highclere Castle to the south of Newbury – made famous as the setting of the series *Downton Abbey* – told conservationist Charles Clover that 'he had been behind a bypass for the past 40 years', but admitted that he 'did not know how much his son, Lord Porchester, had received for the sale of the site of a service station on the proposed new bypass.' To Clover, 'the saga of the Newbury bypass is about more than a road . . . It raises questions about whether we place sufficient value on our country's human and natural history.' The threat of a road, he felt, 'has the ability to bring out a love of land in the strangest people.' Just not, it seemed, in the people who actually owned the land.

The defence of the trees fell instead to a rag-tag army of courageous commoners, many of whom travelled from far and wide. Their tactics delayed the road for months, costing millions; police ended up making over 1,000 arrests. 'Why don't they save their dole money, go to South America and save the rainforests?' sneered one local businessman in a letter to the local paper – a copy of which I pasted into my school project on the bypass, as an example of the calibre of the debate. I remember my mum shedding tears when we went to see the scene of destruction left by the bulldozers, saying it reminded her of images of deforestation in the Amazon. Ten thousand trees were felled along its route. My tree-climbing being strictly limited to trees in our garden, I did what I could. I saved a pine-cone from a tree destined for the chop and grew it into our family Christmas tree.

The unseen influence of other landowning interests may also have been at play in helping determine the route of the road. When the Highways Agency and their private contractor Costain came to my school to tell us what a great job they were making of the bypass, I remember putting my hand up to ask a question. 'Why are you building the bypass through all the nature reserves on one side of Newbury,' I asked, 'when you could just build it through the racecourse on the other side of town?'

I didn't know it at the time, but questioning the sanctity of horse racing in West Berkshire is a bit like doubting the existence of God in the Vatican. Breeding horses is big money here. Newbury Racecourse is one of the country's largest horse-racing tracks, and Lambourn, a village to the north of Newbury, is second only to Newmarket for its stud farms. When I was growing up, classmates at school would joke about folks who lived in Lambourn being inbred. They stopped taking the piss when they got to sixth form and started partying: it was some of the Lambourn stable hands with their ready access to horse tranquillisers who could supply the ketamine.

Venturing out into horsey territory for Sunday walks, it was always obvious how rich the area was. Colonnaded mansions with sweeping driveways sat among rows of stables and well-manicured paddocks. What I didn't know at the time was that most of the racing studs and surrounding fields were owned offshore, in tax havens, and that many of them also receive generous taxpayer-funded farm subsidies. One, Earl's Court Farm Ltd, with an estate of 2,600 acres and an address in Bermuda, was handed £304,300 in 2015. The vast majority of this was as a Single Area Payment, a subsidy calculated on the basis of how much land you own, with few additional strings attached. But when I tried to find who was the ultimate beneficiary of such public largesse, it proved impossible to do so. Combing through a welter of offshore shell companies, the only records I could find indicated that the parent companies were called the Millennium Trust and the Racine Trust – two mysterious organisations with no apparent internet presence, and no named directors or owners.

'Horseyculture' takes up a lot of land in West Berkshire, but it's as nothing compared to agriculture. Seventy per cent of England is given over to farming, and the rolling downland and river valley of the Kennet is a patchwork of pasture and crops. When we think of pressures on the English countryside, we tend to think of encroaching towns and fields being buried under concrete. But it's industrialised farming practices that pose by far the biggest threat to England's green and pleasant land. On this, landowners can have considerable sway, and sometimes for the better.

For years, the multinational pesticides manufacturer Bayer had its UK headquarters in Newbury. The weedkillers and insect sprays it manufactured were sent out into the surrounding countryside, where farmers and landowners doused their crops with them, year after year. Only now are we starting to wake up to the catastrophic effect this chemical inundation has had on ecosystems. One recent study from Germany reports the disappearance of three-quarters of all flying insects over the past twenty-seven years. Another study from France has shown that bird populations have fallen by a third in the past decade and a half. 'There are hardly any insects left, that's the number one problem,' observes one scientist. The UK has seen a 56 per cent decline in farm birds since 1970, with industrialised farming and agrichemicals the key culprits. Neonicotinoid pesticides, in particular, have been shown to pose a major risk not just to insect 'pests' but to many other pollinating insects, including honeybees. Bayer, alongside other pesticide manufacturers, has been making them since the 1980s.

My parents used to keep bees in woodland belonging to the Sutton Estate. I still vividly remember extracting the honey from the big wooden Langstroth hives in our kitchen, spinning the wax-coated frames around in a big barrel, while chewing greedily on pieces of sweet honeycomb. But though we could make sure our bee colony had a good supply of food through the winter, and kept a watchful eye out for any signs of the bee-harming Varroa mite appearing in the hives, there was little we could do to stop surrounding landowners from spraying pesticides on their crops.

At least one landowner in the county, however, decided to treat their land differently. Sheepdrove is an 1,800-acre organic farm, lying to the north of Lambourn's horse-racing studs, owned since 1972 by Peter and Juliet Kindersley. 'Our original aim was to protect ourselves from the polluting chemicals used by farmers all around us and recreate the original downland landscape that we fell in love with so many years ago,' they write. 'We have witnessed the miraculous generosity of nature as the countryside around us has come back to life and, with the return of myriad birds, wild flowers, small mammals, reptiles and insect life, land which was turning into an arid prairie has been transformed to a rich tapestry of wildlife.'

But not all landowners have shared the Kindersleys' philosophy. It's taken much campaigning by environmental groups to eventually achieve an EU-wide ban on bee-harming neonicotinoid pesticides, in the face of considerable opposition from the National Farmers' Union and other landowners' groups.

The impending mass extinction of species poses a profound threat to the survival of human civilisation. A generation ago, a very different threat loomed over Britain: the spectre of nuclear annihilation. Here, too, the decisions of a large landowner in my home county were to have far-reaching repercussions.

West Berkshire's recent history is deeply entwined with both the nuclear establishment and anti-nuclear protests. Since the 1950s, the village of Aldermaston has been central to Britain's nuclear weapons programme, and became the target of the first CND marches towards the end of that decade. Another part of the Atomic Weapons Establishment is based at Burghfield, just down the road. But it was one military site in West Berkshire, above all others, that came to embody the terrifying logic of the Cold War, the struggle against nuclear weapons, and the battle over the land on which they were stationed: Greenham Common.

Comprising nearly a thousand acres of woods and open heathland, Greenham Common had been used as a military training ground for centuries, but was only enclosed when it was requisitioned for an air-field during The Second World War. When I visited Greenham in the spring of 2018, the remains of its huge runway could still be discerned amid the spreading sphagnum mosses and prickly gorse bushes that have now colonised it. It was leased by the Air Ministry, a predecessor department to the Ministry of Defence (MOD), to the US Air Force in 1968. Then in 1980, with Cold War tensions reaching a new peak, Margaret Thatcher agreed to station ninety-six US nuclear Cruise missiles at Greenham Common, making my hometown nuclear strike target number one.

The move represented a significant escalation in tactics by the hawkish new US President Ronald Reagan, who had reversed years of *détente* with the Soviet Union and begun calling it the 'Evil Empire'. Many felt that the MOD – and the British state overall – had sold out British interests for American ones. 'The sign at the gate maintained the pretence of RAF ownership, hence British control,' notes historian George McKay. But 'there is no obligation for the US Government to obtain Britain's consent before firing missiles from Greenham Common.' Instead of feeling safer under the US 'nuclear umbrella', the UK was now in the firing line, more than ever before. The investigative journalist Duncan Campbell, who revealed many of the Government's clandestine plans for nuclear war, noted at the time: 'Cruise missiles may soon be sited at Greenham Common and Molesworth, also US main bases. The Soviet Union would wish to destroy all these bases with considerable speed.' Years later, when I met Campbell in person to interview him, I told him I had grown up in Newbury. 'Oh dear,' he said, shaking his head sadly. 'Yes, that would have gone quickly.'

To local residents who had moved to this leafy Home Counties fastness for peace and quiet, the spectre of nuclear war now loomed terrifyingly large. Greenham Common quickly became a magnet for anti-nuclear protest. In 1981, a group of anti-nuclear protesters called Women for Life on Earth decided to march from Cardiff to Greenham to protest the lunacy of nuclear weapons. Upon their arrival at the base, four of them chained themselves to the fence, while a fifth, Karen Cutler, created a diversion. The lone policeman on guard 'mistook her and the other protestors – as if playing his part in an unsubtle feminist satire – for the base's cleaners.'

Ann Pettit, another of the marchers, was awestruck by the potential for a protest camp at Greenham Common. 'I thought, "My God, it's the Forest of Arden",' she recalled later, referring to the magical woodland in Shakespeare's *As You Like It* where social rules are broken and norms challenged: 'Somewhere to take to the woods and uphold better values than the corrupt court values.'

Historian Andy Beckett argues that Greenham Common 'was one of the best places imaginable to stage a confrontation with the overmighty, transatlantic power structures that had grown up around British-based nuclear weapons. A great sweeping tabletop of gorse heath and grass-land, fringed with deep-green stands of birch and bracken, in 1981 it was one of the few charismatic landscapes left in an increasingly suburban-ized southeast England.'

The MOD and US Air Force had now militarised this landscape, sealing it off from the outside world with miles of fencing and barbed wire. But Greenham's enclosure fence was soon to become synonymous with civil disobedience. On 12 December 1982, in an action called 'Embrace the Base', 30,000 women, including my mum, encircled Greenham Common's perimeter. Others adopted spikier tactics, cutting through the fence with bolt croppers in order to exercise what they argued was their right to walk on common land. A court later found the protesters to be in the right: since Greenham was indeed a common, they couldn't be stopped from walking on it – but damaging the fence in order to actually get in was still a criminal offence. Even so, the MOD opted to introduce new by-laws covering Greenham to ensure future trespassers could be sentenced harshly.

The Greenham Women's Peace Camp maintained a permanent pres-ence at the base for nearly two decades, becoming a rallying point for both anti-nuclear and feminist campaigners. Eventually, with the sudden end of the Cold War, the Cruise missiles left Greenham, and the MOD deemed the site 'surplus to requirements'. It was sold to the local council and a charitable trust, who decided to finally open up the common again. The perimeter fence was torn down, grazing cattle returned, and common access rights restored. Greenham airbase's huge runways were broken up, although this symbolic triumph also had a downside: most of the concrete was used to help build the Newbury bypass.

Only the colossal earthen bunkers that had housed the Cruise missiles remain standing today. On my visit to Greenham Common one spring evening, I stared across the heath at the brooding bulk of the missile siloes. Their silhouettes resembled a cross between aircraft hangars and Bronze

Age burial mounds. But whereas the tumuli that dot Berkshire's chalk downlands were built to remember the dead as they passed into the afterlife, these structures seemed to me to be far more nihilistic: monuments to Mutually Assured Destruction. Up close, the silos appeared even more malevolent. Still shrouded by three lines of fencing, some of it topped by razor wire, they squatted: ziggurats of grassed-over concrete with thick bulkhead doors, defended by menacing MOD signs. THIS IS A PROHIBITED PLACE WITHIN THE MEANING OF THE OFFICIAL SECRETS ACT, read one. UNAUTHORISED PERSONS ENTERING THIS AREA MAY BE ARRESTED AND PROSECUTED.

I patrolled the perimeter of the bunkers, thinking about the peace protesters who'd performed a Situationist rite during the Vietnam War to levitate the Pentagon. Here and there, I was gratified to see, were signs of where the Greenham Women had graffitied slogans onto the concrete fenceposts and cut holes in the fencing. To my disappointment, all of them had been repaired, making easy access to the site impossible. But nature is now slowly doing the job once performed by the protesters. In one place, a silver birch had grown through and around the fence, and was tearing it apart.

It's not just the military who enclose common land and public space, of course. In West Berkshire, as elsewhere across the country, the main culprits are big private landowners. I saw this plainly when I decided to return to the county for a few days' hiking one winter. The Berkshire countryside, beautiful though it is, is also stuffed full of PRIVATE – KEEP OUT signs, letting errant commoners know that the real owners of the landscape would rather you weren't in it.

In some places, the influence of big estates permeates entire villages: a reminder that for a sizeable slice of rural England, feudalism has never died. That much seemed obvious when one freezing December afternoon I walked into the tiny village of Yattendon, on the edge of the Yattendon Estate. Acquired by the media mogul Baron Iliffe in the 1920s, the 8,295-acre estate has reshaped the area's countryside with its vast conifer plantations. It sells 80,000 Christmas trees each festive season.

As I skirted around iced puddles, I noticed something odd about the village. Everything looked the same. All the doors, gates and windowsills in Yattendon were painted in the estate's official dark green, as uniform as the serried ranks of saplings planted in the surrounding fields. Even the telephone box – that staple of quaint old English villages, maintained for tourist selfies long after the landline has been ripped out by vandals – was Yattendon green, rather than the traditional red. The village's noticeboard, proudly displaying a plaque for the award of Best Kept Village of the Year 1974, presented neatly typed minutes from the latest parish council meeting. Out of the grand total of five attendees, they recorded, one had been a representative of the Yattendon Estate. It was hard to shake the sense that, behind the scenes, order was being maintained by some decorous yet shadowy patrician operating out of the Big House on the hill, like something out of the movie *Hot Fuzz*. `

But it isn't merely the colour scheme of villages that landowners have sway over. They also control access to large swathes of the countryside. A 'Right to Roam' was established by the Countryside and Rights of Way Act in the year 2000, but open-access land still only makes up around 10 per cent of England and Wales – a far cry from the situation in Scotland, where the right to roam is now established as the default – and much of that is mountain and moorland. Down south, the countryside is far less open to ramblers. 'Less than 1.5 percent of West Berkshire, for example, is covered, and many of its glorious woodlands remain inaccessible to the large population of London and the Thames valley,' notes Marion Shoard, whose tireless campaigning helped bring about Right to Roam. These tiny scraps of accessible woods include Snelsmore Common and Pen Wood – both of which were cut through by the Newbury bypass – and parts of Greenham Common, which had been closed off to the public for decades because of the airbase. So even these fragments of open-access land have been shut off or defiled by some of the county's major landowners.

The efforts of large landowners to keep people off their estates have, however, proved their undoing when it comes to uncovering what they own.

I was inspired to try to map who owned my home county by the work of John McEwen, who pioneered studies of Scottish land ownership in the 1970s. McEwen set out to find who owned his native Perthshire, but it ended up taking him four years to map just the one county. Fortunately, I discovered a shortcut, and it was all thanks to the territorial behaviour of the landowners themselves.

Under an obscure clause, Section 31(6), of the otherwise extremely boring Highways Act 1980, landowners can prevent new public rights of way from being established across their land by lodging a statement with the local authority. The deposited statements usually last for twenty years, meaning that any public use of the land during this period will not then count towards determining new rights of way. But to protect their interests in this fashion, landowners also have to submit a map delineating the boundaries of their estates. This is then usually published by the council online, or is accessible under the Freedom of Information Act. Possessive landowners are thus hoist by their own petard.

It was this documentation that I was able to draw upon to discover who owns my home county. West Berkshire Council, it turned out, had a remarkably complete set of landowner deposits. I requested they send me their maps in a digital format, to make analysis easier. Combining these with information from a number of other sources, the jigsaw began to fit together. The results astonished me: it was now that I discovered that almost half the county was owned by just thirty landowners.

Their identities offer a telling insight into the landowning elite of modern England. Baronial estates owned by the same aristocratic families for centuries sit next to stately piles snapped up by newly moneyed businessmen (and it *is* nearly always men), organic farms, and horse-racing studs registered in the Cayman Islands. The aforementioned newspaper magnate Baron Iliffe and property mogul Sir Richard Sutton jostle for landowning supremacy with H&M chairman Stefan Persson, Formula One racing legend Frank Williams, and three scions of the wealthy Astor family.

But the single biggest landowner in West Berkshire is Richard Benyon MP. Benyon is the inheritor of the 12,000-acre Englefield Estate; the palatial, turreted Englefield House has belonged to his family since the eighteenth century.

Today, Benyon is the richest MP in Parliament, with an estimated fortune of £110 million. One tranche of this comes from the East India Company; another stems from property, through the development of De Beauvoir Town in the London Borough of Hackney in the nineteenth century. Richard Benyon still owns De Beauvoir today, via the Englefield Estate Trust Corporation, with the Berkshire connection commemorated in the name of Englefield Road. In 2014, his company courted controversy when it took a minority stake in a consortium that bought the New Era housing estate in Hoxton. The consortium threatened to hike rents on the estate, leading Hackney Council to warn of 'enforced homelessness' for nearly half of the ninety-three households living there. When the community rallied in protest, and were joined by comedian-turned-activist Russell Brand, Benyon's firm was forced to back down and sell its stake.

A third income stream flows from farming. In 2017, Benyon's Berkshire estate pocketed £278,180 in farm subsidies, courtesy of the taxpayer. It was through enclosure that the Englefield Estate grew to be so large, and so wealthy. To this day, a large expanse of woodland at Englefield is called Benyon's Inclosure, denoting a former common enclosed by the MP's ancestor.

His deer park was created two hundred years ago by literally moving a village to make way for it. The long flint wall that surrounds Englefield today signals a dark history: people's homes had been demolished to make way for this private pleasure-ground. As the poet Oliver Goldsmith wrote in 1770, in protest at widespread enclosure:

> *Ill fares the land, to hastening ills a prey,*
> *Where wealth accumulates, and men decay.*

But more important than Benyon's sheer wealth is the example he provides of the continuing political influence of landowners. Elected to Parliament in 2005, his political pedigree is impeccable: his father was Conservative MP for Buckingham and Milton Keynes, and his great-great-grandfather was the Conservative Prime Minister Robert Cecil, the 3rd Marquess of Salisbury. The estate's paint scheme, perhaps by coincidence, is of deepest blue. In 2012, shortly after Benyon became a junior environment minister in David Cameron's government, the gravel-quarrying company operating on his estate applied to extend its operations into Benyon's Inclosure. Under the plans, the quarry would expand to cover 217 acres, extracting 200,000 tonnes of sand and gravel annually.

The existing quarry had already wrecked a patch of land called Burnt Common. I visited it one summer: the common looked like the surface of the moon, pockmarked with pits that had filled with water. Despite Burnt Common being marked as open-access land on Ordnance Survey maps, a barbed-wire fence had been erected around it, with signs reading DANGER – DEEP WATER – KEEP OUT.

The local Wildlife Trust protested that the new gravel-extraction plans would lead to the felling of trees, the destruction of ancient woodland and the permanent loss of heathland. As the minister then responsible for wildlife and biodiversity, you might have thought Benyon would have abandoned such plans out of sheer embarrassment. But he pressed on.

This wasn't the only time Benyon's landed interests appeared to clash with his ministerial jurisdiction. The MP also owns an 8,000-acre grouse moor in Scotland, and runs a pheasant shoot at Englefield. Coincidentally or not, as wildlife minister he refused to make it a criminal offence to possess the poison carbofuran, which is used by some gamekeepers to kill birds of prey when they are suspected of predating on game birds.

A second incident during Benyon's ministerial tenure compounded the suspicions of his detractors. Walshaw Moor, a large grouse-shooting estate near Hebden Bridge owned by wealthy businessman Richard

Bannister, was in the process of being prosecuted by the regulator Natural England for damaging protected blanket bog habitat, after its grouse moor management regime had intensified. Then, suddenly and mysteriously, the case was dropped. No explanation was ever offered by Natural England or DEFRA as to why they had abandoned legal proceedings, and Benyon refused to give a straight answer when questioned. Was this another instance of the landed classes coming to a gentleman's agreement behind closed doors?

Even if Benyon had recused himself from such ministerial decisions, what does it say about prospects for meritocracy and democracy in England today when constituencies can still end up being represented by the local lords of the manor? Benyon may stand out for the sheer scale of his estates, but he isn't the only sitting MP to be drawn from the ranks of the landed gentry.

Geoffrey Clifton-Brown MP, for example, owns the East Beckham Estate in Norfolk, for which his estate company received £102,566 in farm subsidies in 2017. Sir Henry Bellingham MP owns land in his seat near the Queen's estate at Sandringham. And the MP for South Dorset is Richard Drax – or Richard Grosvenor Plunkett-Ernle-Erle-Drax, to give him his full quadruple-barrelled surname – owner of 7,000 acres of his constituency, bounded by the longest wall in England. Many MPs nowadays, too, are landlords with rental property portfolios, as the parliamentary register of interests attests.

Nor is the level of land ownership concentration in my home county an anomaly. England as a whole belongs to a tiny number of people and organisations. Just 36,000 landowners – a mere 0.06 per cent of the population – own half of the rural land of England and Wales, according to the Country Land & Business Association, who represent the land lobby in Westminster. That's an extraordinary concentration of land in the hands of so few.

That concentration of ownership is visible in the landscape itself. Once you start looking for them, it becomes possible to discern patterns of land ownership, like invisible ley lines stretching out over the countryside. A hedgerow is no longer simply a tangle of hawthorn to keep out livestock, but a territorial boundary. A set of gateposts, previously remarkable only for the carved eagles perching atop them, takes on a new significance as a display of might: *get off my land.*

To see the world through the lens of land ownership is to survey a landscape of power. Many of England's largest landowners have acquired their land through inheritance; an inheritance that has often been built on the back of conquest and enclosure. And landowners possess great power over how their land is used, for good or ill.

Ill fares the land, indeed. While our last wild habitats face collapse, many landowners continue to turn their land into chemical deserts or flog it off for development, traditional concepts of stewardship seemingly crushed by the lure of pound signs. In our cities, urban space is treated by landowners as an investment opportunity, with homes transformed into assets rather than being places to live in. Urban land is too often wasted, with properties left empty and vacant sites kept as land banks, as owners wait for their value to climb still higher before cashing them in. Shadowy offshore firms swallow taxpayers' money to run horse-racing studs, and lords of the manor are elected to Parliament. Worst of all, the vast majority of people living in England today remain as landless as they have always been. I belong to England; I love its countryside and history. But does any of it really belong to me?

Ramblers and environmental activists, when they gather together around campfires, often sing the songs of the American folk musician Woody Guthrie. They console themselves with the heartwarming lyrics of his most famous piece, a paean to nationhood, land and belonging.

This land is my land, this land is your land . . .

But it isn't true. This land does *not* belong to you or me.

2

ENGLAND'S DARKEST SECRET

There's a huge reluctance to discuss who owns land in England. It's seen as impolite, an expression of the politics of envy. Some of this is a hangover from an earlier era of deference, when the right of the local lord of the manor to his thousands of acres was as unquestioned as his hereditary seat in Parliament.

But there are also deeper ideologies at work. There's a peculiarly English reluctance to debate land ownership, some of which has its roots in the work of the seventeenth-century moral philosopher John Locke. Locke argued that there was a natural right to the exclusive ownership of land, which permitted people to own land as private property just like any other possession. He admitted that 'the earth . . . be common to all men', but argued that any person who cultivated land 'hath mixed his labour with, and joined to it something that is his own, and thereby makes it his property'. Owning land, in Locke's view, was just like a carpenter owning a chair he had made by hand.

Locke's arguments lent a moral respectability to the actions of large landowners through the centuries, shutting down the space for debate. There was just one proviso: taking private ownership of land was only morally justified 'where there is enough, and as good, left in common for others'. That seemed to be true in Locke's day, when the world appeared vast and its population small. But it also provided a convenient excuse for the English gentry to carry on enclosing commoners' land in the name of agricultural improvement, and for the early English colonists in the New World to seize 'wasteland' from Native American peoples. Locke ignored common forms of land ownership, the inherent scarcity of land on a finite planet, and how taking private possession of it becomes a zero-sum game.

Over the past century and a half, Locke's detractors have grown in number, reopening conversations about land. 'Land differs from all other forms of property,' argued Winston Churchill in 1909, at the height of the Liberal Party's push for land reform. 'Land, which is a necessity of human existence, which is the original source of all wealth, which is strictly limited in extent, which is fixed in geographical position – land, I say, differs from all other forms of property in these primary and fundamental conditions.' Churchill was clearly right about this, and it's a view that is once more gaining traction. But it's taken a long time for such ideas to obtain a hearing, and for land ownership to become a permissible topic of debate.

Who owns England has also been literally hidden from plain sight. Large landowners have built high walls around their estates, to keep out prying eyes. The English countryside still bristles with a profusion of KEEP OUT, PRIVATE PROPERTY signs. Rich businesspeople and celebrities live in gated communities protected by private security. For many decades during the Cold War, some Ministry of Defence sites were literally erased from maps.

No one doubts the right to privacy in one's own home, nor the need for security around military bases. But England's laws to protect private landed property go far beyond simply defending the old notion that 'an Englishman's home is his castle'. For many Englishmen whose homes are *actually* castles, their rights also extend far beyond their moats into hundreds of acres of parkland, woods and fields.

The civil offence of trespass means that anyone setting foot on land where no public right of way exists without the consent of the landowner is a trespasser, and can be prosecuted. While access to the countryside has been opened up considerably in recent years, the extension of Right to Roam remains unfinished business, and is a continual reminder that the English remain unwelcome in most of their countryside. And if you can't see it, you're less likely to ask questions about who owns it.

Parallel developments in the 1990s also showed lawmakers to be over-whelmingly on the side of the landowners when it came to dealing with people protesting about land issues. The 1994 Criminal Justice Act created a new, criminal offence – invented by the Major government to squash roads protesters and hunt saboteurs – of 'aggravated trespass', for cases where trespassers were deemed to be impeding the landowner from undertaking lawful activities. This, coupled with the more recent criminalisation of squatting, has closed down the space for taking direct action against unjust and unsustainable uses of land.

Land has also been airbrushed from modern economic theory. All the classical economists – Adam Smith, Karl Marx, David Ricardo, John Stuart Mill – recognised land as a key factor of production, sitting along-side capital and labour as inputs to the economy. Land was different from capital and labour, however, in being of fixed supply, and in having no production costs: nature provided it for free. But neoclassical econ-omists removed land as a separate factor of production, conflating it with capital. Land, despite being finite and thus a constraint upon economic activities, was no longer treated as such.

But most tellingly of all, public discussion of land ownership has been hampered and stymied for centuries by the near-impossibility of obtaining proper information on it. Accurate facts, figures and maps detailing the ownership of land in England are very hard to come by.

Charges of conspiracy are flung about wearyingly often in modern politics. But the long-term concealment of who owns England appears to me to be one of the clearest cases of a cover-up in English history. To understand its depths, we have to go back a thousand years, to Domesday.

The Domesday Book was the first comprehensive survey by any European monarchy of the owners and occupiers of land in their domain. It was, to put it bluntly, a swag list assembled by an acquisitive king. William the Conqueror commissioned Domesday in 1085, nineteen years after his conquest of England, in order to better understand who owned what, so he could tax them more in future. The anonymous scribe behind the *Anglo-Saxon Chronicle* recounts that King William 'sent he his men over all England into each shire; commissioning them to find out . . . what, or how much, each man had, who was an occupier of land in England, either in land or in stock, and how much money it were worth'.

The significance of the Domesday survey is twofold. First, it was the first official state record of who owned England; and second, nothing like it was carried out again for another eight hundred years.

For eight centuries, Crown, Church and aristocracy hid their land-holdings away, fenced off and out of public view. The Domesday Book was preserved and referred to, but mostly as a means for the Crown to extract taxes and settle disputes over legal title to land. There was little sense of it being a public record that might aid demands for wealth redistribution. Occasionally, it was used to try to turn the tables. In 1377, a 'Great Rumour' began spreading among peasants that Domesday Book granted them ancient rights to land that exempted them from feudal duties. The resulting protests, though short-lived, were a precursor to the Peasants' Revolt of 1381. A similar moment of revolutionary possi-bility appeared in the aftermath of the English Civil War. Parliament, freshly victorious, carried out a survey of Crown lands belonging to the recently executed Charles I in order to auction them off. But more radical demands to redistribute land and give every man the vote were brutally quashed by Cromwell.

Yet in the past two hundred years, as England has become an indus-trial democracy, its governments have chosen to survey land ownership on multiple occasions, only to swiftly suppress knowledge of these activ-ities. The past two centuries have seen four 'modern Domesdays' carried out by the authorities: the Tithe Maps of the 1830s; the 1873 Return of Owners of Land; the 1910–15 Valuation Maps; and the 1941 National Farm Survey. In each case these investigations faced huge opposition, were hushed up swiftly after they were carried out, and today have been almost entirely forgotten.

The first of these modern Domesdays occurred in the context of the upheaval generated by the French Revolution, which had caused the boulevards of Paris to run red with the blood of guillotined aristocrats and seen revolutionary Jacobins seize their lands. Napoleon ended the bloodshed but imposed new land taxes to finance wars abroad, levied with the help of a new system of land ownership maps called *cadastres*. These recorded not just the contours of hills and locations of buildings, but also the boundaries of estates – and who owned them. In turn, the Napoleonic Wars prompted the British state to grow, modernise and extend its powers. The British government began counting its population with the first decadal Census, and started to map its territories accurately with the creation of the Ordnance Survey, so that it could better defend them. But in order to impose cadastral maps and land taxes, the authorities would inevitably run into opposition from landowning interests.

In England, it was in fact the Church, rather than the state, that first attempted a system of cadastral maps. The Church was modernising too, through the monetisation of tithe payments. For centuries it had been customary for farmers and landowners to pay to the Church one-tenth of their produce, levied in kind. This continued, despite the Reformation, until modern times. Then in 1836, the Tithe Commutation Act allowed tithes to be paid in cash rather than in goods. As part of the process of commutation, tithe maps were to be drawn up, to show who owned a parcel of land and how much they owed in tithes.

Into this process stepped Lieutenant Robert Dawson, a mapmaker with utopian dreams. Dawson was a cartographer who had been seconded to the Tithe Commission from the Royal Engineers. He knew that for the purposes of collecting tithes, fully accurate maps of land ownership weren't strictly necessary. But Dawson saw this as an opportunity to push a much larger, more ambitious project – a detailed cadastral survey of the entire country.

The Tithe Commission was at first enthusiastic, and backed Dawson's proposals. They implored the government to help fund the accurate mapping of landowners, writing to the Chancellor of the Exchequer, who appointed a select committee of MPs to examine the matter. But while the committee was hearing evidence, 'groups of landowners petitioned the House of Commons requesting that the tithe commissioners' proposals for large-scale maps be defeated'. The English aristocracy feared that a full survey of land ownership might pave the way for new land taxes, as Napoleon's cadastral surveys had on the Continent, or – worse – lead to social upheaval and even revolution. The committee concurred, and 'an opportunity for a cadastral survey of the full kingdom was lost'. Many tithe maps were still produced, but their coverage was incomplete, and in many cases lacking in detail.

Others, however, continued to press for a public register of land ownership. In May 1848, Lord Brougham, a lawyer and former Lord Chancellor, made the case in Parliament for a Land Registry complete with cadastral maps. 'I need hardly dwell on the benefits of a registry for securing titles and facilitating transfers of property,' he told his fellow peers. 'England is nearly the only country which is still without this advantage ... Connected with a registry should be an authentic and detailed map, the result of a survey of each county or smaller district – what the French call a Cadastre.'

Brougham sought to appeal to the landed establishment, explaining that a register of land could 'improve the security of its possessors, and ... increase the facility of its transfer'. It was an argument he felt should appeal 'to the Members of this House, peculiarly the lords, as you are, of the soil of England'. But his speech also hinted at support for land redistribution. 'It was reckoned by Dr. Beke, in 1801, that there were not more than 200,000 owners of land in England,' Brougham related, compared to many millions of small landowners in France: 'No one can believe that the working of any system is good which confines landed property to so few hands.'

His was a lone voice, however, and he had to wait: a Land Registry was eventually established, but not until 1862. Moreover, for decades after its creation, it registered pitifully little land – registration was voluntary rather than compulsory – and it was not a public register.

In the absence of a proper public Land Registry, advocates of land reform had to make do with proxy figures. The 1861 Census provoked a commotion among radicals, as its records seemed to show there were just 30,000 landowners in a population of some 20 million people – although the census said nothing about how much each owned. This was grist to the mill of a new generation of radical liberals and socialists who wanted to see the grinding poverty of the Victorian slums redressed through a fairer distribution of wealth. It was also dynamite for democrats advocating an extension of the electoral franchise and the abolition of the 'property qualification' – the need to own land or capital in order to vote.

The 15th Earl of Derby – himself a major landowner, and the son of the former Conservative Prime Minister – sought to stamp out calls for land reform by disproving these claims. Addressing the House of Lords on 19 February 1872, he asked the Lord Privy Seal 'whether it is the intention of Her Majesty's Government to take any steps for ascertaining accurately the number of Proprietors of Land or Houses in the United Kingdom, with the quantity of land owned by each?' An accurate survey would be a public service, Derby went on, for currently there was a 'great outcry raised about what was called the monopoly of land, and, in support of that cry, the wildest and most reckless exaggerations and misstatements of fact were uttered as to the number of persons who were the actual owners of the soil'.

Viscount Halifax, responding for the government, agreed, opining that 'for statistical purposes, he thought that we ought to know the number of owners of land in the United Kingdom, and there would be no difficulty in obtaining this information'.

Halifax duly tasked the Local Government Board with preparing a Return of Owners of Land. Unlike the original Domesday, this was not produced by sending out surveyors, but by compiling and checking statistics already gathered on land and property ownership for the purposes of the Poor Law. This in itself was no mean feat: as is noted in the preface to the return, 'upwards of 300,000 separate applications had to be sent to the clerks in order to clear up questions in reference to duplicate entries'. No maps were made, but addresses were recorded.

The Return of Owners of Land was finally published, 'after considerable but unavoidable delay', in July 1875. Its initial conclusions gave heart to the landed governing classes: there were, in fact, some 972,836 owners of land in England and Wales, outside of London. Yet 703,289 were owners of less than an acre, leaving 269,547 who owned an acre or above. Even this, the clerks pointed out, was likely an overestimate, based on county-level figures: anyone who owned land in multiple counties would be double-counted.

It fell to an author and country squire, John Bateman, to interpret and popularise the return. In 1876 he published *The Acre-Ocracy of England*, in which he summarised the owners of 3,000 acres and above. It became a best-seller, going through four editions and updates which culminated in Bateman's last work on the subject in 1883, *The Great Land-Owners of Great Britain and Ireland*. Bateman's analysis confirmed the radicals' worst fears: just 4,000 families owned over half the country. Meanwhile, 95 per cent of the population owned nothing at all. The landed elite had been exposed.

The return was swiftly buried because of its embarrassing findings. Landowners hated it. It was set upon by *The Times*, Tory in its politics, which declared that 'the legend of 30,000 landowners has been found to be as mythical as that of St Ursula and her company of 10,000 virgins'. It was castigated by politicians, such as the MP George Brodrick, who criticised it for inaccuracies and double-counting, even though these errors had been easily corrected by John Bateman in his summaries. Radicals failed to fully capitalise on its findings; although a number of MPs stood in the 1885 election on a promise of 'three acres and a cow' for landless farmers, the most they achieved in terms of policy was the 1887 Allotments Act. The moment passed; time moved on; and the return was forgotten.

The third 'modern Domesday' was attempted a generation later. In 1906, the Liberals were swept to power in a landslide election victory, bringing to an end the Conservative hegemony that had dominated British politics since the mid-1880s. The New Liberalism of the twentieth century was committed to much greater state intervention than the *laissez-faire* policies of Victorian Liberals, including a greater willingness to introduce new taxes to pay for social welfare. One aspect of the New Liberalism was a fresh commitment to land reform.

By now land reform had won the support of two of the century's greatest statesmen: David Lloyd George and Winston Churchill. Churchill, then a Liberal MP, wrote in his 1909 book *The People's Rights* about the 'evils of an unreformed and vicious land system'. He railed against 'the landlord who happens to own a plot of land on the outskirts or at the centre of one of our great cities, who watches the busy population around him making the city larger, richer, more convenient, more famous every day, and all the while sits still and does nothing'. Churchill's solution to this social evil was to introduce a land value tax. A 20 per cent tax would be levied on the future unearned increase in land values. To do so, however, would require a full survey of the ownership and value of land across the country.

The Chancellor, Lloyd George, put forward such a tax in the 'People's Budget' of 1909, alongside hikes in income tax for the wealthy and a super-tax on the very richest. When the ensuing vote triggered a constitutional crisis over which chamber of Parliament held the upper hand, the government went to the country to obtain a fresh mandate; the Liberals were returned to power, albeit only with the support of Labour and Irish Nationalist MPs, and the People's Budget was forced through the Lords.

In order to levy the new land value tax, current site values needed to be known; so a valuation survey was set up, dubbed 'Lloyd George's Domesday'. It took five years to carry out and involved the detailed mapping of land ownership across the whole country, using Ordnance Survey maps. This makes it an even more valuable resource than the Return of Owners of Land, which only noted the acreage owned, not where it was. It produced an astonishing volume of data: some 50,000 maps and 95,000 ledgers describing the owners and values of around nine million houses, farms and other properties.

The Liberals' land value tax, however, came to a sorry end. Interrupted by the outbreak of the First World War, and with revenues from it outweighed by the costs of implementation, it was repealed in the 1920 Finance Act, under a government nominally still led by Lloyd George but dominated by the Conservative Party.

I spoke to Professor Brian Short, an academic who has researched the valuation survey extensively, and asked him whether any headline findings exist of who owned England at the time. 'The 1910–15 survey remained unfinished at the start of the war, and stayed that way through to the repeal of the legislation after the war,' he told me. 'There was, unfortunately, no attempt to bring the massive amount of information to any summary conclusion – or at least none that I know of.' He added: 'I fear that the English have been very coy about landownership, and remain so.'

Scottish land reform campaigner Andy Wightman agrees, noting that 'as the twentieth century wore on, people forgot that there had ever been such records. The public had never had access to them in any case and . . . their very existence was very effectively concealed from all but those working in the Inland Revenue and valuation profession.' They were eventually declassified and remain in the National Archives, but have never been digitised.

Frustratingly, the moment was also a missed opportunity to rescue the floundering Land Registry, which continued to register land at a pathetically slow rate. The Land Registry's own official history admits that in 1909, its chief registrar had suggested 'the setting up of a "Domesday Office" – a merger of the Land Registry, Valuation Office and Ordnance Survey. The ownership records being compiled by the Valuation Office would have then been used to create a land register for the whole country . . . Lloyd George was in favour, but Lord Chancellor Haldane was opposed. Had the scheme been adopted, the Land Register would have been completed by now.' Those words were written nearly twenty years ago.

The last and most recent of the modern Domesdays had a rather different aim. It sought not to tax the rich, but to ensure the country could feed itself in the face of total war. With shipping under assault from German U-boats and the country facing the threat of Nazi invasion, Britain embarked on 'Dig for Victory'. The domestic side of this is well known: rationing, allotments, parks dug up for growing vegetables. Less appreciated today is the effort that went into identifying rural land that wasn't being farmed, or had fallen into disuse during the agricultural depressions of the late Victorian period and inter-war years.

To this end, Churchill's War Ministry mandated a National Farm Survey, overseen by the new War Agricultural Committees set up to direct farming. The initial survey was carried out in 1940–1, followed by a larger, two-year survey intended to inform post-war planning. This was seen at the time as a 'Second Domesday' – which tells you how quickly the other modern Domesdays had been hushed up or forgotten.

Though principally an investigation into land *use*, the National Farm Survey also interrogated ownership and tenancy. It covered all farms over five acres – around 320,000 farms in total – covering 99 per cent of agricultural land in England & Wales. However, as an academic paper on the 1941 survey notes, although the 'results were intended to be for use by planners and agricultural advisors, the original records were not made available for general inspection' until 1992. And while various historical studies have now been done using the National Farm Survey, the records remain on paper only, stored in the National Archives. A 2006 report made the case for digitisation of all the maps, but so far, no funder has been found.

What of the languishing Land Registry? Since its foundation in 1862 it had proved an embarrassing failure, and despite several further Acts intended to kickstart it – as well as the missed opportunity of 1909 – its progress remained glacial. Registration of land upon point of sale finally became compulsory after 1925, leading to an increase in activity. All information on who owned land, however, remained tightly guarded.

Incredibly, not even the police were allowed to access Land Registry records without the landowner's permission, thanks to Section 112 of the 1925 Land Registration Act. This clearly hindered efforts to investigate corruption and money laundering. In the 1970s, the Director of Public Prosecutions wrote to the Land Registry pleading for greater transparency. In a document deposited at the National Archives, dated 18 November 1975, an anonymous official refers to the correspondence, and admits: 'the Deputy Chief Land Registrar has told me that the Registry is embarrassed by the extreme restriction imposed by Section 112 and would welcome an amendment'. But he adds: 'On the other hand he did not think a greater liberalisation than that was called for – there was no reason why information about a person's mortgages should be freely available.'

This neurotic secrecy was of a piece with Whitehall's general paranoia during the Cold War. But by the 1970s, a less deferential public and a more inquisitorial press were starting to demand answers from government. The decade also saw a revival of interest in land ownership, prompted by a rise in land and house prices, concerns about financial speculators buying up farmland, and disquiet over wealthy sheikhs snapping up London properties in the wake of the oil crisis.

In 1973, on the centenary of the Return of Owners of Land, a *Sunday Times* journalist, Michael Pye, decided to write a feature story about land ownership for the paper's colour supplement. He wrote to the Ministry of Agriculture, Fisheries and Food (MAFF), 'We plan to contrast the top ten land holdings in 1873 with the largest ten today. I would be very grateful if you could help me in this exercise by letting me have access to a map of your land holdings . . . with perhaps an approximate figure for the total acreage involved.'

It was an anodyne and courteous request, but even this caused ructions at the department. An internal memo from a civil servant dealing with the request advised his superior: 'The problem is to provide the information requested without evoking further questions about politically sensitive matters . . . I trust you are satisfied that this presentation will prove acceptable . . . and will avoid as far as possible any embarrassing enquiries.'

A trade union researcher who dared to enquire about MAFF land-holdings the following year got similarly short shrift. 'Are we required to provide this? – It doesn't seem much of their business!' exclaimed one mandarin in a handwritten note; to which another civil servant responded: 'I suggest a polite reply regretting that the information cannot be obtained without undue effort – provided that is true of course.' It wasn't; the information proved easy to compile.

When the *Spectator* journalist Stephen Glover tried to write a piece on who owned the country in 1977, he found the only way to get the necessary information was to contact the landowners themselves. 'This was usually done on the telephone and naturally entailed difficulties,' he recounted. 'Often, the landowner was out shooting; once he unfortunately turned out to be dead; and once he was drunk. One landowner could not decide whether he owned 10,000 acres or 100,000 acres: "I do find it so difficult to remember what an acre looks like when I drive across the estate."'

MPs had begun asking questions, too. The Labour government that took power in 1974 soon set up two inquiries that aimed to probe the concentration of land ownership. The first of these, the Royal Commission on the Distribution of Income and Wealth, tried to investigate who owned England, but was forced to conclude: 'The paucity of comprehensive up-to-date information on land ownership is remarkable. In the absence of a survey yielding data on the lines of the 1873 survey it is difficult to carry our analysis any further.'

The second, the Northfield Inquiry into the Acquisition and Occupancy of Agricultural Land, got some way further. But although its 1979 report forms a valuable record of the agricultural land then owned by the public sector, financial institutions, and the then small number of overseas buyers, it strangely didn't seek to investigate the large private landowners who own the great majority of land. Then Margaret Thatcher swept into office, and once again the moment for land reform was lost.

By now, however, many NGOs and investigative journalists were determined to break open the 'secret state' regardless of which party was in government. The Campaign for Freedom of Information was set up in 1984, perhaps an appropriate year for founding an organisation dedicated to the rights of the citizen against the overmighty state. It aimed to dismantle the culture of secrecy that pervaded Whitehall, and give people new tools by which to hold government to account. For fifteen years, under the direction of Maurice 'Freedom' Frankel, it campaigned tirelessly for a Freedom of Information (FOI) Act to give citizens the right to know what information was being held by public bodies.

The FOI Act finally came into force in 2005. Now, anyone can request information from any public body, simply by emailing them; the public authority is obliged to respond, and there's a presumption in favour of disclosing information unless it's covered by a specific exemption. Anthony Barnett, whose organisation Charter 88 campaigned for an FOI Act as part of a wider set of constitutional reforms, has written about its 'crippling impact on the old regime'. Certainly, those in government came to regret making such a powerful concession. In his memoirs, Tony Blair castigates himself for being a 'naïve, foolish, irresponsible nincompoop' for introducing FOI, and considers it one of his greatest mistakes; although he may have been forgetting about something.

Freedom of Information requests are one weapon among a small arsenal of tools and data sources that have proven invaluable for uncovering more about who owns England. I'll be referring to these investigative tools throughout this book. Some of them were conceded by the government as the intense secrecy of the Cold War dissipated; others have come about through our membership of the EU, or with the development of digital technology; all have been fought for tirelessly by activists, journalists and citizens.

I've made extensive use of FOIs in asking public sector bodies to release maps of land and properties they own. Also useful are the Environmental Information Regulations 2004 (EIRs), an EU-derived piece of legislation that gives citizens the right to access specifically environmental information. EIR requests are harder for public bodies to refuse than FOIs, and since 2015 they have also applied to the private water companies, thanks to some great campaigning by an environmental law firm called Fish Legal. I've been able to use EIR requests to prise open what land is owned by certain water utilities – though some of them have claimed, bizarrely, that 'land' does not count as 'environmental information'.

It remains harder to find out about private sector land ownership, but here too there has been change for the better. For years, you could only access company accounts at Companies House by paying a fee, making serious investigations prohibitively costly. Then, in 2015, Companies House opened up all its data for free. Its success in providing this excellent resource presents a clear business model for what an open Land Registry should look like.

More recently, Companies House has also started registering 'Persons of Significant Control' – the ultimate owners or beneficiaries of registered companies. This is incredibly helpful for investigating complex corporate networks, and disentangling the inevitable knot of subsidiary businesses, shell companies and investments that the parent firms have set up or taken a stake in. For example, the scandal of ground rent properties – homes that have been sold to people on long leases, but which often contain escalating 'ground rent' charges hidden in the small print, sometimes making the properties impossible to sell. One of the biggest owners of ground rent properties in England is Wallace Estates. They are owned by the Wallace Partnership Group Ltd, who in turn are owned by Albanwise Ltd. But who owns Albanwise? Thanks to Companies House publishing Persons of Significant Control, we now know: a mysterious Italian billionaire called Count Padulli, who also owns a 4,500-acre estate in Norfolk. His country of residence, however, is stated to be the tax haven of Guernsey.

The increasing trend in recent decades to base companies overseas, and often in offshore tax havens, has presented a fresh challenge to obtaining information on who owns England. Offshore jurisdictions like

Guernsey, the British Virgin Islands and Panama aren't just attractive to companies for reasons of 'tax efficiency': they also provide a cloak of secrecy, with less transparent company registries than the UK. If you register a company in the British Virgin Islands, for instance, there is no obligation to reveal the Person of Significant Control who lies behind it.

Anti-corruption charities Global Witness and Transparency International have been pressing for full, public company registers to be implemented in all UK Overseas Territories – including Guernsey and the British Virgin Islands. For years, the government dragged their feet, before being outsmarted by a cross-party group of MPs who forced them to adopt the measures in an amendment to legislation. Even so, the Overseas Territories won't have to publish any corporate registers until late 2020.

Still, there have been big strides in mapping the land owned by offshore companies. In 2015, *Private Eye* investigator Christian Eriksson and data journalist Anna Powell-Smith exposed the thousands of acres of land held by offshore firms, using FOI requests and clever mapping to obtain and display the data from the Land Registry.

Long before offshore tax havens were invented, however, the English aristocracy had perfected a system of avoiding taxes and protecting their inheritances: trusts. Many old landed estates are held in trusts, with trustees managing them on behalf of their beneficiaries, such as the heir to the dukedom or barony. This, too, can conceal the identity of the ultimate owners of land. Moreover, there is no public register of trusts. The Tax Justice Network continues to campaign for such a register, to increase transparency and guard against trusts being used for tax evasion.

Clues as to the extent of an estate can be found, though, via a wholly legal tax exemption wheeze sanctioned by HMRC. The government allows some land, buildings and works of art to be exempted from inheritance tax and capital gains tax, providing they are made available for the public to view for a certain period of time each year. In return, the owner of the 'tax-exempt heritage asset' must deposit a map with HMRC, alongside details of how members of the public can visit the property. Not everyone who has benefited from the scheme, however, has been so keen to let in the great unwashed. In the 1990s, comedian-turned-activist Mark Thomas discovered that Conservative MP Nicholas Soames was avoiding tax on 'a lovely three-tier mahogany buffet, with partially reeded slender balustrade upright supports', but wasn't letting the public view it. He encouraged hundreds of people to make appointments to see the heirloom at Soames's estate in Sussex. Eventually, the MP decided to simply pay the tax.

A similar resource exists where landowners have deposited estate maps with the local council to guard against future rights-of-way claims, using provisions in the Highways Act 1980 Section 31(6), as described in the previous chapter. Thousands of these maps lie buried on council websites; still more are likely gathering dust in council office filing cabinets. A few local authorities have had the good sense to fully digitise the maps and make the data available publicly, though many have not.

Many landowners are also the recipients of millions of pounds in taxpayer subsidies, in the form of various payment schemes for farming, tree-planting and environmental stewardship. These subsidies derive from the European Union's Common Agricultural Policy (CAP), though the UK government shapes how they're distributed. The data on farm subsidies can provide important clues as to the ultimate owner of a piece of farmland. Once again, however, this information hasn't always been public. For years, ministers resisted its release, pressured by landowners' lobby groups, who feared embarrassing stories would emerge about how much taxpayers' money their members were receiving. But campaigners at the group FarmSubsidy. org persisted, and eventually the EU ruled that farm payments data had to become transparent. Some of the largest recipients of farm subsidies in recent years have turned out to be billionaire inventor-turned-landowner James Dyson, a Saudi prince who owns large horse-racing studs, and the Queen, for her private estate at Sandringham.

The data on overall farm subsidies now published by the government doesn't come with maps. That makes it harder to use for locating land-owners' estates. But farm subsidies under the CAP regime come under two 'pillars'. Pillar 1 payments are essentially a subsidy for owning land, with few other strings attached; they make up two-thirds of the money handed out annually. Pillar 2 payments, on the other hand, are allocated for environmental stewardship. Natural England, the government body that was until recently responsible for handing out Pillar 2 payments, publishes maps of where the schemes operate, together with the re-cipients. These maps can be very helpful in pinning down who owns the land – although in many cases the recipients are tenant farmers, rather than the ultimate landowners.

Similar maps still exist for a now-defunct payment scheme for wood-land management administered by the Forestry Commission, called the English Woodland Grants Scheme. Since estates often maintain control of the forests and hedgerows on their estates even where they have leased the fields to tenant farmers, these maps can prove a surer guide to who really owns the area. With Brexit meaning that a huge shake-up of the UK's farm subsidy system is now under way, it's vital that we make future payments to landowners *more* transparent, rather than going backwards to the era of secret subsidies.

Perhaps the biggest underlying change of the past fifteen years that's made exploring land ownership easier is the development of digital tech-nologies. Until the 1990s, cartography was mostly still done on paper. Since then, the growth of GIS (Geographic Information System) mapping tools has transformed how maps can be made and shared. An EU directive called INSPIRE has forced the Land Registry and Ordnance Survey to publish digital maps showing the outlines of all land parcels in England and Wales – but not who owns them, and with licensing restrictions in place on reproducing the maps. Machine-readable data-sets and open-source software have made it easier to analyse complex datasets detailing who owns land, while modern web mapping allows us to create powerful online maps.

Valuation Office to create 'the largest repository of open land data in the world'. Labour's manifesto promised for the first time to consider a land value tax, showing that the resurgence of interest in land spanned the political spectrum.

There is still a long way to go. Despite the government's manifesto commitment, Ordnance Survey's hold over mapping licences makes it very hard to properly map land ownership in England. To Anna Powell-Smith, my collaborator on whoownsengland.org, OS remains 'the great vampire squid wrapped around the face of UK public-interest technology'. And although it has now released details of the one-third of land in England and Wales owned by companies and public sector bodies, the Land Registry remains resistant to overcoming the final taboo: publishing the details of the private landowners who own the remaining two-thirds.

In the thousand years that have passed since the Domesday Book, those seeking to uncover who owns this country have faced obstacles at every turn. Physically and legally excluded from large swathes of the countryside, with debate about land airbrushed from mainstream economics and stymied within political circles by the lobbying of landowners, the general public have had to clamour and campaign for access to the land and for information about who controls it. But it's now possible, at last, to ask questions about who owns England, and credibly hope for an answer.

3

THE ESTABLISHMENT: CROWN AND CHURCH

Somehow, I had expected the Queen's private home to be different. Sandringham House was certainly grand: vast rooms, stuccoed ceilings, great expanses of polished hardwood. Gilded Swiss clocks ticked on marble fireplaces. A statue of Kali, the Hindu goddess of destruction, stood in a gloomy corner of the entrance hall, dancing upon a vanquished enemy. Moth-eaten Union Jacks from doomed polar expeditions hung next to crystal chandeliers. And pinned to the walls were a startling arsenal of knives, scimitars and vicious-looking knuckledusters: the gift of fifty long-dead Indian princes from when Queen Victoria had been crowned Empress of India.

But the house was also curiously parochial. A book on gnomes lay on top of an old edition of the *Guinness Book of Records*. An endless array of mirror-backed cabinets, crammed with onyx carvings and jade elephants and dinner services, gave the place a cluttered feel. Chintz chairs jostled for space with comfy sofas, their padded upholstery perhaps still bearing the imprint of the royal behind. The heavily patterned, Victorian-style carpets looked well worn. This was, after all – as our waistcoated tour guide informed us – the family home of Queen Elizabeth and Prince Philip for many months of the year. It felt like a bizarre mix: at once an old lady's living room, complete with its collections of china dogs and tea sets, and at the same time a regal residence, filled with the tribute of defeated kingdoms. But then, separating out the personal from the public functions of the Crown is always a tricky exercise, as I was to discover.

I had cycled to Sandringham with my flatmate Roger, after taking the train out to King's Lynn. This part of Norfolk has royal connections going back centuries: out in the Wash, it's rumoured, lies King John's buried treasure, submerged in the mudflats when the royal baggage train was caught by incoming tides. But it wasn't until 1862 that the royal family decided to make the area their home. Queen Victoria bought the house for her son, the Prince of Wales – and future King Edward VII – along with an estate that then comprised around 7,000 acres. Today, Sandringham has grown to be even larger: some 20,000 acres of Norfolk, taking in prime farmland, oak woods and landscaped parks.

The whole area is dominated by huge aristocratic estates. As we pedalled through the arid countryside, neighbouring landowners staked their territorial claims through KEEP OUT signs and heraldic carvings. The balustrade of a bridge we cycled over was embossed repeatedly with the letter 'H', denoting the property of Lord Howard of Rising. To the east of Sandringham lies the Marquess of Cholmondeley's Houghton Hall, whose land is registered in the tax haven of Jersey, and who holds the hereditary post of Lord Great Chamberlain, an ancient officer of the Crown.

What makes the Sandringham Estate unusual is not just that it's a royal residence. It's unusual because it's owned by the Queen *in person*, rather than by the institution of the Crown. When Queen Victoria acquired it, she registered it in the name of the Prince of Wales, to avoid it becoming part of the Crown Estate and thereby surrendering its revenues to Parliament. It's his name that's recorded as the owner of Sandringham in the 1873 Return of Owners of Land. The current land title for Sandringham states the registered proprietor to be 'Her most gracious Majesty Queen Elizabeth the Second'. But it omits the crucial line, 'in right of her Crown', which would make it Crown property. The only other royal residence to be owned personally by the royal family is Balmoral in Scotland, and that was bought by Queen Victoria's husband, Prince Albert, before his untimely death. The subsequent

Crown Estates Act allowed the royal family to inherit Balmoral and Sandringham as private residences thereafter.

If all that seems oddly arcane and complex, you're starting to grasp how archaic the British constitution remains. And while this might at first appear an irrelevant quirk of history, the monarchy's survival continues to shape how power is exercised – and how land is owned. But to understand fully, we need to go further down the rabbit hole.

Our tour of Sandringham passed from the kitsch comfort of the drawing rooms into a darkened corridor, hung with drawings of the royals out hunting and lists of the estate's gamekeepers. To my surprise, the walls were lined with cabinets stuffed with dozens and dozens of shotguns. 'This is a .450-bore double-barrelled breach-loading rifle,' recorded one label, 'shot by Queen Victoria.'

'Are any of these used by the Queen currently?' I asked our tour guide.

'Aha, no,' he said. 'The Queen does occasionally go shooting. But under the Firearms Act, you can't publicly display weapons which are in current use. Thanks to Magna Carta, not even the Queen is above the law of the land.'

Well, up to a point, Lord Copper, I thought. Sure, the monarchy nowadays is a shadow of what it once was, its powers tightly constrained, its status mostly symbolic. But when it comes to taxation, for instance, the Queen has a very different arrangement to those which bind her subjects. She has only paid income tax voluntarily since 1993. Up to that point, no monarch had paid taxes since the 1930s, a revelation that sparked a public outcry at the time – particularly as ordinary taxpayers had just been asked to foot the bill for repairing Windsor Castle after it had been gutted by fire. Support for republicanism soared during a decade that saw several royal divorces and the death of Diana; although thirty years on from the Queen's *annus horribilis,* those still calling for the abolition of the monarchy must feel like they're ploughing the loneliest of furrows. Two royal weddings, a diamond jubilee and several more grandchildren have helped restore the royal family's public standing.

The point of this chapter isn't to persuade you to become a republican.

But it *is* intended to show you how the monarchy continues to shape how power and ownership are exercised in the UK. It seeks to outline why the royals – alongside that other great Establishment survivor, the Church – still own so much land after many centuries of existence. Most of all, it explains how the Crown is partly to blame for why land ownership in England remains so unequal today.

The smart-arse answer to the question 'who owns England?' is a simple one: the Crown. All land is ultimately owned by the Crown, and freehold and leasehold titles to land are technically 'held of the Crown', and therefore derived from it. The Crown is 'lord paramount', with land titles held on its sufferance. If you die without a will, any land you owned reverts to the Crown through the law of *bona vacantia*.

In practice, owning a freehold in land nowadays means you can do pretty well what you like with it. No marauding monarch is going to come and take it from you. But that hasn't always been the case.

It was William the Conqueror who declared that all land in England belonged ultimately to the Crown, straight after the Norman Conquest of 1066. At William's instigation, titles in land henceforth would be derived from the Crown. The king sat at the top of this feudal pyramid, and the whole country was now his to carve up as he pleased: a giant cake to be cut into slices and handed out to his cronies.

It's this that lies at the heart of why land ownership remains so concentrated and unequal in England today. William the Conqueror's land grab and system of patronage set the stage for the following thousand years. The king parcelled out land to a small coterie of barons, whose families would continue to inherit such lands for centuries afterwards. By dealing out the pack of cards so unfairly, William skewed the game from the outset. A large part of the blame for the resulting pattern of land ownership has to be levelled squarely at the Crown.

'The public do a very good job of mentally separating the Royal Family from the rest of the aristocracy, but that is not the reality,' admitted one peer with remarkable honesty during a House of Lords

debate in 2013. 'The Royal Family is the core of the aristocratic system.'
As Andy Wightman argues, 'Private landownership in Scotland remains
a small, inter-related and privileged club which is proud to have the
Queen as a member.' The same could be said of England.

Of course, William the Conqueror didn't claim ownership of the
whole of England only to immediately hand it out again to his barons.
He also kept a very large chunk of land for the Crown itself. According
to records in the Domesday Book, the king and his family owned around
17 per cent of England in 1086 – perhaps some 5.4 million acres. Nearly
a thousand years later, the Crown in its various institutional guises still
owns around a million acres of land in England and Wales, or half a
million acres if you exclude the areas comprising foreshore and riverbeds. Looked at from one perspective, that represents a major loss of
land over time. But from another angle, it's an incredible tale of territorial survival. How have the fortunes of this vast estate changed over
time, and how has it managed to survive into the twenty-first century?

If anything, the extent of Crown lands increased in size for a couple of
centuries after the Norman Conquest. In particular, the Norman kings
acquired lots of land to indulge their love of hunting. Another of
William's innovations, besides feudalism, was forest law. Nowadays we
think of a forest as being composed of trees, a large woodland. But
'forest' is actually a legal construct – a term given to an area of land,
whether wooded or not, where hunting privileges were restricted to the
king. William and his successors established vast royal forests, including
the New Forest and the Forest of Dean, where the hunting of deer and
boar was outlawed for anyone save the king and his favoured courtiers.

Since English common law had created a customary right for hungry
commoners to feed themselves by hunting wild game, this was a fright-
ening new encroachment on the rights of ordinary people, in a kingdom
already straining under the Norman yoke. Punishment for poaching in
royal forests was severe. *The Rime of King William*, a furious poem written
a year after William's death by a disgruntled courtier, records that the

king 'established many deer preserves, / and he set up many laws concerning them, / such that whoever killed a hart or a hind / should be blinded.'

By the time of Henry II's reign (1154–89), it's reckoned that royal forests covered somewhere between a quarter and a third of *all* England – a vast area of land subjugated to the private pleasures of one individual at the expense of the public. Royal forests weren't all strictly owned by the Crown – some were established on land belonging to other land-owners – but the constraints and privileges enacted by forest law were so stringent that the Crown might as well have owned the land outright.

The royal penchant for game also inspired many barons to set up their own deer parks and hunting grounds. The thrill of the hunt is still recorded today in place names like Cannock Chase or Cranborne Chase, where nobles took their cue from the king in applying the principles of the royal forest to their own lands. Just as the Crown's division of the spoils of conquest had established a landowning elite, so its act of closing off previously public lands for private gain set a dangerous precedent. In centuries to come, the aristocracy and gentry would begin the process of enclosure, stealing land once held in common and converting it into farmland for private profit.

But the Crown's land grabs didn't go unchallenged. Everyone today has heard of Magna Carta, the contract forced upon the Crown in 1215 by barons fed up with a despotic monarch. Most people have forgotten, however, about the Charter of the Forest, the 'poor man's Magna Carta' which simultaneously pressed the Crown to respect rights customarily held by commoners.

As the historian Peter Linebaugh recounts, 'There were two charters forced on King John at Runnymede. Beside the great charter with which we are all vaguely familiar, there was a second charter in 1217 known as the Charter of the Forest. Whereas the first charter concerned, for the most part, political and juridical rights, the second charter dealt with economic survival.' The Charter ordered that 'all woods made forest . . . shall be immediately disafforested' – which is to say, removed from royal jurisdiction. The rights of commoners to the fruits of the earth – rights which were later to be savagely abused by the aristocracy – were accepted and codified by the Crown. Thereafter, royal rorests and forest law started to shrink in extent and influence. Edward III 'disafforested' the whole of Surrey in 1327, and by 1350 only 15 per cent of England lay under forest laws.

The decline of the royal forests didn't end the Crown's love affair with hunting, of course. Fashions simply evolved as nature's larder was depleted. The last wild boar in England was killed in the seventeenth century. The Hanoverian kings had more of a taste for landscape gardening and hobby-farming, particularly George III, who earned the nickname 'Farmer George'. But under Queen Victoria, the Crown's sponsorship of bloodsports revived in a big way – only this time, the fashion was to buy a keepered grouse moor and blast away at birds with a shotgun. Today, the Queen owns a huge grouse moor estate around Balmoral and another in the North York Moors via the Duchy of Lancaster, as well as hosting pheasant shoots at Sandringham. Once again, the Crown has acted as a trendsetter in the ownership and misuse of land, shaping aristocratic tastes and causing hundreds of thousands of acres of upland England and Scotland to be converted into sporting estates.

Between the Black Death and the Civil War, the story of the Crown lands – as much as is known about them – seems to be one of financial misman-agement and decline. For a time, the monarchy's landed estates had provided adequate income for the royal household to live within its means. But fighting endless foreign wars of aggression, from the Crusades to the Hundred Years War, proved expensive; and soon kings were summoning their barons to plead for more cash. Parliament, the setting for such negotiations, at first delivered the goods – even when it proved ruinous. The levying of the vastly unfair Poll Tax in 1381 sparked a colossal revolt by peasants and labourers that threatened to topple feudalism in its entirety. The revolt was quashed and the landowning order maintained. But increasingly, even landowner-dominated Parliaments came to view the excesses of the Crown with disdain.

Throughout this period, successive kings and queens flogged off and gave away Crown lands with scant thought for the longer term. With the exception of the two duchies – which we'll turn to later – the monarchy's lands were frittered away, handed out to favourites at court rather than managed to maximise incomes. Most profligate of all were the Stuart dynasty, whose thirst for cash resulted in the selling off of land, the creation of new peerages, demands for higher taxes and then, when MPs refused to levy them, the dissolution of Parliament. In fact, the Stuart kings cocked up their finances so badly, it led to civil war and Parliament's execution of Charles I.

For eleven years, England had no Crown. Determined to run things more efficiently, Cromwell's Parliaments carried out an extensive survey of Crown lands. But rather than keep hold of them as an ongoing source of revenue for the nation's finances, they too decided to sell them off. The reason was simple: Cromwell's army was massively in arrears, and its unpaid footsoldiers were getting restless. The Crown lands were sold for about £250 million in today's money, going some way towards settling Parliament's civil war debts. Many of the buyers were existing landed gentry; others belonged to Cromwell's officer class. They didn't get to enjoy their new possessions for long, however: the collapse of the Republic and restoration of the monarchy in 1660 led to the immediate return of all lands to the Crown.

The restored monarchy soon found its freedom to manoeuvre hemmed in by constitutional restraints put in place by a Parliament determined never to have to go to war with the Crown again. When the Stuarts once more proved too big for their boots, MPs invited first the Dutch and then the Germans to come and have a go at wearing the crown. The Hanoverian dynasty proved much more compliant with the wishes of Parliament. In 1760, George III agreed to give up the income from his Crown lands in exchange for an annual stipend called the Civil List. The lands would still technically be his, 'in right of his

Crown', but the revenues would flow to the Treasury and they would be managed by an organisation answerable to Parliament – later called the Crown Estate.

It was a sweet deal for the king, as the Crown lands were in a pretty shambolic state at the time. Revenues remained low, and land holdings had continued to be filched for bribes and the enrichment of court favourites. The Civil List, by contrast, handed the royal family a guaranteed fixed income. And over the next century, the Crown Estate's fortunes were to revive. Staffed with an increasingly professional civil service, its holding of land doubled in size from around 106,000 acres to 220,000 acres over the course of Queen Victoria's reign. More importantly from the government's perspective, revenues grew immensely, bringing in millions of pounds for the public purse. The development of London made some Crown lands stupendously valuable – such as Regent Street, built to link the Prince Regent's mansion on Pall Mall with Regent's Park in the north. And when it was forced to hand over the remaining royal forests to the Forestry Commission in 1924, the Crown Estate quickly made up the lost acreage by investing in farmland instead.

Over the last century, the Crown Estate has become a fully commercial institution, managing its enviable property portfolio with ruthless efficiency. Its holdings have expanded still further to cover 336,000 acres of England and Wales, with huge tracts of prime farmland in Lincolnshire and the Fens, on Romney Marsh, and along the Holderness shore. Comparing maps of what the Crown Estate owns with agricultural land classification maps, you can see that nearly all of its farms are on top-quality Grade 1 and 2 farmland. It also benefited from receiving £366,000 in taxpayer farm subsidies in 2016.

Still, nowadays, there's much more money to be made from Apple iPhones than from apples. The Crown Estate gets more rental income from Apple's flagship store on Regent Street than it does from its *entire* agricultural estate. And though it still bears responsibility for managing the Crown's traditional stamping grounds – Windsor Great Park, for instance – its modern capitalist instincts mean it always has an eye out for new ways to boost its earnings. Where the Crown's landed interests once lay in castles and deer parks, the Crown Estate now prioritises investment in shopping centres and retail parks. That may sound like a moan about creeping commercialisation, but frankly, I'd rather the Crown generate proceeds for the public purse than, say, own a forest for a monarch's exclusive right to hunt boar. The Crown Estate's ownership of the UK seabed has also made it a champion for renewable energy and addressing climate change: what was once an effectively worthless asset has become highly lucrative with the UK's development of offshore wind, which the Estate now has a vested interest in promoting.*

The Crown Estate's motto, 'brilliant places through conscious commercialism', may be a rather nauseating PR slogan, but its contribution to the Exchequer's coffers nowadays is considerable: £329 million in 2017. Subject to Freedom of Information law and with its finances fully open for public scrutiny, the modern Crown Estate's professionalism is a world away from the sloppy venality with which the Crown's lands were managed for many centuries. Still, its transformation into a corporate property agent has its pitfalls: some of the properties it looks after risk succumbing to the overriding imperative for high returns. The Laxton Estate, for instance – the last example of a medieval open field system in England, which has been owned by the Crown Estate since 1981 – was earmarked for sale in early 2018 because it doesn't turn enough of a profit.

Then there's the matter of the reorganisation of the royals' finances in 2012, when the then Chancellor, George Osborne, ended the Civil List and replaced it with a new Sovereign Grant. This new system re-established the link between the health of the Crown Estate and what the royal family receives in income. Now its annual funding is 15 per cent of Crown Estate revenues – so if the Estate posts higher turnover, the Queen and

---

* The Crown Estate owns virtually all of the seabed around England, Wales and Northern Ireland, from 12 nautical miles out to the edge of UK territorial waters. It also owns around half of the UK's foreshore – the coastal land between high and low tides – and many estuaries and riverbeds.

her family get more money. In fact, during the most recent review of the grant, MPs voted to increase the index to 25 per cent of revenues for the next decade, to cover repair works to Buckingham Palace. Not everyone was happy, understandably: as the Labour MP Alex Cunningham pointed out, 'I have always respected the fact that we have a royal family, but I know they also have vast wealth and I don't know what sort of contributions they will be making towards this project.'

Because the Crown's wealth doesn't actually stop with the Crown Estate. There's also the small matter of the other two property empires it owns: the Duchies of Cornwall and Lancaster.

Down a side alley off the Strand, behind the Savoy Hotel, with its cucumber sandwiches and champagne and top-hatted doorman, is an ancient church. This is the Queen's Chapel of the Savoy, and it harbours a well-kept secret. It lies at the heart of the Duchy of Lancaster, one of the oldest property empires in England, and a little-known money-spinner for the monarchy.

When I visited it, the cool air of the chapel was a welcome relief from the sticky heatwave that had been slow-roasting London. Stepping into the sepulchral gloom, I felt the urge to tiptoe: though only yards from one of the capital's busiest shopping districts, the building's thick stone walls muffled all external sound. Blue satin cushions covered empty pews upon a chequerboard floor. Every surface seemed suffused with heraldry. Armorial plates plastered the wood-panelled walls, the coats-of-arms of bygone Knights Commander and Grand Masters of this or that Order. Translucent lions and crosses shone from the stained glass windows; above the altar, one gothic arch framed a depiction of the Holy Grail. It was all very Dan Brown.

Except here, the secret societies and ancient bloodlines are all real. The Savoy Chapel is not only the Queen's personal place of worship, complete with regal throne at the back of the nave. It's also the church for the Royal Victorian Order – an obscure, dynastic order of knighthood that rewards personal service to the monarch. More portentous still are the names that adorn the vaulted ceiling. Commemorated in azure and gold is the royal lineage of the Lancastrians, stretching back to one of the most Machiavellian and capricious bastards in English history: John of Gaunt, Duke of Lancaster, and founder of the Duchy. The chapel is built from the rubble of his luxurious mansion, the Savoy Palace.

Gaunt was the power behind the throne of his teenage nephew, Richard II: the archetypal evil uncle and scheming Grand Vizier *par excellence*. He was also stupendously rich, the largest landowner in England, with vast estates in every county. In 1381, Gaunt was up north hammering the Scots when the Poll Tax rebellions erupted in Kent and Essex. Peasants and townsfolk alike marched upon London, demanding that the king's evil advisers should be hanged – Gaunt chief among them. When the young king refused to hand them over, anarchy ensued. The rebels descended upon the Savoy Palace and began systematically dismantling the wealth of their feudal masters. Tapestries were wrenched off walls, furniture thrown out of windows, and a vast bonfire made of Gaunt's riches. Rather than engage in looting and be written off as mere thieves, the rebels instead opted to smash up the tyrant's vast stash of gold plate so it couldn't be reconstituted. The Savoy – which had cost £35,000 to build, a third of the estimated annual wage bill for the entire English army – was ground to dust.

But Gaunt's ducal lands remained intact. After defeating the Peasants' Revolt, Gaunt was determined to see the House of Lancaster prosper for ever. So when his son, Henry Bolingbroke, murdered Richard II and usurped the throne, his first act was to declare the Duchy to be his and his male heirs' estate for ever more, held separately from other Crown lands. The Duchy of Lancaster has remained the monarchy's personal fiefdom ever since.

Today it runs to 45,674 acres, including five 'rural surveys', which span grouse moors in north Lancashire, moorland in North Yorkshire, dozens of farms near Burton-upon-Trent, and entire villages in Cheshire. In addition, it owns the foreshore along most of the Lancashire coastline, and extensive mineral rights, including valuable gypsum mines. Looking through the Duchy's entries in Land Registry data, the estate's ancient hold over certain areas comes through clearly in the place names: Duchy House, Savoy Road, Lancaster Farm. The Duchy's Savoy Estate in central London, though tiny in extent, rakes in rents from retail, as well as hosting the estate's headquarters at Lancaster House, just around the corner from the Chapel of the Savoy.

The affairs of the Duchy of Lancaster remain cloaked in mystery. Until recently, anyone wishing to look into what the Duchy currently owns had to make do with one grainy map on its website. That's changed with the Land Registry's recent release of more data on land owned by companies and corporate bodies. But in every other way, the Duchy of Lancaster seems to have deflected public attention from its affairs. It's not subject to scrutiny by the National Audit Office, Parliament's financial watchdog. It produces an annual report to Parliament and a Cabinet minister serves as Chancellor of the Duchy, a mostly symbolic role; yet the Duchy has avoided being made subject to Freedom of Information requests from the public. Nor does it pay corporation tax (although the Queen voluntarily pays tax on any income). The Duchy claims that it 'does not receive any public funds in connection with its activities', yet it received almost £38,000 in taxpayer-funded farm subsidies in 2016.

The Duchy is an unreformed anachronism, which owes its survival to the accretions of royal privilege over the centuries. But this archaic body continues to benefit from the modern surge in land and property prices. In 2018, the Duchy of Lancaster posted a £20 million profit – three and a half times larger than what it generated back in the year 2000, and on top of the £76 million received by the royal household thanks to the Sovereign Grant. It seems crazy that we continue to tolerate this set-up, meekly allowing the monarchy to keep a medieval cash cow with minimal oversight and exempt from the tax levied on other businesses. 'Why are we throwing millions of pounds at the Queen,' asks Graham Smith of campaign group Republic, 'when that money could be spent on schools, hospitals and local communities?' Why indeed?

A similar story can be told about the Duchy of Cornwall. It, too, was created in the 1300s, as the personal dukedom of the heir to the throne. Its lands were first gifted to Edward III's son, the Black Prince, and today the Duchy belongs to Prince Charles in his capacity as Duke of Cornwall.

Like its sister body, the Duchy of Cornwall is one of the strangest beasts in England's still quasi-feudal political economy. It's not a company, and so doesn't pay corporation tax. It's neither a charity nor a public body – and it isn't subject to formal parliamentary scrutiny or Freedom of Information requests, though it has to gain permission from the Treasury if it wants to sell off land. The Duchy has even successfully fought off attempts to make it subject to public requests made under the Environmental Information Regulations – something that sits uneasily alongside the Prince's environmental credentials – in a bizarre case involving its ancient ownership of the Fal estuary and its right to allow oyster dredging over it. It is, in short, an anachronism – but one that has survived for nearly seven hundred years and continues to grow in size.

But try to investigate what the Duchy of Cornwall owns, and you'll find it's an even more opaque institution than the Duchy of Lancaster. Its annual reports give a flavour of the properties it possesses, but little by way of detail. The Land Registry, despite releasing data on properties owned by the Duchy of Lancaster, has decided to exclude the Duchy of Cornwall from its Corporate and Commercial dataset – seemingly because it's considered to be the personal estate of one individual, the Duke of Cornwall.

I bought the land title to one of the Duchy's properties, to check out exactly who it was registered to. You need to take a deep breath before reading out the name of the registered proprietor: it's 'His Royal Highness Charles Philip Arthur George Prince of Wales, Duke of Cornwall and Rothesay, Earl of Chester and Carrick, Baron of Renfrew, Lord of the Isles and Great Steward of Scotland'.

Welcome to twenty-first-century Britain, I thought. When I cheerfully emailed the Duchy asking for a map of what they owned, reply came there none. Well, it's always worth a try. But then, concealing wealth is part and parcel of preserving it.

I had more luck leafing through back editions of *National Geographic* at my grandma's house in Cornwall. There, in a feature on the Duchy written back in 2006, was a map showing the outline of its major possessions. That was my starting point for investigating further.

The Duchy does not, contrary to popular belief, own the whole of Cornwall – though it does possess nearly 19,000 acres of it. Its ancient manorial lands encompass the medieval castles of Tintagel, Launceston, Trematon and Restormel; prehistoric stone circles on Bodmin Moor; steep wooded valleys near Herodsfoot and Stoke Climsland; and dozens of idyllic mixed farms, their sunken lanes and high hedgerows as Cornish as clotted cream.

Yet though Cornwall is the heart of the Duchy, its landholdings are spread far and wide. Its biggest possession by far is a 70,000-acre slice of Dartmoor in Devon – most of it leased out to the Ministry of Defence for army training. Further afield, the Prince of Wales has his private home and gardens at Highgrove Farm in Gloucestershire. Some acquisitions are ancient: the Iron Age hill forts of Maiden Castle in Dorset and Ham Hill in Somerset, or the Manor of Inglescombe to the west of Bath. Some are more recent: the Duchy bought the 11,000-acre Guy's Estate in Herefordshire from the insurance company Prudential in 2000.

Nor is it all bucolic farming. Prince Charles has always expressed strong views on architecture, ever since decrying a proposed modernist extension to the National Gallery as a 'monstrous carbuncle'. Much of the public shares the Prince's taste for old-fashioned classical designs; the difference is that he has the land and money to put such ideas into practice.

Poundbury, on the outskirts of Dorchester, is the Prince's answer to building homes that people want to live in – lots of red brick, green open spaces and plenty of Farrow and Ball paintwork. It's certainly pleasant and well-designed, but perhaps just a little too perfect, like something out of *Noddy* or *Trumpton*. Elsewhere, the Duchy's properties include housing estates in Kennington – with clues as to the landlord contained in street names like Black Prince Road, and a nearby pub called the Prince of Wales – and the crown jewels of the Oval Cricket Ground. Still, the Duchy owns a few carbuncles of its own: a Holiday Inn in Reading, a Waitrose distribution centre in Milton Keynes and a quarry in Gloucestershire all number among its possessions.

All told, the Duchy today owns around 130,000 acres of land across England and Wales, nearly twice as much as it did in the Victorian period. This alone is enough to make the Prince of Wales the single largest private landowner in England – even without the additional 100,000 acres of foreshore, 14,000 acres of estuaries and riverbeds, and extensive mineral rights that the Duchy also lays claim to.

By all accounts, the Prince is a well-respected landowner, who's taken a prescient interest in climate change and other environmental issues, and put his money where his mouth is when it comes to long-term estate management. But it's important to distinguish Prince Charles as a person from the Duchy as an institution, just as with Queen Elizabeth and her Duchy of Lancaster.

Both duchies are medieval anachronisms, whose attempts to dodge corporation tax and avoid being subjected to public sector norms of financial accountability and transparency are, essentially, tedious attempts to preserve feudal privilege. The lands owned by the duchies were acquired through the same mix of conquest and confiscation as all the other Crown lands: and yet, where most of these lands today are vested in the Crown Estate, with their revenues flowing into the public purse, the duchies remain private piggy banks for the monarch and heir to the throne. Let's not forget that the Sovereign Grant handed the royal family £76 million in 2017: the duchies brought in £41.9 million on top of this – not to mention the £695,000 in taxpayer farm subsidies handed to the Queen for her Sandringham Estate. And while the Queen and Prince of Wales voluntarily pay income tax on these earnings, future monarchs could readily seek to waive such an arrangement. This is the enduring problem of our uncodified constitution: it's ripe for abuse by changes in personnel. After all, the Prince might respect the traditions of estate management, but he's broken the royal convention of not engaging in political lobbying on multiple occasions, as was revealed with the publication of his infamous 'black spider letters' to ministers.

Surely the time has come for the Duchies of Lancaster and Cornwall to be abolished, and their lands merged with those of the Crown Estate. The Crown Estate has proved itself to be an exceptionally able manager, generating huge profits while being open to scrutiny and mindful of the long term; so why should it not administer the Duchy lands, too? Their revenues would then flow directly to the public purse. MPs could then decide whether to vote for a corresponding increase in the Sovereign Grant – or whether the extra money would be better spent elsewhere, on things like schools and the NHS. The Duchies, being past masters at surviving, would of course put up a fight. Feudalism dies hard: John of Gaunt would be turning in his grave. But there really is no place for it in the modern world.

Before we move on from the Crown, there's just one issue left: the surprisingly vexed question of who owns the royal palaces and parks. 'We all know who owns Buckingham Palace,' states a recent article in *Time* magazine. But do we? The *Daily Express*, admittedly never the most reliable of sources when it comes to the royals, blithely asserts that it's 'owned by the Crown Estate'. But it isn't: their asset maps omit both Buckingham Palace and Windsor Castle.

In fact, both royal residences are under the management of the Royal Household Property Section, yet another part of the Crown's byzantine structure. It, too, hasn't changed much over the years. The 1911 *Encyclopaedia Britannica* stated drily that 'in its main outlines the existing organization of the royal household is essentially the same as it was under the Tudors or the Plantagenets.' Aficionados of Netflix's *The Crown* will be familiar with the hidebound traditions of the Royal Household's management, customs that no doubt irk even the Queen at times. But it might be more accurate to say that *no one* owns Buckingham Palace – or at least, no one has actually registered owner- ship of it. I bought the Land Registry records to check: there's no registered proprietor – only a *caution* from the Crown Estate Commissioners saying that the Queen is 'interested in the land as bene- ficial owner'.

Who owns Hyde Park, Regent's Park and the rest of London's royal parks is an easier question to answer: it's a charity that's grown out of what used to be a government quango. The same is true for the royal residences that are no longer occupied by the royal family – which in England consist of the Tower of London, Hampton Court, Kensington Palace, the Banqueting Hall on Whitehall, and Kew Palace. They're owned and managed by Historic Royal Palaces, a charity that's taken on functions previously carried out by the Department for Culture, Media and Sport. In both cases, what was previously private splendour – enclosed deer parks and palatial homesteads – has now rightly been opened up for public enjoyment.

But strangest of all, and certainly most revealing about where sovereignty really lies under our archaic constitution, is the owner- ship of Parliament. Few people remember today that Parliament was once a royal residence: the Palace of Westminster. It occupies the site next to the tidal Thames where the Danish King Canute once demonstrated to his courtiers the limits of his regal powers by failing to hold back the waves. Canute built his palace on what was then the low-lying Thorney Island; Parliament was still succumbing to floods as recently as 1928.

For centuries, there has been a longstanding convention that no monarch is allowed to enter the House of Commons. At the annual State Opening of Parliament, the Queen sends her emissary Black Rod to knock three times on the door of the Commons, to summon MPs to hear her speech. But the door is slammed shut in his face, symbolising the Commons' independence. This crucial limitation of the monarch's remit dates back to the Civil War. As political theatre, it represents Parliament's subsequent armed rebellion, its execution of the king and imposition of a republic, and its later shaping of a constitutional monarchy. In short, it's an assertion of Parliamentary sovereignty. And yet, it appears that the Queen still quietly asserts her claim to own Parliament.

I discovered this when I chanced across an old parliamentary debate from the Swinging Sixties. The Labour Prime Minister Harold Wilson, having just swept to power on a modernising mission to unleash the 'white heat of technology' and update Britain's tired old institutions, made a special announcement to Parliament in March 1965. The Queen, he declared, had 'graciously agreed that the control, use and occupation of the Palace of Westminster and its precincts shall be permanently enjoyed by the Houses of Parliament'. Control of the building would pass to the Speaker. Wilson's Cabinet colleague Tony Benn must have been pleased: as a diehard republican, he had refused to kiss the Queen's hand when he joined the Privy Council.

Intrigued, I decided to take a look at the Land Registry records for the Houses of Parliament – expecting to find the freehold registered to the Speaker.* But it wasn't. Instead, there was simply a recent caution, similar to that for Buckingham Palace, lodged by the Crown Estate Commissioners, that 'the Queen's Most Excellent Majesty is interested in the land as beneficial owner . . . in right of Her Crown'. Wilson, it seemed, hadn't taken back control at all.

The confusion over who owns Parliament illustrates a broader truth about the muddle of British politics, and how interwoven our modern system of government is with the ancient institution of the Crown. The Crown's formal powers may have withered, but its symbolic soft power remains strong – and its landed wealth is still extensive. Grappling with the archaic customs of the Crown remains essential to understanding

---

* I also submitted an FOI request to the House of Commons to clarify the legal owner-ship status; in their response, they replied: 'we believe the legal position is that the Crown is the owner of the freehold but that the House has use of the parliamentary estate.'

land ownership in England today. Who owns the land on which the House of Commons meets is only a small, perhaps trifling part of that. But symbolism matters in politics. Brexit, we are told, is all about reclaiming parliamentary sovereignty. If that's to be the case, why doesn't Parliament first take back control of the land beneath its feet?

If the story of the Crown has been one of territorial survival, the tale of what's happened to the Church's lands is one of almost complete collapse. Once the country's largest and wealthiest landowner, the Church today is a shadow of its former glory. But what's most surprising is how recently its possessions were lost. Even in the late Victorian period, the Church was the largest single landowner in England. Yet over the past century, it has lost around 90 per cent of its lands. Why? The mystery of who stole the Church's land is a whodunnit worthy of a Brother Cadfael novel.

The medieval Church enjoyed vast wealth. Domesday suggests that bishops and abbots owned over a quarter of the entire kingdom, around 8.3 million acres. By the Reformation, historians' best estimates are that Church lands had declined somewhat, to around 4 million acres. But this was still a colossal area, and it brought in great riches in the form of tithes, rents and agricultural produce. Large areas of England had been settled by the monastic orders, who set to work on draining marshy ground and putting wilderness under the plough. The ordained clergy of priests and bishops also owned plenty of land, not to mention churches and outbuildings. Of course, some of this worldly wealth was reinvested by the Church into building ever-larger cathedrals, and redistributed to the poor in the form of alms. But the senior ranks of the Church seldom went hungry. Over the centuries, various nonconformist and heretical sects – from the Friars and mendicant orders to the Cathars, Lollards and Protestant puritans – poured scorn on the gilded wealth of the Church hierarchy, seeing it as a corruption of the holy poverty of true Christianity.

Henry VIII's decision in 1536 to dissolve the monasteries and seize their lands had no such spiritual motivation. Part and parcel of Henry's break from Rome, it was also a land grab pure and simple, to bolster royal finances and fund foreign wars. A large chunk of the land that Henry took from the monasteries was quickly sold off or handed out to noble cronies. The Russell family, for example – later the Dukes of Bedford – were given the old monastic lands of Woburn Abbey in Bedfordshire. It's still their family seat today. For centuries afterwards, the beneficiaries of Henry's land grab would remain staunch defenders of the Anglican settlement – terrified of losing their possessions should the Catholic Church ever be restored. One of the main reasons why Bonnie Prince Charlie – the Catholic pretender to the throne in the eighteenth century – never succeeded in becoming king was because of the aristocracy's fear of losing their 'Abbey Lands' if he took power.

But the newly created Church of England was hardly poor, either. Only the monasteries had been dissolved; the old bishoprics kept their lands, and the Anglican Church started out with an endowment of land that ensured it would remain very rich. By the time of the 1873 Return of Owners of Land, the Church still owned a vast estate of 2.13 million acres, making it the single largest landowner in England at the time.

Most of this was in the form of land known as 'glebe' – land set aside for the upkeep of parish priests, the lowest and poorest rung of the Anglican clergy. It comprises the land on which vicarages and rectories are built, but also farmland to supplement vicars' incomes. From the Reformation until the twentieth century, parish priests had three main sources of income: fees from performing baptisms, marriages and deaths; tithes, a form of Church taxation levied on other local land-owners and farmers; and glebe land. Glebe could be farmed by the parish priest himself, or rented out to tenants.

Equipped with this huge land bank, and bolstered by the Victorian surge in Christian piety, the Church could feel very secure. Its spiritual grip on the nation was matched by its earthly wealth. But then, over the next century, a quiet catastrophe appears to have overwhelmed the Church's landholdings.

In 1976, a new law, the Endowments and Glebe Measure, centralised the ownership of glebe land, transferring it from parish priests to the Diocesan Boards of Finance that administer to the Church of England's forty-one bishoprics. The law passed without comment at the time. But what emerged much later, thanks to the careful investigations of historian Kevin Cahill and the MP Adrian Sanders, was that 90 per cent of all glebe land had disappeared over the intervening century. Only after a Parliamentary Question was lodged by Sanders in 2002 were the stats released. Having been masters of over 2 million acres in 1873, the Church's glebe lands in 1976 amounted to a pitiable 111,628 acres.

Where had all the Church's land gone? The Church themselves were to prove exceptionally coy about the matter. For years, the subject has remained shrouded in mystery, with the Diocesan Boards of Finance often refusing to answer questions about it. Cahill wrote to every diocese requesting an explanation, but received useful information from less than half. Efforts by Exeter University to investigate the matter in 2012 drew a blank after a 'very disappointing' response rate from Church authorities. The Church is not subject to Freedom of Information laws, even though the C of E is England's established religion and twenty-six bishops sit in the House of Lords making the laws that govern us. But uncovering what the Church still owns today has proved fiendishly difficult, until now.

The Land Registry's release of land ownership information on companies and corporate bodies in recent years means an updated stocktake of the state of Church lands is now possible, and it's even worse than before. A 2015 Freedom of Information request to the Land Registry by *Private Eye* journalist Christian Eriksson elicited figures for the area of land owned by corporate bodies, including each of the Diocesan Boards of Finance. I've checked these figures against the stats on glebe land that a quarter of all dioceses now publish on their websites: in nine out of ten cases, the figures match up well. So, unless there's a backlog of land out there that remains unregistered, we can pretty confidently say that the amount of glebe land has decreased still further over the past four decades. Just 70,000 acres remain. The slide has been universal:

landholdings in Lincolnshire, for example, consistently at the top of the league, declined from nearly 100,000 acres of glebe in Victorian time to 20,000 in 1976; there are now just 12,000 acres left.

The reason why has more to do with the lure of Mammon than with holy scripture. Before the 1976 law change, individual parish priests had the option of selling off their glebe land, alongside simply renting it out, as a way to make some extra cash. We can't be sure, given the Church's silence on the matter, but it seems that many vicars chose to make a quick buck by flogging off the land. After all, faced with the government's abolition of tithes in 1936 (which took place as a result of rural workers' and landowners' campaigns in the wake of the Great Depression), and with dwindling church congregations in an increasingly secular society, some parishes must have felt the need to sell off their assets to make ends meet.

'Stealing land is difficult to do,' muses the land rights activist Gill Barron, who's also looked into the loss of glebe land. 'You can't exactly roll it up in a carpet and carry it away. But . . . the undercover transfer of ownership of land is, in fact, incredibly easy in a country where the records of who owns what are a jealously guarded secret.' And the Church has certainly helped keep the secret closely guarded.

Wresting control of glebe land away from vicars and handing it to dioceses was a belated attempt by the C of E hierarchy to shut the stable door after the horse had bolted. Yet the financial impetus to sell up has clearly remained – hence the continued decline in glebe since the 1970s. 'Because of its original purpose, glebe land is usually situated within a settlement or close on the outskirts of the settlement, with a high chance of it being zoned for development,' write the estate agents Savills. This, they state, 'can make the land very valuable'.

You'll probably have walked past a Glebe Close or Glebe Field near where you live: in some cases, the Church may retain ownership, but usually the site will have been sold on long ago for development. Some of this former glebe land even appears to have found its way into the hands of offshore companies based in tax havens. For example, Land

Registry data lists land at Glebe Farm in Ruislip, West London, as now belonging to Blackfriars Holdings Ltd, based in the British Virgin Islands; while Glebe House in Bedford belongs to Glebe Ltd, registered in the Channel Islands. There are dozens more such examples, and likely countless other glebe fields that have been sold for shopping malls or buried beneath roads.

The loss of glebe lands tells us two things. First, it confirms the great cloak of secrecy that continues to envelop land ownership in England, and how our established institutions continue to promote this – in the case of the Church, perhaps out of embarrassment for what full transparency would reveal.

Second, it's an early case study in the financialisation of land. The Church's sale of glebe lands anticipated the great privatisation of public land later enacted by Margaret Thatcher's government and her successors. In doing so, however, the Church wasn't embarking on some ideological plan; rather, it simply succumbed to that oldest of sins, human greed.

Despite having allowed its clergy to sell off so much of the family silver, the Church today still boasts a property portfolio worth at least £8 billion. Its finances have been kept afloat by the Church Commissioners, a central body set up in 1948 to manage the Church's property assets. The Church Commissioners own land totalling around 105,000 acres, on top of what the dioceses own – and in 2017 this land generated a whopping £226 million of income for the Church.

What remains, however, of the Church's traditional commitment to using its resources to help the poor and homeless? 'The Church of England remains a very large landowner,' admitted Justin Welby, the Archbishop of Canterbury, in a TV interview about the housing crisis. 'We need to be committed to housing development, and, most of all, to community building.'

Welcome as the Archbishop's commitment is, I'm sceptical that the Church will help solve the housing crisis after researching how its

Commissioners have managed their estate. In contrast to the financial mismanagement that's characterised the Church's loss of glebe land, the centralised estate of the Church Commissioners seems to have been very efficiently managed over the last seventy years. But such business acumen has seen them take up the mantle of property developers, and sell off affordable residential housing in favour of more lucrative commercial developments.

'The pressure to generate the investment income needed by the Church of England,' argues housing expert Chris Hamnett, a professor of geography at King's College London, 'has led to an increasingly commercial attitude towards their land and property investments.' Although the Commissioners, he maintains, 'retain a small residual social commitment to "housing the poor"', their properties have 'increasingly come to be viewed as an investment like any other'.

Back when the Church Commissioners were established after the Second World War, the Church had some 60,000 residential properties on its books. Much of its housing stock was of poor quality; some of its London estates around Paddington were even described as slums. But rather than redevelop its properties to provide better-quality accommodation for working-class residents, the Commissioners, finding they generated low profit margins, simply sold off vast swathes of housing. Ninety acres south-east of Paddington were retained and gentrified; house prices there today are an astonishing £11,000 per square *metre*. The Bishop's Avenue, just north of Hampstead Heath, was put on the market by the Church in 1959: today, it's a byword for empty mansions and offshore billionaires. By the 1970s, the Commissioners retained just a tenth of the housing stock they had first inherited.

To fund the upkeep of the clergy and their ageing buildings – like the Archbishop of Canterbury's Lambeth Palace on the banks of the Thames – would take more than the usual church roof fund appeals, the Commissioners decided. This hard-nosed approach saw them diversify the Church's asset portfolio into stocks and shares, and invest instead in commercial property. From the 1950s onwards, they embarked on a string of multi-million-pound redevelopment projects, using their valuable freehold land to build the Angel Centre in Islington, a shopping mall in Birkenhead, and office blocks on the Cartwright Estate near Tottenham Court Road, among other ventures.

Perhaps the biggest moneyspinner of all, however, was the rebuilding of Paternoster Square, next to St Paul's – Church land since medieval times, whose name comes from the Latin for 'Our Father', the opening words of the Lord's Prayer. In 1986, with the City of London booming in the wake of financial deregulation by Margaret Thatcher's government, the Church Commissioners sold a 250-year lease on the land to a consortium of property developers. The deal was worth tens of millions to the Church, who also retained the valuable freehold. Goldman Sachs and the London Stock Exchange would later take up residence in Paternoster Square, transforming it from a place where monks once clutched their rosaries into a temple to modern capitalism.

But it wouldn't be long before the square was filled with the sound of chickens coming home to roost. In the wake of the financial crash of 2008 – the inevitable consequence of City deregulation – Paternoster Square was where the Occupy movement of 2011 first tried to set up camp, before being forced to settle on the steps of St Paul's. The resulting showdown with the Church authorities saw much soul-searching among the clergy over the Church's accommodation with capitalism. The Canon of St Paul's, Giles Fraser, who resigned out of sympathy with the protesters, spoke about the 'very legitimate anger about the way in which wealth has been distributed and the way in which capitalism is currently seen to benefit just a very few people'. Ownership of land and property, of course, remains central to this chasm of inequality.

To be fair to them, the Church Commissioners have always aspired to wealth redistribution – it's just that their remit is to redistribute income between the clergy, rather than among society at large. One example is the fact that the Commissioners today own lots of land and property in County Durham and around Newcastle, stretching from the mouth of the Tyne all the way back to the foothills of the North Pennines. The reason is that the area had once been owned by the local bishop as part of the Palatinate of Durham, an ancient institution where the Church held huge sway outside the jurisdiction even of the Crown. For centuries, the bishop of Durham had been the region's largest and richest landowner. Much of this land was later taken over by the Church Commissioners as part of their efforts to even out some of the inequalities in wealth that had grown up between different branches of the Church, and share out the proceeds from rich bishoprics to poorer ones.

But when it comes to any wider social role, the Commissioners' efforts seem distinctly limited. For a time, the Church had ownership of the philanthropic Octavia Hill Estates, a set of social housing developments across London let out to low-income households for fair rents. Yet low profit margins prompted the Commissioners to dispose even of these in 2011, selling them off in a move that led one local MP to accuse the Church Commissioners of 'putting profit before people'. 'The sleepy old Church of England is a greedy, money-grubbing property tycoon,' spits the journalist Harry Mount, arguing that a ruthless commercialism belies its otherwise affable reputation. Professor Chris Hamnett castigates the Church's outlook as being one of 'philanthropy at 5 per cent': 'While the Church Commissioners engage in a limited amount of what might be termed "social investment", their activities in this sphere are marginal to their major objective of income growth.'

One upcoming test of whether the Church venerates morals above Mammon will be whether it makes use of its extensive mineral rights to profiteer from fracking. In recent years, the Commissioners have been busily laying claim to 585,000 acres of underground deposits of stone, metals and minerals. The Church has explained, reasonably enough, that it's simply re-registering ancient rights as part of an updating process mandated by the Land Registry, and that it has few active plans to exploit such rights with new mines or quarries. But with ongoing efforts by shale gas companies to frack across large swathes of northern England, there are fears the Church could seek to cash in. Rights to oil and gas were nationalised long ago, but the Commissioners could still profit by charging companies wanting to drill through mineral layers belonging to the Church. And though the C of E has divested itself of all investments in coal and tar sands, citing climate-change concerns, it still argues that fracking can be 'morally acceptable' if properly regulated. In 2016, the Church Commissioners gave permission to a fracking firm to carry out underground seismic surveys on their Ormskirk Estate in Lancashire, the first step towards fracking.

The other major test facing the Church over the use of its land is how it responds to the ongoing housing crisis. Warm words from the Archbishop of Canterbury are all very well; but, having allowed vast swathes of land to be sold off, what can the Church practically *do* about it?

It could make a start by confessing to its past sins – by submitting to a searching inquiry into how it permitted its glebe to be flogged off, and how its investment policies have exacerbated the housing crisis by gentrifying key parts of London. Next, the Church Commissioners, having invested heavily in digitising maps of their landholdings in recent years, should publish these maps as a resource for housing associations and local authorities seeking to find local land. Lastly, it should work closely with councils to earmark land for affordable housing, and stipulate that a decent percentage of its land be sold cheaply, at existing use value. At a time when church pews are emptier than ever, the Church needs urgently to engage in some more soul-searching, and show that it retains a social role in modern England.

Old institutions die hard, especially in a conservative country like England. Long after the Crown and Church lost most of their formal powers, they continue to hold sway – kept alive, in part, by their landed wealth. Understanding how these archaic, quasi-feudal pillars of the Establishment operate is crucial to grasping the nature of power in modern Britain, and critical to comprehending why land ownership in England remains so unequal.

The efforts of the Duchies and the Church to evade full scrutiny by Parliament and the public tell us something profound about how privilege tries to perpetuate itself. And the way that both Crown and Church have avoided trying to disclose their landholdings is telling, too: because the concealment of wealth from prying eyes is also critical to preserving it.

These ancient organisations have survived into the modern world by transforming their landed estates from medieval baronies into capitalist property portfolios while still trying to avoid public accountability and wider social responsibility. Some would like to see the Anglican Church disestablished, and the monarchy abolished outright. Personally, I'm ambivalent about that. But on the question of the land they own, it's clear that the estates of the Crown and Church ought to be made to better serve the public interest.

Most of all, the Crown and Church still matter because of the wider Establishment they helped to create. Without William the Conqueror's division of conquered lands to his loyal barons, and without the Church's tacit moral blessing for this unequal hierarchy, England would have no landed elite.

4

OLD MONEY

Once, when asked to give advice to young entrepreneurs on how they could succeed in modern Britain, the now-deceased 6th Duke of Westminster had some sage words. 'Make sure they have an ancestor who was a very close friend of William the Conqueror,' he said.

Class runs deep in English society. Many of the aristocratic families who continue to thrive, prosper and own great swathes of the British Isles can date their bloodlines all the way back to the Norman Conquest. Indeed, 1066 was the making of them: some of the largest landowners in England today owe their territorial empires to the patronage of William the Conqueror a thousand years ago.

The Dukes of Westminster are a case in point. Their family name, Grosvenor, derives from Hugh Le Grand Veneur, the 'great huntsman' of King William's court. Disgruntled commoners took to calling the portly Hugh the 'fat huntsman', or *'gros veneur'*, and the nickname stuck. A statue of the first Marquess of Westminster in Belgrave Square, one of the London estates now owned by the family, bears the proud declaration: 'The Grosvenor family came to England with William the Conqueror and have held land in Cheshire since that time.' Today, the Duke of Westminster is consistently found towards the top of the annual *Sunday Times* Rich List, the inheritor of a £9 billion fortune made from owning a vast, 130,000-acre estate in land and property, built up over centuries.

Nor are the Grosvenors alone in having such an ancient pedigree.

Travel to sleepy Arundel on the edge of the South Downs, and in the middle of the town square you'll find a copper plaque affixed to a wall. 'Since William rose and Harold fell,' runs the inscription, 'There have been Earls at Arundel.' Raise your eyes skyward, and the colossal grey towers and crenellated walls of Arundel Castle loom over the town. The earls, since elevated to become Dukes of Norfolk, continue to lord it over this part of Sussex.

Sitting for a pint in a nearby pub garden overlooking the River Arun, with the Duke's fortress silhouetted against the skyline and the wind hissing gently through the reeds growing on the floodplain, it seemed to me as though little had changed in the past millennium. Feudalism lived on; deference had never died. In the words of that Victorian celebration of the social hierarchy, 'All Things Bright And Beautiful':

> *The rich man in his castle,*
> *The poor man at his gate,*
> *God made them high and lowly,*
> *And ordered their estate.*

A fawning display in the local museum confirmed the impression. 'When the 15th Duke stood on the battlements of his newly repaired keep in 1910', it read, 'he would have had the satisfaction of knowing that almost everything he could see in all directions belonged to him.' Although the Norfolks' estate is thought to have diminished a little in size since then, it's still said to span some 16,000 acres.

Or take Ralph Percy, the current Duke of Northumberland. His ancestor William de Percy appears in Domesday as the owner of a hundred manors in the north of England. Nowadays, the Duke is the second-largest private landowner in England, with at least 100,000 acres in his possession. He runs his estate from Alnwick Castle; local residents complain that it feels like the whole county is run by him.

Such examples give the lie to the widespread notion, perpetuated by scholars, journalists and aristocrats themselves in recent years, that the aristocracy have been consigned to the dustbin of history. In fact, though their wealth and power has waned since their heyday, their stubborn resilience is one of the great success stories of recent English history.

The genteel image of the aristocracy today, epitomised in costume dramas and tea and cakes in country houses, masks an early history that was written in blood. The Norman Conquest was brutal: William's seizure of land was absolute, and he brooked no challenges. Rebellions by the English against their new masters were quickly crushed; the Harrying of the North laid waste huge tracts of northern England. This was one of the most brazen land grabs in history. Four thousand Anglo-Saxon *thegns* were replaced by less than two hundred Norman barons and clergy, and they achieved supremacy through force of arms.

Domesday gives us some idea of how concentrated land ownership became under the Conqueror. The figures are staggering: twenty years after the Conquest, along with the king's 17 per cent, the bishops and abbots owned some 26 per cent of the landed wealth of England, and the 190-odd barons roughly 54 per cent. Even within this elite there was an elite: a dozen of the leading barons controlled about a quarter of the kingdom. One, Alan Rufus – a close relative of the Conqueror – is estimated to have owned about 7 per cent of England's landed wealth on his own, and was one of the richest men who has ever lived.

William and his barons were a tight-knit circle, whose experiences of fighting side-by-side were now being rewarded in the handing out of spoils. Perhaps the best modern analogy is the mafia boss and his cronies, who depend on one another's loyalty and give each other gifts, and will readily spill blood to protect the syndicate's honour. William, the Norman Don Corleone, summoned the nation's biggest landowners to his court upon the completion of the Domesday Book, and is thought to have had them swear oaths of fealty to him as he sat on his throne. The symbiotic relationship between Crown and aristocracy, between monarchical patronage and noble fidelity, has continued ever since.

In later centuries, seizures of land by the gentry continued with the enclosure of the commons. Little of this is remembered or taught in schools today. A powerful folk-memory of the Scottish Highland Clearances rightly persists, but the dispossession of England's peasantry is mostly forgotten. Yet between 1604 and 1914, some 6.8 million acres of common land were enclosed by Acts of Parliament – a fifth of all England. This, of course, was at a time when few 'commoners' could vote to sway what Parliament did. John Clare, the nineteenth-century poet who went mad with grief after witnessing the fencing-off of his beloved countryside, wrote how 'Inclosure came and trampled on the grave / Of labour's rights and left the poor a slave'.

Slavery and colonialism, too, played major roles in the formation of large English estates. Recent research by University College London has mapped over 3,000 British properties that once belonged to slave-owners or people who directly benefited from the slave trade. Large swathes of Bristol, London and Liverpool were built using the wealth that flowed from the sugar and cotton plantations of the Caribbean and North American colonies, where around three million Africans were transported and enslaved over three centuries. One example is Edwin Lascelles, 1st Baron Harewood, who inherited from his father a West Indian fortune which had included a slave plantation. From the proceeds, he had built for him Harewood House in Yorkshire, a vast Palladian mansion complete with parkland landscaped by Capability Brown. The Lascelles family went on to become one of the largest slave-owning families of their era, amassing 27,000 acres in Jamaica and Barbados and nearly 3,000 slaves, for whom life expectancy was a pitiful twenty-five years. Such suffering appeared not to elicit a hint of empathy or remorse from the 2nd Earl of Harewood, who campaigned against slavery's abolition, declaring, 'I, among others, am a sufferer.' He was awarded over £23,000 in 1835 for his loss of 'property'.

The role of violence in the acquisition of aristocratic estates is seldom acknowledged today in the placid displays you see in country mansions. But the stain remains. Gerrard Winstanley, the radical thinker whose group of Diggers sought to redistribute land during the Civil War, lambasted lords who tried to wash their hands of this bloody history. 'The power of enclosing land and owning property was brought into the creation by your ancestors by the sword,' he wrote. Or, as the anarcho-syndicalist peasants in *Monty Python and the Holy Grail* later put it, the violence was inherent in the system. An old joke, told by land reformers and socialists since the late nineteenth century, encapsulates the injustice. A lord confronts a poacher who is trespassing on his estate:

LORD: How dare you come on my land, sir?
POACHER: Your land! How do you make that out?
LORD: Because I inherited it from my father.
POACHER: And pray, how did he come by it?
LORD: It descended to him from his ancestors.
POACHER: But tell me how they came by it?
LORD: Why, they fought for it and won it, of course.
POACHER (taking off his coat): Then I'll fight you for it.

But why own land at all? For centuries, of course, land was the primary source of wealth in England. As the source of food, fuel and shelter for an overwhelmingly agrarian nation, ownership of land conferred great riches – first as feudal dues, and later as monetary rents. But money was only part of the reason for having land; just as important was the power and status it conferred. The 15th Earl of Derby, the Victorian landowner who helped commission the Return of Owners of Land, listed five main benefits of land ownership: 'One, political influence; two, social importance, founded on territorial possession, the most visible and unmistakeable form of wealth; three, power over tenantry; . . . four, residential enjoyment, including what is called sport; five, the money return – the rent.'

Moreover, owning land was a secure investment for the long term, a way of preserving wealth for posterity. Farming was rarely the means of earning a fast buck: it involved considerable outlays, and a poor harvest could cause a major loss of earnings. But in the long run, land would always appreciate in value. A country house and landed estate were the solid, lasting means by which a family's name and fortune could endure down through the ages.

If conquest, enclosure and colonialism were important means by which the aristocracy first acquired their lands, equally important were the inheritance laws that meant they retained them. The crucial rule was male primogeniture – the custom that everything is inherited by the eldest son. This was vital to the maintenance of large estates, because it gave certainty about who was to inherit, and ensured that a lord's landholdings remained intact: owned by one descendant rather than broken up between several. 'If all the children shared the wealth, the properties would be divided and subdivided till the pomp and circumstance of the peerage would disappear,' warned one American admirer of the gentry in 1885. 'In order to retain its importance, the aristocracy must be kept small in numbers.'

The enforcement of male primogeniture has clearly influenced patterns of land ownership across much of England, keeping estates large. In Wales and in Kent, by contrast, estates tend to be smaller; here, and particularly in Kent, the older practice of *gavelkind* – dividing up land equally between all heirs – continued to hold sway. In eighteenth-century France, even before the Revolution sent aristocrats' heads rolling, nobles' estates tended to be smaller than those of their English contemporaries due to inheritance laws which stipulated the *morcellation* of land between all heirs. This gave many more men a stake in the land, though it failed to stop the eventual uprising against aristocratic privilege.

Male primogeniture is also, of course, fundamentally sexist. Occasionally, women have inherited aristocratic titles, and a few duchesses and countesses have become major landowners; but these are the exception rather than the rule. The early twentieth-century poet Vita Sackville-West, who wrote extensively about land and who is perhaps better known as Virginia Woolf's lover, was dismayed not to inherit her family's seat at Knole Castle due to these discriminatory laws of succession. But she struck back at her patriarchal father by buying up Sissinghurst Castle, after discovering the Sackvilles had once owned it. Other aristocratic women have been similarly disinherited. When the 6th Duke of Westminster died in 2016, his 26-year-old son Hugh inherited the entire family fortune over the heads of his elder sisters, making him the richest man under thirty in the world.

In 2013, a group of peers – both women and men – sought to bring an end to male primogeniture once and for all. An Act had recently been passed to change the laws governing royal succession, finally allowing the monarch's eldest daughter to inherit the throne. This 'set the hares running' on whether the same reforms would now be made to noble inheritance, and a campaign group of aristocratic women calling themselves The Hares was formed. A number of peers tried to introduce legislation in Parliament to end male primogeniture. Dubbed the 'Downton Law', after the TV costume drama in which the eldest daughter is forbidden from inheriting the estate, the Equality (Titles) Bill got as far as its committee stage in the Lords.

But Lord Wallace, responding on behalf of the government, was having none of it, and kicked the Bill into the long grass. 'We should take our time, look very carefully at the implications . . . and then perhaps consider further,' he counselled, echoing the arguments of all those who have opposed change within the aristocracy for the past thousand years. Others were more vituperative in their opposition to equality. The Earl of Durham, locked in a dispute with his sisters over inheritance rights, railed against the campaign. 'It is stupid in my view not only to be battling for something that could only possibly appeal to somebody's pride and vanity,' he spat, 'but also something that affects about 0.0001 per cent of the population.' It just so happens that this tiny percentage of people still own a large chunk of the country's landed wealth.

Part and parcel of the aristocracy, and just as important to its formation as a select elite, is the system of hereditary titles. There are five ranks of the peerage, in descending order of importance: dukes, marquesses, earls, viscounts and barons. They're created by the Crown without recourse to Parliament, through legal instruments known as *letters patent*. At present, there are around 800 hereditary peers: 24 dukes (not counting the various honorary dukedoms created for members of the royal family), 34 marquesses, 191 earls, 115 viscounts and 426 barons, as well as 4 countesses and 9 baronesses in their own right. Confusingly, peers can also hold multiple titles as they progress up the ranks, with their heirs adopting the subordinate honours: for example, the heir to the Marquess of Salisbury is styled Viscount Cranborne.* Life peers, meanwhile, are a separate, more recent creation, invented to help modernise the House of Lords, with none of the land and wealth associated with the ancient hereditary peerage.

The whole arcane system of titles has become underpinned over the centuries by byzantine institutions and insignia. Old families proudly bear coats-of-arms, bedecked with heraldic beasts, mottoes and crests recalling their ancestors; the whole flummery policed by the College of Arms – whose head, the Duke of Norfolk, we met earlier. Aristocratic elitism finds its apogee in the voluminous pages of *Debrett's* and *Burke's Peerage*, obsessively compiled lists of current honours and their ancient bloodlines, which read a little like stock-books of good breeding.

The ranks of the peerage may appear convoluted and archaic to outsiders, but their complex, jealously guarded hierarchies are key to keeping the aristocracy exclusive. Sometimes, the closed nature of this club has proven problematic to kings wishing to broaden their pool of supporters and, above all, their income streams. James I ended up creating an entirely new class of hereditary titles, the baronetcies, which he sold to the lesser landed gentry in a seventeenth-century cash-for-honours scandal. Baronets have lower social standing than members of the peerage, but their titles are also hereditary, and their landed domains can be just as extensive. As of 2017, there were 1,204 extant baronetcies

---

* To add further to the confusion, there are actually five separate peerages, created over time as the jurisdiction of the Crown has waxed and waned: peerages of England, Scotland, Ireland, Great Britain and the United Kingdom. 'The Peerage', and the numbers of peers cited above, refer to all of these.

in the UK – meaning that the hereditary, titled aristocracy overall consists of just 2,000 families. Below peers and baronets sit knights and squires: holders of non-hereditary titles ('Sir', 'Dame', 'Esquire'), but nevertheless often significant landowners in their own right. The 'squirearchy' of the early modern period were often lords of the manor across large parts of rural England. In terms of classes of landowners, however, this is where definitions become more blurred, and it gets harder to distinguish between estates that have been inherited and those bought more recently.

But was this exclusive club in fact open to newcomers? Overseas observers of England during the early modern period often marvelled at its political stability, and the fact that it had never suffered a far-reaching social revolution. They attributed this to what they surmised to be England's 'open elite', a ruling class that was willing to welcome the newly wealthy bourgeoisie, and absorb those of middling rank who might otherwise become disgruntled and try to challenge the whole system.

Yet while there was a certain fluidity at the lower end, with merchants sometimes becoming members of the landed gentry, there was also great resistance to new money joining the peerage. Lawrence and Jeanne Stone, surveying the state of the aristocracy between the reign of Henry VIII and Queen Victoria's Golden Jubilee, concluded that 'for 340 years, the elite maintained a highly stable social and political system', in which upward mobility was enjoyed only by a comparative few. Just 157 'men of business' bought their way into the landowning elite over these three centuries and were able to acquire estates of 2,000 acres or more. Throughout this period, 'many of the same families still resided in the same seats', and newcomers attempting to join the landed aristocracy had to overcome 'infinitely resistant lines of snobbery'. Subsequent research has suggested that there were a greater number of wealthy entrants to landed society who succeeded in buying smaller estates of around 1,000 acres; but these were small fry compared to the vast landholdings of the dukes and earls of their day.

By the time of the Victorian Return of Owners of Land, the landed aristocracy was at the peak of its political power. A mere 4,217 peers, great landowners and squires owned 18 million acres of land – half of England and Wales, possessed by 0.01 per cent of the population. In a triumph for trickle-down economics, it had taken eight centuries for England's landowning elite to broaden out from around 200 Norman barons to 4,200 Victorian nobles and gentry. 'In terms of territory, it seems likely that the notables owned a greater proportion of the British Isles than almost any other elite owned of almost any other country,' writes the historian David Cannadine.

What happened next to the aristocracy has often been portrayed as a catastrophe. Between Queen Victoria becoming Empress of India and the killing fields of the First World War, the sun appeared to set on the gilded world of inherited privilege. This perception owes much to the work of the historian F.M.L. Thompson in his 1963 book *English Landed Society in the Nineteenth Century*, later popularised and embroidered in David Cannadine's *The Decline and Fall of the British Aristocracy*. They recount how the entire aristocratic class experienced a sudden loss of territory, wealth and political power – plagued by death duties, assaulted by land reformers and Lords reform, and losing out to the *nouveau riche*. 'The old order is doomed,' bemoaned the Duke of Marlborough in 1919.

No one seriously disputes that the British aristocracy fell from grace after their Victorian heyday. But reports of the death of the aristocracy have been greatly exaggerated. This is particularly true when it comes to the land they own.

Thompson and Cannadine's claims about the rapid territorial losses of the peerage in fact come down to one, rather shaky source. Cannadine states that 'in the years immediately before and after the First World War, some six to eight million acres, one-quarter of the land of England, was sold by gentry and grandees'. Thompson likewise asserts: 'it is possible that in the four years of intense activity between 1918 and 1921 something between six and eight million acres changed hands in England.' For this startling figure, both relied on a single article in one edition of the property magazine *Estates Gazette* from December 1921.

That figure has recently been convincingly challenged by two statisticians, John Beckett and Michael Turner. They examined land sales data from the time and found that 'much less than 25 per cent of England changed hands in the four highlighted years 1918–1921'. Instead, they concluded, it was actually more like 6.5 per cent, and that excitable estate agents at the *Gazette* had massively overstated the case.

Moreover, all sides agree that the highest echelons of the aristocracy were able to cling on to their landed estates with much greater success than the lesser gentry. As Thompson quietly admits in the final pages of his book, 'The landed aristocracy has survived with far fewer casualties . . . Among the great ducal seats, for example . . . Badminton, Woburn, Chatsworth, Euston Hall, Blenheim Palace, Arundel Castle, Alnwick Castle, Albury and Syon House, Goodwood, Belvoir Castle, Berry Pomeroy, and Strathfield Saye are all lived in by the descendants of their nineteenth-century owners.' That Thompson could say this half a century after his supposed 'revolution in landownership' is startling enough. It's even more startling, then, that today, another half-century on, *every single one* of those ducal family seats still remains in the hands of the same aristocratic families.

What may have felt seismic at the time looks a good deal less drastic in retrospect. 'When Thompson wrote in 1963, the great estate seemed to be in terminal decline,' argue Beckett and Turner, 'but the subsequent revival of the fortunes of landed society [have] brought seriously into question the whole business of just how bad things really were.'

At the same time as Thompson was performing the last rites on the aristocracy, another author found them to be in rude health, albeit rather leaner. The journalist Roy Perrott's 1967 survey, *The Aristocrats*, surveyed the acreage held by seventy-six titled landowners. Though most of the estates had significantly diminished in size since 1873, together these individuals still owned a combined 2.5 million acres across the UK. Perrott estimated that this sample represented 'about one-seventh of those owned by the titled nobility', and his definition of that elite totalled around 3,000 people. So, in the era of the Space Race, 0.005 per cent of the UK population still owned 17.9 million acres of the country, or 30 per cent of the total land area.

Drawing on Perrott's work, the geographer Doreen Massey arrived at a similar extrapolation a decade later, concluding that 'in spite of the decline which they have undergone this century, the holdings of the landed aristocracy have by no means been reduced to insignificance'. Stephen Glover's 1977 survey of thirty-three large landowners found that they owned 667,410 acres, a drop of almost two-thirds from the 1,869,573 acres those same estates had owned in 1873. Even taking into account the reduced acreages, Glover concluded, these people 'remain – on paper at least – very rich men', all the wealthier thanks to the rapid rise in land prices that occurred in the 1970s.

More recent estimates, too, strongly suggest that the aristocracy have held their own against the tide of history. Kevin Cahill's *Who Owns Britain*, which draws upon multiple newspaper reports, obituaries and rich lists, presents figures for the 100 largest landowners in the UK and the Republic of Ireland. Altogether, Cahill reckons these select few own some 4.8 million acres. Still, this is only about 6 per cent of the land area of the two countries, and without figures for the rest of the aristocracy, it's hard to conclude from Cahill's research who actually owns the majority of Britain. Nevertheless, his figure for the land owned by the UK's twenty-four non-royal dukes is startling. With a total of over 1 million acres between them, these remain men of very broad acres. Moreover, as we'll see, the *places* they own have increased enormously in value, leaving many of the peerage extremely wealthy.

Or take the figures stated by the Country Land and Business Association (CLA), who represent the landowning lobby in England and Wales; many aristocrats are known to be members. In a 2009 document, the CLA state that 'Our 36,000 members own and manage over 50% of all of the rural land in England and Wales.' A second CLA document from the same year clarifies that the rural land in their members' possession totals five million hectares. So the 36,000 members of the CLA own 12.35 million acres, a third of England and Wales. Dan and Peter Snow, in their 2006 BBC documentary *Whose Britain Is It Anyway?*, came to the similar conclusion that the aristocracy and old landed families still own nearly a third of the UK overall.

Further confirmation that land remains in the hands of the few comes from agricultural statistics collected by the Department for the Environment, Farming and Rural Affairs (DEFRA) on the number and size of farms. Counting the number of farm holdings isn't quite the same as tallying up landowners: many farms are tenanted, and lots will be ultimately owned by companies and councils rather than the aristocracy. But these are still useful proxy figures. DEFRA's 2017 data shows there are 218,000 farm holdings in the UK, covering 43 million acres – 72 per cent of the land area. Even this figure suggests that a tiny fraction of the overall population own the bulk of the land, and given that this includes tenanted farms, it's likely a big overestimate. But the department also publishes statistics for England alone which give a more interesting breakdown of the total acreages owned by farms of different sizes. This allows us to see that the majority of English soil is farmed by a much smaller set of large farms: 25,638 farm holdings cover 16.5 million acres, or 52 per cent of England's land area.

What's more, comparing these with official statistics from 1960, now buried in the National Archives, shows that there are a lot fewer but bigger farms today than sixty years ago. When Thompson wrote about the decline of the aristocracy in the first half of the twentieth century, he described how smaller farmers had started buying up the land sold off by big estates. But since Thompson penned his book, the concentration of land ownership has, if anything, been increasing again.

Pinning down precisely what the aristocracy still own, and what's now owned by the newly wealthy or by smaller-scale farmers, remains difficult. A definitive answer will remain elusive until the Land Registry is fully opened up. From the figures and estimates reviewed here, though, it seems a safe bet to say that around a third of England and Wales remains in the hands of the aristocracy and landed gentry – and that half of England is owned by less than 1 per cent of the population.

The aristocracy, in other words, have adapted, trimmed their sails – and survived. Their tenacity recalls Tennyson's 'Ulysses':

> *Though much is taken, much abides; and though*
> *We are not now that strength which in old days*
> *Moved earth and heaven, that which we are, we are . . .*

As the MP Chris Bryant puts it in his critical history of the aristocracy: 'Far from dying away, they remain very much alive.'

That begs two further questions. What's been the impact of so much land remaining in the hands of so few? And how have the aristocracy pulled off such a stunning feat of survival?

The image that most aristocratic estates present to the world is that of the grand country house, surrounded by beautiful parkland. From the yellow towers of the Duke of Rutland's Belvoir Castle – used as a substitute for Windsor in Netflix series *The Crown* – to the golden limestone frontage of Chatsworth House in Derbyshire, stately homes are the acceptable face of feudalism. Today, a 'cult of the country house' has grown up in England that rightly venerates their sumptuous architecture and historic art collections – though often omitting mention of how such wealth came to be amassed.

We now flock in our thousands to visit these mansions, stroll in their formal parterre gardens, and walk our dogs in their acres of parkland. Less than a century ago, of course, such public access would have been unthinkable. Aristocratic parks were created precisely to keep the masses out, and provide solace for their masters when they returned from the business of court or the hustle and bustle of the city. Many were created by the process of forcible enclosure, during which whole villages were evicted to make way for deer and specimen trees. Now that large swathes of parkland are open to the public for walking and cycling, that violent history has faded.

Aristocratic parkland has also changed our very concept of the English countryside. Much of that is thanks to one man, the individual who has perhaps had the single greatest impact on the English landscape: Lancelot 'Capability' Brown. During the eighteenth century, Brown was the landscape gardener *du jour*; he worked on some 250 sites during his lifetime and his client list included the majority of the House of Lords. Brown literally moved mountains and diverted rivers to create the naturalistic vistas that he and his patrons desired. Graceful curving hillsides were moulded and stands of trees carefully pruned to lead the eye through the parkland towards a distant folly or the setting sun. John Phibbs, Brown's biographer, estimates that he had a direct influence on half a million acres of England and Wales. 'The astonishing scale of his work means that he did not just transform the English countryside,' Phibbs writes, 'but also our idea of what it is to be English and what England is.' None of this, of course, would have happened without aristocratic cash.

Partly because of the scale of their influence, there is also a lingering sense nowadays that the aristocracy are the rightful guardians of our countryside. Many noble families profess their concerns about the environment on their estate websites, and act on them in their management plans. The motto of the Hussey family, inscribed on a crest above the front door of Scotney Castle in Kent, is *Vix ea nostra voco* – Latin for 'I scarcely call these things our own'.*

This notion of the aristocracy as stewards of the landscape is deeply rooted. There seems little doubt that the aristocratic preoccupation with lineage and inheritance gives them a long-term perspective when it comes to managing land. After all, it's in the interests of a lord to look after his estate, because he knows his descendants will inherit it. But

---

* The Hussey family's motto is even more true today than it was when it was inscribed: the castle is no longer their own, but the National Trust's.

asserting you're merely a steward of the land – 'scarcely calling it your own', when your family has in fact had outright possession of it for hundreds of years – can be a convenient excuse for owning so much. 'It doesn't feel to me as if I'm sitting here and owning vast tracts of land, because I obviously share it with hundreds of thousands of people,' the Duke of Northumberland claimed in the 2006 BBC documentary *Whose Britain Is It Anyway?* 'Yes, but – you're the *owner*,' pointed out an incredulous Peter Snow. 'I am the ultimate owner, I suppose,' the duke reluctantly admitted. There's also a risk that the manicured parks and exquisite gardens of the aristocracy blind us to their wider environmental impact. As George Monbiot has argued, 'they tend to be 500 acres of pleasant greenery amidst 10,000 laid waste by the same owner's plough'. And that's not the worst of it.

It was 5 a.m. on a freezing October morning, and I was locked onto a 500-tonne digger in an aristocrat's opencast coal mine.

The coal mine in question had been dug on land belonging to Viscount Matt Ridley, a prominent climate change sceptic, *Times* columnist and member of the House of Lords. I was part of a group that had trespassed on his land in order to shut down the mine for the day, in protest at its contribution to global warming. But our direct action wasn't just intended to highlight the millions of tonnes of coal that had so far been extracted from this gigantic pit. It was also to point out how Viscount Ridley had used his platform in Parliament and the press to cast doubt on climate science, while continuing to draw significant income from a coal mine on his land.

We had entered the vast opencast mine on Ridley's 15,000-acre Blagdon Estate in Northumberland under cover of darkness, making sure we arrived before work started. After climbing up onto the gantry of one of the giant coal excavators, we'd locked ourselves to it with bike locks around our necks. The vast walls of the mine with their exposed seams of anthracite lowered over us. We felt like the hobbits in Mordor. It was around an hour later when we were discovered by security, who initially joked that they thought we were Sunderland supporters coming to rub it in after Newcastle's recent defeat.

The police inspector who arrived later wasn't so amused, particularly after we refused to unlock. We'd come to prevent coal being dug up, and we weren't going to leave quietly. This mine, after all, was on land belonging to an aristocrat who'd stated that 'fossil fuels are not finished, not obsolete, not a bad thing', declared that 'climate change is good for the world', and who was still downplaying its importance just weeks before the opening of the Paris climate talks. Though Ridley admitted his financial interest in the coal mines on his estate, he had never disclosed the size of the 'wayleave', or rental income, that he received from leasing it to a mining company. Investigative journalist Brendan Montague has estimated it to be worth millions of pounds annually.

The arrangement illustrates two things about the aristocracy: their capacity to lobby politically for policies that align with their landed interests; and the way they use their monopoly over large tracts of land to extract rents. Indeed, many members of the peerage own extensive mineral rights across England, in addition to the land itself. The Duke of Bedford, for example, grew rich off the huge copper and arsenic mines that operated on his land at the Devon Great Consols during the Victorian period. The Duke of Devonshire is the only person in the UK to own the rights to any oil beneath his land, because he sank the first oil well on his estate at Hardstoft in Derbyshire before the 1934 Petroleum Act vested such rights in the Crown. He also has other mineral rights stretching far further afield: residents of Carlisle were surprised to receive letters in the post in 2013 notifying them that the Duke was staking his claim to metals and ores beneath their homes.

In fairness to them, many aristocrats nowadays are suspicious of letting extractive industries run riot on their estates. Plenty of large landowners have voiced their opposition to the fracking industry – such as Viscount Cowdray, who's resisted efforts to explore for shale gas in the South Downs, and an alliance of baronets and earls who have refused fracking firm INEOS access to their lands in North Yorkshire.

But the prospect of a fresh source of rental income can be enticing to large estates. Renting out land, after all, requires little effort on the part of the landowner. As historian M.L. Bush argues, throughout its history the English aristocracy has remained 'rigidly divorced . . . from direct production' and 'preferred the *rentier* role' as a means of getting filthy rich without getting their hands dirty.

It's this combination of inherited wealth and rent-seeking indigence that has drawn down much scorn upon the aristocracy in previous eras. 'The rent of land is naturally a monopoly price,' pointed out the classical free-market economist Adam Smith. 'It is not at all proportioned to what the landlord may have laid out upon the improvement of the land . . . but to what the [tenant] can afford to give.'

John Maynard Keynes longed for 'the euthanasia of the rentier', noting that landlords need not work to obtain their income: 'the owner of land can obtain rent because land is scarce'. It's no coincidence that vampires were portrayed in Victorian gothic horror novels as being bloodsucking aristocrats, preying parasitically upon the lower classes. Indeed, Bram Stoker's Dracula is not merely a count but a property magnate, buying up a string of big houses in London as places to leave his earth-filled coffins.

The most lucrative rental income, of course, went to aristocrats who owned land in central London. A 1925 campaigning postcard by radical journalist W.B. Northrop (see opposite) depicts a giant octopus labelled 'landlordism', its tentacles spreading through the streets of the capital. Each tendril curls around the boundaries of one of the 'Great Estates' that own London, listing their acreages and annual rents. 'The Land Octopus Sucks the Lifeblood of the People,' Northrop declared. Tellingly, nearly all of the aristocratic estates shown on the postcard still possess large swathes of the city today. Where they have lost land, they have more than made up for it in soaring property prices on their remaining acres.

You can walk from Sloane Square to Regent's Park without leaving land owned by the aristocracy and the Crown. One hundred acres of

Mayfair and 200 acres of Belgravia are owned by the Duke of Westminster's Grosvenor Estate. The Duke's property empire includes the most expensive street in the country, Grosvenor Crescent – average house price: £16.9 million – and Grosvenor Square, famous as the scene of the 1968 Vietnam War protests and, until recently, the base for the US embassy. The family inherited the land when it was merely swampy fields in the seventeenth century, as the wedding dowry of a marriage between the Grosvenors and infant heiress Mary Davies.

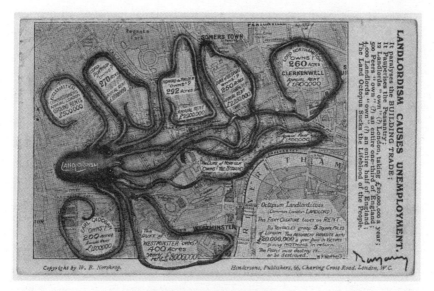

The octopus of 'Landlordism'.

To the north of Oxford Street is the Portman Estate. Comprising 110 acres of properties in Marylebone, the estate was first acquired in 1532 by Sir William Portman, lord chief justice to Henry VIII, who bought it to graze goats. Like the other great estates, the bequest began as farmland and ended up as prime real estate, following a building boom in the Georgian period. Today, the 10th Viscount Portman is the inheritor of a £2 billion fortune, according to the *Sunday Times* Rich List. Next door is the Howard de Walden Estate, consisting of 92 acres of Marylebone and taking in famously fashionable Harley Street. It's been owned by the de Walden family since 1710; the current head of the clan, Mary Hazel Caridwen Czernin, 10th Baroness Howard de Walden, is worth an estimated £3.73 billion.

To the south of Hyde Park is the Cadogan Estate, a 93-acre stretch of Kensington and Chelsea, inheritance of Earl Cadogan. This is the borough of the Grenfell Tower disaster, which left seventy-one dead and hundreds more homeless for months. It's also a borough which, in 2017, had over 1,500 empty homes, many of which are rumoured to be within the Cadogan Estate, dubbed by journalists 'the ghost town of the super-rich'. With an estimated wealth of £6.5 billion, Lord Cadogan's family has a knowing motto: 'He who envies is the lesser man'. Still, that fortune has been subsidised by the taxpayer and built off the back of 'lesser men': the GMB union calculated that in 2014 the Cadogan Estate had received £116,000 in housing benefit from less-well-off tenants.

These four aristocratic estates have a combined wealth of over £20 billion. Almost a thousand acres of central London remains in the hands of the aristocracy, Church Commissioners and Crown Estate. They own most of what is worth owning in central London. The character of the West End, argues the historian Peter Thorold, has been largely determined by the fact that 'a small number of rich families held fast to their land over a long period of time.' This level of aristocratic control has undoubtedly led to some well-planned squares and beautiful architecture. But even Simon Jenkins, the veteran defender of London's historic buildings, admits this has come with its downsides. The Great Estates grew so powerful, Jenkins recounts, that they 'managed for half a century to delay the introduction of a system of local government which might have mitigated the hardship it brought in its train'.

Crucial to the wealth of London's aristocratic estates has been their ability to retain the freehold ownership of their land and properties. For most of their history, this was never in question. Each estate has hundreds of tenants, but they are sold their properties on long leases, so that the landlord retains ultimate control. In more recent decades, however, successive governments have sought to enact leaseholder reform, to allow long-term tenants to extend their leases and eventually buy from their landlords the properties they have lived in for decades. When John Major announced reforms to this effect in 1993, the Duke of Westminster resigned from the Conservative Party in disgust. But the Great Estates are very far from beaten. In a recent landmark court case, attempts to reduce the costs for leaseholders of buying out the properties they rent were quashed, in a victory for London's aristocratic landlords.

While the aristocracy tend to make most of their money from their urban estates, where they spend it has an even bigger impact on the land. It's in the English uplands where the influence of the landed gentry is most marked, and at its most malign: the vast acreages of our countryside given over to grouse moors.

The aristocracy have always engaged in bloodsports: from accompanying Norman kings to hunt deer and wild boar, to rearing pheasants for woodland shooting parties of the sort satirised in Roald Dahl's *Danny the Champion of the World*. Who gets to catch and eat the creatures of the forest has long been a bone of contention between the landed and the landless; for centuries, poaching by hungry commoners was viciously policed. The mantrap in which Danny's father gets snared when out poaching pheasants one night was once commonplace. New Labour's ban on fox hunting was widely seen as retaliation for Thatcher crushing the miners' strike: you routed the working class, so we're bashing the toffs. But though foxhunts and pheasant shoots raise questions about class warfare and animal welfare, neither has anything like the impact on the landscape itself of shooting grouse.

A staggering 550,000 acres of England is given over to grouse moors – an area of land the size of Greater London. But despite the enormous scale of the grouse industry, few are aware of it: until recently there were no public maps showing its extent, and most of the research into grouse is carried out by the Game and Wildlife Conservation Trust and the

Moorland Association, both funded by the owners of grouse moors. A few years ago, the Moorland Association quietly published a map on their website showing the approximate outline of grouse moors in England. After they refused to share the underlying data with me, I was able to extract it from their map with the help of a data analyst, sense-check it against aerial photographs, and publish the results on whoownsengland.org.

The management of driven grouse moors has had a profound and very visible impact on landscapes. Take a look on Google Earth at any of the upland areas of northern England, and you'll soon spot the tell-tale patterns where the moorland heather has been slashed and burned to encourage the growth of fresh shoots favoured by young grouse. But to really appreciate the bleak devastation of a grouse moor, you need to visit one. An estate I walked across in the Peak District looked like a war zone: charred vegetation, scorched earth, deep gullies in the peat worn by rainwater flashing off the denuded soils. Studies by Leeds University have shown that the intensive management of grouse moors through heather burning can dry out the underlying peat, lead to soil carbon loss, and worsen flooding downstream. Residents of Hebden Bridge in West Yorkshire live in the shadow of the huge Walshaw Moor Estate, a grouse shoot so intensively managed that the RSPB lodged a complaint against it with the European Court of Justice. For years, the local residents had warned about the potential ill-effects of having such a degraded ecosystem upstream from them. In winter 2015, disaster struck, with intense rainfall pouring off the hills and inundating many homes, not just in Hebden but downstream as far as Leeds. Grouse moors may seem remote from the lives of most people, but they can still have an impact on those living far from them.

The ecological devastation wrought by grouse moors doesn't stop there. Gamekeepers manage them in such a way as to create a habitat ideally suited to grouse. This has the beneficial side-effect of bolstering conditions for other ground nesting birds, too. But it means curtains for the species that would normally prey upon them. There should be 300 pairs of hen harriers in the English uplands; instead, thanks to illegal persecution by the gamekeepers of grouse moors, there are just four pairs left. Foxes, stoats, weasels and other natural predators of grouse are shot or caught in traps. Even beautiful mountain hares are exterminated, because the ticks they carry can spread disease to grouse.

All this land is owned and managed for the benefit of a vanishingly small number of people. There are only around 150 grouse estates in England. Even the *Spectator* calls grouse shooting 'screamingly elitist'. Through a laborious research process, I've been able to identify the owners of some 500,000 acres of English grouse moors, and around half, by my reckoning, remain in the hands of the aristocracy and landed gentry. These include Baron Raby, who has a 30,000-acre grouse shoot in Upper Teesdale; the Duke of Westminster, whose 23,000-acre Abbeystead estate dominates the Forest of Bowland in Lancashire; and the Duke of Devonshire, owner of Chatsworth House, who also owns a huge 13,500-acre grouse moor at Bolton Abbey.

The other half of England's grouse moor estates have been bought up in recent decades by newly moneyed businessmen, sheikhs and Saudi princes, whose landholdings are examined in more detail in the next chapter. But it's doubtful whether they would have bothered investing in such an unprofitable enterprise were it not also the pastime of the British aristocracy, whose patronage of grouse shooting since Victorian times has lent it a powerful cachet. Owning a grouse moor has been the ultimate status symbol ever since Queen Victoria bought one at Balmoral in the Scottish Highlands, where there are even more grouse moors than in the English uplands.

Grouse moors are also propped up by public subsidies. A survey I conducted of thirty grouse moor estates showed they received around £4 million in annual farm subsidies in 2014. The Moorland Association and other shooting lobby groups claim the subsidies help estate managers foster wildlife habitats: but they are, of course, entirely artificial habitats designed to maximise breeding conditions for what's essentially an upland chicken. It's patently obvious that taxpayers shouldn't have to subsidise elite sports that end up flooding homes. But even were the subsidies to be removed, the social status of having a grouse moor would remain. To end the practice entirely requires a ban on grouse shooting, as ornithologist Mark Avery has called for.

In the meantime, aristocrats who genuinely care for their land ought to wind down their grouse moor estates voluntarily, and dampen the prestige that comes with owning one. If they want to set their sights higher, they should follow the lead of the increasing numbers of landowners who are seeking to rejuvenate nature on their estates, and rewild the English uplands instead.

The aristocracy have preserved their landed estates through a mixture of guile and influence. Faced with an assault on their wealth by various governments during the twentieth century, aristocrats adopted a three-pronged strategy: supplement incomes by sweating their assets and seeking state handouts; find ways to avoid being taxed; and lobby governments to better serve landed interests.

After facing minimal taxation under the *laissez-faire* administrations of the Victorian period – many of whose Cabinets had been stuffed with landowners – the aristocracy faced a rising clamour for higher taxes as the new century dawned. Successive Liberal governments sought fresh revenue streams to pay for the nascent welfare state. Estate duty, an early form of inheritance tax, was first levied in 1894. The Liberal Party was also responding to a wider grassroots movement for land reform that was growing in popularity, and that united farm workers and city-dwellers: its official anthem at the time, sung lustily in conference halls, was entitled 'God gave the land to the people'.

Upon becoming Chancellor in 1908, David Lloyd George, the aristocracy's arch-nemesis, relished the chance to kill two birds with one stone. His People's Budget of 1909 proposed a raid on the pockets of the very well off, to raise funds for the newly introduced state pensions and social security payments. Death duties would be increased, a 'supertax' levied on high incomes, and a 20 per cent tax imposed on the unearned increase in the value of land. Together, these proposals sought to impel landowners to make a fair contribution to society, and to pay back to the community a slice of what they took through their monopoly ownership of land.

Unsurprisingly, these radical measures were vehemently opposed in the House of Lords, which remained stuffed with the landowning gentry. Lloyd George thrived on such confrontation. In his famous Limehouse speech, delivered to a crowd of thousands, he mocked the landed gentry for demanding increased military spending but refusing to cough up. 'We wanted money to pay for [it]; so we sent the hat round. We sent it around amongst workmen ... They all dropped in their coppers.' The Welsh Wizard paused, savouring the punchline; then, 'We went round Belgravia, and there has been such a howl ever since that it has wellnigh deafened us.' The aristocracy, however, viewed this as an outrageous assault on their possessions and privileges. When the Lords duly voted down the Budget, the *Daily News* claimed that the peers who had killed it owned some 10.4 million acres of land between them. But this act, so brazenly self-interested, was to prove their lordships' undoing. The government called a general election and went to the country seeking a mandate to implement their reforms. When they got it, the Liberals not only enshrined their new taxes in legislation, but also saw to it that the House of Lords would never again be able to overrule the Commons on budgetary measures. The 1911 Parliament Act sharply curtailed the political power of the nobility.

But though this dealt a huge blow to landowners' say in parliamentary politics, they were simultaneously inventing new ways to press for their interests outside Parliament. What is today the Country Land and Business Association was founded in 1907 as a campaigning voice for the landowning interest in England and Wales.* Its founders included the Earl of Onslow, the Earl of Harrowby and Viscount Bledisloe. Later,

---

* The CLA began life as the Landowners' Central Association, subsequently the Central Landowners' Association and then the Country Landowners' Association, before adopting its current name.

it took as its offices a grand house in Belgrave Square on the Duke of Westminster's estate. Surrounded by the fluttering flags of foreign consulates, it's tempting to see it as the embassy of the landed classes. Though the CLA was unsuccessful in halting the introduction of Lloyd George's land value taxes, it proved instrumental in their abolition in 1920. Its lobbying later that decade also led to the de-rating of agricultural land, meaning its owners no longer paid council tax on it – something the CLA counts among its greatest victories.

Even so, the burden of taxation proved too much for some estates. When the post-war Labour government hiked death duties and income tax to pay for reconstruction and the new National Health Service, the aristocracy sought new ways to defend themselves. One option was simply to sell up. A new generation of owner-occupant farmers emerged as large estates were broken apart, their fields sold off to former tenants. Other landowners, finding the costs of upkeep on huge draughty mansions to be too much, went for the nuclear option. They would keep their land, but demolish their stately homes.

The result was a huge loss of heritage that clearly benefited no one. Architectural historian Matthew Beckett has gathered records of nearly 2,000 stately homes that were knocked down due to financial difficulties, 'as agricultural or mining incomes fell or due to heavy inheritance tax demands', or otherwise lost to dereliction, dry rot and fire. For just over half of these, he gives a definitive date of demolition, making it possible to chart when the majority of losses took place.

Before the twentieth century, there was a natural attrition rate of one or two stately homes lost annually to fire or bankruptcy. But after the introduction of death duties in 1894, the numbers started to creep up, with the bulk of the damage done over the half-century between 1925 and 1975. The peak of destruction was reached in 1952, when at least forty country houses were lost. One of the casualties that year was Alton Towers in Derbyshire. Owned for hundreds of years by the Earls of Shrewsbury, its fortunes began to decline in the late Victorian period, as its owners haemorrhaged money. Following occupation by US Army forces during the war, its contents were stripped and sold off and the building reduced to a burned-out shell by a deliberate fire. Today the grounds of Alton Towers are, of course, one of the largest theme parks in Britain.

To prevent their family seats succumbing to the wrecking ball – or, worse, becoming a venue for rollercoaster rides – the aristocracy began to innovate. Some sought refuge by deeding over their properties to the National Trust. Others, in the words of historian David Cannadine, 'soiled their hands' by getting jobs in commerce or the City. Others still decided that the time had come to monetise their palatial residences, and threw open the doors to the great unwashed. Sumptuous mansions, previously enjoyed only by their owners, servants and invited guests, were now shared for the first time with the nation at large. Magnificent private art collections were at last put on public display.

The most entrepreneurial patricians sought to attract tourists by setting up safari parks in their grounds, and filled their fields with lions, zebras and giraffes: the Duke of Bedford at Woburn, the Marquess of Bath at Longleat, the Earl of Derby at Knowsley. Fun as it is to watch a tiger prowl around a corner of Wiltshire, you've got to wonder whether the aristocratic fad for safari was sparked as much by nostalgia for the loss of Empire as it was by the desire to draw in crowds. Some peers went further, recoiling at the vulgarity of having to earn a living, and retired to their overseas estates in Kenya and South Africa. To the upper-class socialite Evelyn Waugh, these aristocratic fugitives and reactionaries were engaged in a futile attempt to 'recreate Barsetshire on the equator'. But for the aristocrats who stayed in Blighty, 'the 1950s were a period of recovery such as nobody could have envisaged amidst the privations of World War II and its socialist aftermath'.

Socialism was to prove recurrently popular, however. The 1960s saw a patrician government swept from power by a modernising Labour Party. Deference towards the aristocracy was crumbling, spurred on by the Profumo scandal and rumours of wild sex-parties in the decadent surroundings of Cliveden House. Suddenly, it was no longer fashionable for prime ministers to don tweeds and shoot grouse at weekends, as Tory premiers Harold Macmillan and Lord Alec Douglas-Home were fond of doing. The Labour leader Harold Wilson offered, instead, 'a chance to sweep away the grouse-moor conception of Tory leadership and refit Britain with a new image'. Beyond leaseholder reform, however, little in practice was done by Wilson's first administration to alter the position of landowners. But with Labour's swing to the left in the early 1970s, that soon changed.

Denis Healey, Labour's bushy-eyebrowed Chancellor, never did promise to 'tax the rich until the pips squeak', as the tabloids alleged. But he did warn his party's conference shortly before taking power in 1974 that there would be 'howls of anguish from those rich enough to pay over 80 per cent on their last slice of earnings'. Today such top rates of tax seem unimaginable, though similar levels were imposed by governments of both left and right in the post-war period.

Moreover, Labour had publicly committed itself in its manifesto to 'bring about a fundamental and irreversible shift in the balance of power and wealth in favour of working people and their families'. Part of that intended shift was the abolition of estate duty and its replacement with capital transfer tax, which closed off loopholes employed by the wealthy to gift over their estates while still alive. Most dramatic of all was the suggestion of a wealth tax, levied annually rather than simply at point of death, which Labour MPs voted through in January 1975. 'It means the end of the country estate,' wailed the Duke of Devonshire. In fact, the tide was about to turn in the aristocracy's favour.

Once again, the aristocracy's survival instincts kicked in. Historian Brian Harrison suggests that Labour's threats 'unintentionally prompted the adversary to regroup'. But was it better to engage in a political fight, or in capital flight? Some chose flight. The practice of vesting estates in family trusts to avoid inheritance tax had been honed by tax lawyers over the past century. Increasingly, some large landholdings were now being made over by deed entirely to professional wealth managers, like Rathbones Trust Company Ltd, who today are the registered owners of the Marquess of Northampton's Compton Wynyates estate, among others.

What was new at the time was the increasing registration of landed estates in offshore tax havens. Britain was integral to the development of the modern system of tax havens during the 1960s and 70s. As Nicholas Shaxson has charted, former colonies like the Cayman Islands joined Guernsey, Jersey and the City of London to create a web that would 'catch financial business from nearby jurisdictions by offering lightly taxed, lightly regulated and secretive boltholes for money'.

Now this new overseas empire was to throw a lifeline to the ailing aristocracy by allowing them to escape the burden of taxation being imposed in the motherland. The Marquess of Salisbury was an early adopter, setting up the Jersey-based firms Mysia, Syros and Samos Investments in the 1970s; through these he then registered his 10,000-acre estates at Hatfield and Cranborne. When I contacted the Marquess' estate company to ask why he did so, and whether it was for reasons of 'tax efficiency', they declined to answer, stating they 'do not comment on Lord Salisbury's private affairs'. In later decades, other aristocrats would follow suit: the Marquess of Cholmondeley, for instance, owns his Houghton Estate in Norfolk via the Jersey-based Mainland Nominees Ltd, while Earl Bathurst has vested his 14,500-acre estate in Gloucestershire in a Bermuda-based company.

Alongside such morally dubious – though perfectly legal – practices, the aristocracy also prepared to stand and fight. There were to be two fronts in this war: the first, a battle for hearts and minds, by convincing the public that the aristocracy were the guardians of the nation's heritage; and the second, an alliance with an unapologetically right-wing government who would slash the taxes burdening the landed aristocracy.

In the battle for public opinion, the owners of stately homes clubbed together to make an eminently reasonable case for saving the nation's heritage from being demolished as a result of the new taxes. In a House of Lords debate on the subject in June 1974, Lord Clark argued that 'a wealth tax on the contents of English country houses, large and small, would, in a very short time, lead to their extinction'. Peers queued up to bemoan the fact that, though they might be asset-rich, they were actually rather cash-poor; though as the Earl of Gowrie had the good grace to admit, 'In the public mind, I rather fear we may all appear to be "loaded", as the term is.' He also cautioned that, in the interests of winning over public support, 'a tooth-and-nail opposition to wealth tax might sound more like the squeaks of squeezed pips than [an] anxious chorus'.

Though they clearly had one eye on good PR, the core argument of stately homeowners was difficult to disagree with. Levying an annual wealth tax on all fixed assets, with no means-testing of whether the owners had sufficient cash flow to pay the tax, was likely to lead to a resurgence in the sale and demolition of old country houses. Wealth redistribution was all very well, but destruction of heritage served no one. The public overwhelmingly agreed. A petition protesting at the new taxes, organised by the recently formed Historic Houses Association – president: Baron Montagu of Beaulieu – garnered over a million signatures. In 1974, the V&A's exhibition on 'The Destruction of the English Country House', complete with a hall filled with crumbling columns, attracted huge numbers of visitors. Conservative MP Patrick Cormack, in his book *Heritage in Danger*, complained that faced with the new capital transfer tax and threatened wealth tax, 'the owners of historic buildings are in a siege condition'.

The government backed down. A compromise was made on capital transfer tax: it was waived if the owners of stately homes opened them up for a minimum of sixty days a year. As Labour life peer Baroness Jennie Lee reminded her hereditary colleagues: 'We are not seeking to preserve the best of our country houses in order that they should be for the exclusive use of any one family.' The much-vaunted wealth tax was never implemented. The proposal had been poorly thought through by Labour in opposition, and Denis Healey eventually decided that introducing such a measure would cause more practical and political trouble than it was worth in terms of added revenue.

But the aristocratic fightback didn't stop there. The 1970s saw the rise of free-market neoliberalism, whose staunchest advocates in the

UK included the new leader of the Conservative Party, Margaret Thatcher. Enamoured by her pledges to cut taxes and do away with the encroaching socialist state, many aristocrats felt this was a leader they could do business with. Nigel Lawson, Thatcher's Chancellor for most of the 1980s, had been particularly scathing of Labour's attempts to implement a wealth tax, telling Parliament: 'It has shown its unprincipled exploitation of envy and it has demonstrated its persistent attempts to rekindle the class war.' When he became Chancellor in 1983, he took the 'class war' in the opposite direction. Top rates of income tax were reduced from 98 per cent to 40 per cent over the course of the decade, with lost revenues made up from increases in regressive VAT. Capital transfer tax was first slashed and then replaced in 1986 by inheritance tax, which abolished taxation of lifetime gifts. Furthermore, Lawson granted agricultural land relief from inheritance tax, a boon to land-owners.

By the early eighties, George Howard, grandson of the Earl of Carlisle and owner of Castle Howard, could pen a foreword to a book on Britain's stately homes celebrating that 'the tax environment has been pulled into more or less the right shape'. Castle Howard itself had recently been used as a set for the ITV production of *Brideshead Revisited*, another sign of the growing rehabilitation of the upper classes in Thatcher's Britain. In the new atmosphere of lower taxes and Merchant Ivory costume dramas, '"old money" regained its self-confidence in the 1980s.'

Geographer David Harvey has argued that neoliberalism 'was from the very beginning a project to achieve the restoration of class power'. This perhaps overstates the alignment between free marketeers, with their professed passion for entrepreneurs and opposition to vested interests, and the old aristocracy. The Tories under Thatcher, thought Denis Healey, were a party which she had 'hijacked . . . from the land-owners and given . . . to the estate agents'.

Brash new money was starting to snap up large estates and in some cases supplant the old landed gentry. But there is little doubt that inherited wealth also did very well out of the Thatcher years. Up until then, the wealth and earnings of those at the very top of society had been declining from their Edwardian peak, with British society at its most equal ever in the 1970s. Yet between 1982 and 2007, the top 1 per cent of income earners doubled their share of the national income, from 6.5 per cent to 13 per cent. The upper crust's share of wealth, following a half-century of precipitous decline, also rallied under Thatcher and began increasing again: by 2010, the top 1 per cent owned nearly 30 per cent of the country's wealth.

The Labour government elected in 1997 might have been expected to give the nobility a harder time. It's true that New Labour's relationship with the aristocracy tends to be remembered for being oppositional, thanks to its ban on fox hunting, support for Right to Roam, and reform of the House of Lords. (The Countryside Alliance, formed in the 1990s to campaign primarily against a hunting ban, was bankrolled by peers such as the Duke of Westminster and Duke of Northumberland.*) But though New Labour attacked the political power and cultural customs of the peerage, it left its landed wealth untouched, and even subsidised it further.

Tony Blair continued Thatcher's light-touch approach to taxing wealth, with Peter Mandelson infamously saying Labour was now 'intensely relaxed about people getting filthy rich'. Mandelson's caveat, 'so long as they pay their taxes', was crassly disingenuous when the government was doing so little to crack down on offshore tax avoidance. Moreover, large landowners were also now supplementing their incomes through generous public subsidies for farming and forestry.

Farming subsidies have existed in the UK since the 1950s, and increased after Britain joined the EU, but initially they were tightly tied to food production quotas. From 2003, however, farm subsidies were paid on an area basis. This had been done to end the wasteful 'milk lakes and butter mountains' engendered by production-based payments, but

---

*   The Countryside Alliance's predecessor, the Countryside Movement, was formed in 1995 with similar aristocratic backing, including Lord Peel as its chair.

now meant essentially that the more land you owned, the bigger your subsidy. By my calculations, seventeen of Britain's dukes together received £8 million in farm subsidies in 2015. The following year, fourteen of the country's marquesses were handed £3.5 million, courtesy of the taxpayer. It's no coincidence that the value of agricultural land has skyrocketed since 2003, bolstered by public subsidies.

This unfairness has been compounded by the fact that smallholders of less than 12 acres have ceased to be eligible for subsidies, while for large landowners, there's no upper limit to what you can receive. In 2014, Conservative Environment Secretary Owen Paterson adamantly opposed moves to cap the amount of subsidy any individual landowner could receive, just at the same time as the Coalition government was legislating for a welfare benefits cap.

Brexit now opens up the opportunity for root-and-branch reform of our farm subsidy system, something that current Environment Secretary Michael Gove has enthusiastically endorsed. His welcome plans include capping single area payments at a maximum of £100,000, and ultimately switching the full subsidy system to require recipients of public money to deliver public goods, such as protecting the environment. To their credit, this latter shift is something that the CLA have been proposing for years. But they continue to oppose a cap on payments. It will take courage and tenacity to see through these changes against the wishes of landowning interests. As Thomas Paine wrote: 'The man who is in the receipt of a million a year is the last person to promote a spirit of reform, lest, in the event, it should reach to himself.'

The aristocracy's ancestors stole vast swathes of our land through bloodshed, conquest and enclosure. Today, perhaps a third of England remains in their hands. Holding such a monopoly, they have extracted fortunes in rent, both from their farm tenants and their urban leaseholders. Taxpayers continue to prop up the aristocracy with generous farm subsidies and tax breaks, even as many noble lords seek to dodge taxes by vesting their assets in complex trusts and offshore entities.

The aristocracy may have gifted us half a million acres of beautiful landscaped parkland, but they have also turned another half-million acres of upland into a desert for shooting grouse.

Yet the weakening of aristocratic power and wealth over the past century has forced many peers to become more responsive to the demands of the public, and to work harder for a living. Once-enclosed parks have been opened up, tourists welcomed in; bloodsports have given way, in part, to safaris and zoos. The aristocracy also have an inbuilt eye for the long term, as a result of their inheritance laws and the longevity of their existence. This, they often claim, makes them well-suited to being stewards of the English countryside. But too often this is trumped by the pursuit of short-term profit: the temptation to sell off land for development, lease it for mining, or intensify agricultural production.

If the aristocracy are to remain owners of vast swathes of England for the next century, they cannot merely preside over it as *rentiers*, but need to become active stewards, nursing our land back to health. We face a catastrophic loss of species: half of all our farmland birds have gone, and perhaps three-quarters of all insects. Rather than devote an area of England the size of Greater London to shooting grouse, the aristocracy ought to be giving over that acreage to rewilding our desiccated landscapes. Instead of setting up safari parks, with all their colonial-era baggage, large estates could be bringing back beavers and lynx, restoring England's lost wildernesses and reigniting public enthusiasm for nature. A reformed system of farm subsidies would provide a spur to this, but it will also require the aristocracy's active participation. Will they rise to such a challenge?

5

NEW MONEY

The darkened windows of the vacant house looked like empty eye sockets, staring blankly across the city.

I was standing outside 41 Upper Grosvenor Street, a multi-million-pound Mayfair mansion that had been empty for some fourteen years. The letterbox had been taped up, and a sign next to it read: NO POINT JUNK MAIL IN EMPTY BUILDING.

Post had nevertheless piled up inside the dusty front door. Cobwebs and grime coated the window panes. But the grandiose pillars and imposing height of this classically styled mansion still smelled of wealth.

For a tiny elite of the world's richest people, owning a property in Mayfair isn't about having a home. It's about investing in an asset. House prices continue to soar in the capital, despite the recession and in spite of Brexit. As some sales literature I had found at a nearby Mayfair estate agent brazenly put it, *Don't wait to buy in Mayfair. Just buy in Mayfair and wait, because the best is yet to come.* The empty mansion I was staring at was a symbol of London's housing crisis, the product of an overheated market that had turned bricks and mortar into financial instruments, rather than a roof over someone's head.

But I hadn't come here to view a property to buy. I'd come to plan a protest.

I had found out that number 41 had been bought on a long lease by an offshore company, registered in the British Virgin Islands, a well-known tax haven. Digging further, I'd discovered that the ultimate owner of this company was one Timur Kulibayev, the son-in-law of the president of Kazakhstan – a country that anti-corruption charity Global Witness describes as one of 'the world's worst kleptocratic regimes'. He had bought the leasehold of number 41 for a staggering £28.5 million back in 2007, when it had already been empty for several years. The *Guardian* journalist Helen Pidd found it was still lying vacant two years later, but that there was little that the local council, Westminster borough, could do about it. 'I feel it is a tragedy,' a despairing council officer told her. 'For them to be left vacant and unloved for such a long time, pawns in a real-life game of Monopoly, is disgraceful.'

This empty Mayfair mansion seemed a perfect symbol of our broken housing market, and I was keen to use it as the backdrop for a demonstration against empty homes being planned a few weeks hence. But as I peered through the dust-coated windows, there was an angry shout behind me. Marching towards me down the street was a smartly dressed man, wearing the crisp suit and tailcoat of a hotelier.

'Interested in this building, are you?' he demanded aggressively. 'Thought you might check it out for some squatting, eh?'

I explained patiently that I had no intention of turning the house into a squat, and that I was just interested in the issue of empty properties. He didn't believe me at first, and continued to angrily ask what I was doing. But eventually he softened.

'Look,' he said. 'The owner's an absentee landlord. Very rich. Kazakhstani. I'm the manager of the hotel next door, and they pay me to keep an eye on it – to stop people breaking in, you know.'

Didn't he think it was wrong that it had been left empty for so long?

'It's a shame, I agree. But some people like to waste their money, don't they?'

In fact, Mr Kulibayev hadn't been wasting his money at all. In 2017, his company won a landmark court case against the freehold owner of number 41 – the aristocratic Grosvenor Estate – allowing him to buy out the freehold, despite having never lived in the property. As one legal firm observed: 'Just because this property looked internally like a derelict office, did not mean that it was not, in fact, a house. The tenant of this derelict building was therefore entitled to exercise its right to buy.' Kulibayev's victory seems emblematic of how old landed estates are being steadily eroded and displaced by new money – and how homes are increasingly treated as mere assets by this new elite.

And 41 Upper Grosvenor Street is far from a unique case. London is littered with similar 'ghost houses'. Council figures show that 60,000 properties across the country have stood empty for more than two years. In the neighbouring borough of Kensington and Chelsea, around 1,500 homes were left vacant in 2017. That summer, shortly after the Grenfell Tower fire, I made a Freedom of Information request to Kensington Council asking them if they would release the locations and owners of the empty properties in their borough. They emailed back saying they could only give me topline numbers in an attached spreadsheet. But in fact, the document contained names and addresses for every single one of the borough's empty properties – the council officer had failed to remove them.

Looking through the spreadsheet with Anna Powell-Smith, I was astonished by the names that cropped up. The list read like an address book of some of the world's richest and most powerful people. The former New York Mayor Michael Bloomberg. A British TV executive. Billionaire property developers the Candy Brothers. The Sheikh of Dubai. While some of them no doubt had genuine reasons for leaving their properties empty – refurbishment or visa issues, perhaps – the overwhelming impression was of a gilded, jet-setting elite, who might only pop in on their London homes for a few days a year, and who owned multiple properties around the world.

We decided to take the list to the *Guardian* newspaper, whose investigations team had just been independently sent the same unredacted set of names by Kensington Council. Together, we combed the document for examples we felt were most in the public interest to disclose. To see such wealthy individuals leaving their luxury apartments empty, while hundreds of survivors of the Grenfell fire had yet to be permanently rehoused, really stuck in the craw. It seemed emblematic of how London was becoming so grossly divided by inequalities, just as Charles Dickens had lamented in *A Tale of Two Cities*. There are now a thousand rough sleepers on the streets of the capital. The money being poured into London property is also having a ripple effect, making buying a house unaffordable for everyone else. Professor Chris Hamnett likens it to water pouring into a three-bowl fountain: the money gushes into the super-prime districts first, but it soon overflows, raising house prices in surrounding districts. 'People are being sequentially displaced,' he warns.

Empty mansions are just one, particularly glaring symbol of the increasingly free market in land and property in England, and how the country is being transformed by successive waves of new money. So who are the new plutocrats investing in England's land and property? And what do they own?

My definition of 'new money' in this chapter refers to a group of individuals who have acquired wealth and land since the Industrial Revolution – whether through industry, finance, oil, the entertainment business, or other riches. It's clear that this covers a broad spread of individuals – businessmen and women, City boys, celebrities – many of whom have little in common by way of shared background or interests. Indeed, many of these newly moneyed landowners hail from overseas: Russian oligarchs, Arab sheikhs, American financiers. Compared to the tight-knit aristocratic families of old, they are a disparate bunch, united mainly by the wads of cash in their pockets and their appearance on Rich Lists – although, as we'll see, many have sought to ape the tastes and habits of the aristocracy; some have even joined their ranks. They share one central characteristic, however: whereas the aristocracy have become wealthy as a result of owning and inheriting land, new money tends to have acquired land as a result of becoming wealthy.

This reflects the fact that land, while remaining the bedrock of the economy – our source of food, space for homes and provider of numerous ecosystem services – has ceased being the primary generator of wealth over the past century and a half. Since the Industrial Revolution, fortunes can be made through, for example, holding shares in companies, exploiting fossil fuel reserves, or having well-remunerated directorships in banking. It also stems from the increasingly open market in land and property developed since Britain began dispensing with the legal and social restraints on selling inherited land that existed until the Victorian period. But above all, the rise of the newly moneyed landowners reflects widening inequalities in our society. The UK is today home to a staggering 145 billionaires, behind only China and the US in world rankings. London, meanwhile, has the most billionaires of any city on Earth – ninety-three, with New York trailing a distant second.

The most fervent defenders of free markets like to portray the emergence of the new super-rich as proof of a society in which everyone can 'make it'. 'At last, the self-made rich triumph over old money,' trumpeted the *Sunday Times* in its 2018 Rich List, revealing that 94 per cent of the 1,000 richest people in the UK are now entrepreneurs, rather than inheritors of wealth. That certainly reflects a change in the past thirty years, a result of the tax cuts, deregulation and market liberalisation pursued by Margaret Thatcher and her successors. The first Rich List in 1989 contained no fewer than fifty-seven landowners, making up 28.5 per cent of the entrants – the largest single category of wealth. By 2018, the newspaper classified just 2.9 per cent of the country's richest people as 'having wealth primarily tied up in land'.

But the way the Rich List categorises wealth from land is botched, downplaying the significance of land ownership. 'Yes, land remains a valuable commodity,' it admits. Yet then it adds, nonsensically: 'But today's fortunes are more often to be found in the buildings on the land, with 164 (16.4%) owing their wealth to property.' The distinction is meaningless: the vast bulk of the value of property is not in bricks and mortar, but in the location value of the land it's built on.

Even so, this shift certainly represents a dilution of the wealth and power of the landed aristocracy. But it hardly amounts to a democratisation of riches. Instead, a new capitalist elite has arisen alongside the old feudal order. It's hard to be precise about how much of England they now own; unlike the closed ranks of the titled aristocracy, there are no clearly defined edges to this wealthy group. The newly moneyed landowners profiled in this chapter, who can only ever be a sample, own at least a quarter of a million acres between them in England, rising to over 600,000 acres if you add in Scottish landholdings. Some of them are not major landowners by acreage, but instead possess extremely expensive properties in prime areas of London. Other estimates put the land owned by new money much higher: Dan and Peter Snow, in their 2006 BBC documentary *Whose Britain Is It Anyway?*, reckoned that private, non-aristocratic landowners owned 15 per cent of land in the UK, with celebrities, actors and Premier League footballers owning another 2 per cent. They concluded that 'new money isn't about to drive old money off the land anytime soon.' But though the aristocracy remain past masters at surviving, the momentum now is with the new plutocracy. This is their story.

Four waves of new money have poured into UK land and property over the past century. The first wave arrived in the Edwardian period, when a clique of *nouveau riche* British and American industrialists, grown fat on the profits of their businesses, decided to buy themselves into the aristocracy by acquiring land and titles. Then there was a hiatus of half a century, as increasing taxes and death duties diminished the old aristocracy and bit into the ability of the new capitalists to amass land and wealth. But during the 1970s, things rapidly tilted back in their favour. A second wave of new money arrived on England's shores in the wake of the oil price spike of 1973: suddenly, London was awash with Middle Eastern oil wealth eager to snap up properties. With the collapse of the Soviet Union came a third wave: an invasion of Russian oligarchs, arriving to spend the wealth they had filleted from former state industries and, in some cases, to escape Vladimir Putin. Meanwhile, Thatcher and her followers unleashed a fourth wave of home-grown bucca-neering businessmen, who went on to spend their earnings on lavish mansions and country estates.

But it was the Edwardian plutocrats who got the whole ball rolling. *Fin-de-siècle* England was a playground for the rich, both old and new: a gilded age of imperial complacency and vast inequality. It was a world in which *parvenu* industrialists rubbed shoulders with the landed gentry; where loaded American heiresses married into old English fami-lies, swapping cash for coronets; and where society portrait artists like John Singer Sargent flattered the upper classes with their paintings, the oil on their canvases oozing opulence.

Into this world swaggered William and Edmund Vestey, busi-nessmen extraordinaire, and purveyors of corned beef and cheap eggs to the masses. The Vestey brothers were no two-bit operators: they had built up a global meat-packing empire, buying beef from Argentine cattle ranchers and the Chicago stockyards at rock-bottom prices, shipping it across the world in their Blue Star Line of freight vessels, and delivering it to custom-built cold storage facilities in their native Liverpool. Their business was one of the first fully integrated multi-national corporations. Cheap meat made the Vesteys rich: very, very rich. 'They did not live on the income; they did not live on the interest from their investments; they lived on the interest on the interest,' wrote their biographer Phillip Knightley. But money wasn't enough for these frugal, ruthless merchants. They also craved respect.

Respect was hard to come by among the snooty Edwardian elite, especially if you had to work for a living, and – worst of all – were Liverpudlian. To gain acceptance, you needed land and titles. So the Vesteys set about acquiring them. As an officer of heraldry complains in one of Terry Pratchett's *Discworld* satires: 'Now it seems that as soon as a man opens his second meat-pie shop, he feels impelled to consider himself a gentleman.'

In 1922, William was made Baron Vestey, ostensibly for the great service he had rendered the country during the war by keeping British soldiers fed on cheap meat. But it transpired the peerage had been bought for £20,000 as part of Lloyd George's 'cash for honours' wheeze, in which the wily old rascal had raised funds for re-election by selling titles to 'hard-nosed men' who had done well out of the war. The Prime Minister, as the historian A.J.P. Taylor noted, 'detested titles. This, no doubt, is why he distributed them so lavishly.' It cost Lloyd George his reputation, but Vestey kept his barony.

Undeterred, the Vesteys went on to buy up all the trappings of aristocracy. In 1927 Baron Vestey bought the 5,500-acre Stowell Park Estate in Gloucestershire. It remains the family seat today, registered via a trust fund, and received £450,000 in farm subsidies in 2016. Following the fashions of the landed gentry, they also acquired themselves Highland estates and grouse moors: the 6,600-acre Forest Estate in Argyll and the colossal 55,000-acre Assynt Estate in Sutherland, both still owned and managed by members of the Vestey family. Edmund's side of the family, though lacking the noble titles of William's scions, consoled themselves by purchasing the 17,000-acre Thurlow Estate in Suffolk, which they still farm. Their businesses also acquired vast acreages overseas, including huge cattle ranches in Australia. In a landmark victory for Aboriginal land rights, however, Lord Vestey was forced to return some of these lands to the Gurindji people to whom they originally belonged, following a decade-long struggle led by Vincent Lingiari in the 1970s.

But the Vesteys' landholdings in England and Scotland remain securely theirs. Today, the family has been fully accepted by the landed classes. The 3rd Baron Vestey is a close friend of the Queen, and in 1999 he became Royal Master of the Horse; an appointment that caused mild embarrassment when the Vestey Food Group was implicated in the Findus horsemeat scandal a few years back.

Yet at the same time as inveigling themselves into the establishment, the Vesteys had been pioneering new ways of avoiding the tax authorities. Unbeknown to polite opinion at the time, they created a complex web of trusts and overseas companies that allowed them to become, in Nicholas Shaxson's words, 'among the biggest individual tax avoiders in history'. The brothers domiciled themselves in Argentina for a while and set up a secret trust fund in Paris. It all began perfectly legally, but when the British exchequer finally got word of where they were squirrelling away their millions, they began to investigate. 'Trying to come to grips with the Vesteys over tax is like trying to squeeze a rice pudding,' complained one tax official. When the Vesteys' schemes were finally revealed by a *Sunday Times* exposé in 1980, it transpired that their business had managed to pay just £10 in tax on an annual profit of around £2.3 million. Edmund Hoyle Vestey hardly helped public relations by shrugging: 'Nobody pays more tax than they have to. We're all tax dodgers, aren't we?'

Few contemporaries of the Vesteys were as tenacious at avoiding the taxman, but other self-made men followed their lead in acquiring land and titles, and setting up trusts to manage their landed estates. The plush red benches of the House of Lords began to fill up with plutocratic peers who had made their money in shipping, chemical manufacturing and banking. The era also saw the creation of the first literal press barons, such as Baron Iliffe, part-owner of the *Daily Telegraph* in the inter-war years, whose 8,000-acre Yattendon estate in West Berkshire I traversed in an earlier chapter.

The soap magnate William Lever, whose businesses went on to become the conglomerate Unilever, was ennobled as Viscount Leverhulme and bought himself the 11,000-acre Thornhill Manor estate on the Wirral, a huge expanse of the Scottish Highlands at Badanloch in Sutherland, and the Hebridean islands of Lewis and Harris. He ended up gifting the islands to the local community follo/wing demands for land reform, and the Leverhulme viscountcy became extinct in 2000, but a family trust continues to own the remaining estates.

Weetman Dickinson Pearson, an industrialist who made his fortune buying up land in Mexico to drill for oil, found – like the Vesteys – that a close relationship with Lloyd George did wonders for his social standing. In 1917, he was made 1st Viscount Cowdray, and served briefly in the war cabinet. The cottages on the 16,500-acre Cowdray Estate in the South Downs are still painted in a vibrant chrome yellow, a colour 'chosen due to the 1st Viscount Cowdray's connections to the Liberal party'. (The current 4th Viscount is of a rather different political persuasion: he has donated £65,000 over the past decade to UKIP, the Conservatives and the Vote Leave campaign.) The estate today has an intriguing ownership structure, with some parts of the land registered in the name of Rathbones Trust Company Ltd, a firm of professional wealth managers, and other parts registered to Hudsun Trustees, a division of Rathbones based in the British Virgin Islands.

Other new entrants to the English land and property market at that time began arriving from overseas. A branch of the fabulously wealthy Astor family, whose fortune had been built first on the fur trade and then on New York real estate deals, moved across the Atlantic to set up shop in England. In 1893, William Waldorf Astor I purchased from the Duke of Westminster Cliveden House in Buckinghamshire, a sumptuous mansion where his daughter-in-law Nancy – the first female MP to take a seat in the Commons – would later entertain high society guests; later still, it would become the setting for the Profumo scandal. William was made a viscount for his donations to wartime charities. Though Cliveden is no longer in the Astors' possession, the Astor viscountcy lives on. Its incumbent, the 4th Viscount, is a Conservative hereditary peer, whose wife is the mother of Samantha Cameron, married to former Tory PM David Cameron. Numerous other Astors became Conservative MPs during the twentieth century, and various scions of the family still own thousands of acres in West Berkshire and Scotland.*

Some of the newly moneyed Edwardian landowners mingled philanthropy with self-preservation. Edward Guinness, heir to the brewing fortune and ennobled as the Earl of Iveagh in 1919, found that one way to curry favour with his more blue-blooded but increasingly

---

* The family seat of the Astor viscounts remains Ginge Manor in Oxfordshire. Three scions of the Astors own land in West Berkshire: Robert Astor owns the 861-acre Marlston Estate, James Alexander Waldorf Astor owns the 572-acre Sulhamstead Estate, and Charles John Astor & family own the 1,875-acre Kirby House Estate.

cash-strapped peers was to buy Old Masters from them. Upon his death in 1927, Iveagh's extensive collection of Gainsboroughs and Rembrandts were left to the nation along with Kenwood House in Hampstead, with a stipulation that they be displayed to the public in perpetuity. The 1st Earl also gave generously to the social housing projects established by his father under the aegis of the Guinness Trust. Today, the organisation manages 65,000 homes across England. Still, some of the Trust's practices have attracted criticism in recent years. A 13-acre stretch of land it owned in Wandsworth, left derelict for six years despite housing shortages, was squatted in 1996 by activists from The Land Is Ours, who set up the 'Pure Genius' eco-village in protest at the waste of land. More recently, squatters occupied the Guinness Estate in Brixton in protest at the eviction of tenants and its impending demolition to make way for more expensive housing. What's more, the Earl of Iveagh's 22,500-acre Elveden Estate in Suffolk is today registered offshore in Jersey, presumably for tax purposes. Yet the farming that goes on at the estate is generously subsidised by the taxpayer, to the tune of around £1.2 million annually.

The Edwardian gilded age came to an abrupt end in the slaughter of the First World War, while successive post-war governments hiked death duties and taxes to pay for the expanding welfare state. The old aristocracy fared the worst out of this, but the newly moneyed had their wings clipped, too. For the next half-century, their share of national income and wealth declined as those of the middle and working classes rose.

Then, in December 1973, oil prices suddenly doubled overnight, and the world was turned upside down. Oil-exporting Middle Eastern states, operating through the OPEC cartel, had cut production and hiked prices in retaliation for US support for Israel in the Yom Kippur war. The repercussions for oil-dependent Western economies were immediate and catastrophic. It was a wake-up call for post-imperial Britain: still bewitched by nostalgic dreams about its former grandeur, its standing in the world was fast changing. A BBC interview with Sheikh Ahmed Yamani, Saudi oil minister at the time, distilled the situation:

BBC INTERVIEWER: Doesn't this new, massive increase in the price of oil mean a change in the world balance of power, between the developing nations – you, the producers – and us, the developed, industrialised nations?

SHEIKH YAMANI: (smiling) Yes, it will . . . You have to adjust yourself to the new circumstances.

This shift in the global distribution of wealth was soon brought home to Britons, not just in higher petrol prices at the pump, but in the sudden appearance of rich Arab sheikhs and businessmen on the streets of London. It was the elites of Middle Eastern societies, of course, who did well out of the oil crisis, rather than ordinary people. The mid-1970s brought an influx of newly minted oil wealth from Dubai and Saudi Arabia, looking to buy up English land and property.

'You can hardly open your newspaper these days without reading of some new Arab "takeover",' wrote the *Guardian*'s David Hirst in September 1976. 'Hotels, hospitals, and historic mansions all seem to be falling like ninepins into the hands of the new-rich potentates from the fabulous shores of the Persian Gulf.' Such was the demand among Middle Eastern royalty and traders for luxury properties in places like Kensington and Hampstead that London gained the nickname 'Beirut-on-Thames'.

The English upper crust, still more used to ruling Arabs than having to hobnob with them, were aghast. But some were persuaded to do business when they saw the size of the newcomers' chequebooks. The exclusive gentlemen's clubs and casinos of Mayfair, racist and sexist in equal measure, had traditionally been closed to foreigners; but some were now persuaded to open their doors to Middle Eastern cash. 'It's what one brings to the table,' recalls Marilyn Cole, receptionist at the Clermont Club at the time. 'Arabs knew that they were mixing with the likes of British aristocracy, and their passport was money.' Such money also allowed Arab royalty and businessmen to buy up British land and property – lots of it. One of the first to arrive was Mohamed Al-Fayed. Long before he became famous as the owner of Harrod's, Al-Fayed had attracted notoriety by becoming the proud laird of a Scottish castle, Balnagown in Easter Ross. The 1972 purchase was sniffily described in the pages of the *Observer* as having 'introduced a touch of the mystic East' to the area. Al-Fayed was Egyptian by birth, but his fortune had been made advising the Sheikh of Dubai, Rashid bin Saeed Al-Maktoum, and forging deals with British construction companies eager to begin building in the newly oil-rich United Arab Emirates (UAE). Today, though he has long since sold off Harrod's, Al-Fayed still owns some 34,000 acres of the Scottish Highlands.

Other Arab businessmen were attracted to Britain by the prospect of buying up old English castles. Mahdi Al-Tajir, the former UAE ambassador to the UK, bought Mereworth Castle in Kent for $1.2 million in 1976. To this he later added a Scottish estate and the Highland Spring bottled water company, making him by 2013 the richest man in Scotland, with a fortune of £1.65 billion. Still, this love of quaint old English and Scottish culture – carried almost to the level of parody by some newly wealthy landowners – hasn't stopped Al-Tajir vesting Mereworth Castle in that quintessentially modern capitalist construct, the offshore company.

Al-Fayed and Al-Tajir's ventures onto the British property scene, however, were merely paving the way for the arrival of Arab royalty. The son of the then emir of Dubai, Sheikh Mohammed bin Rashid al-Maktoum – who became the ruler of the emirate and Prime Minister of the UAE in 2006 – started buying land in Britain in the late 1970s. Given his position, it's perhaps unsurprising that he, too, opted to use a series of offshore firms to make his purchases, in an effort to stay out of the public eye. Disentangling the Sheikh's web of land-holding companies has taken some time, but it's now possible to say that today he owns approximately 92,000 acres of land in England and Scotland, acquired over the years in exchange for tens of millions of pounds, making him one of the largest individual landowners in the country. The bulk of this is in the Highlands, but he's also a very significant landowner in England, with luxury flats and houses in Kensington and Windsor owned via SMECH Properties Ltd (incorporated in Guernsey), farms in East Anglia registered under

Tayberry Ltd (Jersey), and horse-racing studs at Newmarket held in the name of Arat Investments (Guernsey). His biggest slice of England, however, is the 14,500-acre Bollihope grouse moor in the North Pennines, registered to the mysterious Arago Ltd (Jersey), whose ultimate owner eluded me for some time. When I visited the address listed for Arago Ltd – a smart townhouse in Belgravia – and spoke to the cleaner who answered the door, she denied any such company was based there, but that it was the offices of UK Mission Enterprise: the Sheikh's logistics company.

In fact, the Sheikh's purchase of Bollihope Moor in 1984 'caused something of a local sensation because of the nationality of the buyer', according to one observer. A mixture of xenophobia and snobbery prompted some journalists to worry that the traditional aristocratic owners of grouse moors were 'fast becoming a dying breed, being squeezed gradually off the moors by more prosperous grouse shooters from abroad, notably consortiums of Dutch and Arab businessmen'.

But in reality, the influx of new money helped revive an ailing sport, whose reputation had fast been going the way of the dodo. An article by veteran class warrior Seumas Milne in 1985 gleefully reported that the Glorious Twelfth that year had been a damp squib owing to 'a shortage of decent victims', but also noted that grouse conservation efforts were now being bolstered with cash from Sheikh Maktoum.

Sometimes there was a slight culture clash; one journalist recounted a story about the ruler of Abu Dhabi, 'who decided to try his hand at the gentry's sport of popping off the odd cartridge at frightened feathered friends, on his luxurious new English estate – and how distressed the gamekeeper was when his new squire turned up with a machine gun'. But nowadays, a new generation has rehabilitated this fusty old blood-sport: photos of the dashing young Crown Prince of Dubai shooting at Bollihope are plastered across the internet.

What Middle Eastern cash did for grouse shooting, it also did for racehorse breeding. Not only had sheikhs invested untold millions in buying up studs and bloodstock, related John Cunningham in a 1982 article; they were also 'gentlemen and sportsmen' – unlike American horsebreeders, who wore 'the wrong sort of check trousers'. When Sheikh Maktoum was once asked by a reporter if horse racing was an investment, he was indignant. 'Certainly not,' he replied. 'Racing is in my family's blood.'

Nevertheless, even the vastly wealthy Saudi royal family have not been above taking public subsidies to fund their horse-breeding hobbies. A Greenpeace investigation found that Saudi Prince Khalid Abdullah's Juddmonte Farms stud at Newmarket had received over £400,000 in Common Agricultural Policy payments in 2015. Prince Khalid is certainly not the only horse-breeder taking taxpayers' money: there are some 34,000 acres of studs in the UK, and a cursory search of government farm payments data turns up dozens of stud farms. But he is definitely one of the wealthiest.

The Prince also owns, via the Guernsey-based company Insite Development Ltd, the 4,000-acre Fairlawne Estate in Kent, which envelops the small village of Shipbourne. One local resident I spoke to complained that 'this humble part of Kent is getting like Park Lane: an outpost of Saudi Arabia', but added: 'To be fair to the owners, they try to cause as little trouble as possible and spend money on looking after their estates. However, they employ major agents who only have pound-signs in their eyes and wouldn't know what wildlife was until they had killed it.' Prince Khalid also ran into trouble in 2011 when he suddenly closed off an historic right of way traversing his estate. 'Fairlawne are good to the village – they do keep it very nice, but then they do things that upset some of us,' commented one local councillor, after villagers protested and had the footpath reopened. 'It was like the great big land owners against little village bumpkins.'

Wealthy landowners pocketing public subsidies and closing down public rights of way is one thing. But there was another, darker side to some of the land purchases by Saudis in the 1980s: they were funded by arms deals. After the oil crisis, the House of Saud poured vast amounts of its new wealth into acquiring missiles and fighter jets to secure its grip on the region. The country most eager to supply the Saudis with such weapons was, predictably, Britain. The British government, working hand-in-glove with the huge UK weapons manufacturer BAE, was desperate to secure lucrative arms contracts with Saudi Arabia, and was prepared to turn a blind eye to bribery to seal the deal. When *Guardian* journalists Rob Evans and David Leigh began investigating the arms deals, former Defence Secretary Denis Healey admitted to them that 'bribery has always played a role in the sale of weapons . . . in the Middle East people couldn't buy weapons unless you bribed them to do so, and that was particularly true in Saudi Arabia.'

Those who brokered such arms deals could expect to receive large commissions. And there was no bigger arms contract than the al-Yamamah deal, brokered in 1985 between BAE, Margaret Thatcher's administration and the Saudi government, worth £43 billion in subsequent sales. Two of the men involved in clinching the deal and accused of taking millions in commissions were Saudi Prince Bandar and his agent Wafic Said. Bandar, son of the then Saudi defence minister, bought the 2,500-acre Glympton Park in Oxfordshire with what are alleged to be his winnings from the al-Yamamah deal. Not to be outdone, Said went on to build Tusmore Park, a grand Palladian house, nearby. Both deny they took bribes. But when the Serious Fraud Office sought to investigate the deal in 2006, Tony Blair personally intervened to shut it down, for fear of it jeopardising ongoing arms sales.

With the Saudi regime's grip on power sometimes appearing shaky, investing in properties in the UK came to seem less of a luxury choice and more of a necessary insurance policy. In the wake of the first Gulf War in 1990, the Saudi royal family bought up no fewer than ten mansions on The Bishop's Avenue in Hampstead, the now-notorious 'Billionaires' Row', peppered with vacant properties and nearly all owned offshore. For over two decades, the Saudi-owned mansions stood empty and decaying, useful bolt-holes for their owners in case Riyadh one day went up in flames. They were eventually sold in 2014 for an estimated £73 million.

* * *

A similar mix of acquisitiveness mingled with fear motivated the third wave of new money to hit England's shores: the Russian oligarchs.

After the collapse of the Soviet Union, Russia's huge state-owned industries were flogged off and asset-stripped in a hyper-capitalistic frenzy. At first, shares in the old enterprises were distributed to ordinary Russian citizens, many of whom didn't appreciate their value and so quickly sold them on. The men who bought up the shares in bulk, however, fast became billionaires. This new class of crony capitalists became not only flush with cash, but also hugely politically powerful. Yet many of the oligarchs didn't reinvest their new-found wealth in rebuilding Russia: instead, they took it overseas, seeking higher returns and greater security than that provided by depleted Russian banks – and fewer questions asked. The IMF estimates that around $170 billion of capital fled the country between 1994 and 2000. Russia's own Trade Ministry puts it slightly higher, at about $220 billion – and says that approximately half of that was 'dirty' money, linked to money laundering or organised crime.

Where to stash all this cash? Where better, of course, than the over-heated property market of central London, and the super-prime districts of Belgravia and Mayfair in particular. As journalist Luke Harding writes, these postcodes have become attractive to 'successive influxes of the international super-rich'. In the early 2000s, the latest was a flood of Russian oligarchs.

Some of the oligarchs' most public acquisitions are well known: Roman Abramovich's purchase of Chelsea Football Club in 2003, or Evgeny Lebedev's buyout of the *Evening Standard*. Indeed, Russians in London for a while became a byword for conspicuous consumption: an orgy of chilled vodka, caviar and bling. But when it comes to the big investments – the acquisition of property and land – most oligarchs are more discreet. The transparency lobbying group ClampK, set up by campaigners connected to Russia's opposition leader Alexei Navalny, runs occasional bus tours around London to show journalists the properties bought up by Russian oligarchs. Along their route, they stop off at Belgrave Square, which became such a popular haunt for Russian wealth that it was once known as 'Red Square'. Formerly, it was home to Putin critic Boris Berezovsky, who died in 2013; the metals tycoon Oleg Deripaska still owns a property there. In April 2018, Deripaska was placed on a US sanctions list of two dozen Russian oligarchs accused of 'malign activity' and 'attempting to subvert western democracies'. A family friend of Putin's, Roman Rotenberg – whose father grew rich through selling pipelines to Russian state gas company Gazprom – lives off Cadogan Lane in Belgravia.

Further afield in north London, as the properties grow larger and more resplendent, the owners seem to become more publicity-shy. Athlone House, just to the north of Hampstead Heath, stood empty for years, until it was acquired in 2016 for an eye-watering £65 million by Ukrainian commodities trader Mikhail Fridman via a Guernsey-based company. Now it's completely covered in scaffolding and cloaked in plastic sheeting, as I discovered on a stroll around the heath. Beechwood House next door is registered to an Isle of Man firm; its ultimate owner, however, is Alisher Usmanov, an Uzbek-born Russian businessman with an estimated £12.8 billion net worth. But most mysterious of all is the gigantic Witanhurst, a 65-room mansion that looms over the heath and comes with five acres of grounds. For years after its most recent sale in 2008, the buyer remained cloaked in secrecy. All that was known was that Witanhurst had been registered to one Safran Holdings Ltd in the British Virgin Islands – and that the owner was spending millions refurbishing it, including installing an underground pool and two-tier cinema. But after some outstanding detective work by Ed Caesar at the *New Yorker* – combing company records, speaking to neighbours and grilling estate agents – he managed to track down the purchaser as Andrei Guriev, owner of Russian agrichemical giant PhosAgro. He had bought it for his daughter: her Instagram account handle is @t_o_p_s_e_c_r_e_t.

Such has been the impact of Russian investment on the capital – and its house prices – that investigative journalist Mark Hollingsworth dubs it 'Londongrad'. By 2006, the Russians had become the biggest foreign buyers in London. It doesn't stop there, however: some oligarchs have acquired a taste for buying up country seats, too. Abramovich, besides owning a townhouse in Chester Square and a £90m pad in Kensington Palace Gardens, bought up the 420-acre Fyning Hill Estate in West Sussex for his daughter some years back. Usmanov, alongside his Hampstead mansion, also owns the 500-acre Sutton Place estate in Surrey. Again, the use of offshore holding companies is near-ubiquitous: Sutton Place is vested in one Delesius Investments Ltd, and tracing its ultimate beneficiary would have been extremely difficult had Usmanov's ownership of the mansion not been revealed through a court case. Still, it appears that most Russians aren't so bothered about acquiring big country estates, and view them like traditional Russian *dachas* – rural holiday homes – with the real deal being high-end London properties.

If cash and a taste for vodka were all that the oligarchs had brought to London, there might be fewer complaints. But they've increasingly become *persona non grata*, for two main reasons. First, there are concerns that a lot of the property purchases being made by Russians in the UK are to launder money from dodgy sources (though there is no evidence to indicate the particular oligarchs profiled earlier have done so). The National Crime Agency (NCA) estimates that £100 billion a year of corrupt foreign money is laundered through the UK, with much of it coming from Russia. 'London is the money-laundering capital of the world,' argues Chido Dunn of campaign group Global Witness. That's hugely concerning, both morally – it means the UK is essentially aiding and abetting criminal activity overseas – and because of the impact it has on our own housing market. 'Prices of high-end properties are artificially driven up by the desire of overseas criminals to sequester their assets here in the UK,' says Donald Toon of the NCA. 'So what that is doing is distorting the market.'

Second, the oligarchs appear to have brought Russian politics with them to the UK – and with it, a spate of extraordinary killings. Some wealthy émigrés from Russia have moved here out of fear for their lives, having fled Putin's increasingly autocratic and vindictive regime: the jailing of Mikhail Khodorkovsky in 2003, a very wealthy businessman who had clashed with Putin, was a particular spur to get out. But it soon transpired that not even the UK was safe. Putin's war against his critics has continued, with the streets of British cities becoming battlegrounds. In 2006, former Russian agent and defector Alexander Litvinenko was poisoned in central London with polonium-laced tea. A public inquiry later ruled that he had been assassinated by FSB agents who were probably acting on Putin's personal orders. The trail of radioactive polonium they used was traced by forensics experts through a series of Mayfair clubs and expensive hotels frequented by Russian oligarchs. Reviewing the events that led up to Litvinenko's death, Peter Pomerantsev, the Soviet-born academic and writer, describes 'Mayfair and all it represents . . . as something potentially, maybe inherently toxic. When does a soft power aimed at attracting investment start to undermine real power?'

Such questions have only become more pressing with the more recent poisoning of Russian double-agent Sergei Skripal and his daughter in Salisbury. The British government has done itself few favours by allowing the UK, and London in particular, to become a prime location for money-laundering by the wealthy, Russian or otherwise, with all the attendant crime and political instability that brings. The answer is not to pander to xenophobia by cracking down on immigration; rather, it's to demand financial transparency from those investing in the land and property market. After all, there are already plenty of unscrupulous London estate agents happy to do business with clients claiming to be spending corruptly acquired cash. In the Channel 4 documentary *From Russia with Cash*, Roman Borisovich, a Russian émigré and anti-corruption campaigner, posed undercover as 'Boris', a Russian government minister looking to buy luxury apartments with money stolen from government healthcare budgets. Even though he was utterly upfront about the source of his ill-gotten gains, every estate agent he spoke to was caught on camera appearing unfazed and happy to help preserve his anonymity. Several even put him in touch with lawyers to discuss structuring offshore vehicles.

Such behaviour is encouraged by the persistent culture of secrecy around the ownership of land and property in England, and the UK's indulgence of offshore business. That's why it's so encouraging to see recent victories, won in the face of government opposition and foot-dragging, to finally shine a light into the dark places used by money launderers. 2018 saw two major steps forward in this fight. Following an amendment to a parliamentary Bill by MPs Margaret Hodge and Andrew Mitchell, British Overseas Territories were finally forced to adopt public registers of companies. This will mean firms registered in tax havens like the British Virgin Islands will in future have to declare their ultimate owners, just like UK-registered companies. A second victory was the introduction of Unexplained Wealth Orders (UWOs), which allows law enforcement agencies to challenge suspicious property purchases, putting the burden of proof on the purchaser to explain how they acquired such wealth. The NGO Transparency International has recommended that police now use these powers to investigate two apartments in Whitehall purchased by Russia's deputy Prime Minister Igor Shuvalov, who bought them for £11.4 million despite a declared annual salary of just £112,000.

Tax avoidance, offshore companies and political intrigue aren't simply foreign imports foisted upon innocent old England by Russian oligarchs and Arab sheikhs. After all, it was the British Vestey brothers who pioneered the art of tax avoidance in the 1920s, and the British government who converted former colonies like the Cayman Islands into tax havens. The blue-blooded Marquess of Salisbury, whose family has been at the heart of political machinations in England since the Elizabethan era, started using offshore firms in which to vest his landed estates in the 1970s. Such practices are now commonplace among Britain's crop of home-grown billionaires, whose ranks have swelled enormously since Thatcherism slashed taxes and deregulated markets.

One glaring example is Jim Ratcliffe, founder of chemicals giant INEOS, owner of a large mansion and grounds near the New Forest, and recently crowned Britain's richest man. The 2018 *Sunday Times* Rich List lauded Ratcliffe as a 'self-made entrepreneur' from a 'humble background'. Yet he also very blatantly avoided hundreds of millions of pounds in corporation tax by moving his company to Switzerland between 2010 and 2016. Ratcliffe has enjoyed extraordinary political access, too: documents I obtained using Freedom of Information requests show that in 2013 he met personally with the then Chancellor, George Osborne, to lobby for a reduction in income tax. Few self-employed businesspeople, struggling to fill in their tax returns every year, could hope to gain the ear of the Exchequer in that way. To cap it all, in August 2018 – having secured his spot at the top of the Rich List, plus a knighthood to boot – Ratcliffe announced he would be moving his fortune to the tax haven of Monaco. It's a classic example of the modern rootlessness of capital.

Other propertied billionaires who have done well out of the post-Thatcherite political settlement have also lobbied the government to reduce taxes further and maintain subsidies for big landowners. Sir James Dyson, the inventor of the bagless vacuum cleaner, has called for the UK to walk away from the EU without a trade deal, slash taxes and regulations after Brexit and become the 'Singapore of Europe'. Leaving Europe without a trade deal would prove devastating for Britain's small farmers, who rely on the EU as their main export market; but Dyson seems blasé about this. He has been busy hoovering up vast quantities of farmland in recent years – amassing some 33,000 acres, mainly in Lincolnshire – in what many observers suspect is a smart move to avoid tax. 'What Sir James is doing is buying up a very handy tax shelter,' suggests one newspaper commentator, explaining that agricultural land is exempt from inheritance tax. Dyson's farms also earned him a whopping £1.6 million in public farm subsidies in 2016. A hard Brexit of the sort he supports would place such strain on government budgets that such subsidies would have to be curtailed: yet he has had the temerity to warn ministers not to cut them.

Other recent examples of wealthy bankers, property dealers and businesspeople buying up land in the UK abound. Paul Dacre, former editor of the *Daily Mail* – whose fervently pro-Brexit headlines included urging May to 'crush the saboteurs' who dared to vote against the EU Withdrawal Bill – has not been above taking generous EU handouts for his farmland in Kent and grouse moor in Scotland. Duncan Davidson, the founder of Persimmon Homes, whose executives regularly complain about a lack of land to build housing on, is not short of land himself: he owns a 26,000-acre farm and grouse moor in Northumberland, the Lilburn Estate. David Ross, the founder of Carphone Warehouse, and Robert Miller, an Anglo-American businessman who made his money from duty-free shops, are two of the more recent buyers of grouse moors in this country; I estimate that at least 250,000 acres of grouse moors in England are now owned by 'new money', as opposed to the old aristocracy and gentry.

Miller's 26,000-acre Gunnerside Moor is registered in the British Virgin Islands, making it probably the largest single overseas-owned estate in England. Running it a close second is the huge Ramsbury Estate that straddles Wiltshire and West Berkshire, registered in Luxembourg and owned by Stefan Persson, the Swedish owner of clothing retail chain H&M. Urs Schwarzenbach, a Swiss banker who owns the Culden Faw estate in posh Henley-upon-Thames via a tangle of offshore outfits, was recently forced to pay £114 million in unpaid duties to Swiss tax authorities in 2017. The professionalisation of football and 'crazy wages' that really took off in the 1990s also created new enclaves of Premier League footballers in places like Alderley Edge in Cheshire and the gated community of St George's Hill in Surrey.

One aspect of the challenge with addressing offshore tax avoidance, the secrecy about who owns what, and the concentration of land and property ownership within an elite, is that so many politicians themselves are now in on the act. At some point between the appearance on TV screens of Harry Enfield's 'Loadsamoney' character and Tony Blair's embrace of 'Cool Britannia', certain members of the British political class grew intensely relaxed about hanging out with the filthy rich. Newly minted stars of Britpop and Young British Artists, from Alex James to Kate Moss and Damian Hirst, started buying up properties in the fashionable Cotswolds in the late 1990s. They were soon joined by media luvvies and politicians. The 'Chipping Norton Set', a cosy cadre of Cotswolds-dwellers that included David Cameron, his advisor Steve Hilton, and the then editor of the *Sun* Rebekah Brooks, became notorious for their lobbying dinners during the phone-hacking scandal and Rupert Murdoch's attempted takeover of Sky.

Power has always socialised with power, but MPs' financial interests seem increasingly to resemble those of an earlier era when politicians were drawn from the ranks of the propertied classes. Nowadays many MPs are landlords with rental property portfolios: the Foreign Secretary Jeremy Hunt, it was revealed in 2018, owns seven flats bought from a Conservative Party donor, but failed to declare them on his register of interests. David Cameron, though pledging to crack down on tax havens, was himself notoriously the beneficiary of an offshore trust fund set up by his late father. When land and property interests are so well-represented in Parliament, it's not surprising that systemic reform of the property market and transparency rules has progressed slowly.

The cast of characters examined in this chapter may seem disparate, ranging from the merely eccentric to the wholly obnoxious. But they all share one thing, at least: owning a disproportionate amount of land and property in this country. Surveying them as a whole, other commonalities start to emerge.

One thing that has united new money in its pursuit of buying up land and property has been, of course, the profits that can be squeezed from doing so. This has led most plutocrats to acquire expensive London apartments and mansions, where a rise in property values can be pretty much guaranteed – often leaving those properties vacant while they jet-set between their many homes. It's also led a few of the very richest to buy up swathes of farmland to take advantage of generous farm subsidies and inheritance tax breaks on agricultural land. Boris Johnson, when Mayor of London, defended foreign investment in the capital, while weakly protesting that the city's houses shouldn't be treated as 'just blocks of bullion in the sky'. But to many of the world's super-rich, they are precisely that. This then has a ripple effect on property prices, worsening the housing crisis.

Many of the newly wealthy clearly want more than simply a financial return: some crave security. Some Russian oligarchs buy London pads seeking a bolthole to escape from Putin; some Saudi princes yearn for a refuge in case the House of Saud one day falls. The UK has long thought of itself as a safe place for political refugees, playing host to everyone from French aristocratic émigrés fleeing the guillotine, to Karl Marx and Friedrich Engels. It's telling, however, that in recent times those most welcome are often those with cash. We tolerate the Saudi royalty leaving vast mansions empty in Hampstead, while selling the Saudi regime bombs to drop on Yemen – but claim not to have room for Syrian refugees.

But it's not just wealthy individuals from unstable nations who seek a bolthole in England – it's also western survivalists. I've found various instances of old Cold War-era nuclear bunkers being bought up by private individuals, whose interest in them, shall we say, may not be purely historical. One London-based private security firm has been quietly advertising a service for installing private nuclear fallout shelters beneath homes, which it markets as protection against a terrorist attack involving a radioactive 'dirty bomb', guaranteeing to keep purchases on the hush-hush by having its staff pretend to be merely installing a septic tank. The recent craze among London's super-rich for massive basements, though spurred on mainly by space and planning constraints, may also be driven by a bunker mentality: one 2018 study found 4,650 basement developments had been granted planning permission in central London in the past decade. The award for most ironic act of self-preservation must go, however, to Jim Ratcliffe. An ardent proponent of fracking whose INEOS petrochemicals business contributes greatly to UK greenhouse gas emissions, fuelling climate change and rising sea levels, Ratcliffe has been seeking permission for the past decade to build himself a 'mansion on stilts' on the Solent that would come fitted with hydraulic jacks to defend it against any sea-level rise. The phrase 'I'm all right, Jack . . .' springs to mind.

While investigating newly moneyed landowners, I was struck by how many seem to have sought respect and belonging in high society by acquiring the trappings of aristocracy. The connection between owning land and having a sense of belonging is far from unique to the wealthy, but they of course invariably have greater means to acquire it than most people. Owning land still bestows social status. Many of the new rich surveyed in this chapter have clearly sought to ape the aristocracy through buying up old English castles and Scottish estates, and copying their fashions by acquiring grouse moors and investing in horse-breeding. Other members of the *nouveau riche* have gone further still, buying up land and mansions right next door to where the royal family live, in a fairly blatant effort to burnish their social standing through proximity to royalty. Kazakh businessman Timur Kulibayev, for example, whose empty Mayfair mansion was described at the start of this chapter, has also snapped up Prince Andrew's former home in the middle of Windsor Great Park. Various oligarchs have purchased houses on Kensington Palace Gardens, next to the royal residence; maps of offshore-owned properties show particular concentrations around Windsor, like moths drawn to a lamp. Most of this is fairly harmless stuff, if a bit sad.

Having acquired the outward appearance of aristocracy, there seems far less sign, however, that England's new super-rich have also absorbed traditional aristocratic codes of *noblesse oblige* towards society, or of becoming long-term stewards of the land. Perhaps such voluntary obligations have always been merely convenient myths, but they seem particularly threadbare now. There are notable exceptions, of course:

from the Guinness family's investments in social housing, to more recent philanthropists like Sir Len Blavatnik. But overall, many newly moneyed landowners seem reluctant to give much back to the country they now own large chunks of. They are only too happy to accept public farm subsidies and take advantage of the tax shelter afforded by owning agricultural land, while simultaneously vesting their estates in offshore tax havens and using their wealth and power to lobby for still lower taxes.

Fundamentally, this is not a question of individual morality, but of how our land and property markets are now structured. We shouldn't be surprised by an erosion in social responsibility when community and human interaction has been reduced to transactional monetary exchanges. The dynamics of capital accumulation mean money seeks ever higher returns: those suddenly flush with cash, whether from oil price spikes or asset-stripping privatisation drives, have been attracted to invest their capital in England's already overheated property market. Over time, each successive wave of new money entering the English land and property market appears more rootless than the last – less concerned by notions of belonging and giving back to the community, and more interested in the cash returns of the assets being acquired. Karl Marx, a political refugee in England who came with little capital but who wrote a lot about it, had a word for this: alienation.

The continued secrecy around who owns land and property in England, and our government's tolerance of the offshore system it created, has also produced an environment conducive to money laundering. And while the defenders of free markets see them as means for democratising wealth, in the case of land it appears that the old landed aristocracy is simply being joined and partly supplanted by a new plutocracy.

Fundamentally, the hyper-capitalism of the newly moneyed has led many of them to treat land and property merely as assets, rather than as places of belonging or homes in which to live. Perhaps the weirdest, most poignant and most apposite example of this is to be found buried deep in the Sussex countryside, outside the village of Uckfield. There, nestled amid overgrown foliage, its vacant windows staring into nothingness, is

Hamilton Palace, the vast, empty mansion of notorious British businessman Nicholas van Hoogstraten.

When I visited, its decaying, unfinished façade put me in mind of the empty Mayfair mansion I stood beneath at the start of this chapter, but on a gigantic scale. Construction began thirty years ago, but has long since ground to a halt. Hamilton Palace is larger than Buckingham Palace, topped by copper orbs, and covered in scaffolding that makes it look a little like a voodoo doll stuck with pins. Perhaps that's appropriate for a house owned by someone once described by a judge as a self-styled 'emissary of Beelzebub'. Van Hoogstraten made his fortune as a landlord with a large rental property empire, becoming infamous for his devil-may-care outbursts and for standing trial for the alleged manslaughter of a business rival. The verdict was later overturned on appeal, but he decided to move to Zimbabwe, where he bought up thousands of acres of farmland and was, for a while, on first-name terms with the bloodthirsty tyrant Robert Mugabe.

Van Hoogstraten still has plans for his crumbling, empty palace, but not as a place to live in. He wants it to become his mausoleum, in which he will be entombed along with all his art collection, like some latter-day pharaoh. By acquiring lands and piling up worldly wealth, perhaps the newly rich seek to attain some measure of immortality beyond their brief time on Earth. Looking up at the pile of decaying bricks and mortar, Ozymandian in its aspirations and now hauntingly empty, I suddenly felt desperately sad. I'm not a religious person, but some phrases from a vaguely Anglican upbringing have stuck in my head. *What shall it profit a man, if he shall gain the whole world, and lose his own soul?*, I thought. Yet this wasn't about individual morality, I reminded myself; van Hoogstraten might be an extreme case, but his individualism and acquisitiveness in many ways simply reflects a country in which our leaders have for too long pretended that society does not exist. It's up to us to fix this broken social contract. The empty homes and bling mansions of today's super-rich may look ugly to us, but they also hold up a mirror to what England has become.

6

PROPERTY OF THE STATE

It was midnight, and a dozen of us were about to descend into an atom-bomb-proof tunnel system two hundred feet below High Holborn.

Minutes earlier, we'd received the WhatsApp message we'd all been waiting for: 'Success, door open.' Finishing last-order pints, we left our rendezvous pub in groups of three, exchanging nervous glances as we walked excitedly through the cold night air. Our mission was a mystery to the late-night revellers we passed enjoying a McDonald's, but we felt conspicuous all the same.

We turned down a darkened side road just beyond Chancery Lane tube – and there was the door, slightly ajar. Hours earlier we had passed it and naively tried the handle, only to find it firmly locked. But our advance party had found a way in. Their method will have to remain a secret, but suffice to say it involved no breaking, only entering.

Behind the black iron door, the beams of headtorches flashed in the gloom, illuminating crumbling paintwork, an ancient lift system and dust-covered signs. ONLY THE AUTHORISED ATTENDANT IS PERMITTED TO ENTER, read one. KINGSWAY TUNNELS, read another. We had gained access to one of London's most secret tunnels, built by the British government during the Second World War and extended during the Cold War.

'This way,' someone whispered, beckoning us over to a metal ladder that descended into the darkness far below. It seemed sturdy enough. But on the way down, we discovered part of the gantry floor that had rusted through. My heart in my mouth, I edged round it to the next ladder, dislodging flecks of corroded metal. As others passed it above me, a gentle rain of rust cascaded down onto our heads, motes of dust illuminated by our headtorches.

With relief, we reached the bottom. Out of the gloom appeared a giant bulkhead door, painted grey, marked with 1950s-style stencil lettering. It felt as if we were approaching the entrance to Tutankhamun's tomb. The door swung back; and there, inside, lay wonderful things.

Two sets of circular tunnels snaked away before us, looking like the ironclad innards of some buried spacecraft. Wires and pipes hung in bunches from the walls. Someone, somewhere was paying a fortune in electricity bills, because the tunnels were well-lit and the bulbs seemed constantly on. There was a pervasive smell of old engine oil, and the air was warm and perfectly still, as if we were close to the earth's core. No breeze permeated this far down, and we were beginning to perspire in our winter coats.

A sudden rumbling overhead alerted us to the fact that we were *beneath* the Underground. Startled at first, overawed by the strangeness of it, and feeling more than a little paranoid, we began to laugh. We'd done it; it was real; we were in. Taking maps out of our bags, we started to chart our route through the tunnels.

All of the passageways bore hand-painted signs, like GOODS ALLEY, SECOND AVENUE and NORTH STREET WEST. Taking the right-hand passage, we soon emerged into a larger room filled with a latticework wall of metal and wires, which turned out to be the main distribution frame of a huge telephone exchange. A ladder hung from the ceiling, affording access to the full height of the frame; a beautiful old telephone, made of shiny black bakelite with a rotary dial, hung from the wall. On the left, neatly stencilled lettering pointed to a FIRST AID ROOM.

The tunnels stretched on and on. In other sections, we found diesel generators, mysterious machines with glass-fronted dials and pressure gauges, and a giant air filtration device proudly badged as THE PRECIP-ITRON. Old circuit diagrams, carefully drawn by hand, were framed on the walls next to the pieces of equipment, lest an engineer needed to fix them. Glass-doored cabinets contained sets of tools. A few, incongruous-looking swivel chairs were slung about the place. In one room, we came across a bank of switches and red lights that looked for all the world like a church organ, but in fact appeared to operate a series of bulkhead doors, sewage pumps and, according to one mysterious label, HOL FLOOD – possibly referring to a set of flood gates located elsewhere in the tunnel system.

Other parts of the tunnels had started to decay. Paint flaked off damp walls. In places, the arc lights would flicker malevolently, casting dramatic shadows. At one point, an alarm sounded, harsh and insistent. We began to panic; would the cops come running? But none did.

At the far end of the tunnel system, we came across an old staff canteen. In the 1980s BBC series *Edge of Darkness*, a nuclear thriller set during the height of the Cold War, the two main protagonists – a Detective Inspector from Yorkshire and an American CIA agent – stumble across a nuclear bunker and find a wall of fine wines set aside for the apocalypse. Sadly, the kitchen we'd discovered contained no such riches. But it did have an industrial-sized potato peeling machine and deep-fat fryer. Something about the mundanity of it, the simple day-to-day-necessity of preparing food, brought home the poignancy of what we were exploring. Even during a nuclear war, people in service of the British state would have to eat; and given the circumstances, the government had conceded that they might as well have chips.

The tunnel system under Holborn was originally constructed as the last redoubt of the British state in the event of a Nazi invasion. Here, deep beneath the streets of the capital, was where the Prime Minister and his war cabinet would have taken refuge had London been overrun. 'We shall fight on the beaches,' run Churchill's immortal words from 1940; 'We shall fight on the landing grounds, we shall fight in the fields and in the streets.' But behind the Churchillian defiance lay preparations for retreat and resistance, and a proviso that 'if . . . this Island or a large part of it were subjugated and starving', the fight would still go on.

Philip K. Dick's novel *The Man in the High Castle* envisions a world in which the Nazis have won the war and the Allies lie vanquished. Oblique references are made to the horrors of Nazi occupation and Churchill's last, desperate efforts to defend his country in the 'Battle of London'. But the Holborn tunnels aren't science fiction. Revealed by investigative journalist Duncan Campbell to be an 'Invasion citadel' and 'headquarters for resistance', it is to these burrows that the territorial boundaries of England would have shrunk had Hitler pressed ahead with sending ground troops to Britain, instead of turning his attention to Russia.

They form just one part of a much broader system of deep-level tunnels constructed by the state beneath the capital, which most Londoners remain oblivious of. The subterranean Cabinet War Rooms – where Churchill's government operated during the Second World War, underneath what is now the Treasury building in Whitehall, protected from bomb blasts by a three-foot concrete ceiling known affectionately as 'the slab' – has become a popular tourist attraction. But the rest of the tunnel and shelter system is much less well-known. During the war, eight deep Tube shelters were constructed to house some 80,000 people in the event of serious bombardment. As things panned out, the Blitz – though destroying large swathes of London and killing around 43,000 people – was actually less destructive than the government had feared. The deep shelters went mostly unused; today a few of them are owned or leased by archival storage companies, but otherwise they have been forgotten.

And how many commuters and tourists walking up Whitehall are aware that a secret tunnel lies beneath their feet? The tunnel, known as Q-Whitehall, was constructed in 1940 to provide a protected run for telephone and telegraph cables run by the General Post Office (GPO) to government departments, starting in Trafalgar Square and running all the way down to Parliament Square. The passageway was also big enough for people to walk along it. One of the few declassified documents on the tunnel reveals that the Postmaster General wrote to

Churchill on 18 August 1941, stating: 'When you visited the Whitehall Tunnel you expressed a wish to know what would be involved in providing an extension of the tunnel to a point under the slab in the Cabinet War room. We now have a report from the Consulting Engineer . . . you will see that the job will take about 18 weeks in all.' To bore the tunnels, a shaft would need to be sunk through a triangular-shaped atrium in the Treasury building above, numbered Court 6. No mention is made of this tunnel in the Cabinet War Rooms displays; but a single key hangs mysteriously on a hook in one corner of the museum. On its red fob are the hand-painted words *G.P.O. Tubes, Court 6*. In the 2017 film *Darkest Hour*, Churchill is shown walking along Q-Whitehall to get between the war rooms, Downing Street and Parliament.

Though I'd heard various urban legends about these tunnels before, I hadn't paid them much attention, until I stumbled across some official documents proving their existence. When, in late 2017, the Land Registry released their Corporate & Commercial dataset, I decided to see if this huge database contained any evidence of the rumoured London tunnels. Astonishingly, it did.

Two entries in the database corroborate the existence of Q-Whitehall. 'His Majesty's Postmaster-General' is listed as the owner of a *Cable Chamber at the corner of Parliament Street and Bridge Street*, with the freehold registered on 10 July 1951; that's just outside the Parliament bookshop, near one of the exits to Westminster Tube. Another entry, referring to a *Vertical Shaft At Basement Level, Old War Office, Whitehall*, points to where the Whitehall Tunnel seems to have been connected to the former headquarters of the British Army. Long buried, the secrets of London's tunnels are slowly being revealed as the state begins to free up its data and release old archives.

The reference that eventually set me off on my adventures beneath Holborn was as obscure as it was mysterious: 'That part of the subsoil which forms part of the underground works which became vested in Her Majesty's Postmaster-General by virtue of the Post Office Works Act 1959 known as the London Works'. Interest duly piqued, I bought the land title and accompanying plan, and then sat staring at them with growing excitement. The plans, overlaid on a 1950s-era OS map, showed a vast and complex tunnel system creeping beneath High Holborn and Chancery Lane.

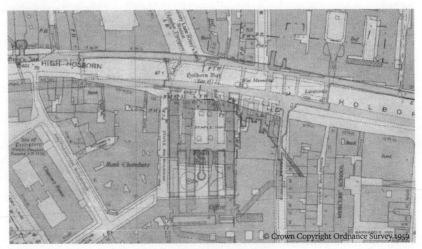

Secret tunnels beneath Holborn.

Though first built to prepare for a Nazi invasion, these tunnels were acquired after the war by the Post Office – then an arm of the state – who began re-purposing them to withstand an even greater threat: the spectre of nuclear war. They were swiftly extended and fitted out to become the atom-bomb-proof telephone exchange called Kingsway. Their existence is an insight into preparations undertaken by the British government to buy up land and construct shelters that they hoped would enable the state to survive a nuclear holocaust.

A single reference to them exists in Hansard, the official transcript of Parliamentary debates. On 20 January 1959, Lord Chesham, introducing the Post Office Works Bill for the government, explained to the House of Lords: 'Shortly after the war small underground shelters which had been constructed mainly in the borough of Holborn for the Ministry of Home Security were taken over by the Post Office. They were extended and they were adapted ... All these works are now complete, and consist of underground rooms with connecting passages more than fifty feet below the surface of the ground. They are used for essential Post Office purposes.'

The Kingsway Exchange connects to the Whitehall Tunnel, and a set of other subterranean exchanges, via twelve miles of deep-level cable tunnels. In 1980, Duncan Campbell, a journalist at the *New Statesman* investigating the government's preparations for nuclear war, discovered an entrance to some of these connecting tunnels and rode a folding bike along them, somehow evading security. 'A manhole cover, gently raised, gives access to one of the Post Office's thousands of subsurface cable chambers,' he wrote in an article for the Christmas edition of the *NS*. Following the tunnels down towards Q-Whitehall, he staged an ironic Christmas party, complete with party hats and tinsel, 'at the entrance to the nastiest bit of government of all' – a side tunnel leading to the Ministry of Defence, where, Campbell claimed, lay a heavily guarded chamber containing the nuclear button.

Campbell's extraordinary exploits were intended to both expose and embarrass the Cold War security state, something he expounded upon further in his book *War Plan UK*. This, after all, was the era of *Protect and Survive* and *When the Wind Blows*, when the government was pretending that households could survive nuclear attack simply by painting their windows white, while building themselves ever-deeper concrete bunkers. 'The real and only priority of civil defence is the protection of government and its war-making capacity,' wrote Campbell.

The Cold War is now mercifully long over, and the British state has changed considerably. It is less secretive, but also much smaller. Once, government envisaged being forced to retreat in the face of external threats. In more recent decades, it has shrunk itself voluntarily. Functions once deemed in the purview of the public sector have been privatised. The Post Office has been dismembered, with BT inheriting the now-defunct Kingsway Exchange. But some of the deep-level cable tunnels remain in use, and are now more carefully guarded by CCTV and motion sensors than in Campbell's day. On our way out of the Holborn tunnels, we lingered by a side alley leading to the deep-level tunnel system. A blog post on an urban exploration website had warned us that the last crew to go down them had lasted five minutes before 'all hell broke loose'. We decided better of it, and returned to the cold night air of London's streets.

In times of war and crisis, the state hunkers down below ground. But to carry out its ordinary functions during peacetime, it possesses an extensive landed estate above ground. To survey this, let's take a walk down Whitehall – at street level, this time.

Begin in Parliament Square, overlooked by Big Ben and the Palace of Westminster, with Whitehall heading off to the north. Parliament Square is roughly one acre in extent, providing a handy visual measure for appraising what the UK government and wider public sector owns. By my calculations, the public sector owns some 2.7 million acres of freehold land in England, or 8.5 per cent of the country. Figure 1 gives a breakdown of this; for the detailed references, please see the Appendix.

Public body	UK-wide	England
Ministry of Defence	505,825 acres	397,098 acres
Forestry Commission	2,064,598 acres	489,814 acres
Highways England	114,314 acres	114,314 acres
Network Rail	129,356 acres	100,525 acres
Other Whitehall departments	165,000 acres	158,957 acres
Local government	1,569,544 acres (England & Wales)	1,326,655 acres
Oxbridge colleges	126,000 acres	126,000 acres
Totals	4,617,568 acres	2,713,363 acres

Figure 1: What central government owns. See Appendix for sources.

Now walk up Whitehall, past the major offices of state. On the left are the grand, neoclassical facades of Her Majesty's Treasury and the Foreign and Commonwealth Office, all columns and balustrades and white Portland stone. The offices of the FCO, which occupy what used to be the Colonial Office, still bear statues celebrating Britain's land grabs across the world: naked female sculptures representing Asia, Africa, America and Australasia offer up the fruits of the Empire to their masters. Only Europa is depicted clothed, sending out her civilising ships and domesticated animals to 'paint the map red', as the arch-imperialist Cecil Rhodes was fond of saying. August and powerful though these great offices of state are, however, neither the Treasury nor the Foreign Office directly owns or controls much land around England or in the UK as a whole. In fact, the Treasury doesn't even own its departmental offices; its land title is registered in the name of the First Secretary of State, a ministerial role that is created from time to time for someone acting as the right hand of the Prime Minister.

Beyond the FCO lies Downing Street. Any politician wanting to wield political power, of course, aspires to enter Number 10, or – if they're willing to settle for the role of Chancellor, Number 11. But from the perspective of governing the Government's own estate, the power resides next door, at 70 Whitehall: the Cabinet Office. It's the Cabinet Office that actually owns the keys to Number 10, and the title to the 'Basement, Ground and 1st–3rd floors', as the government's property register inelegantly records it. Perhaps to the relief of anyone keen to enter through its polished black door and become PM, its status within the government's property holdings is recorded as being 'Core – Inflexible': not even the most ardent small-state neoliberal would sell off Downing Street.

Enter the Cabinet Office via Downing Street (as I did in 2014), and you're reminded immediately that even the government is forced to contend with the lie of the land and the vagaries of nature. An old sign next to the entrance alerts visitors that this is FLOOD PROTECTION LOCATION POINT 15: a hangover from before the Thames Barrier was built, when low-lying parts of Whitehall flooded in 1928 and came close to being submerged during the 1953 Great Flood. Nowadays, however, the Cabinet Office is where the government responds to disasters taking place in *other* parts of the country: Cabinet Office Briefing Room A, the meeting-point for the COBRA committee, is located somewhere in these rooms.

When not fire-fighting emergencies, the Cabinet Office concerns itself with making government run more efficiently, and above all, for less money. Since the onset of austerity in 2010, the CO has taken an increasing interest in mapping what the government owns, and assessing whether it can be sold off to save cash. In 2014, it published, for the first time, an online register and map of all land and property possessed by central government. Now the public could start to better appreciate the true extent of the government's estate, reaching out from Whitehall and spread across the country. Thousands of courts, hospitals, prisons, schools, roads, army barracks, nature reserves, farms, and flood defences, all revealed: the physical manifestation of the public sector as it is today – a provider of healthcare and tanks, of pensions and youth education, of High Speed 2 and pothole repairs. Here was the infrastructure of both the welfare state and the warfare state laid bare: functions of government that have grown and changed immensely since the Victorians built Whitehall, content in the belief that you only needed a streetful of civil servants to run a country – or, come to that, administer to a quarter of the world's population.

But the Cabinet Office's new Government Property Finder was not, of course, intended to provoke reflection on how the role of the state has grown as its citizens have come to demand more of it. An initiative of David Cameron's Coalition government, it was set up, instead, to help shrink the state. The Government Property Finder website invited visitors to 'challenge [us on] whether the land or property is being used effectively . . . If the government cannot justify its use, the land or property will be released and put to better use.' Cabinet Office minister Francis Maude heralded it as a means of 'slashing our own costs'.

Two examples of the Coalition's fire sale of assets can be glimpsed further up Whitehall. On the right – just after the statue of Field Marshal Haig, the butcher of the Somme – is the Old War Office. In 2014, the Coalition vacated it and sold it under a 250-year lease to the billionaire Hinduja Brothers, Indian steel magnates who plan to turn it into a luxury hotel. Perhaps predictably, the company with the lease-hold, 57 Whitehall SARL, is based in the tax haven of Luxembourg. A similar fate has befallen Admiralty Arch, the crescent gateway that straddles the Mall between Trafalgar Square and Buckingham Palace, and which used to provide office space for the Cabinet Office. It was sold in 2012 to Spanish real estate developer Rafael Serrano, who is converting it into an exclusive hotel and private members' club.

These examples only scratch the surface of the huge amounts of public sector land and property that have been sold off and privatised in recent decades. But let's pause and return to pick up these threads again later, because our tour of Whitehall has taken us to the im-posing steel doors of one of the biggest landowning departments in government. With its grey and monolithic exterior, guarded by vast muscle-bound statues and always-armed police, almost Soviet in its architectural style and certainly reminiscent of the ministries in Orwell's 1984, there is little doubt who owns this building: the Ministry of Defence.

Few institutions leave a more distinctive mark on the land they own than the Ministry of Defence. Farmers till their fields; the MOD tends to blow theirs up. Surrounded by miles of barbed wire fences, patrolled by soldiers and dogs, and peppered with intimidating signs warning passers-by to keep out, an MOD site is hard to miss up close. Yet no other landowner is quite so secretive about what happens on their land.

For many decades, hundreds of military-owned sites were literally erased from official maps. Glance at any OS map showing a military installation today, and compare it with a version of that same map published during the Cold War: invariably, you'll see that what is shown now as an airfield or a dense mass of military barracks was previously airbrushed from the official cartographic record. Activist Mark Thomas discovered this to comic effect in his 2002 documentary *Secret Map of Britain*. Turning up outside a military establishment brandishing an Ordnance Survey map, Thomas accosts a puzzled MOD security guard. 'We can't find this place, here, on a map,' he exclaims with exasperation, gesticulating at the high fences, bunkers and KEEP OUT signs, all incontrovertible proof that *here* very much existed.

In the documentary, Dr Chris Perkins, a map curator at Manchester University, claims that around 2,000 to 3,000 sites deemed to be sensitive or critical to national defence were kept off OS maps at the height of the Cold War. There's no small irony in this, given that the military were the first to map the UK with accuracy. It was the drive to defend and fortify Britain against French invasion that resulted in the creation of Ordnance Survey. Perkins argues that 'the most effective mapping . . . has been, and often still is, the exclusive preserve of the military, and the strategic advantages this brings have been jealously guarded by those in power'. 'Maps work,' agrees academic Denis Wood, 'by serving interests.'

Even the MOD, however, are no longer as secretive as they once were. I wrote to them in 2014, asking – perhaps naïvely – whether they would release a map of all their land and property, under the terms of the Freedom of Information Act. They responded, politely but firmly, stating that identifying the location of military bases 'would prejudice the capability and effectiveness of our armed forces'. Two years later, I tried again. Something clearly had changed in the interim – or perhaps an official had just taken pity on me – because this time, they sent me a complete map of every Ministry of Defence site in the country.

The MOD's map confirmed one thing straight away: they own and lease a hell of a lot of land. In fact, the map suggested, the Ministry operates across nearly twice as much land as they ordinarily admit in public. Officially, the MOD says that the estate they own comprises 240,000 hectares across the UK – that's 593,053 acres. But analysing the map I was sent shows that it stretches to some 1,101,851 acres – almost twice as much. This clearly contains a large amount of land that's leased from other landowners, or over which the military have training rights, rather than owned by the MOD outright. That's confirmed by more recently published national statistics, which show that the total land area the MOD owns, leases or has rights over is just over a million acres, with half a million acres owned freehold. Broken down by nation, it becomes clear that England contains the bulk of the freehold defence estate, with some 397,098 acres. The MOD's freehold landholdings in Scotland, Wales and Northern Ireland are all much smaller; but this is partially offset by the huge amount of land in Scotland over which they have training rights.

In England, while some of the biggest and best-known military bases are owned by the MOD outright – like Salisbury Plain, Otterburn in Northumberland and the Stanford Training Area in Norfolk – the armed forces also have access to huge swathes of land where they can train in Kielder Forest (leased from the Forestry Commission), Dartmoor (on loan from the Duchy of Cornwall), and parts of Thetford Forest (rented from the FC and the Crown Estate), among others.

It's a vast area to keep under wraps. But another way the MOD keeps its activities hush-hush is by buying up land that's either sparsely populated or remote from where people live – or, if it comes to it, by moving the people who already live there out of the way. Sometimes, such places are hiding in plain sight. Few Londoners realise, for instance, that they share an estuary with a secret military island that once harboured the UK's atomic weapons research programme, and whose main means of access for pedestrians is via the deadliest footpath in Britain. To show you how the Ministry of Defence can change a landscape utterly, and yet still keep it covered up for decades, let me take you on a journey to the mysterious island of Foulness.

Planning the journey to Foulness – a 6,000-acre weapons testing site off the coast of Essex, not far from Southend – had proved a logistical nightmare. Access to the island is strictly controlled by the MOD. Though it has a civilian population of 150, visitors can only safely get there with a pass, and at very specific times of year. The alternative is to walk the Broomway across Maplin Sands, a vast expanse of mudflats whose treacherous tides have claimed many an unwary traveller. And that, I found when I rang up the authorities, was temporarily closed for long-range weapons testing.

There was one option remaining to me. Barring official 'sponsorship' by a resident, the only reason you're allowed across the single road-bridge connecting Foulness to the mainland is to visit the tiny Foulness Heritage Centre. And that, I discovered, was open on just the first Sunday of each month during the summer, with checkpoints opening at noon and closing by 5 p.m. So I planned ahead. But I forgot to take my bike helmet, and that was my first mistake.

'No access without a helmet,' barked the private security guard as my friend Nick and I rode up to the island's access point, Foulness's equivalent of Checkpoint Charlie. The island, though owned by the MOD, is managed and policed by the private firm QinetiQ, spun out of the Ministry in the 1990s.

'But there was nothing on the website that said I needed to wear one,' I protested, having read every word of the confusing rules and regulations governing access to Foulness. The sun beat down on us and the little queue of visitors waiting to be processed for entry. A sign on the side of the access point read, improbably, NO WAITING AT ANY TIMES.

'This is a Tier One COMAH site,' said the guard, referring to Foulness's top spot on the Control of Major Accidents and Hazards register. 'It's health and safety.' But eventually he relented. Another sign by the gate recorded the number of days since an accident had last occurred on site, like something you might once have seen in an old factory. Nick wandered over to take a picture of it. 'No photography,' instructed our sentry, now enjoying his power trip. 'Photography on Foulness is a criminal offence under the 1935 Shoeburyness Military bylaws.' Needless to say, we later took great pleasure in taking photos of the signs on the island that read NO PHOTOGRAPHY.

Eventually we got our passes, in exchange for leaving our names and phone numbers, and the guard raised the red and white striped barrier blocking the road. 'Back by 5 p.m.,' he growled as we rode off. It felt like we were entering a different country. And in some ways, we were.

Foulness has been owned by the military since the nineteenth century, when it was acquired as a firing range. Later it became a centre for trialling experimental weapons, and the experiments grew more exotic as time went on. In 1947, the island was selected as one of the key testing sites for Britain's atomic weapons programme. No nuclear bombs were exploded here, of course – that was inflicted upon some poor islands in the South Pacific; but other parts of the trigger mechanisms for the bomb were assembled on Foulness. Files in the National Archives relate how Foulness was used for testing beryllium shells in the 1960s and 70s, as part of the development of atomic warheads. Beryllium is very, very nasty if you breathe it in. MOD staff handling it on Foulness were instructed that 'white protective clothing with special shoes or over-shoes must be worn by all'. But as an English Heritage report on Foulness says, 'one of the consequences of these experiments was that beryllium was scattered across sections of the site'. A Land Quality Assessment that I obtained from the MOD under Freedom of Information law shows that large parts of the old atomic weapons testing site on Foulness remain contaminated with heavy metals. At one site, 'for the majority of surface water samples submitted for analysis, concentrations for arsenic, boron, manganese, ammonium and mercury also exceeded human health screening criteria'. Today the island regularly reverberates with explosions from the testing of conventional weapons, and columns of smoke rise from the MOD's ammunitions disposal sites where old shell casings are burned. A sign I found on the coast warning of a nearby firing range was riddled with bullet holes. Despite the hot sunshine, the place seemed suffused with paranoia, a feeling encouraged by the threatening signage that sprouted by the roadside.

When the Americans' A-bomb exploded over Hiroshima, killing hundreds of thousands of people, it also stopped all the clocks in the city. On Foulness, time appears to have stood still since the 1950s. Clapboarded houses, old pickup trucks and rusting farm machinery suggested a bygone England where the present had only been permitted to enter slowly, regulated via the checkpoint. The vast open horizons and hedgeless fields, stretching out before us as we cycled past barbed wire fences and squat military compounds, had an American prairie-like quality. The comparative absence of people has also let nature flourish. Herons and avocets graced the air as we pedalled along the island's one arterial road; starlings sprang from the haze of cow parsley and forget-me-nots lining the verges.

The island is so flat because much of it was won from the sea in the medieval period. Today, the sea yearns to reclaim Foulness. It pounds at its crumbling flood defences and threatens to inundate its many drainage channels with brine. In 1953, the sea won its greatest victory to date. The Great Flood of that year saw Foulness completely submerged by a huge storm surge from the North Sea. Ruth, who we met at the Heritage Centre, told us how she had been ten years old at the time of the flood, and remembered being trapped on the upper floor of her home before rescuers eventually arrived.

Though a flood like that of 1953 has not yet been repeated, sea levels have since risen thanks to climate change, meaning the flood defences need constant maintenance and improvement. I had discovered through a series of FOI requests that the MOD had neglected their sea defences on Foulness for years. Officials at the Environment Agency, the body tasked with defending England from flooding, had grown ever more exasperated by the military's lack of action. There was little the officials could do without the MOD, as landowner, pulling its finger out. Eventually, the repair work was done. But it's a losing battle: with nowhere on Foulness higher than two metres above sea level, and sea levels forecast to rise by two metres over the coming century if global warming and emissions continue at their current rate, it's only a matter of time before the whole island is submerged for ever.

But the MOD can't simply abandon it, because of all the legacy contaminants that stand to leach out if seawater is allowed to cover the island. 'The main constraint for [coastal] realignment is the possibility that the island may contain contaminated materials,' states the official Shoreline Management Plan for Essex. So instead, they keep building the sea walls higher. The MOD knows this isn't sustainable. The military tend to have a better understanding of risk than most government departments, and think long-term. Many MOD bases in England are situated next to the sea or rivers and are at risk of flooding as climate change worsens. An internal review I obtained examining these threats admitted that the 'MOD has to acknowledge that the "Canute syndrome" is changing, and difficult choices are required: abandon, manage retreat, or defend robustly'. But beating a retreat in the face of nature seems, for now, a defeat the MOD is unwilling to concede: the official policy remains one of 'hold the line'.

There is a lingering suspicion, however, that the MOD would rather the remaining population of Foulness abandoned it. Linda, another of the Heritage Centre's volunteer staff, whose family has lived on Foulness for six generations, told us in a hushed voice that there were many empty properties in the village these days. 'The MOD will come in every now and then and install new kitchens and bathrooms in the empty homes, but no one moves in,' she said, indignantly. 'Yet they claim there's a waiting list.' Churchend's village notice board displayed a planning announcement from a few years back stating that a block of terraces was to be demolished and grassed over. Linda mourned the hollowing-out of Foulness's community. In recent years, the pub, shop and post office have all closed; even the church is now fenced off, too derelict to allow in worshippers. 'It would be hard to disagree with whispered conspiracy theories about a silent shut-down, and peaceful long-term removal of the islanders,' alleged a local news report a decade ago.

Foulness remains useful to the MOD: an out-of-the-way expanse of land where access can be strictly controlled and weapons exploded with few complaints from the dwindling population. And so it endures as an extraordinary oddity: a secret military island off the coast of Essex, the land harbouring its secrets and its payload of toxins, waiting for the inevitable day when nature will come knocking and they will be released upon an unsuspecting world.

To understand how the MOD became such a huge landowner, we need to rewind to the trenches and battlefields of the First World War.

In wartime, the state has often resorted to seizing land for military use. The principle of the compulsory purchase of land has existed in English law for some time; numerous Acts of Parliament gave rights of compulsory purchase to the private railway companies at the height of the Victorian railway boom. But the Victorian state itself had remained small, without needing to acquire large amounts of land quickly. That changed after the outbreak of hostilities with Imperial Germany, and the sudden demands of fighting total war drove a rapid expansion in the power of the state.

One week after the start of the Battle of the Somme, Parliament debated the 1916 Defence of the Realm (Acquisition of Land) Bill. Sixty thousand British men had just been slaughtered in the mud of Flanders, and the political mood was febrile. The government chose this moment to push through powers of compulsory purchase of land to support the war effort. Land was urgently needed for new munitions factories, for training soldiers, and for testing the new poison gas weapons that both sides had begun deploying in the quagmire of the Western Front.

The Bill was not without controversy. Landowners were naturally concerned about its implications, and a number of MPs and even ministers regarded it as a flagrant overreach of authority by the state, suspecting the government of using the wartime emergency as cover for a power grab that might extend well into peacetime. Ernest Pretyman, a Conservative MP and Civil Lord of the Admiralty within the coalition government, wrote to Minister of Munitions Christopher Addison to air his objections to the draft Bill. 'It seems to me that it cannot possibly be allowed to pass in its present form,' he opined. 'Property owners have, during the War, most willingly placed their land and houses at the disposal of the Government . . . whilst landowners are risking their lives at the Front, their property is being confiscated at home behind their backs.' Nevertheless, the Bill passed easily.

As things panned out, the impact of the Defence of the Realm Act was less dramatic than some feared. Some 200 munitions factories were built or requisitioned by the government, and various aerodromes were seized; but state intervention in food production did not begin in earnest until 1917, and was much less marked than would be the case in the Second World War.

But these were early straws in the wind. The government had discovered an appetite, and an aptitude, for taking charge of land. This raised big questions for landowners and the wider public about the power of the state, what constituted fair compensation, and the very nature of private property. It also raised the prospect that land could be acquired by the public sector for other uses: not just to build bomb factories during wars, but to build affordable housing in peacetime, too. Indeed, that was what Lloyd George seemed to offer as the hostilities finally drew towards a close, when he promised to build 'homes fit for heroes' for returning soldiers; a promise he never fulfilled.

Many soldiers had fought and died for a vision of England in which they felt they had a real stake in the country, its land and history. In the early years of the war, Rupert Brooke, the most patriotic of the Great War poets, had written:

> *If I should die, think only this of me:*
> *That there's some corner of a foreign field*
> *That is for ever England.*

But as exhausted and shell-shocked soldiers returned home, some corners of English fields were soon to be sealed off for ever.

The military's acquisition of land in the inter-war years was as slow as the rest of its preparations for another armed conflict. Between 1918 and

1939, the War Office acquired just 42,000 acres of land, usually bought at market rates. Few politicians were prepared to acknowledge the growing inevitability of war with fascist Germany. But as appeasement failed and Chamberlain's ultimatums to Hitler expired one by one, that changed dramatically.

The Emergency Powers (Defence) Act of 1939 gave the government sweeping powers to prosecute the coming war, including the seizure of land and property. The subsequent Defence Regulations included two specifically referring to land requisition: DR51 and DR52. These powers ended up being used not only by the War Office, but also by the newly created War Agricultural Committees to direct food production and requisition further vast swathes of land.

Requisitioning began immediately and accelerated during the early years of the war. The increasing mechanisation of warfare had led to a correspondingly greater military hunger for land: bigger and faster tanks needed larger areas to practise manoeuvres; the greatly enlarged air force needed more airfields. At first, the government was reluctant to admit in public quite how much land was being seized for military purposes. An MP's Parliamentary Question to this effect in July 1942 received the terse ministerial reply: 'It would not, I think, be in the public interest to publish these figures.' But further questions were asked, not least because some regions and nations felt they were being unfairly targeted for land seizures. An internal War Office briefing, prepared for the Secretary of State before he met with a deputation of Welsh MPs in the summer of 1942, noted: 'When we were taking over Senny Bridge, the big range near Brecon, we continually met this argument that we were treating the Welsh far worse than the English.' The briefing's author added drily: 'I don't think that the Welsh realise what we are doing in England.'

There was also increasing conflict between the use of land for military purposes and what was needed to boost food supplies. Inter-departmental jostling between the War Office and the Ministry of Agriculture led to the keeping of more accurate shared records. Still preserved in the National Archives, these show that over the course of the war, the War Office alone requisitioned 580,847 acres – on top of what it already owned. Other files relate how most of this land had been seized by November 1942, particularly for large battle-training areas in places like Otterburn, Stanford and Dartmoor, as the War Office scrambled to make up for lost time. But these figures pale in comparison with the vast acreages requisitioned by the state overall, both for military activities and for food production: some 14.5 million acres across the UK – almost a quarter of the entire country. Much of this was done in the last two years of the war, as Allied forces amassed tanks, ordnance and battalions across southern England in preparation for D-Day.

Demobilisation after the Second World War took some time; meat rationing, after all, remained in place until 1954. A decade after the cessation of hostilities, the War Office could happily report that it now possessed only 95,350 acres of requisitioned land, an 80 per cent drop from 1946. But these figures mask how contentious the issue of seized land became after the war – particularly when it was not just fields that had been requisitioned, but people's homes.

Scattered across various military sites to this day are the ghostly remains of villages evacuated during the Second World War to make way for the military. In *The Village that Died for England*, Patrick Wright tells the story of Tyneham, a quintessentially beautiful small English settlement nestled deep in the Dorset countryside, whose inhabitants were moved out to make way for a tank firing range, never to return. The Lulworth Ranges had been gradually acquired by the military in the 1930s, with Tyneham's residents remaining as tenants; but in 1943, with preparations for D-Day under way, the decision was made on the ultimate authority of Churchill's War Cabinet to evacuate the village in secret, so that live firing could be carried out. 'It is regretted that, in the National interest, it is necessary to move you from your homes,' read a letter to the residents from Major General Miller of Southern Command. 'The Army must have an area of land particularly suited to their special needs and in which they can use live shells.'

Moving was a traumatic experience for the whole community. It was 'a dreadful thing to happen to them, and it was a dreadful thing to have to do', recalled John Durant-Lewis, a member of the local council who was tasked with organising the evacuation. Neighbours who had been friends all their lives were billeted far from one another in unfamiliar towns; possessions were lost or broken; some of the older evacuees likely died from shock brought on by the upheaval. But the village filed out with meek good grace, leaving a message pinned to the church door as they departed: 'We have given up our homes, where many of us have lived for generations, to help win the war to keep men free. We shall return one day and thank you for treating the village kindly.'

But worse than the move was the betrayal. 'Churchill's pledge', the official assurance given to Tyneham residents that one day they might be allowed to return to their village, was broken by successive governments. With conscription remaining in place after the war and fresh conflict with the Soviet Union looming, the War Office wished to retain its valuable firing range. The minister dispatched from Whitehall to bear the bad news to the villagers expressed how sorry, truly sorry, he was, but that regrettably, 'training implies having the necessary land on which to train.' To this day, Tyneham remains in the possession of the Ministry of Defence, its buildings dilapidated and roofless, its inhabitants never permitted to return home.

Nor was Tyneham alone in its plight. The Stanford Training Area, an 18,000-acre stretch of sandy heath in Norfolk east of the Fens, was requisitioned in 1942, requiring the evacuation of the residents of West Tofts, Sturston, Langford, Stanford, Buckenham Tofts and Tottington: an episode since dubbed the 'Breckland exodus'. They, too, were never to return. And in December 1943, in preparation for D-Day, the isolated village of Imber, high on Salisbury Plain, was ordered to evacuate. The village and the surrounding ranges had been slowly purchased by the military over the previous forty years, though often opportunistically. A handwritten note in the archives shows that War Office officials acquired the nearby Tilshead Estate legally but perhaps not entirely honourably. The owner of the estate, Mr Farquharson, is noted by a mandarin as being 'about 80 years of age, in a poor state of health and anxious to sell', before adding breathlessly, 'The present provides a most favourable opportunity for us to buy . . . If we can take advantage of it we should save at least £20,000 compared with having to purchase from an unwilling seller.' The residents of Imber, too, proved pliant and willing when asked to move, but were less than happy when the army forbade them from ever coming back. Austin Underwood, a local councillor, demanded a public inquiry into the army's behaviour and campaigned for years to allow the villagers to return, arguing that Imber was a 'murdered village' and, on one occasion, serving the MOD with a mock eviction notice.

These lost villages continued to exert a powerful hold on the public imagination for decades after their evacuation. Around Tyneham, protesting residents were joined in the 1960s and 70s by a hodge-podge of activists drawn from across the political spectrum, and archetypally English in their eccentricities: entomologists, ecologists, retired colonels, even some rural fascists. But though the protestations of the Tyneham Action Group brought the abandoned village to national attention, they failed to make a dent in the MOD's armour, and tanks continued to roll over the soft downland turf. In Imber, a mock Londonderry council estate was constructed for troops training to fight during the Troubles. At Stanford, fake East German villages were thrown up to simulate urban combat during the Cold War. More recent decades have seen the sandy Breckland countryside stand in for the arid deserts of Iraq and Afghanistan.

For residents of Tyneham, Imber and elsewhere, there must have been a particularly bitter irony to the abundant wartime propaganda that urged the public to contribute to the war effort by invoking a deep-seated love of the English pastoral. YOUR BRITAIN, reads one such famous poster, depicting a rural arcadia of rolling downland, stands of oaks, a village nestled in the valley and a shepherd leading his flock home: FIGHT FOR IT NOW.

Defence of the realm.

But not everyone who had their land taken from them remained dispossessed. If you wanted to get it back, it seemed, it helped if you belonged to the landed aristocracy. Crichel Down in Dorset, not so far from Tyneham, comprised 700 acres of agricultural land acquired in 1938 by the Air Ministry. Up until that point, much of it had belonged to the 3rd Baron Arlington as part of his 5,000-acre Crichel Estate, and he had been given compensation of £12,000 (about three-quarters of a million pounds in today's money).

What made Crichel Down controversial was what happened to it after the war was over. Churchill's pledge to Parliament in 1941 had been that all lands acquired under compulsory purchase, or the threat of compulsory purchase, would be offered back to their original owners after the war as soon as they became surplus to requirements. In the case of Crichel Down, the Air Ministry soon had no use for the land; but, ignoring entreaties from Baron Arlington's daughter Mary Anna Sturt and her husband Lieutenant-Commander Toby Marten that they be allowed to buy it back, decided instead to transfer it to the Ministry of Agriculture, on the pretext that it was still needed to maximise food production. This transformed what had been unproductive downland into fields of wheat, increasing its value far beyond what it had been sold for, and meaning that the Martens would have to shell out much more if they ever wanted to repurchase it.

Who was in the right? The Martens clearly had a powerful case: they could point to broken promises, poor process and incompetence on the part of the government. Their plight was presented as that of the plucky individual against an over-mighty central state: not only could it take your money away from you as taxes and demand you fought for it, but now, it seemed, it could also seize your land and never return it. But the state also had a case: Baron Arlington had been compensated for his land; the pledges it had given over the return of land were less clear cut than the Martens presented; and there was a clear public interest in maximising food production in a country that still laboured under rationing. Did private property rights trump this national need? What constituted fair recompense? As ever, the devil was in the detail. But the complex facts of the case became buried beneath a simple fable pitting the Leviathan of the state against a plucky individual.

The subsequent public inquiry in 1954 came down heavily on the side of the Martens, causing the responsible Minister of Agriculture, Thomas Dugdale, to resign. The Conservative Home Secretary summarised the government's change of heart: 'Every citizen of good will sees his land go in time of emergency for Government requirements with as much good will as he can muster; but it is taken for a specific purpose, for a specific need of the State. When that purpose is exhausted, when that need is past, what is wrong, on any consideration of morality or justice in allowing the person from whom the land was taken to have the chance of getting it back?' Former residents of Tyneham would surely have agreed. The free-market *Spectator* portrayed it as a victory for the little guy over big government: 'Lying behind that case was a principle of Government policy, a principle quietly held by the Socialist Government . . . that land once acquired by the State should not be given up to private individuals.'

Of course, not everyone has regarded the Crichel Down affair in that light. The historian I.F. Nicholson, reviewing the case several decades later, found the popular version of the story 'uniquely bedevilled with errors', in which public servants were 'unjustly condemned'. Tim Adams, writing in the *Observer* in 2011, argued that 'the stand-off was seen as the last redoubt of the aristocracy against parliament, and the aristocracy won ... Thereafter any question of land reform, of the breaking up of ancient estates for the common good was shelved.'

Crichel Down may have become surplus to the Air Ministry's requirements; but at what point does it become legitimate to ask whether a few hundred acres out of a 5,000-acre estate are 'surplus to the requirements' of a private landowner? What's more, there seems to have been a stark contrast between how the aristocratic Crichel Estate was handed back its downland acres, and how the residents of Tyneham, Imber and other requisitioned villages were forbidden from returning to their homes.

Nevertheless, Crichel Down set an important precedent, changing the rules on how government has disposed of compulsorily purchased land ever since. The 'Crichel Down Rules', as most recently summarised by the government, 'require government departments, under certain circumstances, to offer back surplus land to the former owner or the former owner's successors at the current market value'. A review carried out in 2000 found that the practical impact of the rules had been limited: out of 3,000 cases where they were considered to apply, the land had been offered back to the owner in fewer than 200 instances. Even so, there is little doubt that the Crichel Down affair marked the high-water mark for the expansive state. That may be cause for relief when it comes to the military, whose justifications for acquiring land in peacetime are clearly much more questionable. But the issues raised by Crichel Down go beyond the military use of land, touching upon other, more pressing reasons why a democratic state might acquire land for the public good: increasing domestic food production, for instance, or providing affordable homes. It seems the pendulum has now swung back in the opposite direction: the default position of governments since Thatcher has been to flog off publicly owned land left, right and centre, regardless of whether this best serves the public interest.

What of the fate of the Crichel Down Estate itself? It remained in the hands of Baron Arlington's descendants, seemingly growing in size to around 10,000 acres by 2012. But then, following the death of Mary Anna that year, it was sold off and the estate broken up. Crichel House was eventually snapped up by an American billionaire, and the land is now registered in the US. Such is the ironic ending of an estate once celebrated for standing up for ancient English rights.

Land and properties seized by the military for airfields and rifle ranges could ultimately be given back to society. But twentieth-century warfare also, of course, saw the advent of chemical, biological and nuclear weapons, whose lasting impacts would result in some corners of England being sealed off for a very long time indeed. To see one such place, I travelled to Porton Down, near Salisbury.

I visited Salisbury about a month after the poisoning of Russian double-agent Sergei Skripal had made the town an international crime scene. The Zizzi's restaurant where Skripal had eaten before falling ill, victim to a Soviet-era Novichok nerve agent, was still closed off with police tape. Weeks earlier, the normally peaceful market town had been crawling with forensics experts in hazard suits and scientists from Porton Down, the government's Defence Science and Technology Laboratory (DSTL), based some seven miles up the road. Its proximity made Skripal's poisoning seem like even more of a calculated insult: Putin's demonstration that he could get away with a chemical attack right under the nose of the British establishment.

A vast amount of nonsense has been written about what goes on at Porton Down. Forget the talk of alien corpses, 'Britain's Area 51' and false-flag conspiracy theories; the truth is far stranger than fiction. This is where the UK's chemical weapons programme began, over a century ago. And it began on land belonging to a land reformer.

I caught the bus out of Salisbury to the tiny hamlet of Porton, and hiked up the hill to the high perimeter fence surrounding the defence laboratory. Few places look eerie in bright sunshine, but Porton Down contrived to do so. There was no one else in view for miles around; the silence of the wide, empty fields was broken only by the distant thrumming of a military helicopter. The author Harold Massingham had it right when he wrote: 'If ever there was an abandoned country, left to the ghosts and the fairies, it is downland.' As the sun beat down overhead, the sweat on my back turned cold, and I felt a prickling sensation on the nape of my neck. Somewhere across the fence, I knew – past the MOD PROPERTY: HAZARDOUS SITE signs, buried under the innocent turf with its covering of vetch and rare orchids – were the remains of some of the most venomous substances known to humanity.

Land at Porton Down was acquired by the military in 1916, as Britain reeled from the Germans' first use of chlorine gas on the battlefields of Ypres the year before. Here, on the rolling downs, the War Office began to test Britain's retaliatory arsenal of poison gas and develop respirators to protect British soldiers from future attacks. Hydrogen cyanide, phosgene, mustard gas; their anodyne names each concealing a formula for cruelty, so bitterly recalled by Wilfred Owen:

> If you could hear, at every jolt, the blood
> Come gargling from the froth-corrupted lungs . . .

An OS map from 1923 shows Porton Down, unlabelled but also unredacted, as a growing complex of workshops and buildings, connected by a light railway system for the transport of shells and equipment. But by now the research was outgrowing the available land, and more was needed. It was to come from a most unusual source.

Take a look at maps of Porton Down today, or aerial photos on Google Earth, and you'll see a strange pattern of trees within the land marked DANGER AREA to the west of the main laboratory; like a set of fields whose hedges have gone wild and seeded the ground with their offspring. When I compared modern images to old maps of the same area, I was surprised to see that this had once been a private estate called Old Lodge, with gardens and a large house long-since demolished. But what really intrigued me was who once lived in that house.

Between 1892 and 1918 it was the estate of one Major Robert Poore, a man whom turn-of-the-century adventure writer H. Rider Haggard once dubbed the 'Don Quixote of the Hampshire Downs'. An ex-soldier who served in the Crimean War, he went on to become a land reformer with a utopian vision. Troubled by the agricultural depression that had blighted rural English communities for a generation, the major bought a farm at Winterslow to the south of Porton Down in 1892, divided it up into smallholdings, and set up a land court to redistribute them to the local populace on very long leases. It was, by all accounts, a great success: the new smallholders began growing crops and selling them, built houses to live in, and halted the village's decline. They're still there today, at a place appropriately called The Common. Like the Diggers' Gerrard Winstanley long before him, Major Poore railed against centralised government and the way land had been taken from the public over the centuries. He advocated a return to a form of local self-government based on Saxon principles, before the imposition of feudalism.

It was a bitter twist of fate, then, that saw this idealist's own land eventually swallowed by the encroaching military machine. Following his death, his 500-acre estate at Porton Down was sold to the War Office, who razed his house to the ground, capped its artesian well, and buried the old major's dreams of land reform beneath barbed wire, bombs and poison gas. A map of the site drawn up a year before the military acquired it contained a foreshadowing of its imminent demise: the land to the west of the lodge had already been labelled 'No Man's Land'.

Worse was to come. Although neither side deployed gas during the Second World War, both amassed huge stockpiles. After the war ended, the Allies discovered that Nazi scientists had been developing even more potent forms of chemical weapons: nerve agents like sarin and tabun that inhibit the functioning of the nervous system, leading to violent convulsions, choking and death. Naturally, the British government decided it had to develop such weapons itself, and instructed Porton Down to get to work. The establishment began by recruiting thousands of volunteers as human guinea pigs on which it would test out nerve agents. In one such experiment, twenty-year-old RAF serviceman Ronald Maddison died after exposure to sarin. Hushed up at the time, his death was finally the subject of a public inquest fifty years later, which led to a verdict of unlawful killing on the part of the military. Today testing is not carried out on humans at Porton Down, but thousands of animals are still used every year. A building within the DSTL complex is referred to in Government Property Finder records as the Centre for Macaques; 116 non-human primates were used in DSTL research in 2016. During my walk around the perimeter fence, I had spotted white smoke emanating from the chimney of a squat, shed-like building. The next day, the papers reported that Sergei Skripal's pets, missing since he had been poisoned, might have been incinerated at Porton Down.

The development and disposal of other nerve agents at Porton Down were also to have long-lasting implications both for land on the site and for ecosystems far from it. Nerve-agent research in the 1950s was helped along by pesticides manufacturers, whose experiments with organophosphates, though directed towards killing large quantities of insects, occasionally threw up novel ways of killing human beings too. In June 1958, an agricultural worker in Kent called Frank Stolton was taken ill after spraying an orchard with an organophosphate pesticide, marketed as Tetram and referred to variously as Amiton and R6199, developed by a subsidiary company of ICI. Admitted to hospital, he was given several doses of atropine – a course of treatment now more widely known as a partial antidote to nerve-agent poisoning.

The pesticide, it transpires, was being produced for ICI by Porton Down's chemical weapons manufacturing outpost at Nancekuke in Cornwall. It was the immediate precursor to VX – the nerve agent made infamous by Hollywood blockbuster *The Rock*, in which Nicholas Cage and Sean Connery battle terrorists armed with the chemical weapon – and one of the deadliest substances ever created. Almost unbelievably, it had been deemed safe to spray on apples. The previous year, ICI's subsidiary had noted that 'the Ministry of Supply are likely to require some share of eventual profits from this project in return for their manufacturing know-how'.

Tetram was soon afterwards withdrawn from public sale, but the cosy relationship between the pesticides industry and the military continued for some time, with deadly results for non-human life. The bioaccumulation of organophosphates in food chains was finally exposed by Rachel Carson's masterpiece *Silent Spring*, but not before bird populations across the world had been hit hard. A number of the most harmful pesticides were banned in Britain and around the world. But at Porton Down, nerve agent development continued – albeit for defensive purposes.

The authorities were, however, becoming increasingly nervous that their activities risked contaminating both land and people. This fear lay behind Porton Down's decision to keep most manufacturing activities at its more remote outpost at Nancekuke. In November 1957, the director of Porton Down, Dr E.A. Perren, wrote to his superiors at the Ministry of Supply setting out the pros and cons of moving the production of chemical weapons back to Porton Down. In a response marked 'Secret and personal', a Ministry official noted: 'The effluent problem may have been underestimated . . . Am I not right in recalling that there was an occasion when a high arsenic content was found in Salisbury's tap water, and that it was suspected that this had resulted from the dumping of DA and DC [two toxic chemicals classified as vomiting agents] in a pit in the old TCS Toxic Compound? . . . Even with a very efficient effluent disposal system there would inevitably be a greater risk of contamination of public supplies (and of Parliamentary or Local Authority "questions") with a plant located at Porton than with one at Nancekuke.'

Then there was the small matter of the safe disposal of nerve agents, whether by land, air or sea. The establishment at Nancekuke tested nerve agents on fish and prawns to understand what the impacts might be of pumping contaminated effluent out into the Atlantic. The results were not encouraging: in a report from 1970, researchers reported that a long-spined sea scorpion, exposed to just 10 parts per million of VX in a tankful of water, had perished after only three minutes.

In the end, it appears that the remaining VX stocks were taken back to Porton Down for storage and disposal. Miles King, a conservationist who specialises in grassland habitats, and who worked for many years on MOD sites, once visited Porton Down. He recalls being shown the way to the zone where they tested V-weapons. 'There were still areas with rusty barbed wire around them and signs saying "no digging", from earlier chemical munition dumps,' he recalls. Small wonder that security at Porton is so tight.

Porton Down is not, however, the only military site with a legacy pollution problem. There are around fourteen MOD properties or former properties around the UK that are still contaminated with old chemical weapons, mainly stocks of mustard gas from the world wars. At Bowes Moor in County Durham, 17,000 tonnes of old mustard gas shells have been stored on a 564-acre stretch of moorland. Drivers on the lonely road that leads past the site are warned not to get any closer. A woodland near Riseley in Bedfordshire became a site for manufacturing mustard gas during the Second World War. After the war, an adjoining landowner reported going on hunts in the woods and seeing foxes and hounds burnt after coming into contact with the contaminated foliage. It's been fenced off ever since, but aerial photos of the area show that the areas used for making and storing weapons haven't been recolonised by vegetation even today.

Similar problems have arisen from the MOD's past experiments in germ warfare, and their use of radioactive materials. The UK's offensive biological weapons programme was relatively short-lived, starting in the 1940s and ending with the brokerage of the Biological Weapons Convention in 1972, in which the UK played a leading part. But cleaning up after it took rather longer. Infamously, Gruinard Island off the coast of Scotland remained contaminated with anthrax until the mid-1980s, whereupon a direct action campaign by anonymous activists – which involved buckets of soil from the island containing anthrax spores being left outside Porton Down – led to the MOD finally decontaminating the land. Low-level radioactivity on various old military bases may take a while longer to address, however: there are at least fifteen sites where the MOD are concerned by the leftover remains of old RAF aircraft, whose control dials used to be painted with radium so pilots could see them in the dark.

A *New Scientist* article reviewing the situation in 1986 was scathing: 'For 40 years, the MoD has coped with its legacy of contaminated land by erecting a fence and tiptoeing away.' Things have improved a little in recent decades: the MOD instigated Project Cleansweep in 2007 to review its key contaminated sites, and carried out extensive land-quality assessments for bases it was considering selling. Left undisturbed, the sites identified would seem to pose only minor risks to human health. But, as with the example of Foulness earlier, it means that large areas of land will remain off-limits to public access, essentially for ever, unless remedial action is taken.

The flipside of the MOD sealing off so much land from normal usage, however, is that many of their sites now tend to be wildlife hotspots. There are 174 Sites of Special Scientific Interest (SSSIs) on Ministry of Defence land; in England, they cover over 70,000 acres of the defence estate. This includes large areas of the unploughed downland pasture on Salisbury Plain, moorland at Warcop, the Thames Basin heaths near Sandhurst, and coastal mudflats at Foulness – though not, curiously, the old experimental testing grounds of the Atomic Weapons Establishment. Porton Down is considered by some ecologists to be 'the single best wildlife site in Britain', particularly for butterflies, and for its species-rich grassland habitat, grazed only by rabbits for the past century.

For many decades, the MOD and its predecessors had little interest in the ecological side-effects of fencing off large parts of the country.

Many MOD sites became green oases in an agricultural desert that was increasingly drenched in pesticides; chemicals that the military had, of course, helped to develop. But the MOD also became more actively aware of its stewardship role, as society's environmental awareness grew: it adopted better site-management plans and employed conservationists, communicating these efforts to a wider public through publications like *Sanctuary*, the Ministry's sustainability magazine.

Of course, all this talk of butterflies rather than bombs is good PR for the military. It's a convenient new military-environmentalist narrative that helps justify the MOD's ownership of a huge swathe of the country. I'm reminded of an old Steve Bell cartoon from the first Gulf War, which depicted the US military seeking to win itself plaudits from green-minded liberals with a missile labelled 'not tested on dolphins'. Still, judging by the amount of wildlife now flourishing on old military sites, it seems the MOD's stewardship is backed up by real action, rather than simply being greenwash.

The question is whether the public really gets to appreciate the natural beauty being nurtured behind the barbed wire fences. There's a genuine trade-off, of course, between creating space in our landscapes for nature to flourish, and allowing untrammelled human activity in those spaces. Some conservationists quietly celebrate the MOD keeping people out; Chris Packham, writing about military sites in an issue of *Sanctuary*, once stated: 'I approve of their lack of access, their level of protection in our overcrowded, over-trampled age.' But there's also a big difference between making the countryside accessible to walkers, cyclists and horse riders, and opening it up to agribusiness, developers and the extractive industries. Intensive crop spraying does much greater damage to an ecosystem than the slight increased risk of footpath erosion and litter left by ramblers.

Many MOD sites have good public-access regimes; others, like the Imber Ranges, could clearly do better. Some former sites have been sold to organisations with greater experience of balancing conservation with public enjoyment, such as the National Trust, who acquired the old

Atomic Weapons Research Establishment testing grounds at Orford Ness in 1993. But for now, the public sector, and particularly the MOD, continues to own much land that's valuable for nature.

Yet the small-state ideology that's infected recent governments has blinded decision-makers to the true value of their land. Lodge Hill in north Kent, for example, is an old disused MOD base, which over the decades has reverted to wilderness and become the number one nesting site in the UK for nightingales. I've walked through part of it, a glorious tangle of hawthorn and oak, and a breath of fresh air for local residents looking to escape the urban sprawl along the Medway. Yet for years the MOD, under pressure from ministers to sell off land for housing, proposed bulldozing Lodge Hill to build 5,000 new homes.

We need to build more homes, no question. Yet rather than fix the real stranglehold on house-building – the hoarding of land by private landowners in pursuit of higher land values – Whitehall has become obsessed with flogging off the remnants of its own estate, regardless of how the land has altered since it first acquired it. The MOD has announced plans to sell off one-tenth of its sites by 2040, covering 32,500 acres – with enough space, it claims, for 55,000 homes. Few will mourn the fact that as the nature of warfare changes, it's possible to let the military estate shrink in size. But will the disposals be done in a way that preserves the habitats that have grown up on many MOD sites; or will they just be sold off to whichever developer offers the biggest pile of cash?

The biggest public sector landowner in England is not in fact the MOD, but the Forestry Commission.* Yet the Commission's origins lie in a similar military imperative. Today, it owns some 489,814 acres of freehold land in England; additional leases and rights give it an overall English

---

*   Technically, the public forest estate is registered in the name of the Secretary of State for the Environment, and the Forestry Commission administers it. MOD land is usually registered in the name of the Secretary of State for Defence.

estate of around 626,383 acres. In Scotland and Wales, its domains are considerably larger – so large, in fact, that it's the single biggest landowner outright, both in England and across the UK as a whole.

The Forestry Commission was set up in 1919, in the wake of a nation-wide timber shortage driven by the wartime hunger for pit props in the trenches. But the first expression of the idea that the state should buy up land to grow trees had come a decade earlier. It was made in the recommendations of the now-forgotten Royal Commission on Coast Erosion and Afforestation, an august Edwardian body set up to investigate various questions on land use, and whose members included the adventure-writer and chronicler of rural England, H. Rider Haggard. In its 1909 report on forestry, the Commission sum-marised the problem: 'The relationship of this country to forestry is peculiar, in so far as it contains a relatively smaller area of land under trees than any country in Europe.' At the time, just 5.3 per cent of England was forested. The Commissioners argued that enough suit-able land could be found to greatly increase tree coverage and afforest 9 million acres. Doing so was seen not just as a way to alleviate military and commercial timber shortages, but also to provide employment in depressed rural areas: the report estimated that a full afforestation programme could permanently employ 90,000 men. But to do so would require concerted state intervention, including the compulsory purchase of land where necessary, since 'it does not appear . . . probable that all owners of suitable land would be ready voluntarily to sell on reasonable terms'.

But the Commissioners' report gathered dust, and nothing was done – until the First World War pushed England's already matchstick-thin timber stocks to breaking point. This time, following a further review by the 1916 Acland Committee, legislation was at last introduced that created the state-owned Forestry Commission. Its first annual report confirmed its militaristic origins: 'Napoleon's maxim that an army marches on its belly had to be brought up to date. The Great War showed that the belly can only move on wood and iron.' With no time to lose, the Commission set about buying up land and planting it with the sorts of cheap, fast-growing softwoods that would come to define its image for decades: conifers.

The Forestry Commission has had a huge impact on England's landscape, sending serried ranks of uniform evergreens marching over hill and vale. Anyone who has ever walked in the Stygian darkness of dense pine forests will know how unnaturally quiet they can be. Standing on a rutted forestry track in plantation woodland, you'll listen in vain for birdsong in the lifeless depths. The Commission's work in the inter-war years made few concessions to beauty. Its square blocks of trees and hard-edged shelter belts, though doubtless masterpieces of function over form, seemed to be executed with the same uncaring nonchalance as the British military cartographers who were then busily drawing straight lines through large chunks of the Middle East.

It was this brutal prioritisation of increasing timber stocks over the wider ecological and amenity values of woodlands that made the Forestry Commission enemies among the nascent conservation movement. The Council for the Preservation of Rural England (CPRE), shortly after its foundation in 1926, pressured the Commission into screening its conifer plantations with belts of native deciduous trees alongside roads. G.M. Trevelyan, one of the early advocates for the National Trust, railed against the creation of 'German pine forests', even if their purpose was for the defence of England. The historian Victor Bonham-Carter could still point in 1971 to the Commission's 'unimaginative planting of conifers, drawn up in parade ground order, without regard to contours or any attempt to diversify species either for ecological or for aesthetic purposes'.

But even in its formative years, the Forestry Commission took a great interest in tree species of all kinds. It cooperated with Kew Gardens in amassing seed banks, and in the 1920s acquired the Bedgebury Estate in Kent with its pinetum, full of rare conifers. The National Pinetum, as it became known, quickly acquired all of Kew's ailing conifer collection, which fared much better in the fresh air far from London's smog. Today Bedgebury plays host to thousands of specimen trees representing over half the conifer species in the world. But out of this rich diversity, it was the Sitka spruce that came to be the staple of the Forestry Commission's monocultural plantations for well over half a century.

The Commission's first trees were planted at Eggesford Forest in Devon in December 1919. The woods remain in their possession today, and you can still see some of the first conifers they planted there a century ago. Forestry Commission estate maps give some interesting insights into where they acquired land subsequently. Two in particular are instructive.

In 1924, the data shows, the Commission was handed a huge area of forest, some 65,000 acres, under the previous year's Transfer of Woods Act. This involved the transfer of the old royal hunting forests – the Forest of Dean and the New Forest – from the Crown Estate to the new state body. In one sense it was merely the passing of lands from one organ of the Crown to another. Yet it was also a symbolic transfer of power: what had once been the private, enclosed deer parks of the Norman kings were now being made over to the public sector.

But the transfer did not, initially, seem to lead to greater public benefits. It fell to the local aristocracy to speak up, unusually, for the rights of both commoners and trees. Lord Montagu of Beaulieu, whose 7,000-acre estate lies to the south of the New Forest, called a debate in the House of Lords when it came to his attention that the Commission had started locking the enclosure gates to the forest for months at a time. 'I have had the courtesy of having a key myself, but I am talking about the ordinary commoner,' he declared. 'If the gates are open to one class they should be open to another.' Worse, the Commission had begun felling ancient oaks in the vicinity. 'The Commission is not primarily interested in any question of beauty,' Lord Montagu argued; he had a point. 'The hardwood trees of the New Forest are one of the wonders of the land. Cutting those trees is like selling your soul.'

Fortunately for the Commission, it was soon able to acquire land far away from such critics, where it could grow and chop down as much softwood pine as it liked. This time, the local lord of the manor provided the land himself. In 1932, the Duke of Northumberland, citing onerous death duties, decided to sell 41,000 acres of land at Kielder in Northumberland to the Forestry Commission. He followed this up by selling them the neighbouring 5,000-acre Marr Estate a few years later. This remote, sparsely populated wilderness on the borders of Scotland proved to be the ideal location for the Commission to create the largest working forest in England. Today, it provides one-fifth of England's entire timber output. Its distance from large settlements has made it something of a draw for other parts of the public sector, too: the MOD's Otterburn Ranges are next door, and large parts of Kielder Forest are leased to the military for army training exercises. In the 1970s, Kielder Water was created by the regional water board, then publicly owned, as a vast reservoir in the middle of the forest – the biggest artificial lake in the UK. There is a sense in which the whole landscape around Kielder resembles the apotheosis of the twentieth-century state and its approach to land: delivering public goods, for sure, but doing so in a way that could be monolithic, monocultural, and unreceptive to local opinion.

Though this book is concerned with land ownership in England, it would be remiss not to mention briefly the impact that the Forestry Commission has had on the landscapes of Scotland and Wales. Initially created as a body covering the whole of Britain, the Commission came to acquire the bulk of its lands in the Scottish Highlands and the mountains of Snowdonia and the Elenydd, with England getting off lightly. In Wales, Forestry Commission plantations came to be resented as an army of occupation. Thousands of acres of once-open hillsides were bought up by the FC and planted with conifers, displacing sheep farmers and in some cases swamping whole settlements. In the hills around Machynlleth in north Wales, where I lived for a few years, I often came across the empty shells of shepherds' cottages and former mining huts lying in the middle of huge forests, enveloped in the silent gloom and half-buried by pine needles. The Commission's activities came to symbolise a form of resource colonialism, which – alongside the instances of drowned Welsh valleys converted into reservoirs to supply

English cities – spurred the resurgent Welsh nationalism of the 1960s. With devolution eventually winning through, the Forestry Commission relinquished its Welsh estate in 2013 to Natural Resources Wales.

In the past half-century, however, the Forestry Commission has become manifestly more responsive and accountable to the public it serves, and much more concerned by the ecological and aesthetic value of the forests it owns. It no longer blankets hillsides in conifers, but instead plants far more native deciduous species, and creates mixed woodland habitats to support wildlife. Widespread clear-felling has given way to thinning, coppicing and more sensitive management practices. The impact of successive waves of tree diseases in recent decades – from Dutch elm disease in the 1970s to sudden oak death and ash die-back more recently – has sparked greater research efforts by the Commission into how to protect our native tree species. It's also poured money into opening up access to the public forest estate: the Bedgebury Estate, for example, is now hugely popular for offroad cycling.

Ironically, the growing public popularity of the Forestry Commission has coincided with increasing attempts by governments to sell it off. Thatcher's first administration passed legislation in 1981 making it easier for the Secretary of State to dispose of Forestry Commission lands. Then, in early 1986, a press rumour did the rounds that the Forestry Commission was to be privatised entirely. The inimitable 'Beast of Bolsover', Dennis Skinner, remarked in the Commons at the time: 'What is this mania for privatisation? . . . A bloke in Bolsover said to me not so long ago, "Don't go down to the woods today. They've flogged off the forest."' As things panned out, the government at the time was far too busy privatising the water industry and electricity sector to get around to forestry too, so it stayed public.

But when David Cameron, a self-confessed Thatcherite, led his party into coalition in 2010, the government decided to have another crack at privatising the forests. This time, however, they ran into far bigger opposition. Half a million people signed a petition by campaigning group 38 Degrees calling on the government to halt the sale. Moreover, the proposals split the Conservative Party's base: many 'Shire Tories' objected to an idea that seemed motivated by short-term financial gain rather than the long-term stewardship of a precious natural resource. The campaign to save the public forest estate claimed the scalp of Environment Secretary Caroline Spelman, and the government did an abrupt U-turn. It was a remarkable moment that spoke volumes about the decades-long rehabilitation of the Forestry Commission: once seen as a remote, uncaring landowner that imposed its foreign trees on local communities, it had been transformed into a national treasure, cherished by the public.

The examples of the Ministry of Defence and Forestry Commission, the two largest institutional landowners in England, illustrate some of the pitfalls and upsides of public sector ownership of land. At its worst, the state as landowner can be secretive, unresponsive, and ride roughshod over the rights of individuals. Over the course of the twentieth century, parts of England were variously requisitioned, fenced off, bombed, carpeted in conifers and choked by contaminants – all in the name of the defence of the realm. But operating at their best, these two landowners also carried out their public functions efficiently, protecting the country during its hour of need and replenishing its natural resources, while proving responsive to public pressure and adaptable to new peacetime priorities.

What's more, these two public institutions represent just one facet of government – the warfare state, rather than the welfare state. From the start of the twentieth century, and particularly after the Second World War, the state began acquiring land to provide for the public's everyday needs – from council housing and state schools, to land on which to build hospitals for the post-war Labour government's new National Health Service. The war had given the lie to notions that the state was incapable of intervening successfully in the economy. Working-class voters left behind by the *laissez-faire* governments of the 1930s, seeing the state's ability to get things done quickly when faced with an external enemy, demanded that the government now intervene in peacetime to end unemployment and provide decent housing. The story of how central and local government acquired land to build New Towns and council homes, as well as help new entrants get into farming via County Farms, is told in more detail in Chapter 8. Other interest groups, too, succeeded in persuading the state to acquire land for public purposes after the Second World War. The early environmental movement scored a victory in pressuring the post-war Labour government to set aside land for National Nature Reserves, while heritage organisations like the National Trust were also given a helping hand by the state.

Some of the biggest transfers of land into public hands came with the Labour government's nationalisation of the 'commanding heights' of the economy, including the water utilities, the railways, the coal mining industry, steelworks and power stations. For three decades, the post-war Keynesian consensus held sway, with both major parties accepting the need for a high level of state intervention in the economy – and for the public sector to own an expanded estate in land.

But increasingly the free-market right demanded the state be pared back. In 1963, under the auspices of a faltering Conservative administration, Dr Richard Beeching presented the findings of his government-commissioned review into the future of British railways. The 'Beeching Axe', as it was quickly termed, would fall sharply: a third of the existing railway network was to be closed. Despite a storm of protest from the rural communities affected, who rightly feared being marooned if they lost their local branch line, the government went along with his proposals.

Beeching's Axe proved short-sighted. He justified his proposals on the grounds of economic rationalisation, but made no recommendations about what to do with the land after the railway lines were closed. This meant that bridges were dismantled, cuttings bulldozed and land flogged off to a panoply of developers – rather than retained in case public demand for rail travel one day revived. Such a revival happened in the 1990s, with the mileage travelled by rail passengers returning to levels not seen since the war. In the meantime, at least some of the trackbeds had been put to good use – reinvented as popular cycle paths by cycling charity Sustrans, and others. But it's hard to know whether to laugh or cry at the announcement by the current Transport Secretary, Chris Grayling, that the government wants to reopen some of the railway lines closed by Beeching – such as the Varsity between Oxford and Cambridge – because it would be beneficial to the economy. To do so, the government will have to buy back the land it so foolishly flogged off half a century ago; only this time, landowners will demand a far higher price than it was sold for.

It was Margaret Thatcher, of course, who took the dismemberment of the public sector to new heights after her election in 1979. Everyone is familiar with her programme of privatising the state-run utilities, the attempt to both shrink the state and mould the public into becoming shareowning entrepreneurs. But much less well-known is how Thatcher presided over a physical shrinking of the state through its disposals of public land. Professor Brett Christophers of Uppsala University, author of a recent book on this subject, calls the Thatcherite fire sale of British public land 'the biggest privatisation you've never heard of'.

By comparing figures on public sector land assembled by the geographer Doreen Massey in the late 1970s with what the government owns today, Christophers estimates that some 5 million acres of land – worth a staggering £400 billion – has been sold off by the public sector over the past forty years. In scale, he argues that it amounts to a 'new enclosure', comparable to the private capture of the public commons in preceding centuries.

The public water boards, for example, had come to own large swathes of England's uplands, which they managed as watersheds to feed their reservoirs and water treatment works. The 1989 privatisation of the water industry saw this estate gifted to nine private companies, a vast asset transfer from the public purse to private shareholders. Today the water companies own some 346,000 acres of England. While most of this is simply managed by the firms for water provision, a good deal is rented out to tenant farmers and to shooting syndicates; United Utilities was even considering at one stage whether to offer up its land for fracking, despite the risks this could pose to groundwater supplies.

Or take the coal-mining industry. Maggie's defeat of the miners is seared into the public consciousness. But less well remembered today was the decision by her successor, John Major, to privatise the coal-mining industry in 1994 – including the disposal of some 273,000 acres of land once owned by the state-run British Coal. The private mining companies who profited from the sale closed many of the deep pits to save on labour costs, and instead expanded into opencast mining – far more environmentally destructive, but requiring many fewer jobs than deep mining. Today, the last few coal mines are shutting up shop; but at least one company continues to prosper – Harworth Estates, the property wing of the old UK Coal, who make their money from building business parks on a handy inheritance of tens of thousands of acres of formerly public land. It's good that derelict land is being redeveloped – but galling to see a private company profiting so much from what could have been retained as public land.

The mania for privatisation has even extended to the management of what are obviously natural monopolies, like the railway network. Mismanagement of the network after its privatisation in 1994 – under the ill-starred company Railtrack – led to the Potters Bar and Hatfield rail disasters and its effective renationalisation under Network Rail. While most of the 100,000 acres that Network Rail owns in England are simply trackbed, some of it is land in very valuable locations, like central London. Austerity budgets and the persistent doctrine of shrinking the state means it's under constant pressure to monetise its assets. Every time a set of sidings or engine sheds become surplus to requirements, there's a feeding frenzy by developers, such as has happened in the King's Cross Central development – where a former goods yard is being converted into a multi-billion-pound suite of posh eateries, offices and flats – and as is set to happen with the Old Oak Common and Royal Park development, as Crossrail and HS2 free up land at an old railway inter-change. Network Rail is also busily engaged in selling off the leases to its railway arches, in the hope of generating higher rents from new cocktail bars and hipster cafés – but in the process pushing out the many small businesses who currently inhabit them and can't afford the rent hikes. Even so, some glimmers of an alternative financing model are starting to appear: in 2017, Transport for London published a landmark study looking at how it might raise funds from local businesses and residents whose property prices benefit from the installation of a new tube station. Such a move would constitute a smart way for the public sector to recoup some of the windfall gains that landowners receive whenever public infrastructure is developed.

The disposal of public land that began under Thatcher continued under New Labour with the development of the Private Finance Initiative. PFI was an attempt to leverage private money into building and servicing schools and hospitals without adding to the public debt, but left the government paying private firms far more in the long run than if they'd financed the work directly from the public purse. Public land sales accelerated with the post-crash austerity programme brought in by David Cameron and George Osborne: the Royal Mail, sold off in 2013; the Government Oil Pipeline, disposed of in 2014; the Green Investment Bank, flogged to the Australian bank Macquarie in 2017. Over 150 courts have been sold by the Ministry of Justice since 2011, with a quarter bought by property developers. The Land Registry itself was earmarked for sale in 2016, only to be saved at the last minute following a concerted campaign by unions and activists.

Reducing the size of the state seems to have trumped all else when it comes to the disposal of publicly owned land. In April 2018, for the first time, the government published its register of public land and property disposals, which gleefully declared that sales under the Coalition had 'helped reduce the total size of the central Government estate by more than 22% and raise £1.8 billion in capital receipts between 2010 and 2015'. Another 1,000 sites have been sold off since then, with many more in the pipeline. No rationale is offered for such a celebration, beyond the one-sided, imbalanced metric of some immediate cash-in-hand, and the implication that this is helping to balance the books. There is no attempt to prove whether the taxpayer got good value for the land and property sold off; no risk assessment presented examining whether the land might credibly be needed again in years to come; no assurances that natural habitats on these sites will be safeguarded, or that the homes promised will be affordable. These things might all have been considered by civil servants behind closed doors. Or they might not have been.

Research by the New Economics Foundation suggests not. Their analysis of public sector land sales in recent years argues that the claimed savings to the taxpayer are a false economy. Rather than just sell off public land, NEF campaigner Alice Martin has argued, 'Maintaining the freehold of land in public or trust ownership and developing new affordable housing to rent and buy would allow councils and public authorities to generate an income stream over time.' Instead, the think tank found that on fifty-nine NHS sites sold off by the government, 80 per cent of the homes being built were going for full market value, unaffordable to an NHS nurse on an average salary; just 10 per cent would be available for genuinely affordable social rent.

'First, all the Georgian silver goes,' the former Conservative Prime Minister Harold Macmillan once said mournfully of Thatcher's privatisation programme, 'then all that nice furniture that used to be in the saloon.' Surely the time has come for the government to stop flogging off land – *our* land – and instead start asking us how we'd like to best use it.

7

CORPORATE CAPTURE

A pub in Manchester; a pint of real ale in my hand. Drinks with work colleagues and activists after a day-long conference. The conversation turns to local politics.

'Tell you what, you know who you should investigate from around here,' says Pete, one of the Manchester Friends of the Earth coordinators. 'Peel Holdings.'

'Sorry, who?' I ask, suspecting I'm about to get a ticking off from Pete for being stuck in my London bubble.

'Peel Holdings! You've not heard of them? They're massive!'

They certainly are. Peel Holdings own the Manchester Ship Canal, ferrying freight from the Mersey into the heart of England's third-largest city. They built the Trafford Centre shopping complex, and more recently sold it in the largest single property acquisition in Britain's history. They're the developers behind the MediaCityUK site in Salford, to which the BBC and ITV have relocated many of their operations in recent years. Airports, fracking, retail – the list of Peel business interests stretches on and on.

And yet, despite owning some 37,000 acres of land, managing a property portfolio worth £2.3 billion, and having control over huge swathes of central Manchester and Liverpool, very few people have even heard of Peel. They operate behind the scenes, quietly acquiring land and real estate, cutting billion-pound deals, influencing numerous planning decisions. Their investment decisions have had an enormous impact, whether for good or ill, on the places where millions of people live and work.

Peel's ultimate owner, the billionaire John Whittaker, is notoriously publicity-shy: he lives in the Isle of Man, has never given an interview, and helicopters into his company's offices for board meetings. His one act of corporate showmanship was to abseil from the glittering glass dome of the Trafford Centre to mark its opening in 1998. Whittaker built Peel Holdings by buying up, in the 1970s and 80s, a series of companies whose fortunes had decayed, but who still controlled valuable land. Foremost among these was the Manchester Ship Canal Company, privatised in 1987 after an 'acrimonious takeover battle' following opposition from local councils. The canal turned out to be valuable not simply as a freight route, but also because of the redevelopment potential on the land that flanked it.

Occasionally, the curtain is drawn back on this unseen corporate force. In 2017, Peel made headlines with their proposals to redevelop the Liverpool docklands, which UNESCO warned could cost the waterfront its World Heritage Status. Peel's plans envision the docks being overshadowed by a set of fifty-storey skyscrapers inspired by the Shanghai skyline, resembling 'a row of gaudy crystal ornaments' in the words of architectural critic Oliver Wainwright. 'Using a common developer tactic, Peel proposed a level of extreme overdevelopment they may have thought would never be accepted,' Wainwright explains. 'But, remarkably, the plans were waved through in 2012.' Lindsey Ashworth, development director for Peel, doesn't however seem to be too fazed by the scheme's critics. 'UNESCO status is a badge on the wall, but we cannot afford to fossilise our city,' she says.

Usually, however, Peel Holdings tends not to show its hand in public. Like many companies, it prefers its forays into public political debate to be conducted via intermediary bodies and corporate coalitions. In 2008, it emerged that Peel was a dominant force behind a business grouping that had formed to lobby against Manchester's proposed congestion charge. The charge was aimed at cutting traffic and reducing the toxic car fumes choking the city. But Peel, as owners of the out-of-town Trafford Centre shopping mall, feared that a congestion charge would lose them 'customers who make long car journeys through central Manchester'. Their lobbying paid off: voters rejected the charge in the local referendum, and the proposal was dropped.

But decisions about the use of public space are seldom subject to popular vote; rather, they're determined through the much more arcane planning process. Though the planning system is fundamentally democratic – anyone can submit an objection, or speak in a council's planning committee hearing – it's also vulnerable to being gamed by large corporate developers who can afford to pay planning consultants and expert lawyers. For example, the restrictions governing usage of a site once development approval has been granted are often contained in what's called a Section 106 agreement. But canny developers sometimes find ways to renege on these, or make subtle alterations so they can change the site use in future.

In 2012, the then MP for Blackburn, Jack Straw, accused Peel Holdings of 'disguising its true intentions from local councils' in respect of a retail park it owned, and using a 'legal subterfuge' that 'verges on calculated deceit' in order to change its agreed use from a warehouse for bulky white goods and furniture to an out-of-town shopping precinct that was drawing custom away from Blackburn's languishing high street. Nor was this instance unique. 'A survey by my council suggests that about a dozen authorities have been caught out by a subterfuge of this kind,' continued Straw. 'What is at stake is the viability of town centres and high streets not only in east Lancashire, but across the country.' Throughout England, cash-strapped councils are being outgunned by corporate developers pressing to get their way.

The situation is exacerbated by a system that has allowed companies like Peel to keep their corporate structures obscure and their landholdings hidden. Indeed, one of the reasons Peel has been able to evade closer scrutiny is their sprawling, byzantine corporate edifice. A 2013 report by Liverpool-based think tank ExUrbe found 'well in excess of

300 separately registered UK companies owned or controlled' by Peel. Tracing the conglomerate's structure is an investigator's nightmare. Try it yourself on the Companies House website: type in 'Peel Land and Property Investments Plc', and then click through to 'Persons with significant control'. This gives you the name of its parent company, Peel Investments Holdings Ltd. So far, so good. But then repeat the steps for the parent company, and yet another holding company emerges; then another, and another. It's like a series of Russian dolls, one nested inside another. Some subsidiaries are based outside the UK: 'Peel (Knowlmere) Company', for instance, owns land in Lancashire but is registered in the Isle of Man, where boss John Whittaker resides. This fact has led MP Margaret Hodge to accuse Peel of dodging taxes, something the company denies.

Until recently, it was even harder to get a handle on the land Peel Holdings own. Sometimes the company has provided a tantalising glimpse: one map they produced in 2015, as part of some marketing spiel around the 'Northern Powerhouse', showcases 150 sites they own across the north-west. It confirms the vast spread of Peel's landed interests – from Liverpool John Lennon Airport, through shale gas well pads, to one of the UK's largest onshore wind farms. But it's clearly not everything. A more exhaustive, independent list of the company's landholdings might allow communities to be forewarned of future developments. As ExUrbe's report on Peel concludes, 'Peel schemes rarely come to light until they are effectively a *fait accompli* and the conglomerate is confident they *will* go ahead, irrespective of public opinion.'

While Peel Holdings is unusual for its spread of business interests and the sheer amount of land it controls, it's also illustrative of corporate landowners everywhere. Corporations looking to develop land have numerous tricks up their sleeve that they can use to evade scrutiny and get their way, from shell company structures to offshore entities. Companies with big enough budgets can often ride roughshod over the planning system, beating cash-strapped councils and volunteer community groups. And companies have for a long time benefited from having their landholdings kept secret, giving them the element of surprise when it comes to lobbying councils over planning decisions and the use of public space. But now, at long last, that's starting to change. If we want to 'take back control' of our country, we need to understand how much of it is currently controlled by corporations.

Companies today own around 6.6 million acres of land, or roughly 18 per cent of England and Wales. Such an assertion was impossible to make until very recently, and is thanks to one journalist's diligent investigations.

In 2015, the *Private Eye* journalist Christian Eriksson lodged a Freedom of Information request with the Land Registry. He asked them to release a database detailing the area of land owned by all UK-registered companies and corporate bodies. Christian later shared this database with me, and what it revealed was astonishing.

Here, laid bare after the dataset had been cleaned up, was a picture of corporate control: expressed in dry statistics and the unpromising format of an Excel spreadsheet, but a compelling picture nonetheless. Here was every limited company, every limited liability partnership, every UK-registered corporation that owns land in this country. Each entry had a square footage of land assigned to it; that was easy enough to convert to acres.

Alongside the utilities privatised by Thatcher and Major – the water companies in particular – and the big corporate landowners were PLCs with multiple shareholders. There were household names, such as Tesco, Tata Steel and the housebuilders Taylor Wimpey, and others more obscure: MRH Minerals, for example, appeared to own 68,000 acres of land, making them one of the biggest corporate landowners in England and Wales.

Gradually, I pieced together a list of what looked to be the top fifty landowning companies, who together own over a million acres of England and Wales. An updated and expanded list of the top 100 is in the appendix to this book. Peel Holdings and many of its subsidiaries, unsurprisingly, features high on the list. But while the dataset revealed in stark detail the *area* of land owned by UK-based companies, it did nothing to tell us *what* they owned, and where.

That would take another two years to emerge. Meanwhile, Christian had been busy at work with his *Private Eye* colleague Richard Brooks and computer programmer Anna Powell-Smith, delving into another form of corporate landowner – firms based overseas, yet owning land in the UK. Of particular interest were companies based in offshore tax havens, a wholly legal but controversial practice, given the opportunities offshore ownership gives for possible tax avoidance and for concealing the identities of who ultimately controls a company. Further FOI requests to the Land Registry by Christian hit the jackpot when he was sent – 'accidentally', the Registry would later claim – a huge dataset of overseas and offshore-registered companies who had bought land in England and Wales between 2005 and 2014: some 279,523 acres of land and property, worth a staggering £170 billion. Some nifty GIS work by Anna allowed *Private Eye* to map all these offshore-owned addresses for the first time.

Private Eye's work revealed that a large chunk of the country was not only under corporate control, but owned by companies that – in many cases – were almost certainly seeking to avoid paying tax, that most basic contribution to a civilised society. Some potentially had an even darker motive: purchasing property in England or Wales as a means for kleptocratic regimes or corrupt businessmen to launder money, and to get a healthy return on their ill-gotten gains in the process. This was information which clearly ought to be out in the open, with a huge public interest case for doing so. And yet the government had sat on it for years.

The political ramifications of *Private Eye*'s revelations were profound. They kickstarted a process of opening up information on land ownership that, though far slower and less complete than many would have liked, has nevertheless transformed our understanding of what companies own. No more than a day after *Private Eye* published its offshore property map, the Land Registry – caught on the back foot by the public interest in its 'accidental' data release – decided to make a virtue of necessity, and announced the publication of its own 'official' database of overseas-owned properties, though without the means to map their locations properly. The following month, the Panama Papers – a huge leak of files from offshore law firm Mossack Fonseca – made headlines around the world. The stories of corporate corruption and dodgy property deals they unearthed added further ballast to efforts to make corporate land transactions more transparent in the UK.

At long last, the Land Registry released its Corporate and Commercial dataset in November 2017, free of charge and open to all. It revealed, for the first time, the 3.5 million land titles owned by UK-based corporate bodies – covering both public sector institutions and private firms – with limited companies owning the majority, 2.1 million, of these. But there were two important caveats. Though we now had the addresses owned by companies, the dataset omitted to tell us the areas of land they owned – the opposite problem to the one we faced before. Sure, we could continue to cite the 2015 acreage data, but it would date over time. Bizarrely, the Land Registry has stubbornly refused to release more up-to-date information on the acreages of land owned by companies, despite repeated FOI requests by myself and others. And without knowing the acreage owned by a company at a particular location, it's hard to say whether the site is a large field, ripe for housing, or a small scrap of verge left over from a previous development. Second, the data lacked accurate information on locations, making it hard to map. After some heroic data-crunching, my collaborator Anna Powell-Smith has mapped the 1.8 million land titles owned by companies and corporate bodies that have postcodes (see corporate.whoownsengland.org). But many have purely descriptive land titles, such as 'Land to the North of Joe Bloggs Road', making them very tricky to pinpoint.

Despite this, what can we now say about company-owned land in England and Wales? Quite a lot, it turns out. We know, for example, that the company with the third-highest number of land titles is the mysterious Wallace Estates, a firm with a £200 million property portfolio but virtually no public presence, and which is owned ultimately by a se-cretive Italian count. Wallace Estates makes its money from the controversial ground rents market, whereby the company owns thou-sands of freehold properties and sells on long leases with annual ground rents. Other players in this market have come under scrutiny in recent years for hiding huge increases in ground rents in the small print of their leasehold contracts – in some cases, doubling ground rents after ten years and locking leaseholders into huge ongoing payments.

We also now know that our old friends Peel Holdings, and their numerous subsidiaries, own at least 1,000 parcels of land across England – not just shopping centres and ports in the north-west, but also a hill in Suffolk, farmland along the Medway and an industrial estate in the Cotswolds. Councils, MPs and residents wanting to keep an eye on what developers and property companies are up to in their area now have a powerful new tool at their disposal.

The data is full of odd quirks and details. Who would have guessed, for instance, that the arms manufacturer BAE owns a nightclub in Cardiff, a pub on Blackpool's promenade and a service station in Pease Pottage, Sussex? It turns out that they're all investments made by BAE's pension fund; if selling missiles to Saudi Arabia doesn't prove profitable enough, it appears the company's strategy is to make a few quid out of tired drivers stopping for a coffee break off the M23.

Or take the huge number of entries in the dataset that list companies owning 'airspace' above residential properties. One such firm, A Shade Greener, has airspace rights registered at over 60,000 homes. At first, this had me stumped. Companies owning even the air above our heads? That sounded more than a little dystopian. Then I realised they all belonged to solar companies who had set up 'rent-a-roof' schemes before government support for solar power was cut. They had secured property rights to the airspace above the roofs on which they'd installed solar panels, to make sure that they weren't overshadowed by other developers putting up tall buildings nearby, thereby reducing the output of solar-generated electricity and costing them revenue.

Some of the details uncovered in the Land Registry's corporate dataset are shadier still. For decades, communities around Heathrow airport have been threatened by plans to build a third runway. Under the various proposals put forward, the villages of Sipson and Harmondsworth have each faced the prospect of total annihilation should expansion of the airport go ahead. Protesters have sought to acquire land along the route of the proposed runway in order to halt it: 'Grow Heathrow', a squat started by climate activists in a field of abandoned greenhouses on the edge of Sipson, has been running for over a decade. But examining the data on what land companies own, it transpires that Heathrow Airport Ltd, too, has been busily buying up dozens of homes in Sipson and land around Harmondsworth – all in anticipation of bulldozing the area to make way for the third runway. What remains unclear is whether they've managed to purchase homes from residents for less than the compensation due under compulsory purchase rules.

The data also lets us peer into the property acquisitions of the big supermarkets, who back in the 1990s and early 2000s were building up huge land banks to construct ever more out-of-town retail parks. Tesco, via a welter of subsidiaries, owns over 11,000 acres of land – and though much of this comprises existing stores, a good chunk also appears to be empty plots, apparently earmarked for future development. One analysis by the *Guardian* in 2014 estimated that the supermarket was hoarding enough land to accommodate 15,000 homes. More recently, however, Tesco's financial travails have prompted it to sell off some of its sites. Internet shopping and pricier petrol have made giant hypermarkets built miles from where people live look less and less like smart investments. In 2016, Tesco's beleaguered CEO announced the company was looking to make better use of the land it owned by selling it for housing, and even by building flats on top of its superstores. As for the supermarkets' internet shopping rival Amazon, whose gigantic 'fulfilment centres' resemble the vast US government warehouse at the end of *Raiders of the Lost Ark* – well, Amazon currently have sixteen of those across the UK. And they've grown very quickly: all but one of their property leases have been bought in the past decade.

As retailers have grown ever larger, so have the industrial farms supplying them with produce. Moy Park Ltd, the largest poultry meat producer in Northern Ireland, also owns or leases at least forty poultry farms in England, according to Land Registry data. Most of these are in the grain belt of Lincolnshire: gigantic sheds that squat amid the flat, open fields, warehousing thousands of broiler chickens. A recent study by the Bureau of Investigative Journalism found that there are now nearly 800 US-style 'mega farms' in the UK, where facilities house more than 125,000 broilers or in excess of 2,500 pigs. Intensive livestock farming by definition doesn't take up much land – the animals are tightly crammed into big feedlot sheds – but the resulting slurry ponds and potential run-off of concentrated pollutants means there can still be significant environmental impacts. Not to mention the welfare implications of treating animals like machines: in 2017, Moy Park was fined £118,000 for allowing hundreds of birds to die during transportation to a slaughterhouse, and letting 300 be put through a disinfectant wash while still alive.

Companies are increasingly taking over previously public space in cities, too. Recent years have seen a proliferation of POPS – Privately Owned Public Spaces – as London, Manchester and other places redevelop and gentrify. You know the sort of thing: expensively landscaped swathes of 'public realm', like Kings Place behind St Pancras, and the 'More London' embankment next to City Hall – all dark granite slabs and hipster restaurants that sell you overpriced slices of avocado served on slate. Aesthetically, they're all very nice. But try to use POPS for some peaceful protest, and you're in for trouble. They're invariably governed by special by-laws and policed by private security, itching to get in your face. I once found this to my cost when staging a tiny, two-person anti-fracking demo outside shale-gas financiers Barclays Bank in Canary Wharf. The whole of Canary Wharf is owned privately by the Qatari Investment Authority, and – bizarrely – photography is banned. Check it out on Google Maps: not even the Google Street View car can get in.

Within a minute of us taking the first selfie on our innocuous protest, security guards had descended en masse, and we spent the next hour running around Canary Wharf trying to evade them.

The Land Registry's corporate ownership dataset contains millions of entries, and much remains to be uncovered. Some of the information appears trivial at first glance – a company owns a factory here, an office there: so what? But as more people pore over the data, more stories will likely emerge. Future researchers might find intriguing correlations between the locations of England's thousands of fast food stores and the health of nearby populations; be able to track gentrification through the displacement of KFC outlets by Nando's restaurants; or spot interesting patterns in the locations of outdoor advertising hoardings owned by companies like JCDecaux and ClearChannel – all of whom have many entries in the Land Registry's corporate dataset.

But to really get under the skin of how companies treat the land they own, and the wider societal repercussions, we need to zoom in on two areas in particular. One is the housing sector, where debates about companies involved in land banking and profiteering from land sales are crucial to our understanding of the housing crisis. The other comprises those companies who've made it their business to dispose of the wastes of consumer society with that classic throwaway solution: landfill.

A walk through the City of London means making your way down a canyon of shiny glass and polished steel. It's a vertical landscape of dark, glittering towers that scrape the sky and blot out the horizon: cathedrals of finance, jostling with one another to win architectural awards. On weekday mornings, this man-made ravine of concrete and girders is filled with a flood of bankers and consultants commuting into work.

But though hundreds of thousands of people work, eat and generate rubbish here every day, the Square Mile is always astonishingly clean. The discarded sandwich cartons, sushi boxes and coffee cups of a quarter of a million hurried working lunches are quickly swept up every day by a silent army of cleaners. Where does it all go? There is a clichéd saying beloved by environmentalists: 'Don't throw anything away – there is no away.' But there *is* such a place, where Londoners have blithely thrown their trash for over a century. It's called Essex.

One morning, navigating my way against the tide of commuters, I caught a train out of Fenchurch Street to discover the lands where Londoners chuck their rubbish. As the coaches clunked and clattered their way out of the metropolis through suburbia, shiny new skyscrapers gave way to rusting bridges coated in peeling paint, leylandii hedges and fences covered in bindweed. For hundreds of years, the Essex marshes have been London's dumping grounds: a hinterland of logistics hubs and vast warehouses, lorry parks and container ports. Here is the hidden physical infrastructure required to keep the wheels of corporate capitalism turning. And here, too, is where the wastes of our consumer society are buried.

Essex is a land of wide-open horizons, very different from the hemmed-in London streets. Yet as my train chuntered across the flood-plains of the Thames Estuary, I noticed oddly situated hills rising out of the otherwise flat landscape. Here and there were mounds of earth that sloped a little too sharply to be natural, a Tellytubby land of artificial hillsides shaped by humanity. On one distant hillside, beneath the striding iron giants of electricity pylons, I could just make out the fumes from moving lorries and a flock of gulls wheeling and diving above them. They seemed attracted by whatever it was the lorries were depositing. Then it struck me: the entire hillside was a landfill site.

Few people are aware of the sheer amount of land taken up by landfill. Huge areas of Essex are devoted to the business of garbage disposal: hundreds of dumper trucks thunder daily down narrow roads, ferrying the wastes of civilisation to burial grounds by the sea. Large chunks of the county are owned by waste disposal companies like Biffa, Veolia and Cory Environmental. Across England as a whole, I calculate that a staggering 270,000 acres of land is taken up by active and historic landfills. In other words, since the Victorian period, we've generated enough rubbish to fill up an area of land almost ten times the size of the city of Manchester.

We may like to think that by giving up plastic straws and taking a tote bag with us for shopping, we've largely solved our waste problem. The good news is the country is certainly recycling a lot more than we used to just twenty years ago: about half of everything households throw away is now recycled or composted. But recycling rates have flatlined since 2010. We still sent a staggering 15 million tonnes of municipal waste to landfill in 2015. And we're running out of land to bury it in: the Environment Agency says we've got less than seven years of available landfill space left. That's before we get to the problem of the old landfills whose corporate operators didn't build them properly – and that are now leaking rubbish.

That's what I'd come to Essex to see. Alighting at Tilbury, I met my guide for the day – Professor Kate Spencer, an environmental geochemist at Queen Mary University. We walked the footpath that winds along the Thames foreshore until we came to a beach that appeared to be entirely composed of man-made rubbish. From where we stood, out to the ominous bulk and towering chimneys of Tilbury power station stretched two kilometres of waste.

Broken glass, bits of china; animal bones, bakelite light switches. The remains of shoes, plastic bottles, textile waste; an antique spoon encrusted in a coppery green patina. The beach crunched and clinked under our boots as we picked our way over a morass of glass and pottery. But this wasn't just rubbish deposited by the waters of the Thames. It was clearly eroding out of the sandy banks next to the shoreline, lapped by high tides, revealing a geological stratum of landfill clearly dateable to the Anthropocene.

Some of the landfill waste was clearly pretty old, and showed little sign of breaking down. At one point, we strayed across a still-preserved scrap of newspaper bearing a photograph of inter-war Prime Minister Neville Chamberlain. Elsewhere, it was obvious the waste was more recent. And this was just the visible stuff: every now and then, we came across old lead car batteries, leaching acid into the Thames. 'Don't touch anything!' Kate warned me. As we walked, she told me about her research into how old coastal landfills are starting to break open and leak their wastes into rivers and the sea. Before the 1990 Environmental Protection Act came into force, landfills were often built without proper linings, and records about what was put into them were often poorly kept or non-existent. Tilbury is just one of the most obviously failing sites: further along the Thames Estuary at Two Tree Island, Kate and her PhD students had found other historic landfills that were leaching heavy metals into the surrounding sands. Incredibly, even the sea walls there had been constructed with household waste as filler, apparently with little thought as to what might happen when the cement and bricks inevitably crumbled.

Whichever company had owned and operated the old landfill at Tilbury clearly hadn't given much thought to its long-term future, either. The remains of a former sea wall, derelict and ineffective, could still be seen below the high-water mark. It was providing no defence at all to the hungry estuary, which had chewed away at the land to reveal layers and layers of landfilled refuse just below the surface. Later, I tracked down the former site owner: the Tilbury Contracting and Dredging Company Ltd, which according to Environment Agency records had last deposited waste here in 1958. But a search of Companies House turned up nothing. Had the company gone bust? Some further digging revealed the firm had passed through various mergers and name changes, later becoming the facilities management conglomerate Interserve, which today has revenues of £3.7 billion annually. Interserve's corporate history webpage still records that during the 1930s, 'the company ... [bought] land at Tilbury for the disposal of refuse'.

But no one today is taking responsibility for clearing up the leaking landfill. The land itself had since been bought by another logistics firm, for unknown reasons. I contacted the local authority, Thurrock Council. They wrote back stating they had no information on the landfill site, and that I should speak to the Environment Agency. So I contacted them. After several weeks, the Environment Agency got back to me – but their reply was dispiriting.

'We are not aware of any leaking/eroding of landfill waste into the

Thames from either of the historic landfills,' they wrote. 'We do not maintain any tidal defences on the historic landfill sites ... Our inspection
teams have never reported that they have observed any issues with pollution or leachate when inspecting the defences or the sluice. As we are not
aware of any leachate we are not aware of any studies into pollution levels.
We are also not aware of any plans to remediate the leaking waste.'

In other words, a corporate landowner had bought the land, dumped
waste there, and walked away, leaving it to gradually erode and leak into
the river. The public sector is understandably keen to turn a blind eye
and unwilling to pick up the tab for this corporate irresponsibility. After
all, Tilbury is far from unique. As Professor Spencer and her colleague
Dr Francis O'Shea have uncovered, there are 20,000 historic landfill
sites spread across England and Wales, with a terrifying 5,000 of them
located in the Environment Agency's flood alert areas. 'The historic
landfill sites situated on actively eroding and low-lying coasts clearly
present a significant risk,' they write. With climate change causing rising
sea levels, increased coastal erosion and worsening flood risk, the
researchers warn that the potential for more of these old landfills to
break open and pollute the surrounding environment represents a
'ticking time bomb'.

But how many of the companies that once owned these landfills
still exist today, and will pay for them to be cleaned up? Not many, I'll
warrant. Limited liability is integral to corporate law, after all. Trash
the environment, make a quick buck, cut and run: far too many companies have treated our land this way. Now the wastes of our throwaway
society, aided and abetted by the companies who've made a killing
from it, are coming back to haunt us. If we want to pass on the land
to future generations in a better state than we found it, we're going
to have to find ways to stop corporations abusing it for short-term
profits, and force them to become better stewards of the land.

Examining corporate control of land is also crucial to understanding the
housing crisis.

One particularly controversial aspect of the housing debate that has generated much heat, and little light, in recent years is the debacle over land banking. In common parlance, land banking is the practice of hoarding land and holding it back from development until its price increases. The American economist Henry George excoriated land banking as a blight on society. One of his followers famously bought a derelict plot of land in the middle of a city and, in a canny piece of political theatre, erected a billboard on which was written: 'Everybody works but the vacant lot. I paid $3600 for this lot and will hold 'till I get $6000.'

Such thinking appeared to move into the political mainstream when in 2016 the then Housing Secretary, Sajid Javid – better known as a follower of Ayn Rand than of Henry George – furiously accused large housing developers of land banking, and demanded that they 'release their stranglehold' on land supply. Housebuilders, not used to such impertinence from a Conservative minister, hit back. 'As has been proved by various investigations in the past, housebuilders do not landbank,' a spokesperson for the Home Builders Federation told the *Telegraph*. 'In the current market where demand is high, there is absolutely no reason to do so.'

So who's right? This is a complex area, but one that's important to investigate. Can the Land Registry's corporate ownership data help us get to the bottom of it?

A decade or so ago, it seemed incontrovertible that a lot of very dodgy land banking was going on. Take the example of Profitable Plots Ltd, a property company registered in Singapore, whose very name should instantly set alarm bells ringing. Among the sites it purchased was a chunk of woodland in Hounslow, West London, which it proceeded to dice up into thousands of small plots. It then marketed the plots to Singaporean investors as a way to profit from the booming British housing market, with TV commercials featuring English footballers urging viewers to 'buy UK land'. What the adverts omitted to say was that the land was in London's Green Belt, and as a result stood very little chance of getting planning permission for development. It was all a colossal scam: Singaporean investors were defrauded of nearly a million dollars, with one man losing nearly all his savings. The British pair behind Profitable Plots Ltd were jailed for fifteen years by a court in Singapore. Land Registry INSPIRE maps still bear the scars – the tell-tale shapes of land cut up into neat square plots, laid out with imaginary roads to give a sense of verisimilitude to the fictitious housebuilding plans. Other similar land banking schemes, mostly based offshore, were eventually investigated and wound down by the UK Financial Services Authority, and the practice seemed to dry up.

Appalling as these land banking scams were, they were clearly of a very different nature to the practices Sajid Javid was accusing law-abiding housing developers of. But other, wholly legal forms of land banking take place all the time.

One such form is practised by UK pension funds and insurance companies, who buy up land as a long-term strategic investment. Legal & General, for example, own 3,550 acres of land which they openly call a 'strategic land portfolio ... stretching from Luton to Cardiff'. Their rationale for buying land is simple: 'strategic land holdings are under-pinned by their existing use value' – such as farming – 'and give us the opportunity to create further value through planning promotion and infrastructure works over the medium to long term'. When I looked into where Legal & General's land was located, however, I noticed something odd. Nearly all of it lay, again, within areas of Green Belt, meaning development is restricted. This time, the company appears to have bought it with the aim of lobbying councils to ultimately rip up such restrictions, and redesignate the site for development in future.

Further digging uncovered that Legal & General had attempted to do precisely this for its land bank on Green Belt farmland outside Luton, submitting proposals to the council for a new business park there and seeking to tear up the existing site allocations in the draft Local Plan. This is a classic tactic of developers with a vested interest in certain sites, and yet another way in which the secrecy around land ownership in England impedes proper democratic debate. There's sometimes a case to be made for redesignating sections of Green Belt if the development need is in the public interest. But why not have that discussion out in the open, rather than have it driven by land speculators who acquire chunks of Green Belt and then lobby councils to chip away at it?

Another form of lawful land banking is when landowners look to profit from the development of neighbouring sites through acquiring 'ransom strips'. The Royal Institute of Chartered Surveyors defines a ransom strip as 'a small but crucial piece of land which is needed to access a property, commonly a development site'. The owners of such strips – which can sometimes just be a few feet wide – can effectively hold potential developers to ransom, by refusing them access to their site unless they give them a slice of the profits. A 1961 court case determined that the owners of ransom strips are entitled to one-third of the increase in the value of the land to which they grant access. Such piratical behaviour has recently prompted centre-right think tank Onward to advocate the reform of compulsory purchase rules so that councils can buy land more cheaply; otherwise, 'there will sometimes be one landowner or someone with a ransom strip who tries to hold out for a windfall profit'.

Offshore fraudsters, pension funds lobbying to rip up the Green Belt and land pirates with their ransom strips are all intriguing examples of corporate malfeasance towards the land. But in the first two of these instances, it's the planning system – the Green Belt – that's (rightly) constraining development, not land banking itself. And none of this implicates the usual bogeymen of the housing crisis, the volume house-builders. By examining what these major developers own, is it possible to say whether they're actively engaged in land banking?

There's no doubt that many of the big housebuilding companies own a heck of a lot of land. Land Registry data suggests that Taylor Wimpey, for example, owned 14,684 acres in 2015, making them one of the largest corporate landowners in England and Wales. In fact, their true landhold-ings are likely very much larger: analysis by Anna Powell-Smith of the land owned by all of Taylor Wimpey's many subsidiary companies suggests they may have as much as 30,000 acres at their disposal. Housing developers themselves talk about their 'current land banks', and publish figures in their annual reports listing the number of homes they think they can build using the pipeline of land where they have planning permission. As housing charity Shelter has found, the top ten housing developers have current land banks with space for over 400,000 homes – about six years' supply at current building rates. The NGO estimates that these housebuilders also have additional 'strategic land banks' with enough room for a further 480,000 homes. These may be further away from getting planning permission, and often may not even be owned outright by the developer, but rather secured through opaque 'option agreements' with landowners – something that doesn't show up in Land Registry records, and is very difficult to investigate.

While having a pipeline of land is understandable for a large developer, Shelter questions 'whether housebuilders should be holding so much land out of the development system for so long when there is such an acute shortage'. Indeed, even though the number of planning permissions has increased in recent years, the number of homes built subsequently – the 'build-out rate' – has failed to keep pace.

Prompted by such statistics, the government ordered a review into build-out rates in 2017, led by Sir Oliver Letwin. Yet when Letwin delivered his draft report, he once again exonerated housebuilders from the charge of land banking. 'I cannot find any evidence that the major housebuilders are financial investors of this kind,' he stated, pointing the finger of blame instead at the rate at which new homes could be absorbed into the marketplace.

Part of the problem is that the data on what companies own still isn't good enough to prove whether or not land banking is occurring. Anna has tried to map the land owned by housing developers, but has been thwarted by the lack in the Land Registry's corporate dataset of the necessary information to link data on who owns a site with digital maps of that area. That makes it very hard to assess, for example, whether a piece of land owned by a housebuilder for decades is a prime site accruing in value or a leftover fragment of ground from a past development.

Second, the scope of Letwin's review was drawn too narrowly to examine the wider problem of land banking by landowners beyond the major housebuilders. As the housing market analyst Neal Hudson commented when it was published, the 'review remit ignored the most important and unknown bit of the market: sites and land ownership pre-planning'. Letwin's report itself accepted that land doesn't diminish in value over time, and so 'it would therefore be perfectly possible for financial investors of a certain kind to seek to make a business out of holding land as a purely speculative activity . . . this is a serious issue for the planning system.' But beyond offering such commentary, his report ducked any deeper analysis.

In fact, if Letwin had raised his sights a little higher, he would have seen there is a whole industry of land promoters out there, working with landowners to promote sites, have them earmarked for development in the council's Local Plan, and increase their asking price. As investigations by the *Telegraph*'s property correspondent Isabelle Fraser have revealed, 'A group of private companies, largely unknown to the public, have carved out a lucrative niche locating and snapping up land across the UK.' One such company, Gladman Land, boasts on its website of a 90 per cent success rate at getting sites developed. Few of these firms appear to own much land themselves; rather, they work with other landowners, perhaps signing options agreements or other such deals. Consultants Molior have estimated that between 25 per cent and 45 per cent of sites with planning permission in London are owned by companies that have never built a home.

For these reasons, I doubt there is a special, dastardly class of speculative investor responsible for all land banking. Rather, the practice of hoarding land awaiting a higher return is something that *all* landowners are liable to do. And that gets us to the heart of the housing crisis. Sure, we need housing developers to build more homes. But most of all we need them to build *affordable* homes. And developers who are forced to pay through the nose to persuade landowners to part with their land end up with less money left over for good-quality, affordable housing. By all means, let's continue to pressure housebuilders whenever they try to renege on their planning agreements. But at root, we have to find ways to encourage landowners of all kinds – corporate or otherwise – to part with their land at cheaper prices.

Since the first appearance of modern corporations in the Victorian period, companies have expanded to become the owners of nearly a fifth of all land in England and Wales. Much of this land acquisition is uncontested: space for a factory here, an office block there. But some of it has proven highly controversial. Huge retailers and property groups like Tesco and Peel Holdings have eroded town centres and high streets by amassing land for out-of-town superstores, and lobbied to maintain a culture of car dependency. Multinational agribusinesses like Moy Park have exacerbated the industrialisation of our food supply and accelerated the decline of small-scale farmers. Property firms like Harworth Estates have made tidy profits from the privatisation of formerly public land – which might otherwise have gone into the public purse, had previous governments treated their assets more wisely.

Though the veil of secrecy around company structures and what corporations own is at last lifting thanks to recent data disclosures by government, there's still much that needs to be done to make sense of this new information. The Land Registry needs to disclose proper maps of what companies own if we're to get to the bottom of suspect practices like land banking, and give communities a fighting chance in local planning battles.

Legally obliged to maximise profits for their shareholders and biased towards short-term returns, companies make for poor custodians of the land. Nor are corporate landowners capable of solving the housing crisis. Hoarded, developed, polluted, dug up, landfilled: the corporate control of England's acres has gone far enough. So how might ordinary people take back control?

8

A PROPERTY-OWNING DEMOCRACY?

A packed conference hall in Blackpool, 17 October 1981. A woman ascends the stage, the squared shoulders of her midnight-blue jacket a dark silhouette in the hot glare of a dozen spotlights. Her carefully coiffured hair seems to recall a flaming torch. As she takes to the lectern, there is rapturous applause.

The figure, of course, is Margaret Thatcher. 'Our concern is to create a property-owning democracy,' she tells the assembled throng of Conservative Party politicians and activists, speaking in her trademark clipped RP. 'It is now our turn to take a major step towards extending home ownership to many who, until now, have been deliberately excluded.'

Margaret Thatcher might seem a strange choice to introduce a chapter whose focus is land reform and redistribution. But in championing a 'property-owning democracy', not only rhetorically but through practical policy, she oversaw a transformation in the ownership of housing during the last quarter of the twentieth century. The year before her conference speech, Thatcher's government had introduced Right to Buy, giving council house tenants the chance to purchase their home from the local authority. Introducing the legislation to Parliament, Environment Secretary Michael Heseltine claimed that 'no single piece of legislation has enabled the transfer of so much capital wealth from the State to the people.' Over the ensuing decade, a million council homes were sold to their tenants.

Thatcher's administrations also enabled millions more to buy private housing by relaxing restraints on bank loans and mortgages, and allowing a supply of cheap and easy credit to flow into property markets. At the start of the 1980s, 55 per cent of the British public owned their own homes. By 2003, 71 per cent did.

The idea of a property-owning democracy had deep roots that pre-dated Thatcher. As a phrase, it was first coined in 1924 by Conservative MP Noel Skelton, in anticipation of the first Labour government taking power and with the spectre of Soviet Russia looming in the background. Skelton argued that capitalism's only bulwark against the rising tide of socialism was to extend individual ownership, and give everyone a stake in the country. During the 1950s and 60s, successive Conservative governments tried to turn this into a reality by overseeing the construction of millions of new homes, by both councils and private developers.

But Thatcher's version of a property-owning democracy was built on shaky foundations. Instead of more council homes being built to replace the ones that were sold off, public sector house building slowed to a crawl in the 1980s and had virtually stopped altogether by the mid-1990s. Right to Buy was a fire sale of public assets – with council homes sold at heavily discounted prices – that delivered a one-off windfall for state coffers without adding to the national housing stock. Councils were simultaneously being stripped of their ability to borrow and to raise local taxes, rendering them incapable of acting as major developers. Rates of home construction by private developers and housing associations never increased sufficiently to cover the shortfall in council homes. At its post-war peak in the mid-1960s, Britain built over 400,000 homes annually. After 1980, this annual rate halved to seldom more than 200,000 new houses per year.

There was still worse to come. The explosion in cheap credit and easy mortgages ushered in by Thatcher's administrations – and blithely presided over by the Major and Blair governments – didn't just lead to more people owning their own homes. It also fuelled a massive increase in house prices. In 1980, the price of an average home was £25,000; by 2008, average house prices exceeded £175,000. Wage growth couldn't hope to keep pace with such a boom, but that didn't matter so long as banks and building societies were happy to sign off on generous mortgages. Then, in 2008, the global financial crash struck, and easy credit dried up. Getting onto the housing ladder was now even harder, and there were even fewer homes being built: in 2013, the UK saw the lowest level of housebuilding for any peacetime year since the 1920s. What began as a housing bubble has become a full-blown housing crisis.

Even if you're an ardent Thatcherite, it's now clear that her vision of a property-owning democracy has failed on its own terms. 'END OF THE HOME OWNING DREAM,' bellowed a *Daily Mail* front-page headline in February 2018. Owner-occupation has gone into reverse. Home ownership among young adults has 'collapsed', according to the Institute for Fiscal Studies, whose research shows that just 27 per cent of middle-income 25- to 34-year-olds own their own house, compared to 65 per cent two decades ago. Millions of millennials now belong to 'Generation Rent', stuck in pricey rental accommodation for years, unable to afford a deposit on a house and at the mercy of private landlords in a system that has neglected tenants' rights for far too long. Theresa May's Conservative government, haemorrhaging support among young voters, has belatedly set about trying to boost housebuilding and revive notions of a property-owning democracy. Yet the rate of construction lags far short of the 300,000 new homes that the Chancellor, Phillip Hammond, admits need to be built in England every year to meet demand.

When you crunch the stats on how much land is now owned by homeowners, you start to see, too, that we don't really live in a property-owning democracy. It's certainly true that far more people own *some* land today than a century ago: the freehold to their house, and if they're lucky, a garden too. But the total area of land owned by England's 14.3 million homeowners remains a tiny fraction of the whole country. The ONS classifies about 9.6 per cent of England and

Wales as urban or built up. But that includes lots of roads, schools, public buildings and parks. The UK National Ecosystem Assessment calculates that domestic buildings take up just 1.1 per cent of England's land area – rising to around 5.4 per cent when you add in domestic gardens. Even that includes rented properties, not just owner-occupied homes; and all of it pales besides the vast areas of land possessed by old and new money. An elite of aristocrats, gentry and City boys owns far more land than all of Middle England put together.

Some argue that the solution to the housing crisis lies in doing away with the dream of a property-owning democracy altogether. Our European neighbours don't seem to share the British obsession with private home ownership; they tolerate higher levels of renting by having much stronger protections for tenants' rights. There's no doubt that Thatcher's pursuit of a property-owning democracy was done both for crudely electoral ends – discounted council house sales to win over working-class votes – and for the ideological goal of weakening the public sector while fostering individualism and acquisitiveness. But it would be too easy to dismiss it all as a neoliberal plot, when the allure of owning your own house and having a place to call your own is clearly so popular. It speaks to a deep-seated desire to belong; to each have a stake in the country we all live in; to have a patch of land to call home. The question is whether these dreams can be satisfied best by buying and selling land and housing on the free market, or whether there are other ways to achieve them. And that opens up all sorts of interesting questions about land reform.

Whenever land reform is mentioned nowadays in British politics, it's jumped on by the right-wing press, who denounce it as the 'politics of envy', crypto-communist, or an incitement to violent dispossession involving pitchfork-wielding peasants. 'LET THE GRAB BEGIN' screamed the Scottish *Daily Mail*'s front-page headline in the wake of the 2003 Scottish Land Reform Act, next to a picture of the then ruler of Zimbabwe, the tyrant Robert Mugabe. To the *Mail*, the Scottish government's mild and sensible legislation – allowing communities to bid to buy land – was tantamount to the bloody land seizures that had recently taken place in rural Zimbabwe. Such offensive comparisons would be laughable if they weren't also an affront to the patient, peaceful work of Scottish communities, who campaigned for decades for some measure of recompense for the violent history of the Clearances. But that just shows you how politically sensitive land reform is as an issue.

In reality, the forcible theft of land in Britain – from the Highland Clearances to the English Enclosures – has always been perpetrated by the haves against the have-nots. England has never undergone a process of wholesale land redistribution to the landless, such as was enacted in France after the 1789 Revolution, or in Mexico after 1910 with the break-up of the *haciendas*. But other parts of the British Isles have seen inspiring and far-reaching efforts to redistribute land. In Northern Ireland and the Irish Republic, the 1903 Wyndham Land Act, passed by a Conservative government, allowed 200,000 tenant farmers to buy from their landlords the land they cultivated. In Scotland, a land reform movement began in the Victorian period and has flowered since devolution, with over half a million acres now in community ownership.

England, too, has a rich and radical tradition of land reform movements. But many of them have been forgotten – or conveniently swept under the carpet. This chapter tells their stories, and seeks to draw lessons for land reform in England today. My journey to uncover them drew me first to an unpromising setting: the stockbroker belt of Surrey.

'Sorry, you can't come in here. It's a private estate.'

I was standing at the entrance to St George's Hill, a gated community of multi-million-pound properties on the southern edge of London. The security guard fixed me with his stare. I decided to act nonchalant.

'Oh, really? I can't just go and have a look around?'

'No.'

'Some big properties here, eh?'

'Yeah.' The guard seemed to relax a bit, then said conspiratorially:

'There's one of them going for £30 million. It's vacant currently.' I gawped. He grinned. 'Watch your back for the Bentleys and Ferraris on the way out.'

But I had no intention of going through the front gate, anyway. I'd come here on a pilgrimage in search of something special that had taken place on the site over three centuries ago. And if I had to trespass to get there, so be it.

Returning to the main road, I began walking the perimeter of the estate, breathing in the ozone belched out by passing Beamers and Rolls-Royces, past gaudy mock-Tudor mansions protected by barbed wire and high fences. All the roads here had Ye Olde English names like Runnymede Close and Chaucer Lane, harking back to a vision of Merrie England when an Englishman's home was his castle. Yet many of the properties here, I knew, were actually owned offshore in tropical tax havens. Even medieval barons had to pay their taxes to the king.

Then, amid ivy-choked trees blackened by constant car fumes, I spotted a hole in the fence. I waited for a break in the traffic, then scrambled over the broken chain-link fencing, pushing past hanging branches, twigs snapping underfoot. I was in. Before me stretched the grounds of an unknown oligarch or wealthy businessman.

But I hadn't come here for them. I had come here because St George's Hill was the birthplace of a radical land reform movement founded during the English Civil War, on this very spot.

In 1649, England was in revolt. The king was dead, his head cut from his body. The whole world seemed to have been turned upside down. That same spring, a group of landless commoners called the Diggers had set up camp at St George's Hill and acted out a bold social experiment. They had come to cultivate land that was not their own. As their leader, Gerrard Winstanley, later recounted: 'I took my spade and went and broke the ground upon George Hill in Surrey, thereby declaring freedom to the creation, and that the earth must be set free from intanglements of lords and landlords, and that it shall become a common treasury for all . . .'

Winstanley's rebellion was part of a ferment of ideas that took hold in the uproar following the civil war and the execution of Charles I. Footsoldiers in Cromwell's army, tired after years of fighting their brethren for little tangible reward, had formed groups calling themselves Levellers and demanded that all men had the right to vote. Others joined millennarian cults, convinced that with the downfall of the monarchy, a new era had dawned.

For Winstanley and the Diggers, that new dawn heralded a chance to overthrow the landowning elite who had enslaved the common people of England since 1066. After the Conquest, the Norman kings declared all land in England belonged to the Crown, theirs to hand out as patronage to favoured barons. Over the centuries, the descendants of the Norman barons had added to their estates by enclosing common land on which commoners had previously been free to graze their livestock and gather firewood – privatising it for their personal use.

It was against this theft of land that Winstanley rebelled. 'Seeing the common people of England', he wrote, 'have cast out Charles our Norman oppressor, we have by this victory recovered ourselves from under his Norman Yoke.' Winstanley's analogy – of labouring commoners yoked to a plough by their tyrannical overlords – encapsulated his visceral anger at the state of the world.

In 1649, St George's Hill appears to have been a patchwork of common land, manorial wastes and Crown land – the ownership of which, following the execution of the king, had become uncertain. It was scrubby heath and woodland used for grazing. Now the Diggers, a rag-tag band of hungry carpenters, cowherds and ex-soldiers, set about digging it up for crops.

Their social experiment didn't last long. Local landowners hated them and sent armed men to beat them up and tear down their makeshift houses. General Fairfax, the commander of the New Model Army, initially took pity on the Diggers, but feared the social consequences if Winstanley's ideas spread. What would happen to England's laws of private landed property if they were allowed to succeed? Unsurprisingly, the Diggers were swiftly evicted from St George's Hill that summer, following a court case based on trumped-up charges.

Although the Diggers failed in their lifetimes, their influence lives on. Winstanley's ideas have been celebrated by radical activists down the ages. But as for the land at St George's Hill itself, history has played a cruel joke. After passing into the ownership of the 'Grand Old' Duke of York – whose men may or may not have marched up to the top of it – it was bought in 1911 by a housing developer, Walter George Tarrant, who immediately set to work cutting down the pines and rhododendrons that covered his 950-acre development site. Two years later, a large swathe of St George's Hill was landscaped into a golf course. Where Winstanley raised the flag of rebellion, today retired businessmen try to lower their handicap. But Tarrant knew that golf alone wouldn't make him rich: so around the course, he began building luxury homes for London's wealthy elite.

It's a supreme irony of history that a place once held in common, and the site of such a radical communal experiment, came to be completely enclosed and privatised. Tarrant's ugly mansions, with names like Oak Tree Cottage, Whitecliff and even Toad Hall, managed to combine crass plutocratic tastes with a faux-historical air, all the while burying the real, radical history of the place beneath neo-Georgian stucco and freshly mown lawns. Even *The Spectator*, hardly a bastion of radicalism, bemoaned the suburbanisation of St George's Hill: 'It is part of the country's history, and ought no more to be in danger of destruction than the documents of the Record Office.' Still worse was to come, however.

In the 1960s, the Beatles bought houses at St George's Hill, and the area acquired over the years a cachet that attracted ever more celebrities, footballers, wealthy businesspeople and Russian oligarchs. Dubbed 'Britain's Beverly Hills', the area today has become a gilded bolthole for the rich. Estate agents Knight Frank say that there are currently 428 luxury properties on St George's Hill. And according to data first uncovered by *Private Eye*, no fewer than seventy-two of these mansions are owned offshore in tax havens, with a staggering collective value of £282 million. In other words, a large chunk of a hill named after England's patron saint is now owned in Panama, Switzerland and the Caribbean.

The final irony about St George's Hill today is that the residents' association mandates every house must have at least one acre of land attached to it – proving once again that old adage: socialism for the rich, capitalism for the poor. If only everyone in the UK were able to have an acre of their own, the Diggers' utopian dreams might start to become a reality.

Treading in the footsteps of Winstanley, trespassing upon land once held in common but now owned offshore, I was making my own gesture of protest. With my bare hands, I dug the earth as Winstanley had centuries before: sinking my fingers into the leaf mould and the thick black loam, smelling its rich peaty scent, the product of a hundred autumns. This soil had once been a common treasury for all. Now it was owned by some wealthy oligarch or businessman, hiding behind their shell company, who probably didn't even live there for much of the year. St George's Hill was lost. But could Winstanley's example inspire fresh efforts today to reclaim the commons?

Common land, as Winstanley well knew, has existed in England since before the Norman Conquest. It is land 'owned in common', in that local communities – commoners – can make collective use of it to obtain food and fuel. Depending on the local customs, commoners may hold different rights relating to such land: on many commons, there is a right to *pasturage* (the right to graze livestock), while on others there is for instance a right to *estovers* (firewood), *piscary* (fish) or *turbary* (a right to cut peat for burning). Medieval peasants had to till their own fields for crops and pay feudal dues to the lord of the manor, but common land provided a social safety net they could rely on in the event of lean harvests and cold winters. As such, some have seen the commons as a sort of medieval welfare state.

Inevitably, just like today's *Daily Mail* headlines lambasting 'welfare cheats' and 'benefits scroungers', there were critics of commons in the early modern period. 'The nurseries of beggars are commons,' ran one such invective from 1607, clearly a tabloid columnist in the making. The feckless poor should work to earn themselves a living, ran the argument, rather than subsisting on the free bounty of the commons. Such reasoning was particularly appealing to the landed gentry, who longed to add to their estates by enclosing common land. 'The poor increase like fleas and lice, and these vermin will eat us up unless we enclose,' exclaimed one presumably puce-coloured pamphleteer. Instead of feeding the poor, the gentry wanted the commons to fatten their sheep for the newly lucrative wool trade. 'They inclose all into pastures, they throw down houses, they pluck down towns,' complained Thomas More in *Utopia*; all to make way for 'sheep, that were wont to be so meek and tame', but who had now 'become so great devourers and so wild, that they eat up, and swallow down the very men themselves.'

It's reckoned that about 27–30 per cent of England consisted of common land around the year 1600. What happened over the ensuing three centuries was a land grab of criminal proportions. Parliament passed Acts that led to the enclosure of 6.8 million acres of commons, a fifth of all England, between 1604 and 1914. Still more land was enclosed privately, without recourse to Parliament. What Winstanley and the Diggers were responding to during the Civil War was the early onset of an orgy of privatisation. By 1873, it's thought that the remaining commons constituted just 5.2 per cent of the country, and even that was to decline subsequently.

Resistance was widespread, but ironically, it was in the cities where enclosure was finally halted, rather than in the countryside. The rapid expansion of Victorian London, with its cholera-ridden poor and over-crowded slums – so memorably depicted in Gustav Doré's nightmarish etchings – prompted a new movement to preserve what was left of urban green spaces. The Commons Preservation Society was founded in 1865 to campaign against further enclosure and protect London's open spaces from being built over. Places like Hampstead Heath,

Clapham Common and Epping Forest were being eyed up by developers, with their landowners desperate to sell. The Society's influential middle-class membership, which included luminaries like Octavia Hill and John Stuart Mill, managed to rally public and legal opinion to their cause, resulting in many commons being protected as public parks. Sometimes direct action was needed: on one occasion, the Society sent 120 workmen to rip down railings that had been illegally erected around Berkhamsted Common.

Despite the efforts of the Victorian anti-enclosers, today only around a million acres of common land remain: just 3 per cent of England. There are around 7,000 registered commons, many tiny in size, with most found in Cumbria and North Yorkshire on poor-quality soils suitable only for sheep grazing. A surprising 24,000 acres of commons have also survived in Surrey, near where the Diggers made their stand at St George's Hill. Quite why is unclear, but their proximity to London suggests that city-dwellers' desire for country air probably contributed to them being saved. Three of the largest commons in England were, for obscure reasons, exempted from registration when common land was codified in 1965: Epping Forest, the Forest of Dean and the New Forest.

Yet even these remaining commons are invariably owned by someone, somewhere. Very little land is now actually 'held in common'. Epping Forest belongs to the City of London Corporation; the New Forest to the Forestry Commission. A fascinating survey of common land registers carried out for the government in the 1990s reveals many of the modern owners of commons: 2,419 out of the 7,039 registered commons are privately owned, either wholly or in part; another 1,230 belong to local councils. The Duke of Northumberland, the Marquess of Salisbury and the Earl of Iveagh all own commons. Appallingly, some commons have fallen into the hands of banks, chemical manufacturers and mining companies: one common in Surrey, for instance, is part-owned by the Worms Heath Gravel Company, and the site 'appears to have been used partially as landfill'.

The pillage of the commons by private owners and corporations gives the lie to the modern myth about the 'tragedy of the commons'. This slander, that common land was a free-for-all where self-interested commoners depleted a shared resource, was propagated by the right-wing ecologist Garrett Hardin as a reason for extending private property rights. It couldn't be further from the truth. Commons were closely regulated by local communities – a fact that can still be glimpsed in the modern registers of ownership, where occasional references to archaic commons officials open windows onto a forgotten world. The 'Piecemaster of Atherstone Common', for example, administers land in Warwickshire at the behest of the commoners, while 'the Constable of the Graveship of Holme' oversees rights to digging peat across seven townships in North Yorkshire. The survival of 'Verderers', 'Fen Reeves' and 'Drove Committees' all point to an ancient, more sustainable relationship with the land that relied on neither market nor state, of the kind analysed by Nobel Prize-winning economist Elinor Ostrom. It was certainly more benign than the free-for-all unleashed by enclosure, which has seen many commons built on, mined and destroyed by private property owners.

Still, it's important not to overly romanticise England's commons. They represent fragments of a world now irrevocably lost. Some activists dream of reversing enclosure and seeing the land taken restored to common ownership. But it's difficult to see how this could be done without overthrowing a thousand years of English private property law. If the Diggers couldn't achieve this during the upheaval of the Civil War, it looks like even more of a lost cause today. Moreover, the relevance of many common rights has withered as England has ceased to be an agrarian society. How many people today would really exercise the right to graze cows on their local common, even if they had the chance? To paraphrase Jarvis Cocker, we may want to live like common people, but we'll never do what common people do.

Today the remnants of commons that remain are arguably most valuable as green spaces where we can stretch our legs and where nature can thrive. As islands of ancient pasture amid a sea of chemical cultivation, they're too precious to be dug up for crops, even communally grown ones of the kind envisaged by Winstanley. We should certainly defend to the death the commons we have left. And we should take inspiration from the concept of the commons, which now has applicability beyond land to things like the welfare state, the internet, and the global commons of Earth's climate.

Most of all, the commons remind us of what has been lost. We need to remember the injustice of dispossession, the fact that huge swathes of land were stolen from the people by the elite, and that today most of us are landless. The next step isn't to get mad, but to get even.

One modern way of reclaiming land for common ownership is finding great success in the Highlands and Islands of Scotland. There, half a million acres of land have been acquired by Community Benefit Societies, often comprised of tenants and crofters who have at last been able to buy their homes and farms from wealthy absentee lairds. Such community buy-outs have received support from the Scottish government in recent years and the legislative backing of Community Right to Buy, which gives community groups a first right of refusal on estates when they come up for sale. My partner Louisa and I paid a visit one summer to the small, windswept Scottish island of Ulva, off the coast of Mull, whose population had been forcibly evicted by the Clearances in the nineteenth century. Today, just six people eke out a living there from farming, fishing and tourism. But we were lucky enough to visit on the very day that the community heard they'd won their bid to buy the island from their absentee owners. We could only sense it vicariously, but it was exhilarating all the same: a feeling that the tide of history had turned, and that the community could now reclaim control of its own destiny.

Another way of redistributing land more fairly is buried in the works of Shakespeare. The opening scene of *King Lear* contains the most famous example of land partition in English literature:

Give me the map there. Know that we have divided
In three our kingdom . . .

Lear, beset by vanity, denies his daughter Cordelia her share of the kingdom because she refuses to flatter him. We rage against Lear's foolishness when he divides up his lands between his other, sycophantic daughters, and ignores the protestations of his loyal courtier, the Earl of Kent.

But what is lost on modern audiences is that Shakespeare likely intended the character of Kent to symbolise an older, wiser way of apportioning inherited land. By speaking up on behalf of Cordelia, Lear's youngest, Kent is defending the Kentish custom of *gavelkind*, which saw inheritances carved up equally between heirs regardless of age. For centuries, the county of Kent has practised this ancient, egalitarian system of land tenure, a survival from a time before the Norman Conquest.

A monument in a churchyard on the outskirts of the Kentish village of Swanscombe commemorates this tradition. Amid old graves and beneath the dark branches of a gnarled yew tree lies a stone memorial, portraying Norman soldiers in chainmail being confronted by Kentish warriors. Beneath the carving is an epigraph:

NEAR THIS SPOT IN THE YEAR 1067, BY ANCIENT TRADITION THE MEN OF KENT AND KENTISH MEN, CARRYING BOUGHS ON THEIR SHOULDERS AND SWORDS IN THEIR HANDS, MET THE INVADER, WILLIAM, DUKE OF NORMANDY. THEY OFFERED PEACE IF HE WOULD GRANT THEIR ANCIENT RIGHTS AND LIBERTIES, OTHERWISE WAR AND THAT MOST DEADLY. THEIR REQUEST WAS GRANTED AND FROM THAT DAY THE MOTTO OF KENT HAS BEEN 'INVICTA', MEANING UNCONQUERED.

The ancient rights and liberties referred to included Kent's custom of *gavelkind*. While William imposed male primogeniture on the rest of England, ensuring land ownership remained concentrated by having only firstborn sons inherit, Kent maintained its ancient tradition of 'partible inheritance', whereby estates were distributed equally between all male heirs. 'The custom of the *gavelkind* tenements, with the advantages which they obviously afforded to the occupier of the soil as over against the lord, held a position unique among regional customs,' argues one legal scholar.

Gavelkind likely affected land ownership in Kent right up to the modern era. 'This subdivision of land in the Middle Ages may well account for the small size of farms in present-day Kent,' suggested the historian D.B. Grigg in the 1960s. Though *gavelkind* was abolished in 1925 – and more recent farm survey data suggests the number of small farms has declined in Kent as it has everywhere else – this custom clearly survived for centuries, defying the 'Norman yoke'. It's surely no coincidence that Kent's stock of independent, unconquered peasants proved a fertile seedbed for rebellion. Wat Tyler, the leader of the Peasants' Revolt, hailed from Maidstone, while Jack Cade's uprising of the 1540s was similarly led by a Man of Kent.

The custom of *gavelkind* shows us how important inheritance laws are to the distribution of land. Among the aristocracy today, abolishing male primogeniture so that eldest daughters could inherit titles and lands as a matter of course would be a small but important step towards equality in this most unequal of British institutions. Legislating for the return of *gavelkind,* and imposing it as the law of the land, would likely cause the break-up of the large aristocratic estates over the course of a few generations. Given peers' resistance even to letting their daughters inherit, however, this seems a distant prospect, and the only beneficiaries would be the younger sons and daughters of the aristocracy. Another option, which would see the value of inherited lands shared with society more widely, could be to close off the inheritance tax loopholes exploited by many large estates today, such as the inheritance tax exemption on agricultural land.

Coaxing lords and kings into sharing out their landed inheritances more equally is one thing. But those who have nothing to begin with have nothing to pass on. What other means exist to enfranchise today's landless tenant farmers and unpropertied millennials?

Modern politicians' support for a 'property-owning democracy' takes on an ironic hue when you realise that, for much of English history, democracy was only available to those who owned property. During the Putney Debates, a series of extraordinary deliberations held during the Civil War over the future direction of the country, the moderate General Ireton rejected the demands of the radical Levellers for all men to be given the vote. 'I think that no person has a right to an interest or share in the disposing of the affairs of the kingdom', he argued, 'that has not a permanent fixed interest in the kingdom.' In other words, if you didn't own land or property, you had no stake in the country, and therefore no right to vote. Of course, there was more than a whiff of self-interest among Cromwell's landed officers in the use of this reasoning. The appropriately named Colonel Nathaniel Rich, inheritor of a huge estate, argued that if the landless poor were given a vote, 'there may be a law enacted, that there shall be equality of goods and estate.'

The 'property qualification' constrained voting rights in England for centuries. The so-called 'Great' Reform Act of 1832 extended the franchise to all men who held land and property worth £10 or more. That may sound like a low bar, but it was a lot of money back then: it meant that a mere 8 per cent of the male population got the vote. It was a transparent attempt at divide-and-rule, to 'detach the discontented and disenfranchised middle classes from the multitude', as one Whig minister put it, and it solicited a furious reaction from the multitude in the form of the Chartist movement. The People's Charter of 1838 demanded universal male suffrage and an end to the property qualification. But after Parliament batted away the millions of petition signatories gathered by the Chartists, one of their leaders, Feargus O'Connor, decided to take a different tack. Instead of abolishing the property qualification so that the masses might vote, he would attempt to enfranchise the masses by collectively buying land and property.

O'Connor's Chartist Land Plan started out optimistically. The essence of his idea, as historian Frank McLynn recounts, was to 'enfranchise more and more Chartists by making them men of property and thus eligible to vote'. It was a utopian scheme that envisaged buying land on the open market with cash raised through what we'd now call crowdfunding. O'Connor succeeded in signing up 70,000 subscribers, who together chipped in £100,000. Such popular interest, notes one observer, confirms 'the widespread and deep longing in Britain for the life of an independent smallholder'. With this money, the Chartist Co-operative Land Society bought its first estate of 103 acres – dubbed 'O'Connorville' – at what is now Heronsgate, on the northern outskirts of London. Plots were handed out to subscribers by ballot, homes built, and a pub founded, still open today and now called The Land of Liberty, Peace & Plenty. Similar settlements were established elsewhere, including Charterville in Oxfordshire and Great Dodford in Gloucestershire, housing 250 tenants in all across 1,700 acres. There was just one problem: O'Connor's plan turned out to be a giant pyramid scheme.

It wasn't that O'Connor was personally dishonest – he sank thousands of pounds of his own money into the project – but that he was rubbish at accounting. The idea had been to acquire land with the crowdfunded capital, use this as collateral to borrow more money, and then reimburse subscribers through a mixture of loans and tenants' rents. But there was sloppy record keeping, rents went unpaid, and it proved impossible to work out who had contributed what. A parliamentary select committee that investigated the Chartist Land Company found that it would have taken 150 years to house or pay back the shareholders and thus satisfy their legitimate aspirations. It was thus not a true company, but a lottery, and a borderline fraudulent one at that. The company was dissolved in 1851, a bitter defeat for O'Connor and the Chartists, whose final monster petition and mass rally on Kennington Common a few years previously had also failed to elicit electoral reform.

But the Chartist Land Company was far from alone in its efforts to enfranchise the working class by buying up land. Over 300 'land societies' were founded in the years 1851–4 alone, constituting a now almost-forgotten working-class movement. The Longton Freehold Land Society, for instance, bought up land belonging to the Duke of Sutherland. The National Freehold Land Society, founded by reformers Richard Cobden and John Bright, later became the building society Abbey National. These schemes seemed to offer an alternative means of political advancement after the failure of the Chartists' moral arguments and threats of physical force. The idea that you could buy political emancipation alongside a nice house, for 'the cost of a single pint of beer a day', as one promotional newspaper put it, was a beguiling one. Even so, behind the family-friendly PR, Cobden harboured radical ambitions; he wanted to take on the 'citadel of privilege in this country', the 'concentrated masses of property in the hands of the comparatively few', and felt this was the only way to do it.

Unfortunately, when equipped with limited capital and faced with entrenched landed interests, there's only so much land redistribution you can achieve through the free market. The freehold land societies succeeded in enfranchising thousands of working-class people and getting them new houses to boot, so they weren't a total failure by any means; the building societies they gave rise to enabled thousands more to acquire homes. But the number of new freeholders they created is estimated to have been only around 20,000, and their political purpose was rendered unnecessary by later Reform Acts in 1867, 1885 and 1918 that extended the right to vote. Market-based schemes, it seemed, could not by themselves fundamentally restructure land ownership in England. But could the state?

Not many MPs have stood for election with the campaign promise of providing their constituents with 'three acres and a cow'. But then, not many MPs have been like Joseph Chamberlain.

'I am in favour of freeing the land,' Chamberlain declared on his stump speeches. 'I am in favour of the repeal of those laws of entail by which more than half of the land in this country is tied up . . . for the supposed benefit of less than 150 families.' Instead, he argued, ordinary people should be leased 'small plots direct from the State, on fair and reasonable conditions'.

A radical Liberal and later a Tory – who was cited by Theresa May as one of her inspirations shortly after she became Prime Minister – Chamberlain was also responding to the pressures of his time. The rabble-rousing American economist Henry George had been stirring up ill-feeling towards landowners with speaking tours to promote his book, *Progress and Poverty*. Fenians were demanding not only Home Rule for Ireland, but also wholesale land reform for Irish farmers struggling under English landlords. Crofters in Scotland had formed the Highland Land League and were occupying land on aristocrats' estates that had been seized from their ancestors. The English countryside languished under a deep and interminable agricultural depression; and English cities were crowded slums, where malnourished families packed into grey terraces yearned for fresh air and fresh veg.

In this febrile environment, Chamberlain embraced radical rhetoric that often far exceeded what he or his party expected to enact in office. But in among the flowery language, his *Radical Programme* made two suggestions that were to have long-lasting practical consequences. 'Besides the creation of smallholdings,' he wrote, 'local authorities should have compulsory powers to purchase land where necessary at a fair market price . . . for the purpose of garden and field allotments.' Over the next few years, the government enacted legislation that produced the first county farms, and gave statutory backing to the humble allotment.

The memories I have of spending time on my parents' allotment as a kid are joyfully happy ones: getting my hands dirty in the earth; the succulent crunch of fresh runner beans picked straight off the cane; wheelbarrow rides with Dad; taking home sticks of rhubarb to make crumbles. Allotments may not, on the face of things, appear revolutionary. There's a nostalgic, English eccentricity and parochialism about them that brings to mind *Last of the Summer Wine* and *Dad's Army*. But there's also something profoundly appealing about their small simplicity – their ramshackle amateurishness, their down-to-earthness – that helps explain their enduring appeal. And at root, they are one of the most successful examples of land reform England currently has.

'Allotments undoubtedly did, and do, extend popular rights to land that would not have been achieved in any other way than the demand for a small, productive plot,' wrote the always-practical anarchist thinker Colin Ward. 'For many of us, the only experience of the land is as an observer ... In the allotment, people participate in *using* the earth.' Working-class demands for allotments in crowded Victorian cities were couched in terms of recompense for the enclosure of the commons, as well as being vital for fresh food and physical exercise. The world wars gave an additional urgency to growing more food: over a million allotment plots were dug during the First World War while 'Dig for Victory' and rationing during the Second saw allotment numbers mushroom to almost 1.5 million.

The Thorpe Report of 1969, the first and only government inquiry into allotments, tried to rebrand them as simply another form of leisure activity. But the productive and political nature of allotments has resisted such assimilation into consumer society. The middle classes 'discovered' allotments in the 1970s, when the BBC sitcom *The Good Life* popularised a new desire for self-sufficiency – and homemade wine – made suddenly urgent by the oil crisis, the three-day week and new-found fears of ecological collapse. Waiting lists lengthened hugely, as they did again three decades later when a fresh spike in oil prices, fears about climate change, and TV gardening programmes sparked a new drive for community gardens. Famously, of course, Jeremy Corbyn is a big fan of allotments. A Steve Bell cartoon depicts Corbyn out digging on his allotment in Islington. 'Is this your allotment, mate?' asks a passing journalist. 'Well, it's mine to work as I please,' replies Corbyn, 'but the land itself belongs to the wider community.' 'So it's a communist plot, then?' wisecracks the snarky hack.

Allotments, it's true, are not owned by their plotholders. Usually, they're on land owned by the local council: plotholders pay a small fee, and local residents who want an allotment are put on a waiting list until plots become available. But what makes allotments really radical is that everyone has a statutory right to one. The 1908 Allotments Act compelled councils to provide land for allotments where there was demand, and defined the size of a plot as being one-twelfth of an acre. In other words, everyone in the country was – for the first time – guaranteed access to an area of land for growing food.

But though having an allotment remains very popular – there are currently an estimated 90,000 people on allotment waiting lists – the area of land given over to them has declined dramatically since their heyday. Two factors are at play: first, councils have tried to break free of their statutory obligation to provide allotments by stalling for years, claiming there isn't enough spare land locally, or pleading they don't have sufficient budget to acquire new land. Second, although some allotments are protected from sale without ministerial orders, other land designated as temporary allotment space has been sold off by cash-strapped councils over the years, especially as austerity bites. Over 100,000 acres of plots existed in 1948; seventy years later, the area of England devoted to allotments has dwindled to just 31,000 acres. Today, we lavish ten times more land on golf courses than we do on allotments.

A similar story of rise and decline can be told about Joseph Chamberlain's other proposal for council-owned smallholdings – the County Farms Estate. After the Smallholdings Acts of 1892 and 1908, local authorities began buying up farmland to let out to young and first-time farmers, sometimes at below-market rents. As such, they became a vital first rung on the 'farming ladder' for newcomers to a sector that has high up-front capital costs. By providing the land and buildings, the public sector has helped inject fresh blood into an industry where the average age today is sixty. The rise of county farms in the first few decades of the twentieth century was meteoric. 'The smallholding movement is unique in modern agricultural history', argues the historian Susanna Wade Martins. 'It is the only occasion on which we see the promotion of small, rather than ever-larger farming units.'

Yet the extent of county farms across England has halved in the past forty years. It's no coincidence that this decline coincides with the era of privatisation and local authority budget cuts ushered in by Thatcher and repeated under the Conservatives since 2010: the area covered has plummeted from 426,695 acres in 1977 to just 215,155 acres in 2017. 'Without council farms there is basically no route into agriculture for people who want to farm on their own account, rather than working with contractors and large corporations,' argues George Dunn, head of the Tenant Farmers Association. Some councils have kept their estates going through careful management: Cambridgeshire, for example, has increased the amount it invests in its county farms, while Norfolk has enshrined a commitment to keeping 16,000 acres of farmland in public hands in its council constitution. But elsewhere the story is one of loss, part of a larger trend of council assets being liquidated to make ends meet. 'It's a beautiful farm, we'll be sorry to leave it,' Herefordshire farmer Steve Clayton told the BBC as the council smallholding he farmed was auctioned off in November 2017. 'The guide price was one-and-a-quarter million. I haven't got that money, and I haven't won the lottery! . . . We're gutted . . . Once you've sold an asset, you've no longer got it, and the money will be gone.'

The allotments and smallholdings movements may have fallen short of securing 'three acres and a cow' for all, and still less a reversal of enclosure. But for well over half a century, councils facilitated land reform on a scale unmatched by any previous tactics. And as they acquired land for new farmers and urban food-growers, they also bought up land for something in even greater demand: affordable housing.

If few people today have even heard of county farms, everyone has an image in their heads of council housing – and it's often a rather forbidding one of a concrete high-rise, looking unloved and dilapidated. Decades of official neglect, slashed public sector budgets and questionable regeneration schemes; decades of politicians talking down council properties as 'sink estates' and talking up the 'aspirational' nature of private home ownership; endless TV crime dramas set in monolithic grey tower blocks – all this has saddled council housing with an image problem, just as councils have had their powers to build new housing deliberately wrested from them. Since June 2017, official attitudes towards council housing have come to be epitomised in a still more grim image: the smoking, charred remains of Grenfell Tower. But it wasn't always like this.

The idea of council housing was born out of the same ferment of utopian ideals and radical ideas that gave us allotments and county farms. Working-class activism had pushed housing to the top of the political agenda: the 1915 Glasgow Rent Strike, led by Govan resident Mary Barbour, saw 20,000 households refuse to pay rent to their money-grabbing private sector landlords. The Labour Party became the official opposition in 1918. Panicking Tory and Liberal politicians, chasing workers' votes, began to accept the need for the state to provide affordable housing outside the free market. 'In this context,' writes historian John Boughton, 'the public housing programme was seen as a quite deliberate and knowing means of placating an insurgent working class.'

Back then, with the promise of 'homes fit for heroes', council housing was aspirational. 'It was unthinkable then that people "sank" in council estates,' writes Boughton. Rather, they were part of a 'programme of "mass upliftment"'. The 1919 Housing Act, championed by interventionist Liberal minister Christopher Addison, stipulated that council housing should be built at a density of no more than twelve an acre, and be 'of cottage appearance'. 'Municipal socialists' on the London County Council and in Progressive-controlled Battersea built public housing that was spacious, well-designed and affordable. The Boundary Estate in Bethnal Green, Britain's first council estate, set a high standard. Now Grade II listed, with Arts and Crafts features, glazed tiling and 'quirky, colourful, streaky bacon-style banded brick-work', it's a world away from 1960s tower blocks and the inhumane designs of Modernist planners obsessed with creating 'machines for living in'.

All this, of course, required both money and land. And although the various inter-war Housing Acts resulted in councils building 1.1 million homes, there was still a long way to go to finally clear away the Victorian slums and rehouse people in affordable, clean, warm accommodation. The Second World War provided the impetus for wholesale change, both by demonstrating the capacity of the state to intervene where the market couldn't deliver, and because the German *Luftwaffe* flattened large parts of British cities. The British public, brought closer together by rationing, shared air raid shelters and an overwhelming desire to build a better future together after the bombs stopped falling, swung sharply to the left during the war. That meant the job of post-war reconstruction fell to Clement Attlee's Labour government, elected by a landslide in 1945.

Britain may have been bankrupted by the most destructive war the world has ever known, but money was still found to make house-building a priority. Nye Bevan's Ministry of Health and Housing, alongside overseeing the construction of 800,000 council homes in just six years, had even greater plans ahead: a National Housing Service to sit alongside the new National Health Service. Bevan lifted the restrictions that meant council housing was only available to the working classes: he wanted public housing to be at least as good as private housing, so that everyone of all classes could aspire to living in a council house. His wife, the politician Baroness Lee of Asheridge, later recalled how Bevan pressured the Treasury into subsidising coun-cils to build with locally sourced materials, so that 'even in those immediate years following the Second World War we were able to build a dream village in the Cotswolds of Cotswold stones'. But to make such dreams a reality required a confrontation with the landowners.

Above all, to carry on building affordable housing, the government needed a way to make land cheap to buy. Some within Labour had long called for the outright nationalisation of land – from Robert Blatchford, bestselling utopian socialist author of *Merrie England* and the pamphlet *Land Nationalisation*, through to Labour's 1918 manifesto. This would have faced enormous political resistance, and required colossal compensation payments to current private landowners. Instead, what the Labour government attempted after 1945 was both more subtle and more effective. It drew upon the thinking of American economist Henry George, whose hugely influential 1879 book *Progress and Poverty* had argued: 'Let those who now hold land retain possession, if they want ... We may safely leave them the shell, if we take the kernel.' To do so, Labour introduced three radical policies: one is still in place, but the other two have since been lost. First, the government essentially nationalised landowners' development rights, through the creation of the planning system under the Town and Country Planning Act 1947 – the basis of today's planning framework. Second, it sought to tax the uplift in land values, so that landowners would have to pay back some of the unearned windfall they received after being granted planning permission. And third, it gave councils the power to buy land cheaply.

What this meant was that landowners still owned their land, but now had to get permission from the local council to develop it – and, crucially, pay a fee, the development charge, out of the inevitable increase in land value after planning permission was granted. Such a charge had been recommended by the 1941 Uthwatt Report, and constituted a variant on Lloyd George's earlier, abortive land value tax. This time, however, rather than tax *all* land, Labour's development charge was only levied on the uplift in land values after development permission had been granted. 'The reputable builder does not normally look for his profits to the sale of land,' commented planning minister Lewis Silkin when introducing the legislation. 'He expects to make a profit out of his building operations, and this he will be able to do when the Bill becomes law just as much as he could before.'

Landowners and developers, however, hated the development charge. Because it was levied at 100 per cent of the increase in land values after development had been granted, it effectively removed the profit motive for developing the land – leading landowners to simply refuse to sell. The charge had been set too high, and the government lacked an effective backstop to compel private landowners and developers into cooperating. A 'landowner strike' ensued, slowing private housebuilding. Landowners sat it out, waiting for the Conservatives to take office and repeal the charge, which they duly did in 1953.

But when it came to the cheap acquisition of land by councils to build homes themselves, they had another card up their sleeve. Thanks to the third and last of Labour's reforms, councils could now buy land at 'existing use value', using compulsory purchase powers if necessary. That meant that if a council wanted to buy a landowner's field, say, for building council homes, the landowner would still be compensated, but only for the field's existing agricultural value – not for the additional 'hope value' the landowner may have hoped to realise one day by selling it for housing. If they refused to sell, the council could issue a compulsory purchase order. 'For 11 years,' writes Daniel Bentley, editorial director at centre-right think tank Civitas, 'councils were able to buy land for their housebuilding programmes at, or close to, existing use value.' Over that same period, about 1.8 million council homes were constructed in England – a third of all the council housing built in the country since the Second World War. Twenty-one entirely new towns – such as Stevenage, Harlow and Milton Keynes – were built by public development corporations under this land purchase framework. Most of the housebuilding took place under Conservative governments, who accepted Labour's reform as necessary to get lots of homes built quickly. Tory housing minister, and later PM, Harold Macmillan proudly oversaw the construction of 229,000 council homes in 1953, the highest-ever annual total.

But the landowners and developers won out in the end. 'LAND OWNERS GET A RAW DEAL,' complained a headline in *The Times* in 1958. Councils had their powers to buy land cheaply taken away from them by the 1959 Town and Country Planning Act and the 1961 Land Compensation Act. Efforts by the later Wilson and Callaghan

Labour governments to reintroduce different forms of development charge were miserable failures. The concept of capturing land values disappeared almost entirely from mainstream political debate under Thatcher. In more recent decades, 'developer contributions', known as Section 106 agreements and the Community Infrastructure Levy, have been introduced into the planning system in an effort to persuade developers to fund public goods, like green space or transport infrastructure, as part of planning deals. But these contributions usually comprise only a fraction of the uplift in land values won through granting planning permission for a development. And they do nothing to get to the root of the crisis in affordable housing, which requires landowners to be prevented from hoarding land while they wait to extract the highest possible price for it. Meanwhile, land values have increased more than fivefold since 1995, according to the ONS.

The current, chronic housing crisis is finally reigniting debate about land reform. There's increasing cross-party support for some form of tax on land values, and for giving councils back the powers to buy land cheaply. The Conservatives' 2017 election manifesto promised to make sure 'communities themselves ... benefit from the increase in land value from urban regeneration and development'. Labour's shadow housing minister, John Healey, has proposed changing the 1961 Land Compensation Act to allow councils to buy land at existing use value once more. A host of organisations, from housing charity Shelter to conservation group CPRE, now support the principle of 'land value capture'. Some free-market Tories, of course, remain highly sceptical about anything that affects the absolute rights of private landowners: Treasury minister Liz Truss tweeted that she found Labour's modest proposals on land value capture 'deeply sinister'. But more sensible Conservative MPs – like Nick Boles, Neil O'Brien and Bim Afolami – seem to understand that without radical reforms to the housing market, the party will lose the support of young people altogether. This message seems to be getting a hearing even in Downing Street. 'Improving the ability of the state to buy land at closer to existing use value, so as to enable land value capture, can therefore be a powerful tool for reducing landowners' ability to extract economic rent,' wrote the housing expert Toby Lloyd in a 2017 book he co-authored while head of policy at Shelter. In 2018, he was appointed Number 10's housing adviser. Hopefully he will be listened to: taxing the uplift in land values and letting councils buy up land at existing use value are the land reforms England most desperately needs today.

England can often seem a deeply conservative country: a place where change seldom happens fast, if at all, and where talk of reforming land ownership can get you labelled a dangerous revolutionary. But there is a buried, radical tradition of English land reform that we too easily forget. It stretches like a golden thread from the rebellious Men of Kent who resisted William the Conqueror's vicious land grab, through Gerrard Winstanley's Diggers and Octavia Hill's Commons Preservation Society, to the late-Victorian social movements that demanded allotments and County Farms. As England ceased to be a predominantly agrarian society, new land reform movements arose to grapple with the problems of scarce urban land, the lack of affordable housing, and landlords pushing up rents.

Anyone despairing about the present-day housing crisis, our declining countryside, or the vast inequalities in English society today, should take heart and inspiration from this lost history of England's courageous land reformers. Some of their methods turned out to be flawed; others proved wildly successful. Either way, there's much we can learn from them.

And if we do, we can start to trace the outlines of a modern agenda for land reform in England. Our starting point should be the historic injustice of the enclosures, and the memory of a time when 30 per cent of England was common land. None of the attempts to redistribute land and property since then have come close to returning such a large area of land to the public, as the statistics in Figure 2 show. But remembering that today we are landless because the commons were taken from us doesn't mean we should be looking to return to some sort of rural

Arcadia, where we all live by toiling in the fields. A modern movement for English land reform is about solving the housing crisis, rewilding our landscapes and reconnecting ourselves to the food we eat. It's about both rural and urban land, and about sharing the wealth that comes from owning land.

Type of land or property holding	Acreage	Percentage of England	Notes & caveats
Domestic homes and gardens	1,749,439	5.4%	Only c.70% of homes are owner-occupied
Allotments	31,712	0.1%	Owned by councils, not individuals; 33,300 acres of UK
County Farms	215,155	0.7%	Owned by councils, not individuals
Common land (2018)	c.1,000,000	3%	Owned by a wide range of private, public & third sector bodies
Totals	2,996,306 acres	9.4%	
Common land (1600)	c.8,640,000–9,600,000 acres	c.27%-30%	

Figure 2: A property-owning democracy?

It's clear that the dream of a 'property-owning democracy' is dead, at least in the free-market terms it was conceived of by Margaret Thatcher. Home ownership at first increased as a result of her reforms, but those same policies – the failure to build new affordable housing to replace the council homes sold under Right to Buy, the property bubble inflated by cheap credit – have proven self-defeating, and undermined the ability of younger generations to buy homes. If we're to solve the housing crisis, we need the government to intervene in the broken land market.

Land reform doesn't mean simply slicing England up like a cake, with a small portion for everyone. The Victorian demand of 'three acres and a cow' for all is now mathematically impossible, given population levels: the UK is roughly 60 million acres in extent, but there are now 65 million of us living here. We could all still become the proud owners of slightly less than an acre each; but who draws the short straw and gets an acre of marshland or mountain-top? And what would most of us do with that acre if we were handed it? But just because a perfectly equal distribution of land is implausible doesn't mean we should stick with the grossly unequal status quo. Fortunately, there are other, better ways of making land ownership in this country more equal, and of sharing out the wealth that comes from the land.

We may never be able to return to the era when commons covered a third of England. But we can still find new ways of making Gerrard Winstanley's dream come true: that the land of England might, at last, become a common treasury for all.

9

IN TRUST FOR TOMORROW

England had just beaten Panama 6–1 in the World Cup when I visited the White Cliffs of Dover, so naturally the town was festooned with flags of St George. They fluttered in the breeze as pubs rang to renditions of 'Three Lions'. But Dover, Britain's gateway to Europe, also displays its patriotism in other ways, all year round. The town square has a huge floral crown, made out of mosses and succulent plants, with its central jewel the crest and motto of Kent – *INVICTA* – celebrating its resistance to foreign invaders. Dover's busy roads, thronged with lorries making their way to and from the continent, are lined with brown heritage signs pointing the way to past English glories: BRONZE AGE BOAT; NORMAN CASTLE. And looming over the port town, overshadowing everything else, are the White Cliffs – property, of course, of the National Trust.

In 2012, as part of a fundraising appeal to acquire a section of the cliffs, the National Trust appointed the philosopher Julian Baggini as the White Cliffs' writer-in-residence. 'Even if we've never been to or seen the white cliffs of Dover, there is a collective sense that they matter,' he wrote. 'My suspicion is that if we look, there is an insightful portrait of the nation to be found engraved in the chalky cliffs of east Kent.' As I walked up to the foot of the cliffs, past Dover's branch of Poundland ('We accept both £ and €') and 40-tonne lorries heading for customs checks, I had to agree. The red paint of the old telephone box next to a cottage named after the poet Matthew Arnold was faded and peeling, but the sunlit cliffs behind were dazzling in their brilliance.

It was this coastline that gave our island its first recorded name. Caesar's Roman invasion force called it *Albion*, from *albus*, Latin for 'white'. Over the past thousand years, the White Cliffs have come to symbolise indomitable England, our seas and soldiers repelling all who would dare conquer this sceptred isle: the Spanish Armada, Napoleon, Hitler. Stare out across the Channel from these windswept headlands, and you can almost hear the thrum of Spitfires above you, and catch strains of Vera Lynn singing about bluebirds. In less clement weather, the clifftops recall that famous Second World War cartoon drawn by David Low, where a defiant Tommy stands on England's edge shaking his fist at the gathering storm over Nazi-dominated Europe, with the caption, 'VERY WELL, ALONE'. Under this weight of national mythology, the White Cliffs signify not just landscape, but *territory*. Small wonder that the National Trust should have chosen to buy them.

And yet, by acquiring them, the National Trust has bought an icon that also carries with it unpleasant baggage. In more recent decades, the White Cliffs have come to symbolise something darker that lurks in the English psyche – an emblem of England's insularity, its hostility to immigrants, its . . . whiteness. The *Daily Express*, one year out from Brexit, notoriously printed a photo of the White Cliffs on its front cover which had been doctored to make the cliffs look even whiter. For many political cartoonists, the White Cliffs provide a perfect metaphor for Brexit itself: a cliff-edge over which hapless politicians madly throw themselves in a suicidal bid for sovereignty at all costs.

Sweating in the midday sun, I'd hauled my way to the top of the cliffs. Down below, amid the grey concrete and diesel fumes of the port of Dover, the knotty, complicated business of trade was giving the lie to simple notions of territorial independence. Duties here, tariffs there; lorries loading and unloading their cargo in a never-ending cycle of give and take. Sometimes, the lorries here contain people: stowaway migrants desperate to make a new home in England, only to find themselves unwelcome upon arrival. In the distance, far from the heady heights of the White Cliffs, I could see the dark shape of Dover

Immigration Removal Centre squatting on the other side of town. A few years back, a march by the far-right English Defence League in Dover town centre had been countered by activists who'd projected an alternative message onto the White Cliffs at dusk: *Refugees Welcome*.

Perhaps wisely, the Trust's visitor centre at the White Cliffs had opted to stay well clear of any debates about national identity, and focus instead on plying tourists with tea and cake. Refreshed, I drank in the landscape. Shorn of their veneer of jingoism, the White Cliffs are simply crushed seashells, a glorious accident of geology. Meandering pathways crisscross the chalk downland of the clifftops, leaving humanity's stark imprint in the turf. But beneath the thin topsoil of petty rivalries and human comings and goings lies the land itself: a billion years of uncaring geography. By the side of one track, I found a pyramid orchid nestled amid the yellow flowers of bird's-foot trefoil, orbited by blue butterflies. Suddenly, customs unions and borders seemed like so much dust.

My phone buzzed, bringing me back to the human world. It was a text message from my service provider. 'O2 ROAMING: WELCOME TO FRANCE,' it said, implausibly. The Normans, it seems, always get the last laugh. And though we might yearn to escape from them, politics and power pervade the landscapes around us. The National Trust is now an entrenched part of that landscape: after all, it owns 614,000 acres of it – 2 per cent of England and Wales, with the bulk of that in England. By becoming the guardian of such a large part of our national heritage, it has inevitably had to make political choices about which landscapes and buildings to preserve, and which to neglect. Whose histories are remembered, and whose forgotten? Is nature best conserved by pickling a landscape in aspic, or by allowing it to change and grow? Whose nation does the National Trust represent, and in whose trust does it own land?

With its cream teas, stately homes and five million members, the National Trust is such an established part of the fabric of England today that it's hard to comprehend how revolutionary it was when it started out. 'The National Trust for Places of Historic Interest or Natural

Beauty' was founded on 12 December 1894. Its three principal founders
– Octavia Hill, Robert Hunter and Hardwicke Rawnsley – were radicals
who railed against enclosure and fought to keep London's green spaces
open for the public.

Octavia Hill was a tireless campaigner, among whose many causes
was the provision of social housing and community gardens for
London's poor. One of her many projects was Red Cross Gardens in
Southwark, an oasis of green amid the city's bustle and alive with bees
and dragonflies, which I visited often while writing this chapter. Her
upbringing had placed much emphasis on the great outdoors; she later
wrote that 'the need of quiet, the need of air, the need of exercise, and
. . . the sight of sky and of things growing seem human needs, common
to all men'. Robert Hunter was a campaigning lawyer for the Commons
Preservation Society and a resolute defender of the commons. 'Any
Commoner whose rights are molested is clearly entitled to throw down
the whole fencing or other obstruction erected,' he wrote. 'The owners
of the soil, if they persist in acts of violence, should be forced before
a Court.' Rawnsley was a curate with a passion for nature. After being
schooled in art by the great Victorian aesthete John Ruskin, he led
some of the first campaigns to protect the Lake District from despo-
liation by reservoirs and railways, and organised mass trespasses along
footpaths closed by large landowners.

These three 'Green Victorians' led a countercultural rebellion
against the assumptions of the Victorian middle classes, that smoke
and grime and ugliness were the unavoidable side-effects of wealth
and progress. You couldn't exactly call them anti-capitalist, but they
sought to put the brakes on the industrialisation of the countryside,
and reasoned that an increasingly urbanised society needed access to
England's still green and pleasant land as a kind of pressure valve.
Their strategy to secure such land was both straightforwardly commercial and startlingly novel: they would buy it, with funds coming from
public appeals and donations.

Some of the Trust's early supporters considered still more radical means of acquiring land. 'We see no reason why for public purposes a bit of beautiful scenery should not be the subject of a forced sale under equitable conditions just as much as a bit of ugly country for a railway,' ran a sympathetic leader in *The Times* following the Trust's first meeting. Such powers of compulsory purchase have never, in fact, been conferred on the National Trust; although going by some of the Trust's early propaganda, you'd be forgiven for thinking they had. 'Why not nationalize the English Lake District?' asked one of its initial fundraising appeals.

What was truly innovative, however, was the legal status given to some of the land acquired by the Trust. In 1907, MPs passed the first National Trust Act, granting the Trust the ability to declare land it owned 'inalienable' – meaning it could not be bought, sold, or compulsorily purchased by the government without a debate in Parliament. This was a radical new concept in land law, unique to the National Trust and giving it powerful protection against the growing state. Not all National Trust land is treated this way; occasionally, over the decades, the Trust has had to dispose of some sites – but the bulk of its land has been granted inalienable status.

Another innovative form of land law deployed by the National Trust has been the use of 'conservation covenants'. These restrict the way land can be used, with the restraints continuing to be effective even after the land changes hands. The 1937 National Trust Act enabled the Trust to broker such covenants with landowners who wished to leave their land to their heirs, but subject to an obligation to maintain the land in a particular state of conservation. Currently, only the National Trust and the Forestry Commission have the power to draw up such covenants.

Given the Trust's reputation nowadays as a guardian of stately homes, the purchases it made in its early years are surprising, too. 'For the first 40 or so years of its existence, from its establishment in 1895 until the 1930s, the Trust was primarily concerned with the acquisition and protection of the countryside,' admits the National Trust's official guide to its historic houses. The few properties acquired by the Trust's founders reflected their interest in small-scale, vernacular architecture rather than grand palaces. 'There was nothing great about them, nothing very striking,' Octavia Hill remarked. The Trust's first-ever acquisition was a few acres of Welsh coastline; the first building, a four-teenth-century thatched cottage in Alfriston, Sussex, badly in need of repair. When it took on Barrington Court in 1907, its first foray into grander houses, trustees deemed it a costly extravagance, never to be repeated. Even with the break-up and sale of many large aristocratic estates in the immediate aftermath of the First World War, the Trust remained uninterested.

Yet from the outset, the National Trust had combined its radicalism with a close relationship with the aristocratic establishment. The Trust's first president was none other than the Duke of Westminster, even then one of the wealthiest landowners in England. Nearly every president and chair since has been a member of the peerage or royal family. And over time, the Trust increasingly began to reflect the interests of the aristocracy at large.

Take tax relief, for example. In 1894, just as the National Trust was being set up, the short-lived Liberal government introduced death duties on landed estates for the first time. At the Trust's inaugural meeting that July, held in the Duke of Westminster's imposing London residence at Grosvenor House, one of the key motions passed was to press ministers to exempt land left for the nation from the new inher-itance taxes. Though the Chancellor gently rebuffed the Trust on this occasion, it would come to lobby the government on the matter again and again.

With the deaths of the original founders, the Trust's acquisitions also started to change. An early straw in the wind was the acceptance on to the Trust's Council of Lord Nathaniel Curzon, the former Viceroy of India. In a strong field, the 1st Marquess Curzon of Kedleston must rank as one of the most pompous, ambitious and disliked aristocrats of all time. Even at Eton, he was taunted by fellow schoolboys with this piece of doggerel:

My name is George Nathaniel Curzon,
I am a most superior person;
my cheeks are pink, my hair is sleek,
I dine at Blenheim once a week!

When he died in 1925, Curzon left Bodiam Castle in Sussex to the Trust, stating in his will that he was leaving it to the nation for the decidedly patrician purposes of 'imbuing it with reverence and educating its taste'. It's certainly a magnificent castle, and very popular with visitors today. But some might argue that imbuing the masses with reverence for the owners of castles was not exactly what the Trust was originally set up to do.

Curzon's biographer, the 2nd Marquess of Zetland, became chair of the National Trust in 1932, and from the outset 'presided over the most significant new direction the Trust had yet taken – the preservation of historic houses'. He invited a fellow peer, the Marquess of Lothian, to address the Trust's AGM in 1934 on the subject of 'England's Country Houses – the Case for their Preservation'. 'Most of these [houses] are now under sentence of death,' intoned Lord Lothian, 'and the axe which is destroying them is taxation, and especially that form of taxation known as death duties.'

Lothian implored the Trust to help landowners by lobbying the government for tax relief. Zetland duly obliged, pressing his fellow Conservatives in the then National Government to throw the aristocracy a bone. It should be remembered, of course, that at the time Britain was weathering the Great Depression, with 2.5 million unemployed by 1933 – almost a quarter of the entire workforce. 'Why should the government award tax concessions to a group of wealthy families in return for limited public access?' asked one later history of the Trust. Why indeed?

But it did. In 1937, a year after hungry workers from Jarrow had fruitlessly marched upon Parliament petitioning for help, MPs passed legislation that set up the Trust's Country House Scheme. The scheme allowed landowners to deed over their properties to the National Trust in lieu of death duties – and, crucially, remain living in them, with the obligation that they open their doors to the public for just thirty days a year. Until 1970, the original owner's descendants were even allowed to carry on living in the property rent-free. It was a significant step towards letting a wider public see the treasures amassed by their social superiors over the centuries, and saved many stately homes from the wrecking ball. But it was also a giant tax dodge for the aristocracy.

It fell to James Lees-Milne, the Trust's first Country Houses Secretary and upper-class socialite, to hob-nob with noble landowners and encourage them to make use of the new scheme. Lees-Milne toured the residences of dukes and earls on his bicycle, eventually acquiring scores of stately homes for the Trust between the 1930s and 1950s, from Lord Lothian's Blickling Estate in Norfolk to Baron Sackville's Knole Castle in Kent. For the environmental campaigner George Monbiot, the Trust was set up 'to protect society from the aristocracy', but lost its way between the wars, and 'came to protect the aristocracy from society'. As one centenary history of the Trust admitted: 'Put bluntly, the Trust became more upper class.'

But there was also another side to this story. Socialists, not just socialites, were coming round to the idea of vesting land and property in the National Trust. Two of the Trust's largest acquisitions in this period came from aristocrats who were ardent left-wingers, rebels against their class. One was Sir Charles Trevelyan, baronet and brother of popular historian George Macaulay Trevelyan – another of the Trust's staunchest advocates – who transferred his huge 13,000-acre Wallington estate in Northumberland to the Trust in 1941. 'Sir Charles Trevelyan is a socialist,' declared the accompanying press release, 'and believes it would be better if the community owned such houses and great estates.' The other was Sir Richard Acland, another baronet who bequeathed to the Trust two enormous estates in the West country, Holnicote and Killerton. He went on to found the left-wing Common Wealth Party during the war, which advocated common ownership of property.

Though the Labour Party's official position at this time advocated much higher taxes on the rich and the full nationalisation of land, many socialists had come to realise that there was little point in destroying beauty and heritage in the pursuit of equality. Stately homes had to be preserved, but opened up properly to the public. A 1935 party pamphlet spoke of securing 'beauty for all, not merely beauty for a few'. The following year, the Labour politician Hugh Dalton praised the National Trust as 'an example of "practical Socialism in action" … A Labour government should give it every encouragement greatly to extend its activities.' Later, as Chancellor in Attlee's post-war government, he built on these warm words by establishing the National Land Fund, endowed with £50 million to support organisations like the National Trust keen to acquire land. The money, however, came with an important condition. As Dalton's successor Stafford Cripps put it, 'you can spend as much of the reserve as you like, so long as it is spent on the National Trust and not on the precious owners.'

This tension – between conserving stately homes or vernacular architecture; preserving aristocratic aesthetics or promoting working-class access – seems to have stayed with the Trust throughout its subsequent history. In the 1960s, it once again changed direction, launching Enterprise Neptune to buy up hundreds of miles of coastline and defend it from development and pollution. The 1970s and early 80s saw another surge in stately homes acquisitions, driven partly by Labour's new capital transfer tax. In the 1990s, the Trust came under fire for the way it handled its tenancies and booted out travellers.

In more recent years, the pendulum seems to have swung back towards recapturing some of its earlier radicalism. In 2001, the Trust acquired the Birmingham Back-to-Backs, the city's last remaining example of Victorian slum dwellings – highlighting the sort of living conditions that Octavia Hill once fought to save working-class families from enduring. It has stepped up its campaigns to resist fracking on its land, and pushed for reform of farm subsidies – of which the Trust is one of the largest single recipients – so that future payments are directed towards environmental stewardship. The past few years have seen the National Trust celebrate the histories of LGBT rights and women's suffrage across its properties, and strive to tell the stories not just of great landowners but also their servants, mistresses and labourers. Such commemorations have inevitably raised the hackles of *Daily Mail* columnists, for whom any attempt by the Trust to reflect modern Britain is an example of political correctness gone mad.

But with its now vast membership, numbering nearly a tenth of the population of England and Wales, the Trust has little choice but to become more democratic, multicultural and representative. Much remains to be done, but the signs are promising: one of the Trust's latest projects is an exploration of the 'colonial countryside' and slave-owners' properties, while its theme for 2019, 'People's Landscapes', focuses on sites of political protest. The battle for the soul of the National Trust will likely continue for as long as it endures. Long may it do so.

To explore a different set of faultlines in the landowning conservation movement, we need to take a trip to a part of the country now dominated by the National Trust: the Lake District.

Today 110,000 acres, nearly a fifth of the Lake District, is owned by the National Trust. No other landscape in England is under the control of conservation groups in quite the same way. You might expect this to have led to the Lake District becoming a world-beating haven for wildlife. But though it's a place of extraordinary beauty, whose dramatic mountains and glassy meres attract millions of visitors every year, three-quarters of the protected nature sites within it are officially classed as being in an 'unfavourable' condition. Why?

The crux of the answer lies in concepts of landscape aesthetics that emerged in the late eighteenth century. The 'Lake Poets' – Wordsworth, Coleridge and other Romantics – lived in and celebrated the topography of the Lakes for its breathtaking vistas, and the effect its awe-inspiring peaks and fells had upon the observer's mood. Wordsworth saw the true value of the landscape as being in its sublime *appearance*, rather than in its wildlife and natural history. The conservation ethic of his 1835 *Guide to the Lakes* was staunchly conservative:

its chapter on 'Changes, and Rules of Taste for Preventing their Bad Effects' opposed all changes that would affect the visual aesthetics of the Lakes, from larch plantations to whitewashed houses.

These notions, in turn, heavily influenced the original founders and supporters of the National Trust as they campaigned to protect the Lake District and started to buy it up. Canon Rawnsley led campaigns in the 1870s against what we might now view as being rather mild, even benign, modern intrusions into the region – the creation of artificial reservoirs to supply northern cities with fresh water, and the coming of the railways. A *Punch* cartoon of the era depicted Rawnsley's ally, the aesthete John Ruskin – who lived near Coniston Water in the Lakes – as a white knight defending the 'lady of the lake' from the iron beast of the steam locomotive, armed only with his artist's palette knife. The National Trust, whose full name and founding articles stresses the importance of 'natural beauty' without really defining what this means, acquired its first land in the Lakes in 1902 at Derwentwater.

And yet, while the march of industry doubtless seemed the greatest threat to the Lake District in the Victorian period, the region's ecology had already undergone huge changes that these early conservationists seemed oblivious to. Wordsworth himself acknowledged that the primeval Lake District had been 'overspread with wood', and that oak and birch had 'skirted the fells, tufted the hills, and shaded the vallies [*sic*]'. Yet he appeared blind to the ecological devastation humanity had since wrought to the Lakes, celebrating instead the 'perfect Republic of Shepherds' whose sheep had nibbled its vegetation to oblivion.

The author Beatrix Potter, who kept a flock of Herdwick sheep and left 4,000 acres of the Lake District to the National Trust upon her death, was even more adamant about the vital role of sheep farming in the Lakes. Continued grazing, she believed, was key to managing the hillsides: 'they will be nothing without the sheep', she wrote. The true threat to the Lake District, in her eyes, was tourists who strayed from the footpaths: she called them 'parasites'. Although the National Trust has wisely ignored Potter's views on ramblers, it has largely followed her advice on grazing: the number of sheep and lambs in the Lakes today is double what it was in the 1950s. Overgrazing is a key factor in the poor state of the region's biodiversity.

No one denies that the Lake District, even in its denuded modern state, remains extremely beautiful. But looking at the landscape through the prism of aesthetics is a very different approach to conservation from that of an ecologists. As the US environmentalist Aldo Leopold put it, seeing the world through an ecologist's eyes is to see 'a world of wounds'. It means realising that chocolate box landscapes may be pretty, but that our concepts of beauty and the sublime are poor guides to the underlying health of an ecosystem. Our land remains green and pleasant, but it's also one where many habitats have disappeared and many species are in freefall. The radical direct action group EarthFirst! once protested against the de-naturing of the Lakes with a spoof tourism poster that read simply 'Come to the Fake District'.

Increasingly, the National Trust has found itself in the crossfire between rival ideas about how landscapes like the Lake District should be managed. The Lakes have 'degenerated into a sheepwrecked waste-land', argues George Monbiot: 'wet deserts grazed down to turf and rock; erosion gullies from which piles of stones spill; woods in which no new trees have grown for 80 years'. Far better, Monbiot and others argue, to halt the intensive management and overgrazing and let nature take its course. Proponents of 'rewilding' point out that landscapes like the Lake District are simply preserving in aspic a degraded environment that's almost entirely artificial. Not only is this a disaster for nature; it's also making flooding worse – torrential rainfall simply flashes off denuded hillsides, drowning nearby towns and villages, as happened in the Lakes during the winter of 2015. But reduce sheep numbers, rewild-ing advocates suggest, and self-willed nature will quickly spring back – bringing with it not only much greater diversity of wildlife, but a far greater resilience to worsening floods and our changing climate.

Of course, allowing the Lakes to rewild would change the character of a landscape that many have grown used to and cherish. Plenty of self-proclaimed conservationists want to conserve the Lake District for its aesthetic beauty, farming traditions and cultural landscape, rather than for the species it supports. 'People ask me why I'm against rewilding,' contends Rory Stewart, the MP for a large part of the Lakes, 'and the answer is because of the human in the landscape . . . these are the hills across which Coleridge walked from Keswick to have dinner with Wordsworth.' Following this approach, conservation resembles pickling a landscape in formaldehyde to preserve human heritage, not nature. This view of the Lake District as for ever more being Wordsworth's 'Republic of Shepherds' has only gained traction in recent years, following the publication of Lakeland shepherd James Rebanks's bestseller *The Shepherd's Life*. Rebanks won powerful backing for this vision of the region as a 'cultural landscape' by advising on the successful bid to have the Lake District awarded UNESCO World Heritage Status in 2017, on top of its existing designation as a National Park.

For all its historic role in preserving the Lakes in its degraded ecological state, the National Trust has been quietly shifting towards a greater acceptance of rewilding in recent years. Its rewilding pilot at Ennerdale has seen a boom in populations of marsh fritillary butterflies, Arctic charr and the native juniper trees that gave the valley its name in Viking times. Professor Alasdair Driver, a veteran ecologist and adviser to the charity Rewilding Britain, calls Ennerdale 'one of England's best rewilding project areas'. But the Trust is also wary of voicing full-throated support for rewilding following the furore it provoked by trying to reforest parts of Thorneythwaite, a 300-acre Lakeland farm it bought in 2016. The charity's supposedly 'secret plan' to rewild the area was subjected to a hatchet-job in the *Daily Mail*, who accused it of a 'betrayal of Beatrix Potter's Lake District legacy'. Frankly, if that means fewer Herdwick sheep, more wildlife and more visitors, so much the better. The National Trust should defy its conservative critics and press ahead with a more ecologically literate approach to managing its land – one that preserves landscape beauty while allowing greater space for nature to flourish.

* * *

Contrary to popular wisdom, national parks in the UK are not owned by the public sector. In the US, parks like Yellowstone and Yosemite are owned by the federal government; but in Britain, National Park Authorities (NPAs) own only a few per cent of the parkland they administer. Instead, England's ten national parks are dominated by private landowners.

The Lake District is the only English national park where a conservation group owns a significant chunk of the land. Ninety-five per cent of the Yorkshire Dales, by contrast, is in private hands, as is 90 per cent of the Norfolk Broads. Dartmoor is largely owned by the Duchy of Cornwall, with a huge section of it leased to the Ministry of Defence. Northumberland National Park, at first glance, appears to be less concentrated in its ownership: only around half of it is in private hands, with the rest divided between the Forestry Commission and the MOD. But on closer inspection, it transpires that the privately owned half is dominated by three huge landowners – the Duke of Northumberland; a deceased businessman's estate called College Valley, now run by a trust; and the colossal farm owned by the founder of Persimmon Homes.

Or take the South Downs, England's newest national park. Just twelve landowners, I discovered, own a quarter of the park – including two dukes, three viscounts, one baron and two baronets. Or the North York Moors, whose upland areas are by my reckoning owned by just fifteen landowners, nearly all of them grouse-shooting estates. These include the Duchy of Lancaster, an earl, two viscounts and the bloke who set up Carphone Warehouse.* One of the largest private landowners in Exmoor

*   The landowners who, by my reckoning, own nearly all of the land above the moorland line within the North York Moors National Park are: the Duchy of Lancaster (Wheeldale, Howl and Goathland Moors); the Earl of Mexborough (Hawnby Moor and Arden Hall Estate); the Strickland Estate (Fylingdales Moor); the Ministry of Defence (RAF Fylingdales); George Winn-Darley, owner of the Spaunton Estate (Spaunton Moor); Sir Richard Beckett QC, baronet, who with two others owns the Bonfield, Bilsdale and Bloworth Moors; Viscount Boyne (Baysdale Estate); Viscount

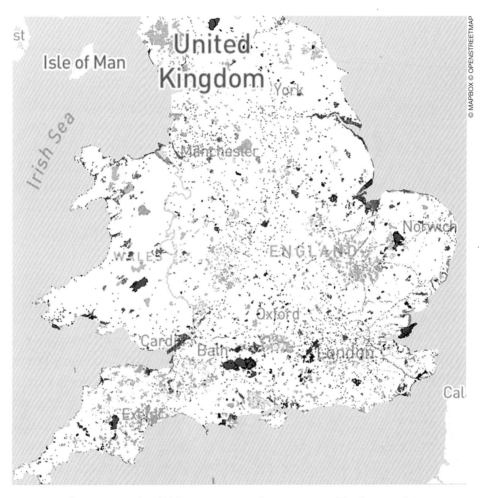

Who owns England? The most comprehensive map of land ownership in England that yet exists. But the secrecy that still surrounds who owns land means it's possible to map only about 10 per cent of the country's landowners. The full, interactive map can be viewed at map.whoownsengland.org. Investigation by Guy Shrubsole, map by Anna Powell-Smith.

The thirty landowners who own nearly half a county. West Berkshire, where I grew up, is a county of huge estates – the largest of which, the Englefield Estate (shown in light blue), is owned by the area's MP, Richard Benyon.

A place for deer, not for people. Richard Benyon MP's deer park, Englefield Estate, West Berkshire, created in the eighteenth century through enclosure and by moving an entire village.

PRIVATE PARK
AUTHORISED ACCESS
ONLY
DOGS MUST BE KEPT ON LEADS

'The most successful direct action in British history.' In April 1932, a group of 400 ramblers staged a mass trespass on the Duke of Devonshire's land, near Kinder Scout in the Dark Peak.

'Since William rose and Harold fell, there have been Earls at Arundel.' Arundel Castle, owned by the Earl of Arundel – who is also Duke of Norfolk – and still lording it over 16,000 acres of Sussex nearly a thousand years since his ancestors first acquired it after the Norman Conquest.

Where the state hunkers down in times of war. 'Kingsway', 200ft below High Holborn in central London, first built as a deep-level bomb shelter for Churchill to retreat to in case of Nazi invasion, later converted into an atom-bomb-proof telephone exchange.

Atmospheric, but lifeless. A typical Forestry Commission pine plantation. The FC's approach to both biodiversity and the amenity value of woodlands has improved in recent decades, but many hillsides remain covered in serried ranks of Sitka spruces.

Like the surface of the moon. A grouse moor in the Peak District. Grouse-moor estates cover half a million acres of England's uplands, an area of land the size of Greater London. The slash-and-burn techniques of intensive grouse-moor management have wrecked the ecosystem, all to satisfy the sporting pleasures of a handful of wealthy aristocrats and City bankers.

An expensive folly. Businessman Nicholas van Hoogstraten's empty mansion in Uckfield, Sussex: still unfinished after thirty years.

Protesters battle for Greenham Common. Nearly a thousand acres
of woods and heathland enclosed by the MOD, Greenham became, in the
1980s, site of ninety-six US nuclear Cruise missiles, and a battleground.

Private – Keep Out. The greeting that ramblers still receive across most of England.
Despite the Right to Roam being introduced in the year 2000, just 10 per cent of
England and Wales is open-access land; 90 per cent remains off-limits to the public.

PRIVATE
NO PUBLIC
RIGHT OF WAY

End empty homes. A protest organised by the Land Justice Network outside a Mayfair mansion that's been empty for fourteen years, and is owned offshore.

Above: 'The Earth must be set free from intanglements of Lords and Landlords, and ... become a common treasury for all.' St George's Hill, birthplace of the Diggers, as it is today: a gated community of offshore-owned mansions. Right: **the Queen's Chapel of the Savoy, heart of the Duchy of Lancaster.** The Duchy has been the monarch's personal estate since 1399.

How corporations often treat the land. A leaking landfill
site at Tilbury in Essex, its contents strewn along the
Thames foreshore; the landfill company has since folded,
and no public authority wants to pick up the mess. Tilbury
coal power station looms in the background.

Whose nation, in whose trust? The White Cliffs of Dover,
property of the National Trust: an emblem of England – but what
do the Trust's choice of properties say about English identity?

National Park, meanwhile, is the mysterious Badgworthy Land Company. It was set up in 1926 by a local hunting syndicate, who snapped up the land to stop it falling into the hands of their arch-nemesis, the League Against Cruel Sports.

The high concentration of private land ownership in our national parks has posed challenges both for conservation and for public access. NPAs are heavily reliant on the goodwill of landowners to implement voluntary estate management plans to conserve the landscapes in their control and properly maintain rights of way. But private landowners naturally want to make a living from their land – whether that's farming, forestry, mining or hunting – and these industries can all too readily come into conflict with nature conservation.

NPAs do have some planning powers which enable them to put the brakes on development within national parks, but these are mostly limited to the built environment and extractive industries. Sir Sebastian Anstruther, for example, one of the major landowners in the South Downs National Park, wanted to dig up 75,000 tonnes of sand every year on his estate, but was dissuaded from doing when his planning application prompted a public outcry. Yet planning constraints within national parks don't prevent Sir Sebastian's neighbour, the Duke of Richmond, from operating a golf course and racecourse on his Goodwood Estate, both of them within the park boundary. And though the planning system reduces landowners' freedom to do whatever they want when it comes to construction projects, it has virtually no control over farming and forestry activities.

Yet as the seminal State of Nature report concluded in 2016, 'the intensive management of agricultural land [has] by far the largest

---

Downe (Danby Estate); Oliver Charles Foster (Egton Estate); the Honourable Fiona Catherine Horton, Sir Josslyn Henry Robert Gore-Booth, and Catherine Mary Wardroper (Whorlton Moor); David Ross, founder of Carphone Warehouse (Westerdale & Rosedale Estates); the North York Moors NPA (Levisham Moor); and the National Trust and Forestry Commission, who own several small sites across the moor.

negative impact on nature, across all habitats and species'. Decades of pesticide spraying and the grubbing up of thousands of miles of hedgerows have taken a terrible toll. A staggering 97 per cent of lowland flower meadows were ploughed up in the decades after the war. Half of all farmland birds in England have disappeared since 1970. Despite such horrifying statistics, intensive farming is still permitted within our national parks, with few questions asked. The International Union for the Conservation of Nature has a ranking system for protected areas worldwide, graded from 1 to 6, with 1 being true wilderness covered by strict protections. Unsurprisingly, all the UK's national parks are classified as Category 5.

As with the National Trust's reasons for buying up so much of the Lake District, landscape conservation rather than ecological preservation lay behind the setting up of the national parks. Still more, however, their origins lie in the grassroots struggle for public access to the countryside. This, too, was a battle over property rights – the rights of people to access the great outdoors, versus the rights of landowners to exclude them.

To Benny Rothman, unemployed and living in the depressed industrial wasteland of 1930s Manchester, 'the only way to enjoy a little fresh air and sunshine was to escape to the countryside'. But the countryside on Rothman's doorstep, the Peak District – the 'lungs of the industrial north' – was under the ownership of the Duke of Devonshire, who used it for grouse shooting. Access to large swathes of it was prohibited under the laws of trespass that had arisen to protect landowners' private property over the centuries. On 24 April 1932, Rothman and a group of 400 ramblers decided to stage a mass trespass on the Duke's land, near Kinder Scout in the Dark Peak. They were met by the Duke's gamekeepers, who, armed with sticks, tried to beat them back. But the trespassers overwhelmed them and pressed on, holding a victory party on the plateau and singing folk songs. The Kinder Scout trespass would ultimately become, in the words of the Labour politician Roy Hattersley, 'the most successful direct action in British history'. Their deeds are still celebrated in song today. *Three Acres and a Cow*, a wonderful travelling show about the history of land rights – founded by the singer and activist Robin Grey – has inspired a new generation with the lyrics of old trespassing folk songs like 'I'm a Rambler'.

Rothman and his fellow trespassers may have been radicals, with Communist Party links and courage that few could muster, but their actions spoke to a far wider yearning for access to the countryside in inter-war England. From the Clarion cycling clubs of the 1890s, through the formation of the Scouts and Woodcraft Folk, to the popular writer S.P.B. Mais leading thousands on a moonlit walk to Chanctonbury Ring, the lure of the outdoors crossed classes and political divides. The Youth Hostels Association and the Ramblers were both founded in the 1930s. But though there had been a string of attempts to pass rights of access legislation since the late nineteenth century, none had yet cleared the fences put in their way by landowning politicians. Kinder Scout dramatised the widespread feeling that, even if the land remained in the ownership of a select few, it should be every citizen's right to walk upon England's mountains green.

After a faltering Access to Mountains Act in 1939, whose enactment was interrupted by the outbreak of war, the post-war Labour government at last passed the 1949 National Parks and Access to the Countryside Act. Besides creating national parks and giving them some measure of protection under the new planning system, the Act also gave fresh powers to councils to map and create rights of way, and to strike agreements with landowners for open-access areas. It was certainly a watershed moment – raising the possibility that trespass might not reign as the unchallenged law of the land for the first time. But it fell far short of the demands of many ramblers for a *right* of open access to all uncultivated land. The land rights campaigner Marion Shoard argued that the access provisions of the 1949 Act proved to be 'one of the most spectacular flops of post-war legislation'. Fifty years after their passage, very few access agreements had been struck between councils and landowners, even in national parks. 'All told,' Shoard estimated, 'land covered by access agreements, orders and acquisition is certainly no more than half of one per cent of the land of the United Kingdom.'

Shoard was a crucial figure in the second wave of movements for public access to land that ultimately bore fruit in the late 1990s. Inspired by her writing, and the resurgent activism of the Ramblers' Association – whose annual 'Forbidden Britain Day' had highlighted glaring instances of land that remained out of bounds – some of New Labour's movers and shakers were converted to the cause of land rights. Chris Smith, then the party's Shadow Environment Minister, told its conference in 1994: 'People have fought for hundreds of years for the right to roam where there is still fresh air and beauty to be enjoyed. We will enshrine that right in law – so that this land can be *our* land – and not just the Duke of Westminster's.'

The exhilarating introduction of a genuine right to roam at last came into existence with New Labour's passing of the Countryside and Rights of Way (CRoW) Act in 2000. Mountains, moorland, downland, commons, heaths and coastlines were all to be opened up for public access, whether landowners liked it or not. It represented a sea-change in how the demands of landowners for the sole and exclusive use of their land were to be balanced against the legitimate rights of the landless to occasionally stretch their legs. Yet as Shoard has pointed out, this right to roam still only covers just 10 per cent of the land of England and Wales. Huge areas remain off-limits. What of woodlands? What of river banks? Why has England settled for so much less than Scotland, where *all* land save cropland and private gardens is now covered by a right to roam? Though the Kinder trespassers' protest proved hugely successful, the achievement of a full right to roam in England remains unfinished business.

So, too, does finding ways to rejuvenate our national parks. Debates about nature conservation within their boundaries have usually ended up focusing on the 'threat' posed by tourists and walkers. While there are some genuine trade-offs between conservation and access – an inevitable increase in litter, disturbance, dogshit and so on – there is at least a process by which to manage this trade-off. The Sandford Principle of

1974 states that where there is conflict between conservation and public enjoyment of a national park, the NPA should prioritise protecting the environment. No such principle or balancing mechanism exists for the demonstrably far greater threat posed to nature by the intensive agriculture that proceeds unchecked within national parks. Seventy years after their creation, and with a fresh government review under way, now is an opportune time to address that imbalance, and bring some wildness back to our national parks.

* * *

My visit to one of England's oldest nature reserves was done unwittingly, without realising I'd be seeing anything out of the ordinary. Wicken Fen in the flat fenlands of Cambridgeshire just looked like a pleasant diversion on a walk I was enjoying one sultry summer's day between Ely and the next train station down the line. Its appearance on the OS map as an oasis of green within the vast white expanses marking agricultural land should have given me a clue. But it was only as I approached its lush reed-lined edges, saw the luxuriant waterlilies floating in the jet-black waters of the drainage channels, and watched the cloud of enormous dragonflies that danced over the water's surface, that I suddenly realised I was looking at something special.

Wicken Fen was acquired by the National Trust in 1899, with some of the first parcels of land donated by one of the founding fathers of British conservation, the financier Charles Rothschild. Today the habitat it conserves is even rarer than when it was founded: 99 per cent of fenland has been lost to arable farming over the past two hundred years.

It was Rothschild who invented the concept of the nature reserve – based on the unarguable notion that 'it is only on land specifically set aside for it that nature comes first'. Of course, landowners had set aside land for *some* forms of nature for centuries: the royal hunting forests of the Norman kings, for instance, or aristocrats' deer parks. But these merely conserved species destined to be shot at and eaten. And the development of poisons, spring-loaded traps and the shotgun

gave the gamekeepers of Victorian landed estates the power to elimi-
nate vast numbers of raptors, pine martens, wildcats and everything
else considered 'vermin'. As the naturalist Richard Perry writes,
between the mid-1800s and the Second World War, 'the survival or
otherwise of Britain's fauna was determined predominantly by the
landed proprietors and their gamekeepers'.

Instead, Rothschild proposed the creation of a set of reserves where
land was left solely for nature, without the selective persecution of
'unwanted' species by landlords. His most extraordinary achievement
was to draw up a list of 284 proposed sites for conservation across
Britain and Ireland, representing the full spectrum of native habitat
types and wildlife hotspots. Rothschild's motivation for doing so was
as much about scientific study as preservation. It was vital, he argued,
to develop a network of reserves for surveying and monitoring –
continuing the work started by amateur naturalists like Gilbert White
over a century before, and honed by Victorian collectors and botanists.

But who could acquire the land necessary for setting up such nature
reserves? At first, Rothschild was an enthusiastic supporter of the
National Trust, joining its council in 1910 in the hope that it would
pursue genuine habitat conservation under the terms of its founding
objectives. Yet when the Trust first purchased Wicken Fen, its management regime 'was for many years scarcely different to any other rural
estate', according to the conservationist and historian Peter Marren,
where 'modern farming and forestry methods that damage wildlife
often went through on the nod'.

Frustrated, Rothschild set up his own organisation, the Society for
the Promotion of Nature Reserves (SPNR), in 1912, and began lobbying
the government to take on the task of acquiring land for nature preservation. But with war looming, the government's interest in land was
squarely fixed on boosting food production. Rothschild's ideas were met
with incomprehension, if not downright derision.

It fell instead to voluntary societies and charities to take on the task
of nature conservation between the wars. Rothschild's SPNR over time

evolved into what today are the Wildlife Trusts, owning and managing a network of around 2,300 nature reserves across the country. The Royal Society for the Protection of Birds (RSPB) began in 1889 as a protest group of middle- and upper-class women against the damaging fashion for rare bird feathers in Victorian hats. It later began acquiring land to set up bird reserves, starting with land on Romney Marsh in 1930. Sites owned or leased by the RSPB across the UK today cover 332,812 acres, of which 127,302 acres are in England: an area of land comparable to that owned, say, by the Duke of Northumberland. Its sites are naturally chosen for their particular significance in terms of bird habitats, with some of the largest being wetland, coastal and estuarine sites: the shingle shorelines of Dungeness, the lagoons of Minsmere in Suffolk, the hauntingly empty Hoo marshes – a landscape immortalised in Dickens's *Great Expectations*.

Land ownership clearly matters for nature conservation. To Peter Marren, 'many a pleasant down or heath would now be a field of rippling wheat or gloomy plantations of spruce if someone had not had the foresight to acquire them with the intention of leaving them as they are.' In his estimation, 'freehold ownership by a conservation body is the safest'. But even Britain's vibrant conservation sector, bolstered by membership in the millions, has struggled to acquire the budgets and land necessary to protect everything that needs protecting. Ecologists concluded that they simply had to persuade the government to intervene, something the state remained reluctant to do, not least because of the sanctity of property rights. To historian Robert Lamb, efforts to create a national network of reserves 'had been stifled time after time by vested land-owning and farming interests at Westminster'.

Perseverance, however, paid off, and in 1949 the same legislation used to set up the first national parks and access agreements also created the first state-designated nature reserves. A new central agency, the Nature Conservancy, was charged with establishing and managing a series of National Nature Reserves (NNRs), staffed with biologists and naturalists. Compared to the Act's provisions for opening up public access to land, the clauses that granted the Conservancy the right to designate and acquire sites for nature reserves excited little controversy among landowners. The sites earmarked for NNRs were small in scale, and considered to be of low economic value; just half a million pounds was set aside to buy land.

Nevertheless, the Nature Conservancy succeeded over the coming years in designating and acquiring a sizeable network of nature reserves, informed in its choice of sites by Rothschild's original list. Today there are 224 NNRs in England covering 233,267 acres, of which around half are owned or leased by the government. Others belong to conservation charities, or in some cases to private bodies: Ashtead Common NNR in Epsom, for example, is owned by the City of London Corporation.

Vital as they remain, National Nature Reserves cover just 0.7 per cent of England. It was recognised from the outset that they could comprise only the central core of official nature conservation in the country, and that other sites of huge scientific and conservation value remained. Accordingly, the Conservancy was given the power to designate additional Sites of Special Scientific Interest (SSSIs or 'triple SIs'). But, astonishing though it seems today, SSSIs originally had no formal protections. A Conservancy official would simply write to a landowner to 'notify' them that their land was of scientific interest, with a sometimes fairly cursory list of the features of note – a community of plants, a suite of lichens, and so on. No restraints were placed on how landowners should treat such sites.

For the first thirty years of their existence, SSSIs were therefore simply lines on a map – and unsurprisingly, large numbers of them were damaged or destroyed by their owners. Mere 'notification' was no protection against the engine of destruction unleashed by post-war mechanised farming. Food production was the overriding priority, bolstered by government subsidies and equipped with an arsenal of artificial fertilisers and bug-blatting pesticides. Thousand-year-old downland fell to the plough; at least 300,000 kilometres of hedgerows were uprooted to make way for ever-larger combine harvesters. The cover of a book written by two environmental campaigners in the early 1980s on the crisis facing the conservation movement captures the widespread despondency. It depicts a landscape laid waste from foreground to horizon by a motorised plough, save only a small patch of wildflowers in the shape of a coffin.

Rising public alarm about the threats to England's countryside was stoked by books like Rachel Carson's *Silent Spring* (1962) and, closer to home, Richard Adams's novel *Watership Down* (1972), in which the rabbits' downland warren is destroyed by developers. A new wave of environmental groups, unafraid of using combative tactics to defend nature, sprang up to challenge the conservatism of the older, landowning conservation bodies. Friends of the Earth's 1980 report, *Paradise Lost*, charted the hundreds of SSSIs that had already been damaged or lost, and demanded proper protections for those remaining.

Fresh legislation to do so began in the dying days of Jim Callaghan's doomed Labour government, and proposed 'a legal responsibility on landowners to ensure proper safeguards over SSSIs on their land as a statutory duty of care.' But when the Conservatives swept into office, three-quarters of the Cabinet were rural landowners. The new Environment Secretary, Michael Heseltine, summoned the head of the RSPB to tell him that 'you are unlikely to find a minister more sympathetic than me.' Yet when it came to actually taking action to protect SSSIs, Heseltine balked, placing great emphasis instead on landowners' beneficence and voluntary action. Even the head of the Nature Conservancy at the time, Sir Ralph Verney, was a Buckinghamshire landowner of ancient lineage who listed his recreational pastime in *Who's Who* as shooting. He meekly accepted the Secretary of State's initial injunction that no further restraints should be placed on private landowners.

But as green NGOs ratcheted up the external pressure, and MPs and civil servants voiced concerns within Whitehall, the government was forced to make crucial concessions. When the Wildlife and Countryside Act eventually made its way onto the statute book in 1981, it obliged

landowners to give advance notice of any 'potentially damaging operations' on an SSSI. The Nature Conservancy was also now empowered
to re-notify the owners of all SSSIs, this time stipulating what activities
they could and could not carry out on their land.

Such effrontery by 'Whitehall bureaucrats' was, of course, a red rag
to some landowners. On the Somerset Levels, outraged farmers burned
effigies of conservationists from a makeshift gallows after West
Sedgemoor was designated a SSSI, and demanded that Sir Ralph Verney
rein in his 'zealots and minions'. The head of the Nature Conservancy
was soon made a political scapegoat and summarily sacked.

Other landowners responded to the new regulations by destroying
the SSSIs on their land before the lengthy re-notification process was
completed. Some farmers ploughed up flower meadows or sprayed
them with weedkiller to make sure they could still use the land for
farming in future, before the screws were tightened. A golf club in
Northamptonshire hired bulldozers to remove the turf and topsoil of
Kingsthorpe Field in order to render it no longer of any scientific
interest. And in Norfolk, a protracted site battle around the newly
designated Halvergate Marshes became what *The Times* called 'the
Flanders of the great war between farming interests and the objectives
of nature conservation'. At issue was the reluctance of local farmers
to desist from draining and ploughing land they owned within the
new SSSI, and the disadvantage this put them at compared to neighbouring farmers who were being paid government subsidies to do the
opposite. Into this fight waded Friends of the Earth's legendary
campaigner Andrew Lees, who organised sit-down protests in front
of farmers' tractors and turned the struggle into a *cause célèbre*. His
intimate knowledge of the landscape once allowed him to gatecrash
a ministerial visit to the area from which he had been excluded, by
navigating the marshy ditches and ambushing them in his waders.

What eventually emerged from these battles was a system of
compensation for landowners that paid them for profits forgone by
not carrying out damaging activities on SSSIs. FOE's Charles Secrett

condemned the inducement as amounting to 'little more than bribes, to compensate landowners for not destroying what had been scientifically determined as our most important wildlife assets'. Some canny landowners exploited the compensation scheme, running rings around the Nature Conservancy and engaging in blatant profiteering.

But it was the price the government was prepared to pay to preserve a still largely voluntary system, and resist growing calls from FOE and others to extend planning controls over farming. Later Acts in 1985 and under the CRoW legislation in 2000 closed some of the loopholes that had allowed farmers to damage SSSIs while they were in the process of notification, and replaced 'ransom payments' for profits forgone with better incentives for positive land management. The Halvergate Marshes became the testing ground for some of the first 'green' farm subsidy payments in Britain, with farmers paid to practise an environmentally benign grazing regime on their land rather than ploughing it up.

The battles over land in the 1980s put the brakes on the wholesale trashing of the country's most important sites for nature. But such victories also shone a light on how much more there was still to do. If even SSSIs were liable to be grubbed up, what hope was there for conserving nature in the rest of the landscape? The episode starkly demonstrated, once again, the power of landowners in resisting measures that interfered with their property rights. And it hints at what still needs to be done to safeguard nature in future.

For over a century, conservation and heritage groups have pursued a strategy of buying up land and property in order to preserve it. The strategy has reaped huge successes – safeguarding hundreds of thousands of acres of beautiful landscapes, giving the public greatly enlarged access to the countryside and a chance to see more of the nation's architectural heritage, and creating thousands of sanctuaries for wildlife.

Yet few environmental groups today – not least landowning charities themselves – would regard this as a sufficient game plan for addressing the ecological crises we face. Even a century ago, when the natural world faced considerably fewer pressures, early ecologists were convinced enough of the threats that they pleaded with the government to use its budgets and influence to set aside land for nature. It's a good job they started the ball rolling so early on, given the resistance and delays they have faced from landowning interests in the decades since. Now many of England's species and natural habitats are experiencing catastrophic decline, and it's clear that safeguarding a few sanctuaries is no longer enough. 'The remaining pockets of habitat are becoming increasingly isolated,' explains the ecologist Hugh Warwick. We need ecosystem-wide measures to save nature, and landowners everywhere must be encouraged, chivvied and pressured into playing their part.

When it comes to land management, voluntarism has reigned for a very long time. UK agriculture generates around 46 million tonnes of greenhouse gas emissions every year – 10 per cent of the UK total – yet farmers and landowners are under no binding obligations to bring these down. Seventy per cent of England is farmland, yet decisions about how this land is best used barely ever come within the ambit of the planning system, where the focus instead is on the built environment. The National Farmers' Union constantly complains about bureaucratic red tape tying up farmers. But history shows that governments have typically remained wary about doing anything at all to infringe the absolute rights of landowners to private property, whether that's around planning, access rights or the operation of SSSIs.

To be sure, there are some inspiring examples of pioneering landowners doing incredible work to safeguard nature voluntarily. The Knepp Estate, owned by Sir Charles Burrell and Isabella Tree, is a 3,500-acre rewilding project deep in the heart of Sussex, whose achievements at restoring lost wildlife have had visiting ecologists waxing lyrical. Free-roaming cattle mimic the extensive grazing patterns of the long-extinct aurochs, creating a mosaic of habitats in which birds and insects thrive: in the space of a decade, Knepp has become the UK's biggest breeding ground for purple emperor butterflies and has 2 per cent of the country's nightingale population. The estate draws income both from 'wildlife safaris' and from selling organic meat, produce of its grazing herds.

If every landowner suddenly followed Knepp's example, we'd have wildlife aplenty. But every sector has its leaders and its stragglers. Rather than rely on voluntary action alone, most industries and interest groups accept common standards that raise ambition over time. Landowners ought to be no different. There are clearly dozens of areas where environmental rules and regulations could be improved, from banning classes of pesticides to promoting soil conservation, so let me instead focus on a few proposals relating particularly to land.

In the 1980s, Marion Shoard, Friends of the Earth and others argued for the extension of the planning system to cover farming and forestry. These sectors had been exempted from the original 1947 Town and Country Planning Act because they were not at that time considered damaging. But as the State of Nature reports have made abundantly clear, intensive agriculture has become the overriding driver of nature's decline in this country. It's time to think again about bringing major decisions over land use into the ambit of planning, and give communities a say over them.

An area of reform already in train, but which needs seeing through to a successful conclusion, is the greening of farm subsidies. DEFRA under Michael Gove has promised to end no-strings-attached subsidies that reward large landowners, and redirect such public money into paying for the provision of public goods – from habitat creation to natural flood measures. But it will be vital to guard against attempts by the Treasury to reduce the overall budget available for doing this, and counter any lobbying by landowners simply wanting money for nothing.

The government should designate a fresh swathe of SSSIs, drawing on lists of sites that have been considered for notification in the past. The conservation charity People Need Nature has proposed that all sites currently classed as 'local wildlife sites' should be given the same level of legal protection as SSSIs.

More broadly, we need to update our notions of landscape beauty so that flourishing ecosystems are prized just as much as chocolate-box views. Seventy years on from their creation, we should review the role of national parks in promoting wilderness, rather than just preserving 'cultural landscapes' denuded by humanity over the past two hundred years.

And looking beyond nature conservation to public access, it's high time England completed the unfinished business of extending right to roam legislation – so that it covers woodland, river banks and ultimately all uncultivated land, as is the case in Scotland.

Lastly, we should learn from the innovative forms of land law that the National Trust has made good use of – the ability to declare land 'inalienable', and the use of restrictive conservation covenants. By accepting obligations about the sustainable use of land in land title deeds themselves, landowners are forced to take on responsibilities alongside rights. It's a potentially powerful way of resetting the social contract between landed and landless, obliging landowners who might otherwise try to make a quick buck from their land to instead look after it for the long term. The Law Commission has recommended introducing a statutory scheme of conservation covenants in England and Wales. Indeed, why not amend the Land Registration Acts and make a basic form of conservation covenant the default setting for all new land titles issued? It could act as a kind of Hippocratic oath for all property owners, prompting them to live up to the public image of landowners as wise stewards of the earth: *whoever owns this land shall leave it in a better state than they found it.*

10

AN AGENDA FOR ENGLISH LAND REFORM

So, who owns England? And what do we do about it?

I started out thinking it might be possible to map England's land-owners as one puts together a jigsaw, one piece at a time. This book has recounted some of that effort: the endless information requests, the geeky analysis of data, the building of maps. But the map is not the territory.

I soon realised that a proper understanding of land ownership in this country can only really come by walking through it; seeing the invisible lines of power within the landscape made corporeal through fences and walls and barbed wire. Trespassing across England, I started to appreciate how the control of land affects the psyche: that feeling of hollowness standing outside an empty mansion; the disgust, as I picked my way over the rubbish lining the Thames next to a company's leaking landfill site; the sense of wonder gazing at butterflies and orchids thriving in a protected nature reserve.

Along the way, the edge-pieces of this giant jigsaw began to click into place. A duke's estate here; an oligarch's house there. But though, step-ping back, the outlines of the picture have started to heave into view, it's also clear how much of the jigsaw remains incomplete, with many pieces missing down the back of the sofa.

Much about land ownership in England remains a mystery. After over two years of investigating the issue, with my collaborator Anna Powell-Smith, the journalist Christian Eriksson and others, the secrecy that persists around who owns land means we still can't arrive at a definitive answer. The Land Registry, despite being a public body funded by taxpayers' money, continues to protect the interests of private land-owners by concealing what they possess. A social taboo continues to stymie questions about land and private property ownership, and makes talk of land reform politically sensitive.

But we now know much more than we did before. We know, pretty clearly, who owns around a third of England and Wales, thanks to the Land Registry being forced to release data on corporate and commercial landowners. Yet maddening deficiencies in the way the information has been published means we can only accurately map the owners of about 10 per cent of our land. It remains very difficult, too, to separate out figures on land ownership by nation. Most frustratingly of all, the Land Registry still refuses to reveal the owners of the other two-thirds of England and Wales – the wealthy aristocrats and businesspeople whose possessions remain conveniently shielded from public view.

Careful investigation and number-crunching can, however, take us closer to the overall picture. In some cases, the state of the data means we can only hazard a guess at the truth. But with that caveat, let me set out my best estimate of who owns England.

Who owns England: the summary figures

Let's start with the landowning sectors where we can have greatest confidence in the figures. The public sector – central and local government, and universities – has tended to be the most open about the land it owns. Central government has also been willing to voluntarily release information about the size of its estate in recent years, though partly in order to flog it off.

Careful crunching of data obtained from FOI requests and published maps (see Chapter 6) leads me to conclude that the public sector – central government, councils, and the Oxbridge colleges – together own 2.7 million acres of England, or 8.5 per cent of the country. Many of these bodies also own and lease additional land in Wales, Scotland and Northern Ireland; a full breakdown and sources can be found in the Appendix.

The traditional 'Establishment' bodies – the Crown and the Church of England – have not been nearly so forthcoming about the extent and nature of their landholdings. But it's possible to say that the Church Commissioners and Anglican dioceses together own around 175,000 acres, or 0.5 per cent of England. And totting up the English acreages of the Crown Estate, the Duchies of Cornwall and Lancaster, and the Queen's personal estate at Sandringham, gives a total for Crown land of 456,482 acres, or 1.4 per cent of England. This figure would almost double if you included the Crown's ownership of large stretches of foreshore and estuaries, but these semi-submerged lands aren't usually counted in measurements of England's extent. Again, sources are given in the Appendix.

Conservation charities, with their vast memberships and public accountability, are generally very transparent about the land they own. By my reckoning, the National Trust, RSPB and Woodland Trust own almost a million acres of England and Wales, or 636,000 acres if you look at England alone – 2 per cent of the country.

So, that means the public sector, Crown, Church and conservation groups together own almost 4 million acres, or around 12.4 per cent of England. The other 88 per cent of the country, therefore, must be in private ownership, belonging to companies, individuals, charities and trusts.

This is where things get trickier – particularly if we want to break down the available figures for England only.

It's possible to say with some certainty, thanks to Land Registry data released following FOI requests by the journalist Christian Eriksson, that limited companies and limited liability partnerships – both those registered in the UK and those based overseas or offshore – own 6.6 million acres, or 18 per cent of England and Wales. But it's currently impossible to break down this total between the two nations, because the Land Registry – which covers both England and Wales – refuses to release maps of the land, or any data that would allow us to assign acreages to location. As things stand, the best we can do is assume the acreage owned is split proportionately between England and Wales, and stick with an estimate that corporations own 18 per cent of England. The 100 largest landowning companies are listed in the Appendix.

What about individuals? After all, don't we now live in a 'property-owning democracy', as politicians keep telling us?

At one end of the spectrum, the bulk of the population in fact owns very little land – or none at all. While the majority of people now own a home, homeowners' share of England only amounts to about 5 per cent of the land. Yet for many, even the prospect of homeownership is now a distant dream, with millions struggling to get onto the first rung of the property ladder.

A select few, however, have acquired the cash needed to buy their way into the ranks of major landowners. The handful of newly moneyed industrialists, oligarchs and City bankers profiled in this book own around 250,000 acres between them in England (or 600,000 acres if you take into account their Scottish estates). These, however, are only a snapshot of a broader – though still extremely small – segment of high society. One estimate puts the overall total area of land owned by 'new money' at around 17 per cent of the country.

But in the end, it's old money that still lords it over the rest of us, at least when it comes to land ownership. I estimate that the aristocracy and gentry still own around 30 per cent of England. This is based on others' estimates, historical surveys, and the declarations of landowning bodies like the Country Land and Business Association. The outright refusal of the Land Registry to release information on land owned by individuals or trusts, however, makes it very difficult to be more specific. It's proven feasible to investigate the landholdings of the uppermost echelons of the aristocracy, whose numbers are small and whose lands remain vast; but painting a comprehensive picture of what is owned by all 2,000 peers and baronets, let alone the broader ranks of the gentry, remains a formidable task. But on this, I am sure: a few thousand dukes, baronets and country squires own far more land than all of Middle England put together.

Adding all these figures together accounts for around 82 per cent of England. By coincidence, the Land Registry is still only around 83 per cent complete – 17 per cent of England and Wales remains unregistered, of unknown ownership. The most likely owners of these 'missing acres'

Landowner	Percentage of England
Crown	1.4%
Church	0.5%
Public sector	8.5%
Conservation charities	2%
Companies & LLPs (UK and overseas)	18%
Aristocracy & gentry	30%
New money	17%
Homeowners	5%
TOTAL	82.4%
Unaccounted for	c.17%

Figure 3: Who owns England? My estimates. Full table with sources in Appendix.

are the aristocracy, many of whose lands have remained in the same families for centuries, and which consequently may never have undergone a market transaction that would have seen them registered. Or it may be that this unregistered land actually belongs to a wide range of individuals and organisations, from councils who've never got around to registering what they own properly, to unclaimed estates now taken over by the Crown under the custom of *bona vacantia*.

The scale of inequality in land ownership

Looked at another way, the inequality of land ownership in England is even starker. There are no official statistics on how concentrated land ownership is in England – even though the Land Registry could easily compile them if it wanted to. But a good proxy dataset is the Department for the Environment's annual farm survey. This tells us how many farms there are in England, how many fall into different size categories – between 50 and 100 acres, say, or bigger than 250 acres – and how much land is farmed by small, medium and large farmholdings. Many farms, of course, are part of larger estates whose owners rent them out to tenant farmers – so counting the number of farms in England will actually overestimate the number of landowners. But crunching the numbers, we can see that a small set of large farms utterly dominate the countryside.

The figures are staggering: we can conclude from them that 25,000 landowners – far less than 1 per cent of the population – own half of England. Nor is this just an issue with farmland. We can see from looking at central London, for example (see Chapter 4), that huge swathes of prime real estate lies in the hands of a very few 'Great Estates'. Or we can point to the fact that just thirty landowners own nearly half of West Berkshire (Chapter 1), or that fifteen landowners own almost all the moorland in the North York Moors (Chapter 9). Land ownership in England is astonishingly unequal, heavily concentrated in the hands of a tiny elite.

Perhaps worse is how little has changed over the centuries. At the time of the Domesday Book in 1086, some 200 Norman barons owned half of England. Thanks to the miracle of trickle-down economics, that elite expanded over time – so that a mere eight centuries later, half of England lay in the hands of 4,000 aristocrats and members of the gentry. It's certainly the case that the aristocracy subsequently declined from their late-Victorian heyday. For a while, between the 1920s and the 1970s, there was greater equality of land ownership in England as some of the old estates were broken up and a new generation of tenant farmers were able to buy their own farms. Redistribution of wealth by successive governments was partially mirrored in the redistribution of land through the expansion of county farms, allotments and council housing. But throughout all this, the landed aristocracy survived to a far greater extent than is commonly realised. From the 1970s onwards, they were joined by a newly minted plutocracy who today are keeping up the landowning traditions of a territorial elite.

Why unequal land ownership is a problem

Land remains the bedrock of our economy. Trade Secretary Liam Fox likes to claim that we now live in a 'post-geography' world, but this is arrant nonsense. We need land to grow our food, build our homes, and provide space for the ecosystems that clean our air and provide us with fresh water. In England, roughly speaking, we devote 10 per cent of our land to towns and cities and 70 per cent to farming, with 20 per cent left over for nature.

But any discussion about how best to use our land is inherently skewed by the grossly unequal pattern of land ownership. Imagine inviting 100 people to a birthday party. Then, when you get to the stage of cutting up the birthday cake, one of the guests steps forward to announce that half the cake is already theirs – and not only are they having their cake, they're eating it too. How different is this, really, from the numerous 'stakeholder meetings' that civil servants hold about how best to use our land, day in, day out? Invariably, the attendees and lobbyists at such events – the CLA, the NFU and so on – represent 'landowning interests'. They have every right to be heard, but they represent a tiny fraction of the population – the 1 per cent who own half the land deciding how to use a common resource that everyone depends on. The same is often true of the notionally democratic planning process – skewed by landowners and developers with options on land, who can afford the consultants to bludgeon cash-strapped, beleaguered councils into accepting their proposals.

The present unequal concentration of land ownership, moreover, is the sanitised end-result of a history drenched in blood. It's a social and economic hierarchy first established through the land grab instigated a thousand years ago by William the Conqueror, who doled out the spoils of conquest to his barons – a surprising number of whose descendants remain major landowners today. Aristocrats were able to pass on their landholdings intact by adopting the sexist, feudal practice of male primogeniture; many added to their estates by stealing common land from the peasantry and getting rich from the slave trade. The passage of time has cloaked these crimes, but they ought to weigh heavily on today's large landowners when considering their social responsibilities.

To those who own it, land often confers huge unearned benefits. The location value of land is generated by the community who live and labour on it, and by public investment in transport and amenities – yet it's the landowner who reaps the resulting unearned increase in land prices and property rents. The Duke of Westminster's Mayfair estate, for instance, started out 300 years ago as marshy fields. It would still be marshy fields today if it hadn't been for the expansion of London – the toil of millions of people congregating together to make the capital a desirable and fashionable place to live and work, replete with publicly funded roads, Tube stops, hospitals and schools. Now, a property in Mayfair is worth £21,000 per square metre. Is it really too much to ask landowners to give a little of this collectively generated wealth back to the community in some way?

And yet, landowners have always ferociously lobbied to preserve their privileges and resist any infringement of their absolute private property rights over land. Landowners, for instance, lobbied hard to exclude farming and forestry from being included within the planning system when it was first set up, ensuring it remained focused on urban land use decisions. Landowners clubbed together to abolish the country's only attempt at levying a land value tax a century ago, and overcame all subsequent attempts by progressive governments to put in place development charges on land. Landowners successfully campaigned to exempt agricultural land from council tax in the 1920s, and from inheritance tax in the 1980s. For centuries, landowners have made use of trespass laws to deter and prosecute anyone who dares stray across their land, and bitterly resisted more recent efforts to open up access to the countryside. Some landowners in the 1980s, faced with the prospect of having to moderate their damaging land use practices or be reprimanded under a new set of protections for Sites of Special Scientific Interest (see Chapter 9), even opted to destroy the nature reserves on their land rather than face curtailment of their freedoms.

Enough is enough. Land is a common good and ought to be treated as such – used carefully, for the good of everyone, and protected for the long term. If we're going to make better use of our land, however, we have to grapple with ownership. And to do that, England needs a programme of land reform.

An agenda for English land reform

It's time for a serious political debate about land reform in England.

We face a housing crisis of generational significance; a collapse in species and natural habitats; a farming sector facing huge challenges over Brexit; and spiralling inequality. Land reform is central to all of these challenges.

There's a huge amount we can learn from other countries who have undergone successful land reform programmes – not least Scotland, whose land movement has flowered in the last twenty years. In Scotland, access to the land has been opened up to the public; island communities have revived themselves for the first time since the Clearances as a result of community buy-out legislation; and steps are being taken towards addressing the sky-high land values that are driving the housing crisis. But we can also look to England's own history of land reform and land reform movements – a radical past that's often forgotten, or conveniently buried. And we can look to the nascent movement for land reform that exists in England today: the housing activists, land workers, community food growers, ramblers, cyclists, environmentalists, students, homelessness charities and many others, of all political stripes, who have seen that the route to a better future lies in uniting around the common issue of land.

What follows is a suggested agenda for land reform in England: a set of ten demands that, I propose, would help fix many of the problems with how land is owned, used and abused in this country. Most of these proposals have been inspired by conversations with other campaigners in England's growing land-reform movement, or are ideas that already have common currency. They are far from being an exhaustive list; there are many more good proposals out there that I simply didn't have space to include. By all means, disagree with them. You may think them too moderate, or too radical, or simply unworkable. All I ask is that you come up with better solutions, and push for those instead. Because one thing is clear – simply talking about the policies needed is never sufficient to win. To become a reality, land reform in England will need to be campaigned for, vociferously and tirelessly.

Two overarching proposals frame my more detailed suggestions. First, we need a Land Reform Act for England. This would encompass some or all of the proposals I make below, and should be a flagship piece of legislation for any reforming government seeking to resolve the housing, farming and nature crises that we face. Second, we need a Land

Commission for England, following the excellent example of the Scottish Land Commission, which was set up in 2017. Like its Scottish cousin, it would be a public body tasked with investigating and reporting on all manner of issues relating to land and land reform. An English Land Commission would be an important institution for generating informed public debate about how we use and share out land in England, and carefully thinking through some of the most complex and contentious aspects of land reform.

But many big steps towards land reform in England need not wait. There's plenty we can be getting on with and campaigning for straight away. Here, then, are my ten proposals for land reform in England.

1. End the secrecy around land ownership – tell us who owns England

It's time to lift the veil of secrecy that has cloaked who owns land in this country for too long.

Other countries deal with this so much better. It's only really England that nurses its particular emotional hang-up over land ownership. In France, you can go into your local town hall and ask to see the *cadastre*, the set of maps showing who owns land in your neighbourhood. Denmark has had a national cadastral map since 1844, which today is fully digitised, and updated daily. The US began surveying and parcelling up land shortly after the War of Independence, to redistribute land to American soldiers as a reward for their service. The state of Montana has put all its land ownership maps online for free: zoom in and click on a land parcel, and you can see the owner, the value of the land and whether it's used for forestry, farming or housing. New Zealand, meanwhile, has an almost comprehensive digital record of who owns it, and allows anyone to download the data for free.

It's time England got to grips with this too. The government must open up and complete the Land Registry. That means, first, dropping the fees that prevent people seeing the full picture of who owns England.

The Land Registry has already conceded the principle of releasing free datasets of what's owned by companies and corporate bodies – now it should extend that to cover land owned by individuals.

To assuage legitimate concerns about invasion of privacy, any free data release of land owned by individuals could exclude residential properties. There seems no serious reason, however, why the same courtesy should be extended to the extensive personal estates of dukes and earls, or those vested in trusts. Opening up the Land Registry is about shining a light on the great mass of land owned by the aristocracy and wealthy businesspeople.

But the Land Registry also remains incomplete, despite 160 years of operation. It needs to be finally completed, and soon: the organisation's own aspirational target of completing its work by 2030 is far too late. One way of speeding up the process would be to mandate that any landowner in receipt of public farm subsidies must register their land. Better still, the government should use the opportunity of the next census in 2021 to carry out a modern Domesday Survey of all land ownership.

The opening up of data could shed light on dark corners in other ways, too. The government has finally relented to pressure and ordered all British Overseas Territories to publish proper company registers that reveal the ultimate owners of firms. Anyone wanting to dodge taxes or launder money by buying up UK property and registering it to a company in the Cayman Islands will find it much harder to hide from public scrutiny in future. But there's also much more that could be done to improve transparency at home. We need a public register of trusts – of the kind used by many members of the aristocracy in which to vest their landed estates – to expose this ancient, home-grown form of legal tax avoidance. We need a public register of options on land, to address land banking and property speculation, by revealing currently hidden agreements between landowners and developers. And we need greater transparency around the planning system, with better online maps matching up land ownership, options and planning permissions, so the public can see who benefits from the planning process, and better engage with it themselves.

2. Fix the housing crisis: stop landowners hoarding land and leaving homes empty

At its heart, the housing crisis is a land crisis. The real cost of a house isn't the bricks and mortar, but the land underlying it – and land prices have spiralled upwards 400 per cent since 1995. Politicians can talk all they like about building more homes, or slashing planning regulations to free up developers. But fail to tackle sky-high land prices, and all you'll end up with is a bunch more unaffordable houses.

Housing developers are often accused of land banking to bolster their profits, but in reality all landowners have a propensity to hoard land – and to demand as high a price as they can get when they come to selling it.

Over the past 150 years, the government has negotiated the right to compulsorily purchase land when it's deemed in the national interest to do so – from allowing companies to obtain land for the first railways, to acquiring military training grounds during the Second World War. Compulsory purchase is often attacked as Stalinist by its free-market detractors – and this book hasn't shied away from examining times when the state's acquisition of land has gone badly wrong, as in the case of Tyneham, the village requisitioned by the MOD and never returned. But in a democratic, rules-based society, there are two vital constraints on compulsory purchase. One is the planning system. The other is the principle that landowners will always, rightly, be fairly compensated for land acquired under compulsory purchase. The question is what constitutes fair compensation.

The homes built between Attlee's post-war Labour government and the start of the 1960s were not only built under the modern planning system – that bugbear of neoliberal think tanks today, who decry it as the source of the housing crisis; they were also built under a set of land compensation rules that let local authorities buy land much more cheaply than they can today. Where land was acquired compulsorily, landowners were fairly compensated, but at prices close to the existing agricultural use value of their land – rather than with the 'hope value' of future development baked in. That system lasted until lobbying by landowners persuaded the government to revert to full market prices (see Chapter 8) – after which, land prices began their inexorable and continuing rise.

It's time for a rethink. Faced with a housing crisis of national and generational significance, it's time to give councils the power to buy land cheaply again so that they can build more affordable housing. A rising chorus of voices from across the political spectrum agree: from housing charity Shelter to the conservation group CPRE; from think tanks on the left, such as IPPR and the New Economics Foundation, to those on the right, like Civitas, the Centre for Policy Studies and Onward. The idea was even hinted at in the Conservative Party's 2017 General Election manifesto. Any political party that wants to solve the housing crisis has to grapple, sooner or later, with how to deal with high land prices. And any party that fails to do so will surely face the wrath of Generation Rent at the polls.

We also have to end the national scandal of empty homes. This, too, is partly a function of the broken land market, where rocketing prices have encouraged the wealthy to treat housing as an asset rather than as a place in which to live. The 60,000 homes across the UK left empty by their owners for more than two years – a waste of land even if there were no housing crisis – are an obscenity when thousands sleep rough on our streets. The government should hit long-term vacant properties with a 300 per cent hike in council tax. Theresa May's government has already accepted the principle of doing so, and increased the surcharge from 50 per cent to 100 per cent. But at current levels, it's unlikely to do much to discourage the wealthy, offshore owners who leave them empty. If a 300 per cent council tax premium on empty homes still proves too low, why not do as Boris Johnson suggested when he was Mayor of London, and raise the rate to 1,000 per cent?

Beyond these two measures, the English Land Commission should be tasked with reporting on the best form of land value tax to levy in England. Land value tax is often proposed by land activists as a solution to the housing crisis – indeed, to some devotees of the thinker Henry George, land value tax is a silver bullet solution to *all* our woes. I don't agree, though I do think it's a proposal that has many merits. But the devil is in the detail. Do you just change business rates to reflect land values, for instance – or go the whole hog by abolishing council tax in favour of a land value tax on residential properties? And what would be the social ramifications of doing so – not to mention the political risks if it were designed in the wrong way? Part of the reason why there's been no attempt at implementing a land value tax for decades is because there's been no serious political discussion about one. When Labour's 2017 manifesto dared to even hint at exploring land value taxation, it was jumped on by the Conservatives, who slammed it as a 'garden tax'. My proposal would be to open up the political space for a grown-up debate about land value taxes via the new Land Commission, armed with the data and resources needed to model different scenarios and make a clear recommendation.

3. Fix our farming system: stop handouts to wealthy landowners simply for owning land, and farm in harmony with nature

One of the many ways in which land ownership is currently rewarded is through our present system of public farm subsidies, which effectively gives large landowners a hand-out for simply owning land. Every year, hundreds of millions of pounds of taxpayers' money is paid out to farmers and landowners in the form of area-based payments, with minimal strings attached. The larger your estate, the more money you tend to get.

Meanwhile, smallholders with a farm of less than 12 acres are excluded from receiving payments, on the pretence that dealing with lots of small claims would be a waste of public money – as if no-strings handouts to wealthy landowners weren't already a far larger waste of public money.

Brexit provides the opportunity to radically reform this system of farm payments as we leave the EU's common agricultural policy. First, the Government should cap area-based farm subsidies at a maximum of £100,000 per landowner annually. After all, it has already legislated for a benefits cap of £20k – so capping state hand-outs to landowners at five times what poor households are permitted is already more than they deserve. Environment Secretary Michael Gove has hinted that he's prepared to implement such a cap, as part of a transition to a new system of payments, but has come under pressure from the Country Land & Business Association to reverse course. He should resist such vested interests and press ahead. With the spare funds freed up by such a cap, the government should restore payments to smallholders.

Second, the whole system of farm payments needs to be radically overhauled from being area-based, with few questions asked, to one of paying out public money in return for public goods. That means land-owners being paid to invest in things like environmental protection, natural flood measures such as tree-planting and blanket bog restoration, and agro-ecological forms of farming.

Incentives for best practice are all well and good, but how to deter bad behaviour, and the short-termist abuse of land? After all, it wasn't long ago that landowners were ripping out hedgerows and even destroying nature reserves in the pursuit of profits. The destruction nowadays may be less blatant, but the rot is more insidious: decades of pesticide overuse and intensified agriculture has damaged soil structures and decimated our wildlife. Scientists are clear that agriculture is the main driver of species loss in Britain today.

We have a mechanism for deciding how to constrain urban sprawl; it's called the planning system. But ever since the Town and Country Planning Act was introduced in 1947, landowners have vociferously resisted extending its remit to cover farming and forestry operations. In the 1980s, amid mounting evidence that intensive agriculture had displaced urban sprawl as the driver of environmental destruction, campaigner Marion Shoard proposed applying planning 'to the task of rescuing our land-scape'. Today, it's time to reopen that debate. A future Land Commission should consider whether major changes in rural land use should become subject to planning decisions – for example, the conversion of ancient pasture to arable, the felling of woodland, or the drainage of wetland to grow crops. After all, it takes centuries for a species-rich flower meadow to grow, but an afternoon to plough it up. Why shouldn't such dramatic changes be subject to some democratic oversight?

4. Restore nature's abundance: end unsustainable land uses like grouse shooting, and bring wilderness back to our uplands

Fixing our unsustainable, pesticide-drenched farming system is the main way to reverse the catastrophic decline in English wildlife. But if we want to free up large tracts of land for wild nature, it makes sense to do so in areas of sparse population, and where agricultural productivity is low. That makes the English uplands a prime candidate. And yet currently half a million acres of upland England are subjected to the ravages of intensive grouse-moor management. By turning an area of land the size of Greater London into a glorified upland chicken run, a few landowners have had a disproportionate impact on the natural world, and on the communities living nearby. Burning the moorland heather to increase grouse numbers dried out the underlying peat, releasing climate-changing greenhouse gases, and destroying the natural ability of the soils to resist wildfires in summer and floods in winter. Yet grouse-moor estates remain buttressed by millions of pounds of public farm subsidies.

The government should end taxpayer hand-outs to the owners of grouse moors, ban the burning of blanket bog and outlaw grouse shooting. It's a nineteenth-century practice in a twenty-first-century world – popularised by Queen Victoria, taken up by dukes and earls keen to copy royal fashions, and imitated today by City boys who enjoy playing at being toffs. But in a world beset by climate change, where wildfires and flash floods strike with ever-increasing frequency, it's no way to be treating a vast swathe of our uplands.

Of course, grouse-moor owners – many of whom are Conservative donors and members of the House of Lords – continue to hold considerable sway over the policies of Conservative governments. A few years ago, a 100,000-signatory petition to ban driven grouse shooting, started by respected ornithologist Mark Avery, drew frenzied opposition from landowners and their friends in the Commons. I've no doubt that an outright ban is some way off, perhaps awaiting a change in government. In the meantime, enlightened aristocrats could do nature and the public a favour by voluntarily ending grouse shoots on their estates and taking up the challenge of rewilding England's degraded uplands. Fashions, after all, change with the times. Rather than persist with Victorian bloodsports – or that staple of 1950s aristocratic nostalgia for Empire, stately homes with safari parks – there is much more to be gained nowadays by rewilding your landed estate and opening it up for eco-tourism, as the Knepp Estate in Sussex has done so successfully. Aristocratic patronage in the eighteenth century allowed Capability Brown to create half a million acres of beautiful landscaped parkland. Will today's lords and ladies rise to the ecological challenges we face, and let wild nature roam free again over their vast lands?

I'm doubtful that voluntary action by a few benevolent landowners will be sufficient to reverse the tide of destruction, so we also need the public sector to step up to the plate. One clear way it can do so is by bringing more wild nature into our national parks.

As Chapter 9 showed, national parks are not, in fact, owned by the nation – rather, the vast majority of them are owned by private landowners – but National Park Authorities and central government do have ways of influencing land use within them. Professor Alasdair Driver has proposed creating 'designated wild areas' within National Parks that, in the uplands, 'equate to 10–50% of the park area'. We may not be able to aspire to the large-scale wilderness that characterises national parks in the US, Driver reasons, but he is 'certain we can achieve a better balance overall between those areas where natural processes prevail, and those where intensive management dominates.'

A second way the government can restore ecological processes throughout our landscapes is by designating more Sites of Special Scientific Interest. Conservationist Miles King argues that there are hundreds of places across England that merit such a designation, but which government regulators have shied away from protecting, knowing the fuss this would generate among landowners. Over a hundred years after Charles Rothschild drew up his list of sites deserving of protection, it's time to complete the network and create the space for nature to recover.

5. Abolish the last vestiges of feudalism in our system of land ownership

It might seem bizarre to be demanding an end to feudalism in the twenty-first century – but that's England for you, I'm afraid. England's an old country, and large parts of it continue to live in the past. As I've seen clearly on my hikes and trespasses around the country, there are whole villages owned by estates where deference to the lord of the manor seems alive and well, and constituencies – like West Berkshire, where I grew up – that still send the largest local landowner to Parliament. In some places, feudalism has never died.

For one thing, we should end the archaic, sexist practice of male primogeniture within the aristocracy. In the age of #MeToo and resurgent feminism, it's a scandal that England's largest landowners can get away with excluding women from inheriting land and titles from their fathers. The Crown changed its own sexist rules of succession back in 2015 – although with Prince Charles, Prince William and Prince George next in line to the throne, we look set to be ruled by male monarchs for some time to come. Yet there are hundreds of female aristocrats who will lose out on inheritances in favour of their younger brothers. 'The buildings and countryside of England are the very lifeblood of my being, and I feel very, very strongly about it,' argues Lady Lucinda Lambton, whose father's estate and titles will pass to her brother. 'So yes, I do mind not inheriting.'

Of course, fixing this feudal anachronism would only bring a modicum of equality to what is an inherently elitist institution. To go further, I would task a future Land Commission with considering changing the laws on inherited lands and titles back to the older and more equitable tradition of gavelkind. Reintroducing *gavelkind* as the default law of the land would be controversial and require careful consultation, but it would certainly break up the large landed estates within a few generations.

An alternative way of sharing out the proceeds from inherited landed estates more broadly with the rest of society is by closing the loopholes used by large landowners to avoid inheritance tax. Some of this would be impossible without addressing the complex thicket of family trusts that the aristocracy have developed for vesting their estates in; hence my earlier suggestion of a public register of trusts. But any willing Chancellor of the Exchequer could go some way to clawing back lost inheritance tax receipts by ending the tax-exempt status of agricultural land. To protect small farmers and family farms, an area threshold could be brought in to keep the exemption in place for smallholdings.

There are few larger inheritances than those inherited by the monarch and the heir to the throne – and none that so starkly demonstrate the persistence of feudalism in modern England. The Government should abolish the Duchies of Cornwall and Lancaster and merge their lands with those of the Crown Estate. The Duchies are medieval anachronisms that serve no purpose in the modern age beyond being additional moneyspinners for the Queen and Prince of Wales. They are unaccountable, opaque anomalies that avoid proper parliamentary and public scrutiny and dodge corporation tax, yet still swallow public subsidies. Merging them with the Crown Estate would still allow them to be efficiently and sustainably managed, while also contributing to the public purse. It would then be up to MPs whether to vote to use this extra income to spend on schools, hospitals and public services, or whether to increase the size of the (already generous) Sovereign Grant (see Chapter 3) that pays for the public and private expenditure of the Royal Household.

The Church, that other pillar of the English establishment, has some questions to answer, too, about how it's mismanaged its extensive land-holdings. Parliament's Public Accounts Committee should hold an inquiry into the Church's sell-off of glebe lands, and how it intends to use its remaining land to provide more affordable housing. With the Archbishop of Canterbury professing his keenness for the Church to use its land to help fix the housing crisis, taking part in such an inquiry is surely the least it can do.

6. Curb the ways that corporate capitalism uses land to avoid tax and abuses it for short-term profit

As Chapter 7 explored, the ways in which companies use and abuse land are manifold – some necessary and uncontentious; some downright dodgy. And as Chapter 5 related, the fact that large chunks of England have been bought up by the newly wealthy can be seen as evidence of entrenched, aristocratic privilege crumbling in the face of the market. But when corporations and wealthy individuals, seeking ever-higher returns, start treating land and housing as assets – and start using complex offshore structures to avoid tax, and launder dirty money through the UK property market – then you start to get problems.

Some of this can be resolved by improving transparency and reporting, as discussed in my first recommendation above. Corporate capitalism's propensity to treat homes as assets and leave them empty is also addressed in earlier proposals, while pressuring landowners to steward their land for the long term, rather than for quarterly profit margins, is something I deal with in my final recommendation below.

But all this would be made a lot easier if we simply banned companies and trusts registered in offshore tax havens from owning land and property in England.

Implementing such a ban wouldn't stop non-British nationals from owning land in this country; they'd just have to do so, reasonably, through companies registered in the UK or other normal tax jurisdictions, rather than tax havens. Indeed, the biggest impact would likely be on those British aristocrats and businesspeople who pioneered the use of offshore ownership in the first place. But banning the offshore ownership of land and property would mean greater transparency, far less scope for money laundering, and more people paying their taxes. Brexiteers played upon fears of immigration and campaigned to end freedom of movement – but it's the freedom of capital to do whatsoever it pleases that's the real problem.

7. Stop the fire sale of public sector land and property

The enclosure of the commons by aristocrats and gentry robbed the public of millions of acres of land, dismantling the medieval 'welfare state' that allowed the poor and hungry to live off the fruits of nature. When this outrageous land grab was finally halted in the late Victorian period, some sought to make amends for the theft of common land by pressuring government to provide land for the people, through initiatives like council housing, allotments and County Farms.

Over the last forty years, huge amounts of publicly owned land have been taken away from us. Waves of privatisation and austerity have disposed of public sector assets and pared local government to the bone – what academic Brett Christophers calls the 'new enclosure'.

Neoliberal politicians' ideological commitment to shrinking the state has led to public sector land being viewed as an asset that must be liquidated for maximum returns, rather than taking a longer-term view on the true value of the land. A more sensible approach to managing public land would surely be to factor in its wider environmental and social value when deciding how best to use it, and whether to dispose of it at all.

We need a new screening process to put the brakes on public land being flogged off, forcing officials to factor in the full social, economic and environmental value of the land in question. The New Economics Foundation suggests that government should become far more open to keeping land in public ownership but leasing it out, thereby generating income for the public purse but retaining the valuable freehold. Gwyn Williams at RSPB points out that when the water utilities were privatised back in the 1980s, the government included a legislative lock on the subsequent disposal of water company land – much of which includes nature-rich SSSIs. If one of the newly privatised water companies wanted to sell off some land, it had to consult Natural England – the government's conservation regulator – who could place restrictions on future use, and even organise a 'sponsored sale', giving first dibs to conservation charities to acquire the land. This provision seems to have been mostly forgotten in practice, but reviving it and applying it to all public sector land could be a good way to halt the fire sale, and more sensibly manage how public land is best used for the long term.

One area where the frittering away of public land is causing particular harm is the ongoing sale of county farms (see Chapter 8), whose extent has *halved* in the last four decades. We must stop the sell-off of the county farms estate, and protect them from future asset-stripping with a ministerial lock on sales. Councils have to get approval from ministers before selling off statutory allotments, and there are rules on schools disposing of playing fields – so why not extend this principle to county farms?

The 200,000-acre county farms estate is, after all, the legacy of England's last, forgotten era of land reform. By protecting and rejuvenating county farms, we could make them beacons of sustainable smallholding practice, trialling nature-friendly forms of farming and producing fresh food for nearby schools, hospitals and councils keen to adopt the 'Preston model' of local procurement. They could become a vital way to reacquaint people with where their food comes from – hosting open days, school visits, and local residents prescribed a dose of healthy outdoor exercise by their GPs. We may not all be able to own three acres and a cow, but a revived County Farms estate could reconnect many more people to the land.

8. Give people a stake in the country and let communities take back control of local land

One of England's buried pieces of radical legislation is everyone's statutory right to an allotment. It may not sound like much, but when you think about it, a legal right to demand land on which to grow your food is a revolutionary idea. It goes against both feudal and capitalist forms of land ownership, harking back to the ancient, egalitarian concept of the commons as a place where communities could gain their sustenance.

Allotments remain hugely popular today – and yet we have let this icon of English land reform languish. We devote ten times more land to golf courses nowadays than we do to allotments. And cash-strapped councils have tried to break free of their obligation to provide allotment sites by stalling for years, claiming there's no land available locally and leaving tens of thousands of people waiting for allotment plots.

We need to give people a stake in the land by strengthening everyone's statutory right to an allotment. Not only do allotments give people the chance to grow their own fresh food, have contact with nature, and socialise with other allotmenteers; they're also a way of giving people a sense of belonging, a patch of earth to cultivate and call their own. The Allotments Acts should be amended to cut waiting list time to a maximum of one year. If councils are allowed to buy land cheaply again (see proposal 2, above), local authorities will find it less of a drain on their budgets to acquire sites for allotments.

In London, a special case where food-growing space is physically constrained by the density of development, a more creative solution is called for. We need to make London's Green Belt better serve the city's inhabitants, by using more of it for community food growing and for nature. Currently, too much of the Green Belt is a welter of golf courses and land banks owned by shadowy firms. Free marketeers argue that we simply need to tear up the Green Belt and build housing on it. But quite apart from the massive urban sprawl and congestion this would generate, it would do little on its own to address the housing crisis – since land-owners in the Green Belt would simply pocket huge windfall gains from the spike in land values, and the new housing would end up being sold at unaffordable prices. What we need instead is to rejuvenate the Green Belt so that it better fulfils its original purpose of providing green space and recreation for the public. Planning guidance on the use of Green Belt land could be amended to prioritise the provision of allotments, community farms and nature reserves.

We also need to learn from Scotland's recent successful embrace of land reform, and introduce a strong Community Right to Buy in England that allows communities to take back control of land they need. Community groups in England have some existing, rather weak powers in this regard under the Localism Act, such as the ability to designate local 'assets of community value' – such as a local pub, post office or library – and a 'community right to bid' should that asset come up for sale. But in Scotland, community groups can get first right of refusal to buy *any* land or property that comes onto the market – as well as access to public funds to help raise the necessary finance.

While the Localism Act has in many ways just provided cover for cuts to public services in the name of 'Big Society' voluntarism, the Scottish Community Right to Buy hands communities real power. Scottish islands depopulated by the nineteenth-century Clearances are rebuilding them-selves by setting up Community Land Trusts and buying out their absentee landlords. The isle of Eigg, one of the first such community buy-outs, has completely rejuvenated its economy as a result, with its own microbrewery, booming tourist industry and 100 per cent renewable electricity grid.

Why shouldn't English communities have this same right? It could be a shot in the arm for towns and villages run down by decades of deindustrialisation and the decline of the high street; a chance to *really* take back control of your neighbourhood from big corporate landowners. Imagine the renewed sense of pride a community would get from building its own affordable housing. Or the sense of security that, say, a flood-prone town would gain if it were able to acquire the denuded moor lying upstream from it, and plant it with trees to help prevent future floods. Half a million acres of land are currently estimated to be in community ownership in Scotland; we should aim for a million acres of England to be owned by community groups by 2030.

9. Complete the unfinished business of opening up access to England's green and pleasant land

England has some staggeringly beautiful countryside, but we still aren't welcome in vast swathes of it. Despite the right to roam introduced by the Countryside & Rights of Way Act back in 2000, only 10 per cent of England and Wales is covered by open-access rights. It's time to let us, the public, feel at home in our own country, rather than be treated as trespassers in someone else's land.

The government should extend the right to roam to all uncultivated land. Extending open-access rights to woodlands and riverbanks in the first instance would open up lots more countryside in the South and Midlands; most open-access land tends to be in the North, and in Wales, over mountain and moorland. But the end goal should be to follow Scotland's lead, and have a genuine right to roam over all land that's not being used for growing crops, and naturally leaving private gardens off-limits. This right has existed in Scotland since 2003, and in many Scandinavian countries for much longer. It's a crucial part of resetting the social contract between landowners and the landless: land ownership remains in the hands of a tiny few, but we should all get a chance to share in the natural beauty of the land we live in.

10. Instigate a new land ethic: that land owner-ship comes with responsibilities as well as rights

The American conservationist Aldo Leopold wrote of fostering a new 'land ethic', to encourage humanity to treat the earth with care for future generations. Many landowners, particularly aristocratic ones, foster a public image that they are the true stewards of the land, protecting its best interests for the long term. Some genuinely believe this, and act on it accordingly – but certainly not all.

My final proposal is that England should change its laws around land ownership to embed stewardship of the land at the heart of what it means to be a landowner. The National Trust has made use of 'conservation covenants' for many decades, brokering agreements with landowners to restrict development on their land when they die and pass it on. A conservation covenant might stipulate, for example, that an estate's woodlands be conserved in perpetuity, binding future owners into respecting these wishes.

But I'd go further. Why not legislate so that *all* land ownership titles, when sold on, contain a simple, basic clause – an obligation on the land-owner to *leave the land in a better state than they found it*. It could be a form of Hippocratic oath for landowners: a pledge to 'do no harm', ecologically speaking, and act as good stewards. Strict legal enforceability isn't my main aim here. I'm talking about a cultural change – embedding the idea that land ownership comes with responsibilities, not just untrammelled rights; the idea that we belong to the earth, rather than the earth belonging to us.

Taken together, these proposals could transform the way land is owned and used in England. They would result in a boom in affordable housing, fewer empty properties, and more people being able to get a secure roof over their heads. Communities would be free to take back control of the land they depend on locally. Landowners would contribute more to society in taxes and public goods, and start to repay some of the unearned windfall gains they have enjoyed from spiralling land values.

Our food would be more sustainably produced, by a greater diversity of small farms, with the current trend towards ever-larger megafarms reversed. Those yearning to grow food themselves, whether on a humble allotment or a council-owned smallholding, would be able to do so. The parlous state of England's wildlife and habitats would have turned a corner, its vast uplands rewilding in the wake of the abolition of grouse shooting; communities living downstream would suffer fewer floods. The last, archaic vestiges of feudalism that still exist within our system of land ownership would finally be abolished, and the worst excesses of irresponsible offshore capitalism reined in. The public would at last be welcome in the countryside rather than treated as errant trespassers. More than that, we would share a greater sense of belonging and have a larger stake in the country, with a proper say in how the land – *our* land – is best looked after to serve as a 'common treasury for all'.

In essence, land reform in England needs to do the following. Firstly, we need to give everyone a stake in the land. The rousing battle-cry of Edwardian land reformers was 'the land for the people'. That doesn't mean everyone suddenly being handed a field and a pitchfork. It means fixing the broken land market so that everyone can afford a roof over their heads, giving communities the power to take control of land that they depend on, strengthening our statutory right to an allotment for anyone who wants one, and extending Right to Roam across the whole country.

Secondly, we need to reset the social covenant between the landed and the landless. Some of the taxes and inheritance law changes proposed in this chapter, if enacted, would undoubtedly lead to a gradual break-up of large estates and a redistribution of land over time. But equally important is shifting the attitude and actions of land-owners by altering the terms on which land is owned. The ownership of land should come with formal responsibilities, not simply rights. The benefits of owning land should be tempered with a number of obligations: the acceptance of everyone's right to access the country-side; the submission of major decisions over land-use changes to the democratic planning process; the need for landowners to contribute to public goods and pay into the public purse, rather than treating land as a mean of avoiding tax.

Lastly, land reform in England has to result in land being better protected for the long term. We need to encourage more nature-friendly forms of farming through a reformed farm payments system; set aside more land for nature with new reserves and rewilded parts of our National Parks; and ban outright the most wasteful and damaging ways in which land is currently used, such as for grouse shooting. Titles to land should themselves be altered to reflect landowners' obligation towards future generations. In sum, landowners who like to claim that they are the true stewards of the land should be held to their word.

But enough of words. As Gerrard Winstanley, founder of the Diggers, once wrote: 'thoughts run in me that words and writing were all nothing and must die, for action is the life of all, and if thou dost not act thou dost nothing.'

If you want to see the housing crisis fixed, nature restored and land ownership become more equal, put down this book and take action. Join the rising tide of people in this country now demanding land reform: you can find a list of active groups in this book's Appendix. Then do everything you can to make change happen: speak to the media, pressure your MP, start a community group, protest, campaign – act.

This land *is* our land. Let's take it back.

ACKNOWLEDGEMENTS

If it takes a village to raise a child, it takes a movement to write a book. This book couldn't have been written without the help, support, inspiration and love given to me by many friends, colleagues and activists within England's growing movement for land reform.

Firstly, I'd like to thank my agent, James MacDonald Lockhart; my editor, Tom Killingbeck, and the rest of the team at William Collins; and my employers, Friends of the Earth, who allowed me to take six months' sabbatical to write this book.

I owe a special debt of gratitude to a group of friends without whom I couldn't have written the book, and who have given me countless hours of their time. My huge thanks to Robin Grey, songwriter and storyteller, whose fantastic show *Three Acres and a Cow* everyone should see; Nick Hayes, a force of nature, with whom I've shared many a fine day trespassing and whose own forthcoming book on trespass is set to be a treat; Tom Kenny, whose understanding of land and the planning system is just awesome; and Miles King, whose knowledge of the grassland ecosystems on old MOD sites is matched only by his stock of wry anecdotes. In particular, I'm extremely grateful to Anna Powell-Smith, data journalist and computer programmer, who's been my collaborator on the Who Owns England blog as its Technical Lead since 2017, and whose mapmaking skills are second to none.

I'm very grateful also to Christian Eriksson, Ben Allen and Nick Riley, whose investigations, generosity and self-confessed data geekery furnished me with many of the datasets that inform this book. Thanks to my dear friend Roger Geffen, with whom I've spent many late nights discussing land rights over beer. Most of all, thank you to my partner Louisa Casson, who has been my daily inspiration; I love you.

Then there are the countless numbers of people whom I've had the pleasure of talking to about this book as it gestated, who shared ideas and wisdom and who encouraged me to write it. My heartfelt thanks to them all, and my apologies to those I've not had the space to name here. My great thanks to Marion Shoard, Andy Wightman, Kevin Cahill and George Monbiot, pioneers in writing and campaigning on land issues, whose work and correspondence has been inspirational. Thanks to Adam Dyster, Peter Jackson, Darren Beatson and everyone at the National Trust who generously gave their time and granted me access to the Trust's archival documents and datasets; to Professor Brian Short, for corresponding about the requisitioning of land during the world wars, and about 'modern Domesdays'; to the investigative journalist Xavier Greenwood, for sharing his findings on what the Oxbridge colleges own; to Simon Fairlie, Gill Barron, Mike Hannis and everyone at *The Land* magazine; to Ferdia Earle, Kate Huggett, Maria Sanders, Bonnie van der Stein and everyone involved in the Land Justice Network; to Kate Swade, Mark Walton and all the folks at Shared Assets; to Toby Lloyd, Catharine Banks, Laurie Macfarlane, Dr Beth Stratford, Sara Mahmoud and Joe Beswick, for many a conversation about housing and land value taxes; to Vicki Hird, Ruth Davis, Gwyn Williams and Lord Maurice Glasman, for discussions about County Farms, the politics of land and the role of the public sector and voluntary groups in protecting nature. My thanks to Christopher Price at the Country Land and Business Association, for his wisdom, wry humour and ability to disagree amicably; to Mark Avery and Ruth Tingay, for chatting grouse moors and who owns them; to Rob Evans, for discussions about corrupt money and arms deals, and for his inspirational journalism taking on vested interests; to Duncan Campbell, for meeting up to discuss secret tunnels beneath London; to Caspar

Henderson, whose kind advice was crucial in getting this book underway; to Jake White and Naomi Luhde-Thompson, who have been endlessly generous in sharing their legal and planning wisdom; to Dr Beth Parkin, for giving me access to some invaluable journals; to Professor Alasdair Rae at the University of Sheffield, for his assistance in crunching numbers on golf courses and allotments; and to Professor Kate Spencer at Queen Mary University of London, who took me to explore the leaking landfills that line the Thames. I'd also like to thank everyone who's read, followed and tweeted about whoownsengland. org over the years – and the many people who've got in touch to offer information and help off the back of reading it. Any errors in this book are, of course, my own.

Lastly, I want to thank my parents, who taught me to love the land and gave me the best childhood anyone could dream for, and to whom this book is dedicated.

APPENDICES: FIGURES ON WHO OWNS LAND

Table 1: The size of England – and the rest of the UK's nations

	Land area	Population
England	32 million acres	55.6 million
Wales	5 million acres	3.1 million
Scotland	20 million acres	5.4 million
Northern Ireland	3 million acres	1.8 million
United Kingdom	60 million acres	66 million

Land area: Office for National Statistics, rounded to nearest million.
Population figures: Office for National Statistics, current as of June 2018.

Table 2: Land owned by the public sector, Crown, Church, and conservation charities

These are the best approximate figures available at September 2018, based on a patchwork of research sources, including FOI requests and organisations' self-declared ownership statements. Some numbers are approximate and rounded. Details of sources are supplied in the footnotes; see also relevant chapters for discussion of the data. Figures are for freehold ownership.

Organisation	Acreage – UK	Acreage – England	Percentage of England
Forestry Commission	2,064,598	489,814	8.5%
Ministry of Defence	505,825	397,098	
Highways England	114,314	114,314	
Network Rail	129,356	100,525	
Other Whitehall departments	165,000	158,957	
Local authorities (England & Wales)	1,569,544	1,326,655	
Oxbridge colleges	126,000	126,000	
Public sector	4,674,636	2,713,363	
The Crown Estate	336,000	264,233	1.4%
Duchy of Cornwall	130,894	130,639	
Duchy of Lancaster	45,674	41,610	
Sandringham Estate	20,000	20,000	
The Crown (landward acres)*	532,568	456,482	
Church Commissioners	105,000	105,000	0.5%
Diocesan Boards of Finance	70,000	70,000	
Church of England	175,000	175,000	
National Trust for England & Wales	614,000	474,641	2%
RSPB	332,812	127,032	
Woodland Trust	64,000	34,241	
Conservation charities	1,010,812	635,914	
TOTAL	6,393,016	3,980,759	12.4%

The Crown owns an additional 545,378 acres of foreshore and estuarial riverbeds across England & Wales.

Table 3: Land owned by companies

Land Registry data on land owned by companies covers both England and Wales, and cannot currently be broken down by nation. Figures for UK limited companies and LLPs acreage come from a Land Registry spreadsheet released in response to a FOI request by Christian Eriksson in May 2015. Overseas and offshore companies figure comes from Land Registry data obtained under FOI in 2015 by Christian Eriksson and mapped by Anna Powell-Smith; see http:// www.private-eye.co.uk/registry.

Organisation	Acreage – England & Wales	Percentage of England & Wales
UK-registered limited companies & LLPs	6,376,627	
Overseas & offshore companies	279,523	18%
Companies (UK-registered & overseas)	6,656,149	

Table 4: The top 100 landowning companies in England & Wales

These figures come from a Land Registry spreadsheet released in response to a FOI request by Christian Eriksson in May 2015. All subsequent attempts to get updated figures have been rejected by the Land Registry. The figures relate to land held by the companies in both England and Wales; it's not possible currently to break them down by nation. This list was compiled by cleaning up the data, and in some cases combining subsidiaries of the same company. As a result, it won't be definitive, but it should be reasonably indicative. The full dataset will be published on whoownsengland.org.

	Company name	Acreage	Nature of company
1	United Utilities Water Ltd	140,124	Water utility
2	Dwr Cymru Cyfyngedig (Welsh Water)	77,975	Water utility
3	Yorkshire Water Services Ltd	68,927	Water utility
4	MRH Minerals Ltd	67,935	Mining company based in Cumbria
5	Harworth Estates	67,159	Property wing of former mining firm UK Coal
6	Severn Trent Water Ltd	51,668	Water utility
7	Lafarge	48,557	Industrial products conglomerate (concrete, cement, aggregates)
8	UK Power Networks Services (Contracting) Ltd	48,262	Electricity distribution firm
9	L.E.T. Nominees 1 Ltd	34,234	Trust company run by the aristocratic Lowther Estate in Cumbria
10	Gunnerside Estates Ltd	27,258	Grouse moor in the North Pennines belonging to businessman Robert Miller
11	The Boughton Estates Ltd	25,516	Aristocratic estate in Northamptonshire belonging to the Duke of Buccleuch
12	Cemex UK Operations Ltd	25,340	Cement manufacturers
13	UK Coal Kellingley Ltd	25,247	Coal mining (company now dissolved)
14	Albanwise Ltd	22,361	Farm estate belonging to Italian Count Luca Padulli
15	Beeswax Farming (Rainbow) Ltd	21,891	Farm business belonging to Sir James Dyson, with land mostly in Lincolnshire. Total estate known to be larger
16	Woburn Estate Company Ltd	21,474	Aristocratic estate belonging to the Duke of Bedford
17	Ramsbury S.a.R.L.	21,373	Estate registered in Luxembourg belonging to Stefan Persson, founder of H&M; land in Wiltshire and West Berkshire

18	Northumbrian Water Ltd	21,032	Water utility
19	Elveden Estates Ltd	20,664	Estate in Suffolk belonging to the Earl of Iveagh
20	Hanson Quarry Products Europe Ltd	20,534	Mining company
21	Swangrove Estates Ltd	20,502	Aristocratic estate in Gloucestershire belonging to the Duke and Duchess of Beaufort
22	Corlands Minerals Ltd	20,371	Mining company
23	Featherstone Estate Ltd	18,119	Grouse-moor estate in Cumbria, ultimate owner unknown
24	Ham Nominees Ltd	17,908	Aristocratic estate owned by the Tollemache family
25	Rathbone Trust Company Ltd	17,854	Wealth management firm that appears to own land on behalf of various large estates
26	Anglian Water Services Ltd	17,607	Water utility
27	Mainline Pipelines Ltd	17,216	Multi-fuel pipeline company
28	Tata Steel UK Ltd	16,692	Steel manufacturers
29	Wemmergill Estates LLP	16,001	Grouse-moor estate in North Pennines owned by businessman Michael Cannon
30	Thames Water Utilities Ltd	15,987	Water utility
31	South West Water Ltd	15,816	Water utility
32	Weardale Estates Ltd	15,523	Grouse-moor estate owned by former City banker Michael Stone
33	Peel Estates	15,041	Property and retail conglomerate founded by John Whittaker. Total acreage thought to be considerably higher
34	Taylor Wimpey UK Ltd	14,684	Housing developer. Thought to own much more land via other subsidiaries
35	Knarsdale Estate Ltd	14,538	Grouse-moor estate registered in Jersey, owned by two US businessmen
36	Arago Ltd	14,533	Grouse-moor estate belonging to the Sheikh of Dubai

37	Methley Trustees Ltd	14,397	Trust company run by the aristocratic Mexborough Estate for the Earl of Mexborough
38	Pencelli Ltd	14,209	Military training ground in the Brecon Beacons owned by the Honourable Artillery Company
39	British Gypsum Ltd	13,661	Mining company
40	Ford & Etal (Trustees) Ltd	13,622	Aristocratic estate in Northumberland owned by Baron Joicey
41	Strutt & Parker (Farms) Ltd	13,463	Agribusiness in Essex and Suffolk
42	Percy Northern Estates Ltd	13,193	Aristocratic estate owned by Duke of Northumberland
43	Grimsthorpe & Drummond Castle Trust Ltd	12,870	Aristocratic estate in Lincolnshire owned by Baroness Willoughby de Eresby
44	Sibelco UK Ltd	12,739	Mining, cement and aggregates producer
45	Farmcare Trading Ltd	12,615	Agribusiness owned by the Wellcome Trust (formerly Cooperative Farms)
46	Badgworthy Land Company Ltd	12,526	Hunting society with land in Exmoor
47	College Valley Estates Ltd	12,395	Estate in Northumberland once owned by businessman Sir James Knott, now managed by a board of directors
48	Englefield Estate Trust Corporation Ltd	12,168	Estate in West Berkshire belonging to Richard Benyon MP
49	Rose Chaplet Nominees Ltd	12,129	Estate, owner unknown
50	The Birdsall Estates Company Ltd	11,942	Aristocratic estate in Yorkshire Wolds owned by the Willoughby family
51	Blankney Estates Ltd	11,909	Agribusiness in Norfolk
52	Imerys Minerals Ltd	11,880	Mining company
53	Tesco Stores Ltd	11,743	Supermarket

54	The Cowdray Trust Ltd	11,538	Estate in South Downs belonging to Viscount Cowdray; total area of estate known to be larger
55	Insite Development Ltd	11,411	Estate company based offshore, ultimately owned by Saudi Prince Khalid Abdullah, that runs his estate in Kent and grouse moor in Yorkshire
56	Port Of Sheerness Ltd	11,164	Port in north Kent
57	The Channel Tunnel Group Ltd	11,107	Channel Tunnel railway firm
58	Fim Forest Funds General Partner Ltd	10,707	Investment management fund
59	Parkers of Leicester Ltd	10,688	Farm business with land in Leicestershire and Norfolk
60	SLA Property Company Ltd	10,476	Insurance company (Suffolk Life Assurance)
61	National Grid	10,186	Electricity grid owner
62	Compton Beauchamp Estates Ltd	10,031	Racehorse business in Oxfordshire
63	G.E.T. Nominees Ltd	10,022	Aristocratic estate in Denbighshire, Wales, owned by Lord Newborough
64	Burghley House Preservation Trust Ltd	9,894	Company and charity which administers to estate of Marquess of Exeter in Lincolnshire
65	Persimmon Homes Ltd	9,839	Housing developers; known to own considerably more land via other subsidiaries
66	RWE	9,837	Energy utility
67	The Goodwood Estate Company Ltd	9,751	Aristocratic estate in South Downs owned by the Duke of Richmond
68	Zurich Assurance Ltd	9,348	Insurance company
69	Arat Investments Ltd	9,151	Horseracing studs at Newmarket and other land registered offshore, owned ultimately by the Sheikh of Dubai

70	British Telecommunications Plc (BT)	9,015	Telecomms company
71	Yattendon Estates Ltd	8,900	Aristocratic estate in West Berkshire owned by Baron Iliffe
72	Dale Ltd	8,827	Grouse-moor estate in North Pennines registered in Liechtenstein, ultimate owners unknown
73	Vanbrugh Trustees Ltd	8,775	Company that manages Blenheim Palace and surrounding estate in Oxfordshire, property of the Duke and Duchess of Marlborough
74	Catlin Estates Ltd	8,736	Grouse moor in North Pennines owned by the Catlin family
75	Walshaw Moor Estate Ltd	8,592	Grouse-moor estate near Hebden Bridge owned by businessman Richard Bannister
76	The Edward James Foundation Ltd	8,335	Charitable foundation managing estate left by surrealist patron Edward James
77	Muggleswick Estate Ltd	7,799	Grouse moor owned by hedge-fund manager Jeremy Herrmann
78	Farmland Reserve UK Ltd	7,716	Farmland in Cambridgeshire owned by the Mormon Church
79	Penllergaer Estates Ltd	7,704	Estate in south Wales now owned by a trust
80	BDW Trading Ltd	7,382	Housing developers (Barratt/David Wilson Homes)
81	British Agricultural Services Ltd	7,309	Agribusiness
82	Landlark Investments Ltd	7,231	Civil engineering firm
83	Tayberry Ltd	7,112	Farming estate, registered offshore, owned ultimately by the Sheikh of Dubai
84	Glympton Services (Jersey) Ltd/Glympton Park Holdings Ltd	7,004	Estate in Oxfordshire, registered offshore, owned by Saudi Prince Bandar
85	B.S. Pension Fund Trustee Ltd	6,982	British Steel pension fund

86	The Willey Estates (1994) No1 Company Ltd	6,873	Aristocratic estate and game shoot in Shropshire owned by Lord Forester
87	Wessex Water Services Ltd	6,862	Water utility
88	Annington Property Ltd	6,682	Property company that bought 50,000 army homes from MOD in 1990s
89	Ireland Moor Ltd	6,632	Unclear: possibly a hunting society
90	Cokenach Ltd	6,549	Mysterious estate in Hertfordshire, potentially owned overseas, ultimate owner unknown
91	Place Newton Estate Shoot Ltd	6,499	Partridge and pheasant shoot in Yorkshire Wolds, ultimate owner unknown
92	Glebe Mines Ltd	6,326	Fluorspar mining firm
93	Stublick Estates Ltd	5,985	Estate owned by hedge-fund manager Jeremy Herrmann
94	Betchton Ltd	5,984	Estate in Cheshire, ultimate owner unknown
95	Walters Mining Ltd	5,973	Coal-mining firm with mothballed mines in South Wales; subsidiary of US firm
96	Farmland Investments Ltd	5,950	Grouse-moor estate (the Reeth Estate) in North Pennines, ultimate owners unknown
97	The Croglin Estate Company Ltd	5,772	Grouse moor in Cumbria owned by a businessman
98	Hotspur Forestry Ltd	5,741	Estate company owned by the Duke of Northumberland
99	Badlesmere Ltd	5,552	Estate, appears to be registered in Jersey, owner unknown
100	Southern Water Services Ltd	5,506	Water utility
	TOTAL	1,723,335 acres	

Table 5: Land owned by the dukes, and the subsidies they get

The table below lists the acreages owned by Britain's twenty-four non-royal dukes (therefore excluding the Duke of Cornwall and the honorific dukedoms bestowed upon other members of the royal family). The 1873 acreages are sourced from the Return of Owners of Land; the 2001 acreages are all drawn from Cahill, Who Owns Britain, *and refer to landholdings across the UK, rather than England only. Cahill reached these figures by compiling publicly available statements from sources such as the Sunday Times Rich List. More information on what the dukes own can be found in Chapter 4.*

Farm subsidy data is drawn from the government's farm payments database at www.cap-payments.defra.gov.uk. Details of all the dukes' companies and trusts in receipt of payments are given in my blog post, 'The Dukes, their tax breaks and an £8 million annual subsidy', https://whoownsengland. org/2017/05/08/the-dukes-their-tax-breaks-an-8million-annual-subsidy/.
'Single area payments' refers to that portion of farm subsidies that are dispensed according to the area of land being farmed, and thus are essentially a subsidy for land ownership.

Title	Land (acres)		Farm subsidies	
	1873	2001	Total 2015	Single area payments
Duke of Buccleuch and Queensberry	460,108	270,700	£1,643,510	£707,036
Duke of Grafton	25,773	11,000	£835,559	£495,320
Duke of Westminster	19,749	129,300	£815,805	£462,775
Duke of Devonshire	198,572	73,000	£768,623	£218,856
Duke of Beaufort	51,085	52,000	£688,097	£345,075
Duke of Bedford	86,335	23,020	£543,233	£431,163
Duke of Marlborough	23,511	11,500	£526,549	£284,468
Duke of Norfolk	49,866	46,000	£449,166	£259,605

Duke of Richmond, Lennox, and Gordon	286,411	12,000	£379,085	£253,038
Duke of Roxburghe	60,418	65,600	£361,919	£175,938
Duke of Rutland	70,137	26,000	£358,430	£314,531
Duke of Northumberland	186,397	132,200	£327,403	£133,553
Duke of Sutherland	1,358,545	12,000	£191,802	£170,419
Duke of Atholl	201,640	148,000	£172,436	£60,287
Duke of Fife	(Title did not exist then)	1,500	£169,905	£144,364
Duke of Argyll	175,114	60,800	£120,097	£0
Duke of Wellington	19,116	31,700	£80,878	£66,486
Duke of Montrose	103,447	8,800	n/a	n/a
Duke of Somerset	25,387	2,000	n/a	n/a
Duke of Hamilton	157,368	12,000	n/a	n/a
Duke of Abercorn	78,662	15,000	n/a	n/a
Duke of St Albans	8,998	4,000	n/a	n/a
Duke of Manchester	27,312	0	n/a	n/a
Duke of Leinster	73,100	0	n/a	n/a
Totals	3,747,051	1,148,120	£8,432,497	£4,522,914

Organisations campaigning on land issues

- Land Justice Network – *activists' network that advocates for land reform and organises demonstrations* www.landjustice.uk
- Land Workers Alliance – *a grassroots union representing farmers, growers and land-based workers* landworkersalliance.org.uk
- Three Acres and a Cow – *a travelling show telling the history of land rights and protest in folk song and story* threeacresandacow.co.uk
- Shared Assets – *a think-and-do-tank that supports people managing land for the common good* www.sharedassets.org.uk
- The Land – *an occasional magazine about land rights* www.thelandmagazine.org.uk

- Friends of the Earth – *environmental campaigning group* friendsoftheearth.uk
- Shelter – *housing and homelessness charity* www.shelter.org.uk
- New Economics Foundation – *think tank proposing ideas for a new economy where people really take back control* neweconomics.org
- IPPR – *centre-left think tank advocating land reform*
- Civitas – *centre-right think tank advocating land reform*
- Who Owns Scotland – *campaigner Andy Wightman's fantastic maps and blog about Scottish land ownership, one of the inspirations for this book* www.whoownsscotland.org.uk

For more about Who Owns England, including blogs, interactive maps and tips about exploring land ownership, visit whoownsengland.org

NOTES

INTRODUCTION

1   an indication of Doreen Massey and Alejandrina Catalano, *Capital and Land: Landownership by Capital in Great Britain* (Edward Arnold, 1978), p. 7.

1   Land . . . is by far Winston Churchill, *The People's Rights* (Hodder & Stoughton, 1909), pp. 117–19.

2   increased *fivefold* since 1995 Office for National Statistics, 'The UK national balance sheet: 2017 estimates', 5 December 2017, https://www.ons.gov.uk/economy/nationalaccounts/uksectoraccounts/bulletins/nationalbalancesheet/2017estimates

2   over half the UK's wealth ONS, 'The UK national balance sheet estimates: 2018', 29 August 2018, https://www.ons.gov.uk/economy/nationalaccounts/uksectoraccounts/bulletins/nationalbalancesheet/2018. See also Phillip Inman, 'UK's wealth rises as land values soar by £450bn in a year', *Guardian*, 29 August 2018.

2   The land enters Speech given in Bedford on 11 October 1913, cited in Richard Wilkinson, *Lloyd George: Statesman or Scoundrel* (I.B. Tauris, 2018), p. 72.

3   It is not the individual Churchill, *The People's Rights*, p. 125.

5   It is far easier Marion Shoard, *This Land Is Our Land: The Struggle for Britain's Countryside* (Paladin, 1987), p. 213.

1 THIS LAND IS NOT MY LAND

7   thirty individuals and organisations All figures here are detailed on my blog post, 'The thirty landowners who own half a county', 17 April 2017, https://whoownseng-land.org/2017/04/17/the-thirty-landowners-who-own-half-a-county/

8   The land to be lost Jim Hindle, *Nine Miles: Two Winters of Anti-road Protest* (Underhill Books, 2006), pp. 58–9.

9   Alice's Meadow Conversations with Friends of the Earth campaigners.

9   Sir Richard Sutton Richard Jinman, 'A cup of tea but tight lips in historic land-owner's fiefdom', *Guardian*, 23 March 2005.

9   The Sutton Estate George Monbiot, 'A land reform manifesto', 22 February 1995, http://www.monbiot.com/1995/02/22/a-land-reform- manifesto/

9   Claiming that he was Monbiot, 'A land reform manifesto'.

10   he had been behind Charles Clover, 'Prepare to be appalled', *Spectator*, 30 September 1995.

11   Earl's Court Farm Full details on my blog post, 'The thirty landowners who own half a county'.

12   One recent study C.A. Hallmann, M. Sorg et al. (2017), 'More than 75 percent decline over 27 years in total flying insect biomass in protected areas.' PLoS ONE 12: 10, e0185809. https://doi.org/10.1371/journal.pone.0185809

12   There are hardly any Agence France-Presse, '"Catastrophe" as France's bird population collapses due to pesticides', *Guardian*, 21 March 2018.

12   56 per cent decline Claire Marshall, 'Farmland birds show rapid decline', BBC News, 23 October 2014, http://www.bbc.co.uk/news/science-environment-29728558

12   since the 1980s Bayer microsite, 'Beecare', https://beecare.bayer.com/what-to-know/pesticides/neonicotinoids.

12   At least one landowner Cally Law, 'Publisher Peter Kindersley: from farmhouse to basement flat', *The Times*, 30 March 2008.

12   Our original aim http://www.sheepdrove.com/our-farm/how-it-all-began/

13   considerable opposition See e.g. https://www.cla.org.uk/advice/briefing-note-neonicotinoids-and-bees

13   Greenham Common See the website Greenham: A Common Inheritance, http://www.greenham-common.org.uk, webpages entitled 'Clouds of War' and 'Taking a Stand'.

14   The sign at the gate George McKay, *Senseless Acts of Beauty: Cultures of Resistance since the Sixties* (Verso, 1996), p. 193, footnote 38.

14   Karen Cutler Andy Beckett, *Promised You a Miracle: UK 80–82* (Allen Lane, 2015), p. 163.

14   I thought, 'My God . . .' Ibid., p. 164.

14   was one of the best Ibid.

15   A court later found BBC News, 'Special Report: The Women's Peace Camp', 10 November 1999, http://news.bbc.co.uk/1/hi/special_report/1999/11/99/greenham_common/503679.stm

15   It was sold 'Greenham common – a chronology', *Guardian*, 5 September 2006.

16   80,000 Christmas trees BBC news, 'Christmas tree farm at Yattendon prepares for December', 2 December 2017, http://www.bbc.co.uk/news/av/uk-england-hampshire-42201400/christmas-tree-farm-at-yattendon-prepares-for-december

17   Less than 1.5 percent Marion Shoard, 'Into the woods', *The Land*, 22 (January 2018).

18   John McEwen Author's correspondence in March 2017 with Kevin Cahill. Another pioneer of land ownership studies, Cahill told me that McEwen, 'the grandad of land ownership writing in the UK, thought he could do his home county first, in a couple of months using Roger Millman's maps. It took him four years to do one county.'

18 Section 31(6) For a full discussion of such landowner deposits and maps, see 'Stand and deliver! How the Highways Act helps unmask landed wealth', 30 January 2017, https://whoownsengland.org/2017/01/30/stand-and-deliver-how-the-highways-act-helps-unmask-landed-wealth/.

18 thirty landowners Full details on, 'The thirty landowners who own half a county'.

18 Englefield Estate see http://www.englefieldestate.co.uk/about-us/our-history

19 Englefield House See David Nash Ford's Royal Berkshire History website, http://www.berkshirehistory.com/castles/englefield_house.html

19 Englefield Estate Trust Corporation See Benyon (De Beauvoir) Estate website, http://thebenyonestate.com

19 The consortium threatened Aditya Chakrabortty, 'New Era estate scandal: families at the mercy of international speculators', *Guardian*, 19 November 2014; Amelia Hill and Peter Walker, 'New Era tenants take rent battle to US after Tory MP's firm sells stake', *Guardian*, 14 November 2014.

19 In 2017, Benyon's Berkshire estate DEFRA online farm subsidies database, 2017 payments total arising from search results for 'Englefield Est Trust Corporation', 'Englefield Estate Forestry', and 'Englefield Home Farms'.

19 His deer park http://englefieldhistory.net/new-park.html Oliver Goldsmith, 'The Deserted Village', 1770.

20 Under the plans Planning application documents can be viewed online at https://planning.basingstoke.gov.uk/online-applications/applicationDetails.do?activeTab=externalDocuments&keyVal=ZZZTB2CRBJ276

20 As the minister George Monbiot, 'Richard Benyon, the minister destroying what he is paid to protect', *Guardian*, 20 April 2012.

20 No explanation See for example Dr Mark Avery, 'Wuthering Moors 1', 19 March 2012, https://markavery.info/2012/03/19/wuthering-moors/; Dr Avery's continued investigations into the case, e.g. 'Wuthering Moors 28', 15 October 2012, https://markavery.info/2012/10/15/wuthering-moors-28/; and Charlie Cooper, 'Wildlife minister Richard Benyon under fire in another game-shooting case', *Independent*, 30 May 2012.

21 Geoffrey Clifton-Brown Parliamentary register of members' interests, July 2017: https://publications.parliament.uk/pa/cm/cmregmem/ 170707/170707.pdf. Mr Geoffrey Clifton-Brown is recorded in Norfolk Council's Highways Act 1980 Landowner Deposit Register as the owner of the East Beckham Estate. Farm payments data can be found online at http://www.cap-payments.defra.gov.uk/Search.aspx; search results for 'East Beckham Estate'.

21 Sir Henry Bellingham Parliamentary register of members' interests, July 2017: https://publications.parliament.uk/pa/cm/cmregmem/ 170707/170707.pdf

21 MP for South Dorset Tim Adams, 'Who owns our green and pleasant land?', *Observer*, 7 August 2011.

2 ENGLAND'S DARKEST SECRET

23 the earth . . . be common John Locke, *Second Treatise of Civil Government*, 1690.

23 where there is enough Ibid.

24 Land differs Churchill, *The People's Rights*, p. 117.

25   Land was different Josh Ryan-Collins, Toby Lloyd and Laurie Macfarlane, *Rethinking the Economics of Land and Housing* (Zed Books, 2017), pp. 39, 48–51.

26   sent he his men *Anglo-Saxon Chronicle*, entry for 1085, http://www.britannia.com/history/docs/1083-86.html

26   The resulting protests Juliet Barker, *1381: The Year of the Peasants' Revolt* (Harvard University Press, 2014), Ch. 3.

26   The past two centuries See also 'A guide to modern Domesdays', 5 March 2017, https://whoownsengland.org/2017/03/05/a-guide-to- modern-domesdays/

27   started to map James C. Scott, *Seeing Like a State* (Yale University Press, 1998), p. 33.

27   a detailed cadastral survey Roger J.P. Kain and Elizabeth Baigent, *The Cadastral Map in the Service of the State: A History of Property Mapping* (Chicago University Press, 1992), p. 237.

28   groups of landowners Roger J.P. Kain and Hugh C. Prince, *The Tithe Surveys of England and Wales* (Cambridge University Press, 1985), p. 79.

28   an opportunity for Kain and Baigent, *Cadastral Map*, p. 249.

28   I need hardly dwell Lord Brougham, speech on the Criminal Law Consolidation and Amendment Bill, House of Lords debate 12 May 1848, Hansard, vol. 98, cc877–925.

28   a Land Registry Land Registry, *A Short History of Land Registration in England and Wales* (2000), pp. 7–9: http://webarchive.nationalarchives.gov.uk/20101213175739/http:/www.landreg.gov.uk/assets/library/documents/bhist-lr.pdf

29   The 1861 Census Discussed in Kevin Cahill, *Who Owns Britain: The Hidden Facts Behind Landownership in the UK and Ireland* (Canongate, 2001), p. 30.

29   whether it is The Earl of Derby, 'Number of Land and House Owners: Question to the Lord Privy Seal', House of Lords debate 19 February 1872, Hansard vol. 209 cc639–43.

29   upwards of 300,000 Local Government Board, *Return of Owners of Land 1873* (July 1875), Vol. 1.

30   In 1876 he published John Bateman, *The Acre-Ocracy of England* (1876), available online at: https://archive.org/details/acreocracyenglaoobategoog

30   Bateman's last work John Bateman, *The Great Land-Owners of Great Britain and Ireland,* 1883, available online at: https://archive.org/details/greatlandowners ooobateuoft

30   the legend of 30,000 Cahill, *Who Owns Britain*, p. 39.

30   It was castigated Ibid., pp. 49–53.

30   Radicals failed Roy Douglas, *Land, People & Politics: A History of the Land Question in the United Kingdom, 1878–1952* (Allison & Busby, 1976), pp. 11 and 49–50.

31   evils of . . . does nothing Churchill, *The People's Rights*, pp. 116–30.

31   valuation survey Rose Mitchell, 'Edwardian place and society: the Valuation Office survey', National Archives blog, 15 December 2016, http://blog.nationalarchives.gov.uk/blog/place-society-edwardian-england/. See also National Archives research guide on the Valuation Office Survey, http://www.nationalarchives.gov.uk/help-with-your-research/research-guides/valuation-office-survey-land-value-ownership-1910-1915/.

32   as the twentieth century Andy Wightman, *The Poor Had No Lawyers: Who Owns Scotland (And How They Got It)* (Birlinn, 2015), p. 132.

32   the setting up Land Registry, *A Short History of Land Registration in England and Wales*, available online at http://webarchive.nationalarchives.gov.uk/20101213175739/http://www.landreg.gov.uk/assets/library/documents/bhist-lr.pdf, p.11.

33   Second Domesday National Archives research guide on the National Farm Survey of England and Wales 1941–1943, http://www.nationalarchives.gov.uk/help-with-your-research/research-guides/national-farm-survey-england-wales-1941-1943/

33   results were intended Brian Short and Charles Watkins, 'The National Farm Survey of England and Wales 1941–3'. *Area* 26: 3 (1994), pp. 288–93.

33   A 2006 report Humphrey Southall, Report to the Countryside Agency, 'Digitising the 1941 National Farm Survey: An Initial Assessment' (January 2006), http://webarchive.nationalarchives.gov.uk/20101219013602/http://countryside-quality-counts.org.uk/publications/1941-Farm-Survey.pdf

34   the Deputy Chief 'Land Registry: disclosure of information about land ownership', 1974–1976, National Archives HO 241/617.

34   The problem is MAFF, 'Estates Management Committee properties: requests for statistical information; includes details of extent of MAFF holdings', 1968–1976, National Archives MAF 348/49.

35   Are we required Ibid.

35   This was usually Quoted in Shoard, *This Land Is Our Land*, pp. 214–15.

35   The paucity of comprehensive Quoted ibid., p. 216.

35   its 1979 report HMSO, *Report of the Committee of the Inquiry into the Acquisition and Occupancy of Agricultural Land* (July 1979).

36   Anthony Barnett, whose organisation Anthony Barnett, 'Goodbye Charter 88: A new epoch for democratic resistance has begun', *OpenDemocracy*, 20 November 2011, https://www.opendemocracy.net/ourkingdom/anthony-barnett/goodbye-charter-88-new-epoch-for-democratic-resistance-has-begun

36   In his memoirs Martin Rosenbaum, 'Why Tony Blair thinks he was an idiot', *BBC News* Open Secrets blog, 1 September 2010, http://www.bbc.co.uk/blogs/opensecrets/2010/09/why_tony_blair_thinks_he_was_a.html.

37   scandal of ground rent For more information, see the work of the Leasehold Knowledge Partnership, https://www.leaseholdknowledge.com/

37   a mysterious Italian Isabelle Fraser, 'Grounds for concern over firms that snap up freeholds', *Telegraph*, 16 December 2017.

37   Persons of Significant Control see https://beta.companieshouse.gov.uk/company/01359468/persons-with-significant-control

38   forced them to adopt Anushka Asthana, 'May to set timetable to reveal foreign owners of UK property', *Guardian*, 17 January 2018.

38   Private Eye investigator More details at http://www.private-eye.co.uk/registry

38   continues to campaign e.g. Andreas Knobel, 'The case for registering trusts – and how to do it', Tax Justice Network briefing, 3 November 2016, https://www.taxjustice.net/wp-content/uploads/2013/04/Registration-of-Trusts_AK.pdf

39   tax-exempt heritage asset HMRC webpages on tax-exempt heritage assets,

including maps of the estates covered: http://www.hmrc.gov.uk/gds/heritage/lbsearch.htm

39   Not everyone who has benefited See also Mark Rowe, 'How the rich cheat you of your right to roam', *Independent*, 5 March 2000.

39   a lovely three-tier Adam Jacques, 'Mark Thomas interview: The social-activist comedian talks opera, charity shops, and Nicholas Soames', *Independent*, 31 October 2015.

39   a Saudi prince Roger Harrabin, 'Farm subsidies: Payment to billionaire prince sparks anger', 29 September 2016, http://www.bbc.co.uk/news/uk-politics-37493956

41   Information wants Stewart Brand, cited in R. Polk Wagner, 'Information wants to be free: intellectual property and the mythologies of control', *Columbia Law Review* 103: 995 (2003), https://www.law.upenn.edu/fac/pwagner/wagner.control.pdf

41   millions of acres Department of Communities and Local Government (DCLG), Housing White Paper, 'Fixing our broken housing market' (February 2017), p. 76, https://www.gov.uk/government/uploads/system/uploads/attachment_data/file/590463/Fixing_our_broken_housing_market_-_accessible_version.pdf

41   You can buy Author's conversations with Land Registry. See also data.gov.uk: https://data.gov.uk/publisher/land-registry

41   Osborne had moved Vincent Moss, 'Final nail in your coffin: Chancellor moves into new home as UK stripped of AAA rating', *Mirror*, 24 February 2013.

42   be a massive step Catharine Banks, 'Briefing: The case for greater land market transparency', Shelter, November 2016, http://england.shelter.org.uk/professional_resources/policy_and_research/policy_library/policy_library_folder/briefing_the_case_for_greater_land_market_transparency

42   Housing White Paper DCLG, 'Fixing our broken housing market'. For a discussion of the Land Registry-related elements of this, see https://whoownsengland.org/2017/02/08/thanks-to-the-housing-white-paper-an-open-land-registry-is-now-much-closer/

43   the great vampire squid Anna Powell-Smith, 'How to use Land Registry data to explore land ownership near you', 14 March 2016, https://anna.ps/blog/how-to-use-land-registry-data-to-explore-land-ownership-near-you

3. THE ESTABLISHMENT: CROWN AND CHURCH

46   Queen Victoria bought Helen Walch, *Sandringham: A Royal Estate for 150 Years* (The Sandringham Estate, 2012).

46   Sandringham has grown Ibid., map on pp. 118–19.

46   tax haven of Jersey Land Registry land titles show that Houghton Hall and its surrounding estate is registered in the name of Jersey-based company Mainland Nominees Ltd. See also the entry for Mainland Nominees Ltd on Companies House, which states it to be registered in Jersey. On Jersey's status as a tax haven, see John Christensen, 'Portrait of a tax haven: Jersey', 5 November 2017, https://www.taxjustice.net/2017/11/05/portrait-tax-haven-jersey/

46 Balmoral in Scotland In fact, the situation with Balmoral is even more compli-
    cated: it's owned by a trust, of which the Queen is the principal beneficiary. For
    full details, see Wightman, *The Poor Had No Lawyers*, pp. 151–4.

47 She has only paid Sarah Ann Harris, 'Does the Queen Pay Taxes? A Guide to
    the Royal Finances After the Paradise Papers Leak', *Huffington Post*, 6 November
    2017, https://www.huffingtonpost.co.uk/entry/does-the-queen-pay-taxes_uk_
    5a005b59e4b04cdbeb34b73e

48 *bona vacantia* see https://www.gov.uk/government/organisations/bona-vacantia

48 A large part See Shoard, *This Land Is Our Land*, pp. 17–19, and Cahill, *Who Owns
    Britain*, pp. 20–2.

48 The public do The Earl of Clancarty, House of Lords Second Reading debate on
    the Equality (Titles) Bill, Hansard, 25 October 2013, col. 1317, https://publications.
    parliament.uk/pa/ld201314/ldhansrd/text/131025-0001.htm

49 Private landownership Wightman, *The Poor Had No Lawyers*, p. 152.

49 17 per cent Thomas Hinde (ed.), *The Domesday Book: England's Heritage, Then and
    Now* (Hutchinson, 1986), p. 14. The figure is a simple extrapolation: 17 per cent of
    the 32 million acres that comprise England – though necessarily a rough figure,
    since the kingdom of England in 1086 was not of its present extent.

50 established many deer preserves Translated from Old English in Seth Lerer,
    Inventing English: A Portable History of the Language (Columbia University Press,
    2007), p. 43.

50 a quarter see Shoard, *This Land Is Our Land*, p. 28.

50 a third see e.g. Chris Given-Wilson (ed.), *An Illustrated History of Late Medieval
    England* (Manchester University Press, 1996), p. 28: 'The area covered by forest
    law was greatest in the mid-twelfth century, when around 150 royal forests
    covered perhaps a third of England's land surface.'

50 There were two charters Peter Linebaugh, *The Magna Carta Manifesto: Liberties
    and Commons for All* (University of California Press, 2008), p. 6.

50 all woods made forest Modern English translation in Harry Rothwell (ed.), *English
    Historical Documents, Vol. 3, 1189–1327* (Eyre & Spottiswoode, 1975), pp. 337–40.

51 only 15 per cent of England Given-Wilson (ed.), *An Illustrated History of Late
    Medieval England*, p. 28.

52 Many of the buyers Sidney Madge, *The Domesday of Crown Lands: A Study of the
    Legislation, Surveys, and Sales of Royal Estates Under the Commonwealth* (George
    Routledge & Sons, 1938); Ian Gentles, 'The Sales of Crown Lands during the
    English Revolution', *The Economic History Review* 26(4), 1973, pp. 614–35. Gentles
    states the Crown lands sold for around £1.5 million; to convert the value of the
    sales in 1649 to today's money, I used the Bank of England's historical inflation
    calculator, online here: https://www.bankofengland.co.uk/monetary-policy/
    inflation/inflation-calculator

53 doubled in size Cahill, *Who Owns Britain*, p. 73.

53 336,000 acres Statistic from The Crown Estate's Annual Report and Accounts
    2015/16, p. 3, https://assets.publishing.service.gov.uk/government/uploads/
    system/uploads/attachment_data/file/537945/crown_estate_annual_report_.pdf.
    Land owned by the Crown Estate is mapped at http://map.whoownsengland.org/

53   Comparing maps Author's analysis of GIS maps of land owned by the Crown Estate, released following a FOI request, with Natural England's Agricultural Land Classification maps, available for download on data.gov.uk.

53   receiving £366,000 Data for 2016 and 2017 published by DEFRA at http://www.cap-payments.defra.gov.uk/Search.aspx.

53   more rental income Matthew Naylor, 'How to make more money from Apple than apples', *Farmers Weekly*, 7 January 2018.

54   £329 million The Crown Estate, Integrated Annual Report and Accounts 2017/18, https://assets.publishing.service.gov.uk/government/uploads/system/uploads/attachment_data/file/719587/The_Crown_Estate_Integrated_Annual_Report_2018.pdf

54   The Laxton Estate Dan Churcher, 'Laxton: village rooted in the past faces an uncertain future', *Newark Advertiser*, 18 January 2018.

54   15 per cent https://www.royal.uk/royal-finances-0

55   I have always respected Francis Elliott, Fariha Karim, Oliver Wright, 'Palace repair bill is double estimate', *The Times*, 19 November 2016.

56   ground to dust Frank McLynn, *The Road Not Taken: How Britain Narrowly Missed a Revolution 1381–1926* (Vintage, 2013), pp. 22–3.

56   monarchy's personal fiefdom ever since Cahill, *Who Owns Britain*, pp. 93–6; Duchy of Lancaster, Report and Accounts – Year ended 31 March 2018, https://www.duchyoflancaster.co.uk/wp-content/uploads/2018/07/2018-DoL-Annual-Report-and-Accounts.pdf

56   45,674 acres https://www.duchyoflancaster.co.uk/properties-and-estates/.

56   grouse moors . . . Cheshire Overview of estate lands gleaned from author's analysis of Land Registry Corporate and Commercial dataset entries for the Duchy.

57   one grainy map See https://www.duchyoflancaster.co.uk/boundary-map/

57   National Audit Office . . . corporation tax Matthew Weaver, 'Queen's private estate records £20m profit but could take Brexit hit', *Guardian*, 20 July 2018.

57   Freedom of Information requests see e.g. FOI Wiki, 'Organisations and officials with public responsibilities that are not subject to the Freedom of Information Act', https://foiwiki.com/foiwiki/index.php/Organisations_and_officials_with_public_responsibilities_that_are_not_subject_to_the_Freedom_of_Information_Act#Duchy_of_Lancashire

57   does not receive https://www.duchyoflancaster.co.uk/2018/07/20/duchy-of-lancaster-annual-report-and-accounts-for-year-ended-31st-march-2018/.

57   almost £38,000 http://www.cap-payments.defra.gov.uk/Search.aspx

57   £20 million profit Duchy of Lancaster, Report and Accounts – Year ended 31 March 2018

57   £76 million Sovereign Grant Report 2017–18, https://www.royal.uk/financial-reports-2017-18

57   Why are we throwing Weaver, 'Queen's private estate records £20m profit but could take Brexit hit'.

58   It's not a company See http://duchyofcornwall.org/frequently-asked-questions.html#question_13

58   gain permission from the Treasury See Public Accounts Committee,

'Twenty-fifth report: The Duchy of Cornwall' (Part 2: The role of the Treasury), 14 October 2013, https://publications.parliament.uk/pa/cm201314/cmselect/cmpubacc/475/47506.htm. The Duchy is not subject to formal parliamentary scrutiny in the sense that it is, like the Duchy of Lancaster, not bound to open its finances to the National Audit Office. The Duchy's battles over its Falmouth oyster farm go back years; see e.g. BBC News, 'Prince of Wales' Duchy of Cornwall wins oyster farm scrutiny appeal', 4 April 2016, https://www.bbc.co.uk/news/uk-35958262. The Duchy sold the oyster farm in 2017.

58   His Royal Highness Land Registry land title no. CL251882 for Restormel Farm in Cornwall.

59   a feature on the Duchy The 2006 *National Geographic* article and map used to be available online, yet now seems to have disappeared into the ether; but a copy of the map is reproduced on my blog at https://whoownsengland.org/2017/03/15/what-land-does-the-duchy-of-cornwall-own/.

59   nearly 19,000 acres 18,800 acres, to be precise: see Duchy of Cornwall, Integrated Annual Report 2018, http://duchyofcornwall.org/assets/pdf/DuchyOfCornwall IAR2018.pdf. See p. 84 for a breakdown of landholdings by county.

59   Its biggest possession Maps and more details on all these landholdings and more are contained in my blog about the Duchy of Cornwall.

60   Holiday Inn . . . Waitrose Cahal Milmo, 'Revealed: Prince Charles's secret property deals – including £38 million industrial carbuncle', *Independent*, 14 June 2013.

60   quarry in Gloucestershire Hanson Aggregates' Biodiversity Action Plan for Daglingworth sand quarry, 2010, mentions the Duchy as landlords: https://www.hanson.co.uk/system/files_force/assets/document/bap-daglingworth.pdf?download=1

60   130,000 acres of land Duchy of Cornwall, Integrated Annual Report 2018, p. 84, states the Duchy to be 52,970 hectares (130,894 acres). (The 2006 National Geographic map stated the Duchy to be 135,526 acres, while Kevin Cahill in *Who Owns Britain* reckoned it was 141,000 acres.)

60   twice as much The 1873 Return of Owners of Land recorded the Duchy as owning 74,113 acres: see Bateman, *The Great Land-Owners of Great Britain and Ireland*.

60   100,000 acres . . . 14,000 acres Cahill, *Who Owns Britain*, p. 84.

60   the Sovereign Grant handed In 2017–18, royal income was as follows: Duchy of Cornwall, £21.7m in profits; Duchy of Lancaster, £20.2m in profits; Sovereign Grant Fund, £76m (derived as a percentage of The Crown Estate's £329m in profits); farm subsidies to Sandringham Farms, £695,000 = £118.6 million total. Sources are the previously-cited annual reports for the Crown Estate and both Duchies, the Sovereign Grant Fund Report, and DEFRA CAP payments website.

61   black spider letters Robert Booth and Matthew Taylor, 'Prince Charles's "black spider memos" show lobbying at highest political level', *Guardian*, 13 May 2015.

61   We all know who owns Jacob Davidson, 'The world's 10 most expensive houses – and who owns them', *Time* ('Money' supplement), 14 November 2014, http://time.com/money/3585583/worlds-most-expensive-houses/

61   owned by the Crown Estate Reiss Smith, 'Who owns Buckingham Palace? A look inside the Queen's home in pictures', *Daily Express*, 18 November 2016.

61   asset maps https://www.thecrownestate.co.uk/en-gb/our-places/asset-map/

62   Who owns Hyde Park https://www.royalparks.org.uk/about-us/who-we-are

62   the Tower of London https://www.hrp.org.uk/about-us/who-we-are

63   graciously agreed House of Commons debate on the Palace of Westminster, 23 March 1965, Hansard, vol. 709, cc328–32, https://api.parliament.uk/historic-hansard/commons/1965/mar/23/palace-of-westminster#column_328; Wilson's more detailed note on the 'Control and custody of the House of Commons' is online at https://api.parliament.uk/historic-hansard/commons/1965/mar/23/control-and-custody-of-the-palace-of.

64   8.3 million acres Hinde (ed.), *The Domesday Book*, p. 14, states that bishops and abbots possessed around 26 per cent of England in 1086; 26 per cent of 32 million acres is 8.32 million.

64   4 million acres J.P. Cooper, 'The Social Distribution of Land and Men in England, 1436–1700', *Economic History Review*, New Series 20: 3 (December 1967), pp. 419–40.

65   One of the main reasons McLynn, *The Road Not Taken*, pp. 273–4.

66   111,628 acres See Cahill, *Who Owns Britain*, pp. 163–7.

66   very disappointing Matt Lobley et al., 'Making land available for woodland creation', University of Exeter Centre for Rural Policy Research, June 2012, p. 58: https://www.forestry.gov.uk/pdf/Exeterreport.pdf/$FILE/Exeterreport.pdf

67   just 12,000 acres left Land Registry, Corporate and Commercial dataset, released June 2015. To obtain the figures listed here, I searched the dataset for all entries for Diocesan Boards of Finance and added up the totals.

67   abolition of tithes See http://www.nationalarchives.gov.uk/help-with-your-research/research-guides/tithes/; Patrick Wright, *The Village That Died For England: The Strange Story of Tyneham* (Vintage, 1996), pp. 166–7.

67   Stealing land is difficult Gill Barron, 'God's Own Acres: Adios to the landed clergy', *The Land* 20 (Summer 2016), http://www.thelandmagazine.org.uk/articles/adios-landed-clergy

67   Because of its original purpose Rosie Ogg, 'In plain English: glebe land', 7 November 2017, https://www.savills.co.uk/blog/article/223664/residential-property/in-plain-english-glebe-land.aspx

67   Land Registry data Author's search of the Land Registry's overseas company dataset, June 2018; these are just a couple of examples out of dozens.

68   £8 billion Rob Preston, 'Church Commissioners assets increase to £8.3bn', *Civil Society*, 14 May 2018, https://www.civilsociety.co.uk/news/church-commissioners-assets-increase-to-8-3bn.html

68   Church Commissioners, see 'Church Commissioners digitise mapping database', https://www.ordnancesurvey.co.uk/business-and-government/case-studies/church-commissioners-digitise-mapping-database.html

68   £226 million https://www.churchofengland.org/about/leadership-and-governance/church-commissioners

68   The Church of England Madeleine Davies, 'Church must use land holdings to promote affordable housing, says Archbishop of Canterbury', *Church Times*, 27 November 2017.

69   The pressure to generate C. Hamnett, 'The Church's Many Mansions: The Changing Structure of the Church Commissioners' Land and Property Holdings, 1948–1977', *Transactions of the Institute of British Geographers* 12: 4 (1987), pp. 465–81.

69   £11,000 per square *metre* Land Registry Price Paid dataset, mapped against postcode areas by Anna Powell-Smith at https://houseprices.anna.ps/

69   The Bishop's Avenue . . . By the 1970s Hamnett, 'The Church's Many Mansions'; see also Shirley Green, *Who Owns London? A Revealing In-depth Investigation* (Weidenfeld & Nicolson, 1986), pp. 19–25.

70   From the 1950s Details of these property deals, in which the Church Commissioners sometimes had part-stakes with other developers, can be found in Green, *Who Owns London?*, pp. 19–25; and in Massey and Catalano, *Capital and Land*, pp. 82–91.

70   Paternoster Square see Shirley Green, *Who Owns London?*, p. 22; https://www.paternostersquare.info/history.aspx

70   retained the valuable freehold Land Registry records show that the freehold land title for Paternoster Square is still owned by the Church Commissioners today.

70   very legitimate anger Alan Rusbridger, 'Canon of St Paul's "unable to reconcile conscience with evicting protest camp"', *Guardian*, 27 October 2011.

71   Palatinate of Durham For more detail see the Durham University Archives, https://archiveshub.jisc.ac.uk/search/archives/674a2ea7-c359-3b3d-a8b8-e1ee0d70bc7c

71   putting profit before people 'Octavia Hill Estates sale is "end of affordable housing in Waterloo" says MP', 24 March 2011, http://www.london-se1.co.uk/news/view/5174

71   The sleepy old Church Harry Mount, 'Why the sleepy old CoE is just a greedy, moneygrubbing property tycoon', *Spectator*, 20 January 2018.

71   philanthropy at 5 per cent Hamnett, 'The Church's Many Mansions'.

71   re-registering ancient rights Kaya Burgess, 'Church of England tells landowners it owns their mineral rights', *The Times*, 9 January 2018.

72   morally acceptable Emily Gosden, 'Fracking is acceptable, says church', *The Times*, 19 January 2017.

72   first step towards fracking Ruth Hayhurst, 'Fracking awareness campaign launched as Aurora prepares for seismic surveys', *Drill Or Drop*, 26 May 2016, https://drillordrop.com/2016/05/26/fracking-awareness-campaign-launched-as-aurora-prepares-for-seismic-surveys/

72   a decent percentage Some have been calling on the Church to do this for years. The Christian campaigning group Housing Justice called for the Church to make its land available for affordable housing in 2015: see Jonathan Owen, 'Church of England "should sell off its £2bn land estate for housing"', *Independent*, 10 June 2015. More recently, such calls have come even from the centre-right: see Harry Phibbs, 'The Church of England has a moral duty to provide new housing', Conservative Home, 15 June 2018, https://www.conservativehome.com/localgovernment/2018/06/the-church-of-england-has-a-moral-duty-to-provide-new-housing.html

4. OLD MONEY

75   Make sure they have an ancestor Cited by Sam Roberts, 'Gerald Grosvenor, British Duke and Billionaire, Dies at 64', *New York Times*, 15 August 2016.

75   £9 billion fortune See the *Sunday Times* Rich List 2017.

76   16,000 acres Alastair Jamieson, 'Duke of Norfolk and 80 other landowners seek hunt protest ban', *Telegraph*, 19 October 2008.

76   local residents complain Author's conversations with Alnwick residents.

76   at least 100,000 acres In the 2006 BBC documentary *Whose Britain Is It Anyway?*, the Duke of Northumberland is stated to own 135,000 acres, but 35,000 of these are thought to be in Scotland.

77   Four thousand Anglo-Saxon *thegns* Christopher Dyer, *Making a Living in the Middle Ages: The People of Britain 850–1520* (Yale University Press, 2002), Ch. 3.

77   26 per cent . . . 54 per cent Hinde (ed.), *The Domesday Book*.

77   a dozen http://nationalarchives.gov.uk/domesday/world-of-domesday/nobles. htm

77   One, Alan Rufus Philip Beresford and William Rubenstein, *The Richest of the Rich: The Wealthiest 250 People in Britain since 1066* (Harriman House, 2007).

78   some 6.8 million acres https://www.parliament.uk/about/living-heritage/ transformingsociety/towncountry/landscape/overview/enclosingland/

78   Inclosure came and trampled John Clare, 'The Mores', in Eric Robinson (ed.), *John Clare: Major Works* (Oxford University Press, 2008).

78   over 3,000 British properties 'Legacies of British slave-ownership', https://www. ucl.ac.uk/lbs/maps/

78   around three million Africans http://www.nationalarchives.gov.uk/help-with-your-research/research-guides/british-transatlantic-slave-trade-records/

78   Edwin Lascelles . . . 2nd Earl of Harewood See 'Legacies of British slave-owner-ship', entries for Edwin Lascelles, 1st Baron Harewood, https://www.ucl.ac.uk/lbs/person/view/2146638741, and for Henry Lascelles, 2nd Earl of Harewood, https://www.ucl.ac.uk/lbs/person/view/6180. The latter gives a breakdown of the compensation he was awarded, appearing to total over £26,000.

78   over £23,000 Simon Smith, 'Slavery and Harewood House', BBC Leeds website blog, 22 February 2007, http://www.bbc.co.uk/leeds/content/articles/2007/02/22/ abolition_harewood_house_feature.shtml. Harewood House is still owned by the Lascelles family today; the current owner is the 8th Earl of Harewood. https:// harewood.org/

79   The power of enclosing Quoted in Christopher Hill, *The World Turned Upside Down* (Penguin, 1972), p. 132.

79   An old joke Adapted from Eva Guillorel, David Hopkin and William Pooley (eds), *Rhythms of Revolt: European Traditions and Memories of Social Conflict in Oral Culture* (Routledge, 2018).

79   One, political influence 15th Earl of Derby, 'Ireland and the Land Act', *Nineteenth Century*, October 1881, p. 474. Cited in Shoard, *This Land Is Our Land*, p. 12.

80   A country house See Lawrence Stone and Jeanne C. Fawtier Stone, *An Open Elite? England 1540–1880* (Oxford University Press, 1986), p. 11.

80   If all the children Adam Badeau, *Aristocracy in England* (1885), pp. 43, 51.

80   aristocratic privilege William Doyle, *The Oxford History of the French Revolution*, 2nd edn (OUP, 2002), Ch. 1.

80   Vita Sackville-West See her poem *The Land*, 1926.

81   26-year-old son Hugh Keith Dovkants, 'Hugh Grosvenor: How the richest man in the world under 30 stays normal', *Tatler*, 8 August 2017.

81   The Hares Matthew Bell, 'To the manor born: the female aristocrats battling to inherit the title', *Independent*, 14 June 2013.

81   We should take our time House of Lords committee stage debate on the Equality (Titles) Bill, 6 December 2013.

81   It is stupid Bell, 'To the manor born'.

82   hereditary peers Debrett's, 'Ranks and Privileges of the Peerage', https://www. debretts.com/expertise/essential-guide-to-the-peerage/ranks-and-privileges-of-the-peerage/

82   1,204 extant baronetcies List compiled by the official Standing Council of the Baronetage, September 2017, https://www.baronetage.org/wp-content/uploads/2011/01/Analysis1September-2017.pdf

83   Yet while there was a certain fluidity Stone and Fawtier Stone, *An Open Elite?*, pp. 303–4.

83   but these were small fry Mark Rothery, 'The wealth of the English landed gentry, 1870–1935', *Agricultural History Review* 55: 2 (2007), pp. 251–68.

84   In terms of territory David Cannadine, *The Decline and Fall of the British Aristocracy* (Penguin, 1990), pp. 18–19.

84   This perception owes much F.M.L. Thompson, *English Landed Society in the Nineteenth Century* (Routledge, 1963).

84   The old order Quoted ibid., p. 330.

85   much less than 25 per cent John Beckett and Michael Turner, 'End of the Old Order? F.M.L. Thompson, the Land Question, and the burden of ownership in England, c.1880–c.1925', *Agricultural History Review* 55: 2 (2007), pp. 269–88.

85   The landed aristocracy Thompson, *English Landed Society*, pp. 343–4.

85   When Thompson wrote Beckett and Turner, 'End of the Old Order?'

86   about one-seventh Roy Perrott, *The Aristocrats* (Weidenfeld and Nicolson, 1967); see table on pp. 150–5 for the acreages owned by the landowners concerned (56 in England & Wales, 23 in Scotland, but with an overlap of three). His figure for 3,000 nobles and landed gentry is on p. 13. The ONS estimates that the UK's population in 1967 was almost 55 million (see https://www.ons.gov.uk/file?uri=/peoplepopulationandcommunity/populationandmigration/populationesti-mates/adhocs/004356ukpopulationestimates1851to2014/ukpopulationestimates18512014.xls), so 3,000 people out of 55 million is 0.005 per cent of the population.

86   in spite of the decline Massey and Catalano, *Capital and Land*, pp. 58–60.

86   very rich men Stephen Glover, 'The old rich: a survey of the landed classes', *Spectator*, 1 January 1977.

86   Our 36,000 members CLA, 'Environmental standards in farming: consultation response from the Country Land and Business Association', 27 May 2009,

https://www.cla.org.uk/sites/default/files/A0938084%20Environ.Standards%20Resp.pdf

87   five million hectares CLA, 'Response to the Commission for Rural Communities Inquiry into the Future for England's Upland Communities', April 2009, https://www.cla.org.uk/sites/default/files/CRC upland farming resp.pdf

87   a third of the UK overall *Whose Britain Is It Anyway?*, BBC2, 2006, https://www.youtube.com/watch?v=VMUkgRzRhik

87   DEFRA's 2017 data DEFRA, Agriculture in the United Kingdom datasets, 2017, https://www.gov.uk/government/statistical-data-sets/agriculture-in-the-united-kingdom

87   25,638 farm holdings DEFRA, June 2017, https://www.gov.uk/government/statistical-data-sets/structure-of-the-agricultural-industry-in-england-and-the-uk-at-june. Under the England heading, select 'results by type of farm' and within the spreadsheet select the tab named 'Farm sizes (area and holdings)'; see the columns for numbers of farms >=100ha and the total farmed area under farms of this size.

87   a lot fewer but bigger MAFF agricultural statistics from 1960 show there were 48,039 farm holdings in England covering 15.3 million acres, or 48 per cent of the country. See MAFF, 'Planning Unit: study on agricultural land prices; land ownership and structure of agriculture', National Archives, MAF 428/27

88   Though much is taken Alfred, Lord Tennyson, 'Ulysses', *Poems* (1842).

88   Far from dying away Chris Bryant, *Entitled: A Critical History of the British Aristocracy* (Doubleday, 2017), p. 11.

89   During the eighteenth century Dr Oliver Cox, 'Why was Lancelot "Capability" Brown so important?', https://www.nationaltrust.org.uk/features/why-was-lancelot-capability-brown-so-important

89   The astonishing scale John Phibbs, *Place-Making: The Art of Capability Brown* (English Heritage, 2017).

90   they tend to be 500 acres George Monbiot, 'A Land Reform Manifesto', 22 February 1995, http://www.monbiot.com/1995/02/22/a-land-reform-manifesto/

91   fossil fuels are not Matt Ridley, 'Fossil fuels are not finished, not obsolete, not a bad thing', 22 March 2015 http://www.mattridley.co.uk/blog/fossil-fuels-are-not-finished-not-obsolete-not-a-bad-thing/.

91   climate change is good Matt Ridley, 'Why climate change is good for the world', *Spectator*, 19 October 2013.

91   millions of pounds annually Brendan Montague, 'Banks Family Mining Millions in Profit from Climate Sceptic Matt Ridley's Coal', DeSmogUK, 11 May 2015, https://www.desmog.co.uk/2015/05/11/banks-family-mining-millions-profit-climate-sceptic-matt-ridley-s-coal. The piece states that 'Banks Group spent £5.1m in the last year on "operating lease rental for land and buildings"', and that '£3.1m of the lease rental would relate to coal mined from the Blagdon Estate'.

91   ores beneath their homes 'Duke lays claim to mineral rights in Carlisle area', *Cumberland News*, 5 July 2013.

91   Viscount Cowdray 'Lord Cowdray speaks out against fracking', BBC News, 7 September 2013, http://www.bbc.co.uk/news/uk-england-23994674

91   an alliance of baronets Ruth Hayhurst, 'Yorkshire landowners back National Trust in INEOS legal challenge', *Drill Or Drop*, 23 February 2018, https://drillordrop.com/2018/02/23/yorkshire-landowners-back-national-trust-in-ineos-legal-challenge/

92   rigidly divorced M.L. Bush, *The English Aristocracy: A Comparative Synthesis* (Manchester University Press, 1984), p. 190.

92   The rent of land Adam Smith, *An Inquiry into the Nature and Causes of the Wealth of Nations* (1776), Book I, Ch. XI.

92   the euthanasia John Maynard Keynes, *The General Theory of Employment, Interest and Money* (1936), ch. 24.

92   Bram Stoker's Dracula An 1882 cartoon from San Francisco depicted landlords as vampire bats, squeezing rents from their tenants before enjoying champagne and a rich meal. See https://commons.wikimedia.org/wiki/File:VampireLandlord1882.jpg

92   The Land Octopus W.B. Northrop, 'Landlordism causes unemployment', postcard, 1925.

92   Tellingly, nearly all Frank Jacobs, 'The Landlord Octopus, Still Stalking London', BigThink.com, 2017, http://bigthink.com/strange-maps/the-landlord-octopus-still-stalking-london

93   the most expensive street Rupert Jones, 'Grosvenor Crescent rated the most expensive street in England and Wales', *Guardian*, 23 December 2017.

93   Comprising 110 acres The Portman Estate's guide, 'Marylebone – guide to shopping and eating out' (March 2016), contains a map of their estate; see http://www.portmanestate.co.uk/downloadcentre/download-centre.aspx

93   Like the other great estates On the history of the estate, see 'Rich List 2012: No. 4 – Viscount Portman', *Birmingham Post*, 23 January 2012.

94   fashionable Harley Street Howard de Walden Estate website, https://www.hdwe.co.uk/about-us.aspx

94   an estimated £3.73 billion Statistics on the wealth of all the great estates in this section taken from the *Sunday Times* Rich List 2017.

94   To the south The Cadogan Estate's website has a map of its land and property: http://www.cadogan.co.uk/locations. For another map and more details of the estate, see Mark Shepherd, 'To the Manor, Seaborn', *Property Week*, April 2009, http://www.propertyweek.com/news/to-the-manor-seaborn/3138754.article (£).

94   the ghost town Joshi Herrman, 'The ghost town of the super-rich: Kensington and Chelsea's "buy-to-leave" phenomenon', *Evening Standard*, 21 March 2014.

94   He who envies Deidre Hipwell, 'Chelsea never goes out of fashion for the Cadogan family', *The Times*, 30 May 2014.

94   £116,000 in housing benefit GMB, 'Landlords hit housing benefit jackpot', 25 February 2014, http://www.gmb.org.uk/newsroom/landlords-hit-housing-benefit-jackpot

94   Almost a thousand acres For maps and acreages of all these estates, see 'Who owns central London?', 28 October 2017, https://whoownsengland.org/2017/10/28/who-owns-central-london/

94   a small number Peter Thorold, *The London Rich: The Creation of a Great City, from 1666 to the Present* (St Martin's Press, 1999), p. 112. See also Green, *Who Owns London?*, p. 36.

94   managed for half a century Simon Jenkins, *Landlords to London: the story of a capital and its growth* (Book Club Associates, 1975), p. 272.

95   extend their leases Pemberton Greenish solicitors, 'A short guide to Enfranchisement and Lease Extension', October 2013, https://www.pglaw.co.uk/wp-content/uploads/2013/10/A_Short_Guide_to_Enfranchisement_Web.pdf

95   Duke of Westminster resigned Stephen Bates, 'The Duke of Westminster obituary', *Guardian*, 10 August 2016.

95   attempts to reduce Patrick Collinson, 'Property market braces for shockwaves from landmark leasehold case', *Guardian*, 14 January 2018.

95   in a victory Knight Frank estate agents, 'Mundy vs the Sloane Stanley Estate: Victory for freeholders as lease extension costs upheld', 25 January 2018, http://www.knightfrank.co.uk/blog/2018/01/25/mundy-v-the-sloane-stanley-estate-victory-for-freeholders-as-lease-extension-costs-upheld

96   publish the results See my blog, 'Who owns England's grouse moors?', 28 October 2016, whoownsengland.org, https://whoownsengland.org/2016/10/28/who-owns-englands-grouse-moors/

96   Studies by Leeds University Leeds University, EMBER study, 2014. See Leeds University press release, 'Grouse moor burning causes widespread environmental changes', 1 October 2014, and underpinning report: https://www.leeds.ac.uk/news/article/3597/grouse_moor_burning_causes_widespread_environmental_changes

96   For years, the local residents George Monbiot, 'This flood was not only foretold – it was publicly subsidised', *Guardian*, 29 December 2015.

97   four pairs left Paul Rincorn, 'Hen harrier plunges towards extinction in England', BBC News, 28 June 2017, http://www.bbc.co.uk/news/science-environment-40422732.

97   spread disease to grouse For more on the ecological impact of grouse moors, see Mark Avery, *Inglorious: Conflict in the Uplands* (Bloomsbury, 2015), as well as his blog: https://markavery.info/blog/. For more about grouse moors in general, see David Hudson, *Grouse Shooting* (Quiller, 2008).

97   150 grouse estates The UK National Ecosystem Assessment 2011 states there are 450 grouse shooting moors in the UK, with 296 in Scotland and 10 in Wales, meaning that England has c.144. See Ch. 5, 2011, p. 25: http://uknea.unep-wcmc.org/LinkClick.aspx?fileticket=CZHaB2%2FJKlo%3D&tabid=82. An earlier study puts the total slightly higher, at 153 grouse moor estates in England: see P.J. Hudson, *Grouse in Space and Time* (Game Conservancy Trust, 1992).

97   screamingly elitist Dominic Prince, 'The ultimate trophy asset for the new-money elite', *Spectator*, 12 March 2008.

97   Baron Raby 'Grouse shooting at Raby, County Durham', *Shooting Gazette*, 22 August 2011, http://www.shootinguk.co.uk/shooting/shoot-reports/grouse-shooting-at-raby-county-durham-11249

97   Forest of Bowland Roger Borrell, 'How Bowland's shooting estates have shaped the

Lancashire landscape', *Lancashire Life*, 13 August 2012, http://www.lancashirelife. co.uk/people/how-bowland-s-shooting-estates-have-shaped-the-lancashire-landscape-1-1571196

97   Bolton Abbey http://boltonabbey.com/the-estate/sporting/

97   even more grouse moors Mure Dickie, 'After 150 years, are the days of grouse shooting numbered?', *Financial Times*, 11 August 2017. For who owns Scotland's grouse-moor estates, see Andy Wightman's work at http://www.whoownsscotland.org.uk/.

97   around £4 million Damian Carrington, 'Grouse shooting estates shored up by millions in subsidies', *Guardian*, 28 October 2016.

98   'People's Budget' Bruce Murray, '"The People's Budget" a century on', *Journal of Liberal History* 64 (Autumn 2009).

99   We wanted money David Lloyd George, Limehouse Speech, 30 July 1909, http://www.parliament.uk/about/living-heritage/evolutionofparliament/houseoflords/house-of-lords-reform/from-the-collections/peoples-budget/limehouse/

99   10.4 million acres Quoted in Wightman, *The Poor Had No Lawyers*, p. 130.

99   Its founders included See Charles Clover, 'History of the CLA', 2007, https://web. archive.org/web/20150403002255/http://www.cla.org.uk:80/about-cla/history-cla.

99   Viscount Bledisloe See Hansard's record of tributes to the late viscount on 8 July 1958, https://api.parliament.uk/historic-hansard/lords/1958/jul/08/the-late-viscount-bledisloe.

100   among its greatest victories Clover, 'History of the CLA'; see also Edith H. Whetham, *The Agrarian History of England and Wales*, Vol. 8 (1914–1939) (Cambridge University Press, 1978), pp.161–2.

100   2,000 stately homes Figures derived from lists compiled by Matthew Beckett on his excellent *Lost Heritage* blog, http://www.lostheritage.org.uk.

100   One of the casualties Matthew Beckett, Lost Heritage blog, http://www.lost heritage.org.uk/houses/lh_staffordshire_altontowers.html

101   soiled their hands Cannadine, *Decline and Fall of the British Aristocracy*, p. 649.

101   recreate Barsetshire Quoted in ibid., p. 442.

101   the 1950s were a period Ibid., p. 651.

102   a chance to sweep away Quoted in Dominic Sandbrook, *White Heat: A History of Britain in the Swinging Sixties* (Little, Brown, 2006), p. 8.

102   howls of anguish Denis Healey, 1973 Labour Party Conference, quoted in *Telegraph* obituary, 3 October 2005.

102   It means the end Quoted in Brian Harrison, *Finding a Role? The United Kingdom 1970–1990* (Oxford University Press, 2010), p. 133.

102   unintentionally prompted Harrison, *Finding a Role?*, p. 134.

103   catch financial business Nicholas Shaxson, *Treasure Islands: Tax Havens and the Men Who Stole the World* (Vintage, 2012), p. 103.

103   The Marquess of Salisbury See 'The Marquess of Salisbury's offshore estates', 10 July 2017, whoownsengland.org, https://whoownsengland.org/2017/07/10/the-marquess-of-salisburys-offshore-estates/

103   the Marquess of Cholmondeley *Private Eye* offshore ownership maps, http://www.private-eye.co.uk/registry) show the Houghton Estate in Norfolk,

family seat of the Marquesses of Cholmondeley, to be registered in the name of Mainland Nominees Ltd, based in Jersey.

103   Houghton Estate see https://www.houghtonhall.com/

103   14,500-acre estate https://www.cirencesterpark.co.uk/about-us/history-of-cirencester-park/

103   a Bermuda-based company Land Registry offshore company dataset, displayed on map.whoownsengland.org. See also *Private Eye* special report, 'Selling Britain by the offshore pound' (2015), http://www.private-eye.co.uk/special-reports/tax-havens.

103   a wealth tax House of Lords debate on wealth tax and historic houses, 26 June 1974, Hansard, https://api.parliament.uk/historic-hansard/lords/1974/jun/26/wealth-tax-proposal-and-historic-houses-1

104   In the public mind House of Lords debate on wealth tax and historic houses, 26June 1974.

104   the owners of historic buildings Patrick Cormack, *Heritage in Danger* (New English Library, 1976), p. 186.

104   We are not seeking House of Lords debate on wealth tax and historic houses, 26 June 1974, Hansard, https://api.parliament.uk/historic-hansard/lords/1974/jun/26/wealth-tax-proposal-and-historic-houses-1#column_1514

104   more practical and political trouble Cited by Howard Glennerster, 'Why was a wealth tax for the UK abandoned?: lessons for the policy process and tackling wealth inequality', *Journal of Social Policy* 41: 2 (2012), pp. 233–49. See also Harrison, who argues: 'The owners of landed estates banded together to ward off taxation, and especially the threat of a wealth tax, through admitting the public more widely to their homes, through diminishing their tax liability by creating trusts to manage them, and through cultivating a public image for promoting tourism, providing film sets, and conserving national traditions and treasures' (*Finding a Role?*, p. 134).

105   It has shown Nigel Lawson MP, Commons debate on Dividends Bill, 27 July 1978, Hansard: http://hansard.millbanksystems.com/commons/1978/jul/27/dividends-bill#S5CV0954P0_19780727_HOC_363

105   the tax environment George Howard, foreword to Sibylla Jane Flower, *Debrett's The Stately Homes of Britain (Personally Introduced by the Owners)* (Book Club Associates, 1982).

105   'old money' Harrison, *Finding a Role?*, p. 137.

105   was from the very beginning David Harvey, *A Brief History of Neoliberalism* (Oxford University Press, 2007), p. 16.

105   hijacked . . . from the landowners Cited in Harrison, *Finding a Role?*, p. 140.

106   the top 1 per cent Harvey, *A Brief History of Neoliberalism*, p. 17.

106   30 per cent of the country's wealth Thomas Piketty, *Capital in the Twenty-First Century* (Harvard University Press, 2014), fig. 10.3.

106   The Countryside Alliance Anthony Barnett, 'Prince named as secret backer of hunt lobby', *Observer*, 26 September 1999.

106   fn Lord Peel as its chair Nicholas Schoon, '"Secret" pro-hunt group to go public', *Independent*, 16 November 1995.

106   intensely relaxed Peter Mandelson, quoted in the *Financial Times*, 23 October 1998.

107   £8 million in farm subsidies See 'The Dukes, their tax breaks, and an £8 million annual subsidy', 8 May 2017, https://whoownsengland.org/2017/05/08/the-dukes-their-tax-breaks-an-8million-annual-subsidy/.

107   handed £3.5 million See 'The Marquesses and their 100,000 acres', 13 August 2017, https://whoownsengland.org/2017/08/13/the-marquesses-and-their-100000-acres/.

107   It's no coincidence Savills, 'UK Agricultural Land Market Survey' (2015), graph on p. 5 showing the rise in agricultural land prices since 2003, http://pdf.euro.savills.co.uk/uk/rural---other/alms-2015.pdf

107   ceased to be eligible Rural Payments Agency, 'The Basic Payments Scheme in England' (2015), p. 13, https://assets.publishing.service.gov.uk/government/uploads/system/uploads/attachment_data/file/649753/BPS_Handbook_-_final_v1.0.pdf

107   adamantly opposed moves Owen Paterson MP, DEFRA Oral Questions, 12 June 2014, Hansard, https://hansard.digiminster.com/Commons/2014-06-12/debates/14061240000027/CAP(CommonLand)#contribution-14061240000104.

107   His welcome plans 'Post-Brexit farming funding set out by Michael Gove', BBC News, 4 January 2018, http://www.bbc.co.uk/news/uk-politics-42559845; Ben Webster, 'Gove's plan to cut subsidies for landowners', *The Times*, 27 February 2018.

107   The man who is Thomas Paine, *The Rights of Man*, 1792.

5 NEW MONEY

110   the world's worst Global Witness blog, 'First test for White House Kleptocracy Initiative – have Oil – will Travel', 28 September 2006, https://www.globalwitness.org/en/archive/first-test-white-house-kleptocracy-initiative--have-oil--will-travel/

110   £28.5 million Land Registry land title documents for 41 Upper Grosvenor Street. See also https://whoownsengland.org/2018/02/27/the-mayfair-mansion-thats-been-empty-for-14-years/

110   I feel it is Helen Pidd, 'Unoccupied, unloved: London mansions left to crumble by elusive offshore owners', *Guardian*, 16 October 2009.

110   Just because this property Lodders Solicitors, 'What is a "house"?', 5 April 2017, http://www.lodders.co.uk/blog/what-is-a-house/

111   60,000 properties Rowena Mason, 'Over 11,000 homes have stood empty for at least 10 years, data shows', *Guardian*, 1 January 2018.

111   The former New York Mayor David Batty, Niamh McIntyre, David Pegg and Anushka Asthana, 'Grenfell: names of wealthy empty-home owners in borough revealed', *Guardian*, 2 August 2017.

112   a thousand rough sleepers Ministry of Housing, Communities & Local Government, 'Rough Sleeping Statistics, Autumn 2017, England', 16 February 2018, https://assets.publishing.service.gov.uk/government/uploads/system/uploads/attachment_data/file/682001/Rough_Sleeping_Autumn_2017_Statistical_Release_-_revised.pdf

112   People are being Quoted in Ed Caesar, 'House of secrets: Who owns London's most expensive mansion?', *New Yorker*, 1 June 2015.

113   the most billionaires The *Sunday Times* Rich List 2018, 13 May 2018, table on p. 7.

115   Their business Shaxson, *Treasure Islands*, p. 34.

115   They did not live Phillip Knightley, *The Rise and Fall of the House of Vestey* (Sphere, 1993). See also 'Heirs and disgraces', *Guardian*, 11 August 1999, https://www.theguardian.com/theguardian/1999/aug/11/features11.g2

116   bought for £20,000 Millar and Brummer, 'Heirs and disgraces' Chris Bryant MP, 'How the aristocracy preserved their power', *Guardian*, 7 September 2017; Martin Linton MP, contribution to Commons debate on the House of Lords Bill, 16 March 1999, Hansard col. 978, https://publications.parliament.uk/pa/cm199899/cmhansrd/vo990316/debtext/90316-32.htm

116   'hard-nosed men' See Cannadine, *Decline and Fall of the British Aristocracy*, pp. 315–18, esp. p. 317

116   detested titles Cited ibid., p. 314.

116   5,500-acre Stowell Park See www.stowellpark.com

116   registered via a trust fund Land Registry title deed for Stowell Park Estate reveals it to be registered in the name of a firm of solicitors, who presumably administer to Baron Vestey's trust.

116   £450,000 in farm subsidies See http://www.cap-payments.defra.gov.uk/Search.aspx.

116   6,600-acre Forest Estate Entries for the Vesteys' Forest Lodge and Assynt estates can be found on Andy Wightman's maps of Scottish land ownership at whoowns-scotland.org.uk.

116   Edmund's side See www.thurlowestate.co.uk

116   17,000-acre Thurlow Estate David Harrison, 'Estate owners vow to defy ban on hunting', *Telegraph*, 15 September 2002.

116   Findus horsemeat scandal David Batty, 'Queen's official supplied horsemeat to Sodexo', *Guardian*, 14 March 2013.

116   among the biggest Shaxson, *Treasure Islands*, p. 34.

117   Trying to come to grips Ibid., p. 47.

117   just £10 in tax Phillip Knightley, who led the *Sunday Times* investigation into the Vesteys, recounts this finding in conversation with Charles Miller, 'Six lessons from a career in investigative journalism', BBC 'College of Journalism' blog, 4 August 2011, http://www.bbc.co.uk/blogs/collegeofjournalism/entries/bd9691f7-3459-33ce-917a-c6e21aeea1d2

117   Nobody pays more Quoted in Blue Star Line online obituary for Vestey, http://www.bluestarline.org/edmund_vestey2.htm. See also *Telegraph* obituary, 28 November 2007, https://www.telegraph.co.uk/news/obituaries/1570710/Edmund-Vestey.html.

117   such as Baron Iliffe Iliffe was made a baron in 1933. See *The London Gazette*, 27 June 1933, 33954, p. 4296: https://www.thegazette.co.uk/London/issue/33954/page/4296. On other early press barons, see Cannadine, *Decline and Fall of the British Aristocracy*, p. 200.

117   viscountcy became extinct The 3rd Viscount Leverhulme died without a son

in 2000, and the contents of his Thornhill Manor estate were put on the market; see John Martin Robinson, 'Going, going, gone for ever', *Telegraph*, 10 March 2001.

117 **Badanloch** Andy Wightman's maps at whoownsscotland.org.uk state that the executors of the will of the late Lord Leverhulme still hold 28,424 acres at Badanloch.

117 **a family trust** See http://www.leverhulmeestates.co.uk.

118 **chosen due to** 'Telling an estate by its colours', *Country Life*, 8 August 2011.

118 **donated £65,000** Electoral Commission data on political donations by 'Viscount Michael Cowdray' and 'Michael Cowdray', http://search.electoralcommission.org.uk/

118 **Rathbones Trust Company** The Land Registry's land title for Cowdray House, as of September 2017, was registered to 'Hudsun Trustees Limited and ACE "Advice & Corporate Engineering" International SA'. The website for the Hudsun Trust Company Limited states: 'HUDSUN TRUST COMPANY LIMITED is a fully licensed British Virgin Islands trust company . . . It has been the choice of clients for the past twenty years as Rathbone Trust Company (BVI) Limited, a member of the internationally known Rathbones Group of Companies.' See http://www.hudsuntrust.com/index/about_us. ACE International SA, meanwhile, is a Swiss firm of accountants and lawyers who were also acquired by Rathbones in 2009; see: http://www.ace-international.ch/about-us.

118 **William Waldorf Astor I** Ian Sansom, 'Great dynasties of the world: The Astors', *Guardian*, 26 March 2011.

118 **various scions** See author's blog at https://whoownsengland.org/2017/04/17/the-thirty-landowners-who-own-half-a-county/

118 **thousands of acres . . . Scotland** The children of the current 4th Viscount Astor are the beneficial owners of the 18,700-acre Tarbert Estate in the Scottish Highlands, according to whoownsscotland.org.uk.

119 **left to the nation** English Heritage, 'History of Kenwood', http://www.english-heritage.org.uk/visit/places/kenwood/history-stories-kenwood/history/. **65,000 homes across England** http://history.guinnesspartnership.com/about/

119 **A 13-acre stretch** The Land Is Ours, http://tlio.org.uk/past-camapigns/wandsworth-eco-village-1996/. See also account and photos from the protest on Urban75: http://www.urban75.org/photos/protest/eco-village-wandsworth-squat.html

119 **squatters occupied** Alexandra Rucki, 'Squatters move into flat in protest against Brixton housing estate evictions', *Evening Standard*, 17 February 2015.

119 **registered offshore in Jersey** Land Registry overseas and offshore company dataset, first released November 2017, records that Elveden Estates Limited, a Jersey-based company, registered numerous land titles making up the Elveden Estate between 2000 and 2002.

119 **around £1.2 million** DEFRA farm subsidy data for Elveden Farms Ltd and its subsidiaries shows that they received £1.4 million in 2015 and £1.2 million in 2016: http://www.cap-payments.defra.gov.uk/

119   A BBC interview Archival footage featured in Adam Curtis's BBC documentary 'The Mayfair Set', Episode 1: Who Pays Wins, 42 minutes in: https://www.youtube.com/watch?v=234H8X1-JiA

120   You can hardly David Hirst, *Guardian*, 27 September 1976; see also Dominic Sandbrook, *Seasons in the Sun: The Battle for Britain, 1974–1979* (Penguin, 2012), p. 93.

120   Beirut-on-Thames Abdel Bari Atwan, *A Country of Words: A Palestinian Journey from the Refugee Camp to the Front Page* (Saqi Books, 2007), ch. 7.

121   introduced a touch Ian Mather, 'The sheikhs who live in the glen', *Observer*, 25 January 1976.

121   British construction companies See also e.g. Kathleen Phipps, 'The United Arab Emirates: An open door to the businessman', *Guardian*, 14 December 1976.

121   some 34,000 acres http://www.balnagown.com/about/overview-of-the-three-estates/. The estate has been mapped by Andy Wightman at whoownsscotland.org.uk.

121   Mereworth Castle 'Britain: Dinner for 370,000, please, James', *Time*, 2 August 1976, http://content.time.com/time/magazine/article/0,9171,914443-2,00.html. See also Historic England, entry for Mereworth Castle, https://historicengland.org.uk/listing/the-list/list-entry/1000938

121   a fortune of £1.65 billion BBC News, 'Highland Spring owner Mahdi al-Tajir "richest man in Scotland"', 21 April 2013, http://www.bbc.co.uk/news/uk-scotland-22238445

121   offshore company Land Registry data shows that Mereworth Castle is registered in the name of Kent Campbell Holdings Ltd, a British Virgin Islands company.

121   approximately 92,000 acres Author's analysis of Land Registry data; see further references below.

121   in the Highlands The Sheikh owns the 61,961-acre Killilan and Inverinate Estates in Scotland, registered under SMECH Properties, according to whooownsscotland.org.uk. At least part of this was bought as early as 1985: see 'Scots estate for sheikh', *Guardian*, 29 August 1985, p. 3.

121   Kensington and Windsor Other London and Windsor houses owned by SMECH Properties (formed 1976, according to the OpenCorporates database) are recorded in the Land Registry's overseas and offshore dataset.

122   Tayberry Ltd is also listed in the same dataset, and the farmland it owns overlaps with that of Saker Estates, a company whose Person of Significant Control is recorded in Companies House as being HH The Ruler's Court, Dubai: https://beta.companieshouse.gov.uk/company/06475753/persons-with-significant-control.

122   studs at Newmarket Arat Investments Ltd (formed 1978: OpenCorporates), as revealed by *Private Eye* (http://www.private-eye.co.uk/registry), overlap with the Godolphin Stables, long publicly known to belong to the Sheikh; see e.g. https://www.godolphin.com/about-us/our-founder/.

122   Arago Ltd Land Registry land title for the Bollihope Estate.

122   the Sheikh's logistics company See e.g. Murray Wardrop, 'Sheikh's British palace staff worked in "culture of fear"', *Telegraph*, 15 March 2011. Companies House accounts for UK Mission Enterprise Ltd show it to be ultimately owned by the Government of Dubai: https://beta.companieshouse.gov.uk/company/05600850/persons-with-significant-control

122   caused something Olivia J. Wilson, 'Land ownership and rural development in theory and practice: case studies from the north Pennines in the 19th and 20th centuries', Durham theses, Durham University, 1990, http://etheses.dur.ac.uk/6250/1/6250_3605.PDF, p.333.

122   fast becoming Julian Taylor, 'Plenty to grouse about as Glorious Twelfth draws near', *Guardian*, 7 August 1978.

122   a shortage of decent victims Seumas Milne, 'Glorious Twelfth goes off half-cock', *Guardian*, 13 August 1985.

122   who decided to try Frank Keating, 'Barrels of fun . . .', *Guardian*, 24 September 1977, photos of the dashing young Crown Prince e.g. https://www.pinterest.com/pin/372321094167936722/

122   gentlemen and sportsmen John Cunningham, 'Britain's Horse Caliphs', *Guardian*, 2 October 1982.

123   over £400,000 Harrabin, 'Farm subsidies: Payment to billionaire prince sparks anger'.

123   34,000 acres PwC, 'The British Thoroughbred Breeding Industry: Economic Contribution & Opportunities (Vol 1)', 25 March 2014, https://www.thetba.co.uk/wp-content/uploads/2014/10/Economic-Impact-Study.pdf.

123   farm payments data See http://www.cap-payments.defra.gov.uk/Search.aspx

123   Insite Development Ltd a Guernsey company set up in 1979; see https://opencorporates.com/companies/gg/1-8123.

123   4,000 acre Fairlawne Estate Companies House records for the Fairlawne Estate Company Ltd show its ultimate owner to be Saudi Prince Khalid Abdullah: https://beta.companieshouse.gov.uk/company/01882355/persons-with-significant-control; a landowner record for the Fairlawne Estate deposited under the Highways Act 1980 s31.6, gives the figure of 4,173 acres: https://www.kent.gov.uk/__data/assets/pdf_file/0005/13694/Deposits-register-2014.pdf. The same document also reveals the land is registered to Insite Development Ltd

123   Fairlawne are good 'Villagers defeat Saudi Prince in footpath battle', *Telegraph*, 25 November 2011.

124   bribery has always David Leigh and Rob Evans, 'Secrets of al-Yamamah', *Guardian*, 2007, https://www.theguardian.com/baefiles/page/0,,2095831,00.html

124   Prince Bandar David Leigh and Rob Evans, 'The BAE files: cast of characters: Prince Bandar', *Guardian*, 7 June 2007, https://www.theguardian.com/world/2007/jun/07/bae5

124   alleged to be his winnings David Leigh and Rob Evans, 'Friend of the world's leaders: man at centre of arms deal', *Guardian*, 7 June 2007, https://www.theguardian.com/world/2007/jun/07/bae12.

124   2,500-acre Glympton Park Chris Koenig, 'Saudi Prince's Oxfordshire estate', *Oxford Times*, 1 May 2008, http://www.oxfordtimes.co.uk/business/profiles/2239673.Saudi_Prince_s_Oxfordshire_estate/

124   Said went on David Leigh and Rob Evans, 'The BAE Files: cast of characters: Wafic Said', *Guardian*, 7 June 2007, https://www.theguardian.com/world/2007/jun/07/bae17

124   personally intervened David Leigh and Rob Evans, 'Blair called for BAE inquiry

to be halted', *Guardian*, 22 December 2007, https://www.theguardian.com/baefiles/story/0,,2231496,00.html

124 peppered with vacant properties Robert Booth, 'Inside 'Billionaires' Row': London's rotting, derelict mansions worth £350m', *Guardian*, 31 January 2014.

125 around $170 billion Figures cited in Mark Hollingsworth and Stewart Lansley, *Londongrad* (Fourth Estate, 2009), p. 61.

125 successive influxes Luke Harding, *A Very Expensive Poison: The Definitive Story of the Murder of Litvinenko and Russia's War with the West* (Guardian Faber Publishing, 2016).

125 occasional bus tours http://clampk.org/2016/01/20/kleptocracy-tours/

126 still owns a property Luke Harding, 'Mega-rich homes tour puts spotlight on London's oligarchs', *Guardian*, 4 February 2016.

126 a US sanctions list Lauren Gambino, 'Trump administration hits 24 Russians with sanctions over "malign activity"', *Guardian*, April 2018.

126 A family friend Harding, 'Mega-rich homes tour puts spotlight on London's oligarchs'.

126 Athlone House Thomas Burrows, 'Ukrainian billionaire oligarch gets the go-ahead to turn derelict mansion into one of London's finest private homes complete with cigar room, gym and yoga room and worth £130 million', *Daily Mail*, 14 September 2016.

126 Mikhail Fridman See https://www.forbes.com/profile/mikhail-fridman/

126 Beechwood House Lucy Hanbury, 'Arsenal billionaire buys £48m London estate', *Evening Standard*, 19 May 2008.

126 £12.8 billion See https://www.forbes.com/profile/alisher-usmanov/

126 Safran Holdings Ltd Witanhurst (41 Highgate West Hill) can be seen on Private Eye's offshore property map to be registered to Safran Holdings Ltd; see http://www.private-eye.co.uk/registry

126 underground pool Zoe Brennan, 'Move over Buckingham Palace! Furious locals, a massive underground extension, and the mystery owner of London's most incredible home', *Daily Mail*, 24 June 2011.

126 outstanding detective work Ed Caesar, 'House of secrets: who owns London's most expensive mansion?', *New Yorker*, 1 June 2015.

126 biggest foreign buyers Hollingsworth and Lansley, *Londongrad*, p. 134.

127 townhouse in Chester Square Graham Norwood, 'Why London's Chester Square remains a premier address', *Financial Times*, 18 March 2016.

127 £90m pad Ryan Kisiel, 'Welcome to the neighbourhood! Chelsea boss Roman Abramovich buys £90m home on Britain's most expensive street', *Daily Mail*, 29August 2011.

127 Fyning Hill Estate Fyning Hill was first acquired by Abramovich via the BVI company Rosle Estates Ltd; see, for instance, this South Downs National Park Authority planning application for the property: http://planningpublicaccess. southdowns.gov.uk/online-applications/applicationDetails.do?activeTab= details&keyVal=NKSQC6TUN2800. Abramovich's ultimate ownership is detailed in Hollingsworth, *Londongrad*, p. 124.

127 500-acre Sutton Place Approximate area derived from measuring the map polygons: http://www.private-eye.co.uk/registry.

127   Delesius Investments See http://www.private-eye.co.uk/registry

127   through a court case 'Arsenal tycoon's stately home was a "sweetener in deal with oligarch"', *The Times*, 11 February 2012.

127   £100 billion a year Jim Armitage, 'Britain's £100bn-a-year money-laundering problem: police only acted forcefully on seven reports of grand corruption last year', *Independent*, 10 June 2015.

127   London is the money-laundering capital Quoted in *From Russia with Cash*, Channel 4, 8 July 2015, http://www.channel4.com/programmes/from-russia-with-cash

127   Prices of high-end properties Quoted in *From Russia with Cash*.

128   jailing of Mikhail Khodorkovsky Reuters, 'Russian court delays verdict on oil tycoon Mikhail Khodorkovsky', *Guardian*, 15 December 2010.

128   Putin's personal orders BBC News, 'President Putin "probably" approved Litvinenko murder', 21 January 2016, http://www.bbc.co.uk/news/uk-35370819

128   Mayfair and all it represents Peter Pomerantsev, 'Murder in Mayfair', *London Review of Books*, 31 March 2016.

129   public registers of companies Dan Sabbagh, '"Dirty money": U-turn as Tories back plans to make tax havens transparent', *Guardian*, 1 May 2018.

129   two apartments in Whitehall Transparency International, 'Unexplained Wealth Orders in use: here's at least 5 cases the police should consider today!', 31 January 2018, http://www.transparency.org.uk/uwo-consider-today/#.WqhZDZPFLUQ

130   moving his company Nick Mathiason, 'Ineos tax deal sparks fury as firm plans to move to Switzerland', *Guardian*, 4 March 2010.

130   documents I obtained See Rob Edwards, 'Ineos boss lobbied Osborne to bust unions and back fracking', *The Ferret*, 27 February 2017, https://theferret.scot/ineos-boss-lobbied-osborne-unions-fracking/

130   tax haven of Monaco Jillian Ambrose, 'Britain's wealthiest man Sir Jim Ratcliffe leaves the UK to move to Monaco', *Telegraph*, 8 August 2018.

130   walk away from the EU Will Heaven, 'James Dyson: If Brexit talks fail with the EU it's "no big deal"', *Spectator*, 29 July 2017; John Arlidge, 'Exclusive interview: Sir James Dyson reveals the secrets of his success', *Sunday Times* Rich List 2017, 7 May 2017.

130   busy hoovering up Philip Case, 'Brexiter Dyson warns government not to cut farm subsidies', *Farmers Weekly*, 28 July 2017, http://www.fwi.co.uk/news/brex-iteer-dyson-warns-government-not-cut-farm-subsidies.htm

130   33,000 acres, mainly in Lincolnshire See 'Why is James Dyson hoovering up land?', 19 September 2017, https://whoownsengland.org/2017/09/19/why-is-james-dyson-hoovering-up-land/

130   What Sir James is doing Gary Rycroft, *Lancaster Guardian*, 11 January 2015, http://www.lancasterguardian.co.uk/news/opinion/gary-rycroft-column-1-7039313

131   temerity to warn ministers Case, 'Brexiter Dyson warns government not to cut farm subsidies'

131   generous EU handouts One 'Dacre, P' of Wadhurst in Kent received £28,219.15 in 2016 and £32,482.63 in 2017 in farm subsidies under the EU CAP; see http://www.cap-payments.defra.gov.uk/SearchResults.aspx

131   farmland in Kent Dacre owns the East Lymde estate near Wadhurst and a

grouse-moor estate near Ullapool in Scotland; see Kevin Rawlinson and Jasper Jackson, 'Daily Mail editor received £88,000 in EU subsidies in 2014', *Guardian*, 30 March 2016.

131   26,000-acre farm Acreage obtained by measuring the area of land covered by Environmental Stewardship payments to Lilburn Estate according to Natural England maps.

131   David Ross see Dominic Prince, 'The ultimate trophy asset for the new-money elite', *Spectator*, 12 March 2008.

131   recent buyers of grouse moors See http://grousemoors.whoownsengland.org/ and accompanying blog, 'Revealed: the aristocrats and City bankers who own England's grouse moors', 12 August 2018, https://whoownsengland.org/2018/08/12/revealed-the-aristocrats-and-city-bankers-who-own-englands-grouse-moors/

131   Gunnerside Moor I have mapped Robert Miller's Gunnerside Estate at 'Who owns England's grouse moors?', 28 October 2016, https://whoownsengland.org/2016/10/28/who-owns-englands-grouse-moors/

131   registered in the British Virgin Islands Land Registry land title documents for Gunnerside Moor reveal it to be registered to Gunnerside Estates Ltd, a company based in BVI.

131   Ramsbury Estate see http://www.private-eye.co.uk/registry; *Private Eye*, 'Selling Britain by the offshore pound.'

131   Culden Faw estate See *Private Eye*, 'Selling Britain by the offshore pound'.

131   £114 million in unpaid duties see Jim Armitage, 'Prince Charles pal and trading veteran hit with £114m tax fine', *Evening Standard*, 21 November 2017.

132   Chipping Norton Set Caroline Dewar, 'Who's who in the Chipping Norton set', *Telegraph*, 5 March 2012.

132   Conservative Party donor Rob Davies and Rajeev Syal, 'Jeremy Hunt got "bulk discount" on seven flats from Tory donor', *Guardian*, 18 April 2018.

132   beneficiary of an offshore trust Robert Booth, Holly Watt and David Pegg, 'David Cameron admits he profited from father's Panama offshore trust', *Guardian*, 7 April 2016.

133   just blocks of bullion See http://www.bbc.co.uk/news/uk-england-london-25776687

133   nuclear bunkers For instance, a large Cold War bunker at Hope Cove in Devon, auctioned off in 2014, was bought by one Hope Cove Salcombe Ltd. See BBC News, 'Cold War concrete bunker in Devon to be auctioned', 14 July 2014, http://www.bbc.co.uk/news/uk-england-devon-28292148; Companies House entry for Hope Cove Salcombe Ltd registering the charge: https://beta.companieshouse.gov.uk/company/09261321/filing-history

133   private nuclear fallout shelters Westminster security, 'Underground "Nuclear Bomb" Fallout Shelter For Sale in London', 10 January 2016, https://www.westminstersecurity.co.uk/underground-fallout-shelter/

133   4,650 basement developments David Batty, Caelainn Barr and Pamela Duncan, 'What lies beneath: the subterranean secrets of London's super-rich', *Guardian*, 7 May 2018.

134   mansion on stilts Darren Boyle, 'Billionaire plans to fit new £4 million mansion

with hydaulic stilts that will keep it safe from rising sea levels', *Daily Mail*, 18 April 2015.

134   Prince Andrew's former home Guy Adams, 'The truth about Andrew's £15m house sale', *Daily Mail*, 22 May 2016.

134   Kensington Palace Gardens Anna Edwards, '£100m mansion for sale on London's Billionaire's Row (but Saudi Prince owner wants transaction to remain a secret)', *Daily Mail*, 29 July 2013.

134   offshore-owned properties See maps of offshore property at http://map.whoownsengland.org/ and http://www.private-eye.co.uk/registry.

135   more recent philanthropists Sir Len Blavatnik has donated £55m to Tate Modern and the V&A, for example; see *Sunday Times* Rich List 2018.

136   emissary of Beelzebub David Millward, '"Emissary of Beelzebub" who revels in his own notoriety', *Telegraph*, 20 December 2005.

136   made his fortune BBC News, 'An "emissary of Beelzebub"', 22 July 2002, http://news.bbc.co.uk/1/hi/england/2143994.stm

136   his mausoleum Lynn Barber, 'Nasty Nick', *Observer*, 15 January 2006.

136   *What shall it profit* Mark 8:36 (King James Version).

6 PROPERTY OF THE STATE

140   'Invasion citadel' Duncan Campbell, *War Plan UK* (Burnett Books, 1982), p. 104.

141   When you visited 'Whitehall Tunnel. Proposed extension to War Cabinet Basement'. Letter from Postmaster-General to Prime Minister covering memorandum and minute by Prime Minister thereon, 21 August 1941, National Archives CAB 80/30/7. Digitised and available online at http://discovery.nationalarchives.gov.uk/details/r/C9196810.

142   The plans, overlaid For details of the land titles and plans mentioned here, see https://whoownsengland.org/2017/12/15/how-land-registry-data-reveals-londons-secret-tunnels/

142   Shortly after the war http://hansard.millbanksystems.com/lords/1959/jan/20/post-office-works-bill

143   A manhole cover Duncan Campbell, 'A Christmas party for the moles', *New Statesman*, 19–26 December 1980.

143   real and only priority Campbell, *War Plan UK*, back cover.

144   all hell broke loose 'GES227 – Kingsway Exchange, London', 6 April 2013, http://www.guerrillaexploring.com/gesite/public_html/index.php?option=com_content&view=article&id=355:ges227-kingsway-exchange&catid=5:subterranean&Itemid=10

145   First Secretary of State Land Registry Corporate & Commercial dataset, entry for the Treasury building.

145   Basement, Ground As recorded in the Government Property Finder, https://www.epims.ogc.gov.uk/government-property-finder/SearchForPropertyAndLand.aspx. The Land Registry land title that covers 10–12 Downing Street and 68, 70 and 72 Whitehall states that the owner is the Secretary of State for Communities and Local Government, care of the Cabinet Office.

145 low-lying parts of Whitehall See Antony Milne, *London's Drowning* (Thames Methuen, 1982).

146 slashing our own costs 'New tool that maps government property', 20 August 2014, https://www.gov.uk/government/news/new-tool-that-maps-government-property

147 57 Whitehall SARL Ian Hay, Ministry of Defence, 'MOD completes sale of historic Old War Office', 2 March 2016, https://insidedio.blog.gov.uk/2016/03/02/mod-completes-sale-of-historic-old-war-office/

147 Rafael Serrano 'Government completes historic Admiralty Arch deal', 18 June 2015, https://www.gov.uk/government/news/government-completes-historic-admiralty-arch-deal

148 We can't find Mark Thomas, *Secret Map of Britain*, Channel 4, 2002. Available to watch on YouTube: https://www.youtube.com/watch?v=itqMwuB8gOk

148 the most effective mapping Perkins, C., Dodge, M., 'Satellite imagery and the spectacle of secret spaces', *Geoforum* (2009), doi:10.1016/j.geoforum.2009.04.012, available online at http://personalpages.manchester.ac.uk/staff/m.dodge/cv_files/spectacle_of_secret_spaces.pdf.

148 Maps work Denis Wood, *The Power of Maps* (Routledge, 1993).

148 240,000 hectares Ministry of Defence Guidance note, 'The defence training estate', published 12 December 2012, last updated 13 January 2015, https://www.gov.uk/guidance/defence-infrastructure-organisation-and-the-defence-training-estate

149 just over a million National Statistics: MOD land holdings bulletin 2017, https://www.gov.uk/government/statistics/mod-land-holdings-bulletin-2017. In 2014, the Cabinet Office's Government Property Finder website accidentally published details of the MOD's military and civil properties, and quickly took them down again – though not before I had downloaded a copy. These showed the MOD's land and property holdings to sum to 220,434 hectares, or 544,705 acres – presumably these were just freehold (and possibly leasehold), rather than land over which the Ministry simply possessed training rights.

151 white protective clothing Note circulated by J.D. Davies for the Director of AWRE Aldermaston to issue to workers on Foulness on 11 February 1975: National Archives ES 17/4, 'Firing of experimental assemblies containing beryllium at Foulness: safety of employees and local population; beryllium dispersion trials.

151 one of the consequences English Heritage, 'Atomic Weapons Research Establishment, Foulness, Essex: Cold War Research & Development Site: Survey Report', Research Department Report Series no. 13 (2009), p. 19, http://research.historicengland.org.uk/Report.aspx?i=14729

151 for the majority Grontmij Group Ltd for Defence Estates, 'MOD Shoeburyness – Fleet: Phase 2 Land Quality Assessment – Prioritised Areas', May 2009, p. 10. Report obtained under Freedom on Information laws; the author holds a hard copy.

153 The main constraint Essex and South Suffolk Shoreline Management Plan 2, October 2010, p. 226.

153 MOD has to acknowledge Defence Estates, 'Impacts of Climate Change on the MOD Estate', April 2007, unpublished by the MOD but obtained by the author under FOI and online at: https://friendsoftheearth.uk/sites/default/files/

downloads/impacts-climate-change-mod-estate-45473.pdf. For a news article written off the back of this and other FOI'd documents, see Sam Marsden, 'Military "may have to abandon flood-prone bases"', *Telegraph*, 21 February 2014.

153   It would be hard Bernie Friend, 'Foulness: Secret island of beauty and terror', *Basildon, Canvey and Southend Echo*, 11 April 2009.

154   a number of MPs Hansard, Defence of the Realm (Acquisition of Land) Bill 2016, Second Reading transcript, 5 July 2016: https://api.parliament.uk/historic-hansard/commons/1916/jul/05/defence-of-the-realm-acquisition-of-land. Final Act published at http://www.legislation.gov.uk/ukpga/Geo5/6-7/63

154   It seems to me Letter from E.G. Pretyman MP to Minister Addison, 2 July 1916, National Archives WO 32/2655, http://discovery.nationalarchives.gov.uk/details/r/C2539192.

155   200 munitions factories Historic England, First World War Centenary Project, 'First World War: Munitions Factories', https://historicengland.org.uk/whats-new/first-world-war-home-front/what-we-already-know/land/munitions-factories/

155   If I should die Rupert Brooke, 'The Soldier', 1914.

156   just 42,000 acres Letter from C.L. Bayne in the War Office to J.C.P. Langton in the Ministry of Agriculture, 1 February 1941, National Archives WO 32/16666, 'Acreage of land requisitioned by War Office'.

156   DR51 and DR52 Brian Short, *The Battle of the Fields: Rural Community and Authority in Britain during the Second World War* (The Boydell Press, 2014), p. 160 lists the different Defence Regulations pertaining to land requisitioning.

156   further vast swathes See e.g. http://www.nationalarchives.gov.uk/help-with-your-research/research-guides/land-requisitioned-war/

156   It would not Hansard, Parliamentary Question from Sir H. Morris-Jones MP to the Minister of Agriculture, 23 July 1942: https://api.parliament.uk/historic-hansard/written-answers/1942/jul/23/requisitioned-land#S5CV0382P0_19420723_CWA_25

156   When we were taking C.L. Bayne, War Office, 'Internal notes on Brief for S. of S' Deputation of Welsh MPs re Cambrian Battle Training Area', 27 July 1942, National Archives, WO 32/16666, 'Acreage of land requisitioned by War Office', http://discovery.nationalarchives.gov.uk/details/r/C2549812

157   580,847 acres Note from Miss D. Lambert in the Land Branch of the War Office to Mr E.H. Lawrence in the Ministry of Agriculture, 29 August 1946, National Archives WO 32/16666.

157   14.5 million acres See http://www.nationalarchives.gov.uk/help-with-your-research/research-guides/land-requisitioned-war/, section 7.1: '14.5 million acres of land, 25 million square feet of industrial and storage premises and 113,350 non-industrial premises were requisitioned during the Second World War.' While an archival reference is given for War Office totals, no source appears to be given for this statistic. I have also discussed this with Prof. Brian Short, who confirms that at least 11.5 million acres of land across Great Britain were requisitioned for military use by 1944, much of it very temporary; additional land was requisitioned to be brought into agricultural use under DR52.

157   only 95,350 acres Letter dated 9 July 1956, drafted by a War Office civil servant

for Secretary of State Sir Walter Monckton MP to send to the Ministry of Defence and other service ministers summarising War Office landholdings, National Archives WO 32/16666

157   It is regretted . . . Moving was a traumatic experience . . . training implies Wright, *The Village that Died for England*, pp. 207, 208–10, 223.

158   The Stanford Training Area Mark Nicholls, 'Touring the STANTA ghost villages', 17 June 2006, *Eastern Daily Press*.

159   the nearby Tilshead Estate Handwritten note from War Office official (name illegible), 22 February 1933, National Archives WO 32/21837, 'Imber, Wiltshire: purchase of land, Tilshead Estate'.

159   murdered village Cited in Marianna Dudley, *An Environmental History of the UK Defence Estate, 1945 to the Present* (Continuum, 2012), pp. 123–6.

159   Your Britain Frank Newbold, 'Your Britain – fight for it now', poster issued by the Army Bureau of Current Affairs, 1942. Imperial War Museum Art. IWM PST 14887.

160   Crichel Down in Dorset For an overview of the Crichel Down case, see Roger Gibbard, 'Whose land was it anyway? The Crichel Down Rules and the sale of public land', *Working Papers in Land Management and Development* 01/02, http://www.reading.ac.uk/LM/LM/fulltxt/0102.pdf.

160   three quarters of a million Calculated using Historical Inflation Rate calculator, http://inflation.iamkate.com/.

160   Churchill's pledge Wright, *The Village that Died for England*, p. 230.

161   Every citizen Sir D. Maxwell Fyfe, House of Commons debate on Crichel Down, Hansard col. 1292, 20 July 1954, https://hansard.parliament.uk/Commons/1954-07-20/debates/8443e7eb-d5e5-45f2-9af4-b7504c3a583b/CrichelDown.

161   Lying behind that case 'Remember Crichel Down', *Spectator*, 23 July 1954, p. 6, http://archive.spectator.co.uk/article/23rd-july-1954/6/remember-crichel-down

162   uniquely bedevilled I.F. Nicholson, *The Mystery of Crichel Down* (Clarendon Press, 1986), pp. vi–viii.

162   Tim Adams, writing in the *Observer* Tim Adams, 'Who owns our green and pleasant land?', *Observer*, 7 August 2011.

162   Crichel Down Rules Government guidance on the Crichel Down Rules on land ownership, published 12 December 2012:https://www.gov.uk/guidance/crichel-down-rules-on-land-ownership.

162   out of 3,000 cases Department for Communities and Local Government, 'The operation of the Crichel Down rules', 2000, http://webarchive.nationalarchives. gov.uk/20120919234653/http://www.communities.gov.uk/documents/planning andbuilding/pdf/158478.pdf. For very helpful details on the Crichel Down case see pp. 23–8.

163   Crichel House Jim Durkin, 'American billionaire buys Crichel House', *Daily Echo*, 24 July 2013, http://www.bournemouthecho.co.uk/news/10567790.American_ billionaire_buys_Crichel_House/

164   If ever there was H.J. Massingham, *English Downland* (B.T. Batsford, 1936), p. vi.

164   Land at Porton Down An overview of the history of Porton Down is given in 'War Office, Ministry of Supply, Ministry of Defence: Chemical Defence Experimental

Establishment', National Archives WO 189: http://discovery.nationalarchives.gov.uk/details/r/C14396

164   *If you could hear* Wilfred Owen, 'Dulce et decorum est', in *Poems*, 1921 (Viking Press).

165   Don Quixote H. Rider Haggard, *Rural England: Being an account of agricultural and social researches carried out in the years 1901 & 1902* (Cambridge University Press, reprinted 2010), pp. 9–18.

165   Major Poore railed For more on Major Poore, his estate at Porton Down and his experiment in land reform at nearby Winterslow, see Wiltshire Council's community history webpages: https://history.wiltshire.gov.uk/community/getcom.php?id=253.

165   local self-government See the Poore family's papers at the Wiltshire and Swindon History Centre: http://discovery.nationalarchives.gov.uk/browse/r/h/5eec33e1-8225-4083-aff2-c628afo50ecb

165   sold to the War Office The Poore Estate was sold to the military in 1924; see 'Contract, with plan, for the sale by Poore Ltd to the War Department of the 554 acre estate sometime part of the Porton Down Experimental Establishment', 1924, Wiltshire and Swindon History Centre 1915/13: http://discovery.nationalarchives.gov.uk/details/r/422b6459-cd91-48f4-a424-695b2c520ed4

165   No Man's Land Ordnance Survey six-inch map series for Hampshire & Isle of White XXX.SE, revised 1923.

166   public inquest Rob Evans, 'Scandal of nerve gas tests', *Guardian*, 3 September 1999.

166   verdict of unlawful killing BBC News, 'Nerve gas death was "unlawful"', 15 November 2004, http://news.bbc.co.uk/1/hi/england/wiltshire/4013767.stm.

166   A building within FOI response 12 June 2017, https://assets.publishing.service.gov.uk/government/uploads/system/uploads/attachment_data/file/627152/2017-05600.pdf

166   Sergei Skripal's pets Haroon Siddique and Luke Harding, 'Sergei Skripal's cat and guinea pigs die after police seal house', *Guardian*, 6 April 2018.

166   Frank Stolton MAF archival records, 'Amiton poisoning case: F Stolton', 1958–9, National Archives MAF 284/128, http://discovery.nationalarchives.gov.uk/details/r/C1436262

166   produced for ICI Dr Brian Balmer of University College London, in a presentation to the WHO on the history of nerve agent development, notes on slide 8 on the development of the V-series agents: 'Pesticide research at Plant Protection Ltd (PPL) produced "Amiton" ... Technology transfer from PPL (via ICI) to military took place between 1951 and 1953': http://www.who.int/global_health_histories/seminars/Brian_Balmer_presentation.pdf. A report dated 6 August 1968 listing all past projects at Porton Down's manufacturing outpost at Nancekuke – in which the first project in the list is production of R6199 for ICI in 1955–6 – is contained in War Office file WO 188/2259, 'Case for retaining chemical agent production facilities at Nancekuke, 1957–70', http://discovery.nationalarchives.gov.uk/details/r/C11395503

167   the Ministry of Supply Extensive evidence of the collaboration between ICI's subsidiary Plant Protection Ltd and the Ministry of Supply, which then controlled

Porton Down and Nancekuke, can be found in PPL's minutebooks held at the Wellcome Institute. The minutebook covering 1955–8 (WF/C/S/18/04) is particularly enlightening. A note from 30 October 1956 states in relation to R6199 that 'Manufacture at Nancikuke [*sic*] will, for the present, be allowed to proceed'. A note of 29 January 1957 refers to the company's contract with the Ministry of Supply for an annual supply of 25 tons of R6199. A note of 25 May 1957 states that 'the Ministry of Supply are likely to require some share of eventual profits from this project in return for their manufacturing know-how'.

167   Secret and personal Letter from G.D. Heath on behalf of Mr Haddon, Ministry of Supply, to Dr Perren, head of CDE Porton Down, 31 December 1957, National Archives WO 188/2259, 'Case for retaining chemical agent production facilities at Nancekuke, 1957–70', http://discovery.nationalarchives.gov.uk/details/r/C11395503

167   two toxic chemicals Alfred M. Sciuto, Urmila P. Kodavanti, *Handbook of Toxicology of Chemical Warfare Agents*, 2nd edn (Academic Press, 2015), ch. 36, 'The Respiratory Toxicity of Chemical Warfare Agents'. See https://www.sciencedirect.com/topics/veterinary-science-and-veterinary-medicine/vomiting-agents

168   a report from 1970 Results of test, dated 17 February 1970, National Archives WO 188/2453, 'Disposal of toxic agents at Nancekuke 1954-74'; see http://discovery.nationalarchives.gov.uk/details/r/C11395528

168   old chemical weapons MOD briefing on Project Cleansweep, July 2011, https://www.scribd.com/doc/60530845/MoD-Briefing-on-Project-Clean-Sweep-July-2011

168   At Bowes Moor Rob Edwards, 'MoD investigates former chemical weapons factories for contamination', *Observer*, 24 July 2011.

168   foxes and hounds Judith Perera and Andy Thomas, 'Mustard gas at the bottom of the garden', *New Scientist*, 13 February 1986.

168   Biological Weapons Convention John Walker, *Britain and Disarmament: The UK and Nuclear, Biological and Chemical Weapons Arms Control and Programmes, 1956–1975* (Ashgate Publishing, 2012).

168   Gruinard Island 'Biological warfare: Dark Harvest', *Time*, 9 November 1981.

169   Low-level radioactivity Rob Edwards, 'MoD reveals 15 radioactive UK sites', *Guardian*, 20 December 2011.

169   For 40 years Judith Perera and Andy Thomas, 'Mustard gas at the bottom of the garden', *New Scientist*, 13 February 1986.

169   174 Sites MOD SSSI factsheet, 2015: https://assets.publishing.service.gov.uk/government/uploads/system/uploads/attachment_data/file/33339/sites_of_special_scientific_interest_SSSIs.pdf.

169   over 70,000 acres FOI response from the MOD, 21 October 2010: https://www.whatdotheyknow.com/request/32754/response/121843/attach/4/20101019%20MOD%20SSSI%20list%20U.pdf

169   the single best Michael McCarthy, 'The secret of Porton Down: behind its defences, it has created Britain's finest wildlife reserve', *Independent*, 11 August 2003

170   better site management Dudley, *An Environmental History of the UK Defence Estate*, p. 197.

170   military-environmentalist narrative see ibid., p. 198.

170   I approve of their lack Chris Packham, Foreword to *Sanctuary* 46 (2017), https://assets.publishing.service.gov.uk/government/uploads/system/uploads/attachment_data/file/660061/Sanctuary_2017_Complete_-_lo-res.pdf

171   Lodge Hill in north Kent An excellent overview of this case can be found on Miles King's A New Nature Blog: https://anewnatureblog.wordpress.com/category/lodge-hill/.

171   proposed bulldozing Ownership of Lodge Hill has more recently been passed, ominously, from the MOD to Homes England, whose purpose is rather summed up in their name. At the time of writing, Lodge Hill was still under threat of development: see Nicola Jordan, 'Medway: Plan for 5,000 homes at Lodge Hill back on the table', *Kent Online*, 1 February 2018, http://www.kentonline.co.uk/medway/news/plan-for-5000-homes-back-159464/

171   one-tenth of its sites Jessica Elgot, 'MOD to sell tenth of UK defence sites including D-day training ground', *Guardian*, 7 November 2016.

172   626,383 acres Author's analysis of Forestry Commission GIS maps, available for download at https://www.forestry.gov.uk/datadownload. The GIS data covers both England and Scotland, and all forms of tenure; here I have isolated the freehold and leasehold figures for England. The public forest estate in Wales has been owned and managed by Natural Resources Wales since 2013.

172   The relationship Second Report (on Afforestation) of the Royal Commission on Coast Erosion, Reclamation of Tidal Lands, and Afforestation, 1909, Part I.

172   it does not appear Second Report (on Afforestation) of the Royal Commission on Coast Erosion, Reclamation of Tidal Lands, and Afforestation, paras 91–2.

172   legislation was at last 'History of the Forestry Commission', https://www.forestry.gov.uk/forestry/cmon-4uum6r

172   Napoleon's maxim First Annual Report of the Forestry Commissioners (1920), p. 11, https://www.forestry.gov.uk/PDF/FCAR_1920.pdf/$FILE/FCAR_1920.pdf

173   pressured the Commission Peter Waine and Oliver Hilliam, *22 Ideas That Saved the English Countryside: The Campaign to Protect Rural England* (Frances Lincoln, 2016), p. 174.

173   German pine forests Ibid., p. 175.

173   unimaginative planting Victor Bonham-Carter, *The Survival of the English Countryside* (Hodder & Stoughton, 1971), p. 181.

174   Sitka spruce As the Forestry Commission state on their website, 'Sitka spruce is the most productive and most economic species to grow across virtually all of the Forest District. It currently accounts for 70–80% of the conifer element.' See https://www.forestry.gov.uk/forestry/infd-6xjf34

174   handed a huge area National Archives, 'Records of The Crown Estate and predecessors', explains how the Crown Estate's ownership of the Royal Forests passed to the Forestry Commission in 1923–4: http://discovery.nationalarchives.gov.uk/details/r/C62

174   65,000 acres Author's analysis of Forestry Commission GIS maps.

174   I have had the courtesy Lord Montagu, House of Lords debate on the New Forest, 6 July 1927, Hansard, https://api.parliament.uk/historic-hansard/lords/1927/jul/06/the-new-forest#S5LV0068P0_19270706_HOL_47

174   the Duke of Northumberland The Duke's Northumberland Estates website states that 'death duties forced the Estate to sell 47,000 acres of land at Kielder. In 1932 this land was planted up by the Forestry Commission to create the largest man made forest in Northern Europe.' See http://www.northumberlandestates.co.uk/about/.

175   41,000 acres . . . 5,000-acre Author's analysis of Forestry Commission GIS maps shows it acquired 41,000 acres of Kielder in 1932, and the Marr Estate in 1937.

175   it provides one-fifth Forestry Commission news release, 'Ever wondered how a working forest works?', 22 July 2014, https://www.forestry.gov.uk/newsrele.nsf/webnewsreleases/1c4c120f199b7f4580257d1d0055897c

176   legislation in 1981 Sylvie Nail, *Forest Policies and Social Change in England* (Springer, 2008), p. 59.

176   a press rumour Forestry Commission, 66th Annual Report 1985–6, p. 18, https://www.forestry.gov.uk/PDF/FCAR_1985-1986.pdf/$FILE/FCAR_1985-1986.pdf

176   What is this mania Dennis Skinner MP, House of Commons debate on the Forestry Commission, 10 April 1986, Hansard col. 95 cc329–31, https://api.parliament.uk/historic-hansard/commons/1986/apr/10/forestry-commission#S6CV0095P0_19860410_HOC_57

176   Half a million people Johnny Chatterton, 'Victory! Government to scrap plans to sell our forests', 17 February 2011, https://home.38degrees.org.uk/2011/02/17/victory-government-to-scrap-plans-to-sell-our-forests/

179   government wants to reopen Christopher Hope, 'Reversing the 1960s Beeching rail cuts will help tackle the housing crisis, says Chris Grayling', *Telegraph*, 14 December 2017.

179   biggest privatisation Brett Christophers, 'The biggest privatisation you've never heard of: land', *Guardian*, 8 February 2018; see also Brett Christophers, *The New Enclosure* (Verso, 2018).

179   346,000 acres For full details of what each water company owns, see 'Liquid assets: land owned by the water utilities', 29 August 2016, https://whoownsengland.org/2016/08/29/liquid-assets-land-owned-by-the-water-utilities/.

180   United Utilities Emily Gosden, 'United Utilities opens talks with Cuadrilla over fracking deal', *Telegraph*, 20 July 2013.

180   273,000 acres Response to Parliamentary Question by Jim Lester MP in 1975. Hansard, Written Answers (Commons), 'National Coal Board (Land Holding), 13 March 1975, https://api.parliament.uk/historic-hansard/written-answers/1975/mar/13/national-coal-board-land-holding

180   Harworth Estates https://harworthgroup.com/about-us/. See also 'The 50 companies that own over a million acres of England & Wales', 12 December 2016, https://whoownsengland.org/2016/12/12/the-50-companies-that-own-over-a-million-acres-of-england-wales/

181   selling off the leases See the website of the campaign group Guardians of the Arches, https://www.guardiansofthearches.org.uk/

181   landmark study TfL, 'Land value capture: final report', February 2017, https://www.london.gov.uk/sites/default/files/land_value_capture_report_transport_for_london.pdf

181   Over 150 law courts Tamsin Rutter, 'The big HMCTS sell-off: buyers of 152 former courts revealed', 23 March 2018, *Civil Service World*, https://www.civilserviceworld.com/articles/news/big-hmcts-sell-buyers-152-former-courts-revealed

181   helped reduce the total Cabinet Office, 'Transparency report: Government's land and property disposals in 2015–16 and 2016–17', April 2018, https://assets.publishing.service.gov.uk/government/uploads/system/uploads/attachment_data/file/697082/Transparency_report_Government_s_land_and_property_disposals_2015-16_and_2016-17.pdf

182   Maintaining the freehold Alice Martin, 'Making the case for affordable housing on public land', 31 July 2017, http://neweconomics.org/2017/07/affordable-housing-public-land/

182   just 10 per cent Joe Beswick and Hanna Wheatley, 'No homes for nurses: how NHS land is being sold off to build unaffordable homes', 9 January 2018, http://neweconomics.org/2018/01/no-homes-for-nurses/

7 CORPORATE CAPTURE

183   Trafford Centre Graham Ruddick, 'Capital Shopping Centres seal £1.6bn Trafford Centre deal despite Simon Property Group's concerns', *Telegraph*, 27 January 2011.

183   MediaCityUK See http://www.mediacityuk.co.uk/

183   some 37,000 acres See http://peellandp.co.uk/. Peel state they own 15,000 hectares, which is around 37,000 acres.

184   His one act 'John Whittaker – the publicity shy billionaire', *Telegraph*, 24 November 2010.

184   Whittaker built 'Profile: John Whittaker', *Scotsman*, 28 March 2010.

184   acrimonious takeover battle 'Peel Holdings milestones', *Manchester Evening News*, 30 June 2005.

184   a row of gaudy Oliver Wainwright, '"Final warning": Liverpol's Unesco status at risk over docks scheme', *Guardian*, 1 July 2017,

185   customers who make Andrew Bounds, 'Manchester congestion charge divides business', *Financial Times*, 20 October 2008.

185   disguising its true intentions Jack Straw MP, House of Commons debate, 'Peel Holdings', Hansard, 16 May 2012, col. 662, https://publications.parliament.uk/pa/cm201213/cmhansrd/cm120516/debtext/120516-0004.htm

185   well in excess of 300 ExUrbe, 'Peel and the Liverpool City Region: Predatory Capitalism or Providential Corporatism?', March 2013, http://media.wix.com/ugd//440822_22c65849313bcedd42dc15d57426cd04.pdf

186   Peel (Knowlmere) Company See https://opencorporates.com/companies/im/006301C.

186   land in Lancashire Peel (Knowlmere) Company is shown on the overseas & offshore property maps compiled by *Private Eye* as owning land near the Forest of Bowland in Lancashire. See http://www.private-eye.co.uk/registry.

186   dodging taxes Jennifer Williams, 'Property giant Peel Group accused of "tax dodging"', *Manchester Evening News*, 11 June 2013.

186   one map they produced Peel Group, 'Investing in the North: Peel 150 in the

Northern Powerhouse', 1 October 2015, https://www.peel.co.uk/wp-content/uploads/2018/03/Peel-150-map.pdf

186   Peel schemes rarely Peter Kilfoyle, foreword to ExUrbe, 'Peel and the Liverpool City Region: Predatory Capitalism or Providential Corporatism?', March 2013, http://media.wix.com/ugd//440822_22c65849313bcedd42dc15d57426cd04.pdf

187   6.6 million acres This figure consists of 6,240,593 acres owned by UK-registered limited companies, 136,034 acres owned by UK-registered limited liability partnerships (LLPs), and 279,523 acres owned by overseas-registered companies. All figures for May 2015.

187   the top fifty See 'The 50 companies that own over a million acres of England and Wales'.

188   Some nifty GIS work See *Private Eye*'s online maps of offshore ownership at www.private-eye.co.uk/registry

189   its own 'official' database Land Registry press release, 'Land Registry publishes Overseas Companies data', 17 March 2016, https://www.gov.uk/government/news/land-registry-publishes-overseas-companies-data.

189   the Panama Papers See e.g. Luke Harding, 'What are the Panama Papers?', *Guardian*, 5 April 2016.

189   company-owned land For a breakdown of the ten companies with the most land titles, see Anna Powell-Smith, 'The companies and corporate bodies who own a third of England and Wales', 14 November 2017, https://whoownsengland.org/2017/11/14/the-companies-corporate-bodies-who-own-a-third-of-england-wales/

189   £200 million December 2017 accounts for Wallace Estates filed with Companies House https://beta.companieshouse.gov.uk/company/04216645,/filing-history. The same set of accounts states that the company is part of a group of companies headed by Albanwise Ltd, whose Companies House profile reveals its Person of Significant Control to be Count Luca Rinaldo Contardo Padulli: https://beta.companieshouse.gov.uk/company/01359468/persons-with-significant-control

190   huge increases in ground rents Patrick Collinson, 'Leasehold houses and the ground rent scandal: all you need to know', *Guardian*, 25 July 2017. See also the website of the campaigning group Leasehold Knowledge Partnership, www.leaseholdknowledge.com

191   One analysis Simon Goodley and Leila Haddou, 'Revealed: Tesco hoarding land that could build 15,000 homes', *Guardian*, 26 June 2014.

191   sell off some of its sites Jon Yeomans, 'Tesco raises £250m from sale of 14 sites', *Telegraph*, 15 October 2015.

191   even by building flats Ashley Armstrong, 'Tesco Towers: supermarket enters the fray with a radical new solution to the housing crisis', *Telegraph*, 19 November 2016.

191   currently have sixteen James Sillars, 'Amazon to create 400 jobs at new UK fulfilment centre', Sky News, 29 January 2018, https://news.sky.com/story/amazon-to-create-400-jobs-at-new-uk-fulfilment-centre-11227459

192   all but one Land Registry Corporate & Commercial dataset entries for 'Amazon UK Services Ltd' and 'Amazon.co.uk Ltd'.

192   at least forty Land Registry Corporate & Commercial dataset entries for 'Moy

Park Ltd' turns up eighty land titles, of which forty appear to be distinct farmsteads with postcodes, and the remainder additional land parcels attached to them.

192   nearly 800 Andrew Wasley, Fiona Harvey, Madlen Davies and David Child, 'UK has nearly 800 livestock mega farms, investigation reveals', *Guardian*, 17 July 2017.

192   Moy Park was fined Matt Atherton, 'Moy Park to pay £118,420 for animal welfare offences', 7 July 2017, https://www.foodmanufacture.co.uk/Article/2017/07/07/Chicken-processor-fined-for-animal-welfare-failings

194   270,000 acres GIS analysis by the author measuring two datasets produced by the Environment Agency: maps of historic landfill (204,784 acres) and 'Authorised Landfill Site Boundaries', i.e. current landfill (66,425 acres).

195   recycling rates have flatlined DEFRA, Digest of Waste and Resource Statistics, March 2017, p. 37, fig. 3.6: https://assets.publishing.service.gov.uk/government/uploads/system/uploads/attachment_data/file/607416/Digest_of_Waste_and_Resource_Statistics__2017_rev.pdf

195   15 million tonnes DEFRA, Digest of Waste and Resource Statistics, fig. 3.4, p. 35.

195   less than seven years Andrea Lockerbie, 'Landfill in England to run out in seven years', *MRW*, 7 September 2017, https://www.mrw.co.uk/latest/landfill-in-england-to-run-out-in-seven-years/10023208.article

196   other historic landfills James Brand and Kate Spencer, 'Assessing the risk of pollution from historic coastal landfills. Executive Summary for the Environment Agency', 2017, http://www.geog.qmul.ac.uk/media/geography/staff/academicstaff/191752.pdf.

196   last deposited waste Environment Agency, Historic Landfill map and dataset.

196   revenues of £3.7 billion http://www.interserve.com/about-us. For more on the Tilbury Contracting and Dredging Co Ltd, and how it became Interserve, see their entry in Grace's Guide to British Industrial History, https://www.gracesguide.co.uk/Tilbury_Contracting_and_Dredging_Co, and the Wikipedia entry for Interserve.

196   the company ... bought 'Our history', http://www.interserve.com/about-us/our-history.

197   The historic landfill Kate Spencer and Francis T. O'Shea, 'The Hidden Threat of Historical Landfills on Eroding and Low-lying Coasts', ECSA Bulletin 63, Summer 2014, http://www.geog.qmul.ac.uk/media/geography/staff/academicstaff/145301.pdf

197   ticking time bomb Francis T. O'Shea and Kate Spencer, 'Contamination of Coastal Sediments from Historic Landfills: A ticking time-bomb', 9th International SedNet Conference, Krakow, Poland, 2015, https://www.researchgate.net/publication/282097595?channel=doi&linkId=5604ff8108aea25fce320723&showFulltext=true. See also Tom Bawden, 'Landfill dumps across UK "at risk of leaking hazardous chemicals"', *Independent*, 21 February 2016.

198   release their stranglehold Sajid Javid MP, speech to Conservative Party Conference, 3 October 2016, http://press.conservatives.com/post/151284016515/javid-speech-to-conservative-party-conference

198   As has been proved Rhiannon Curry and Isabelle Fraser, 'House builders hit back at landbanking claims', *Telegraph*, 3 October 2016.

199   one man losing Leong Chan Teik, 'I lost more than $200k in UK land investment,

now I work as a security guard', *Next Insight*, 20 February 2016, https://www.nextinsight.net/story-archive-mainmenu-60/938-2016/10577-i-lost-more-than-200k-in-uk-land-investment-now-i-work-as-a-security-guard

199 **jailed for fifteen years** K.C. Vijayan, 'High Court dismisses appeals by directors of Profitable Plots', *Straits Times*, 23 June 2015.

199 **Other similar** The FSA investigated one such scheme, UK Land Investment International Limited, in 2006, concluding that the scheme was unlawful and should be wound down. See BBC R4 *Face the Facts*, transcript of episode broadcast 1 August 2008, http://www.bbc.co.uk/radio4/facethefacts/transcript_20080801.shtml. Other similar schemes, however, escaped censure for some time afterwards: see Nick Duxbury, 'Unregulated land banking firms escape FSA ruling', *Property Week*, 24 April 2009, https://www.propertyweek.com/news/unregulated-land-banking-firms-escape-fsa-ruling-/3139070.article

199 **strategic land portfolio** 'Strategic Land', http://www.legalandgeneralcapital.com/our-investments/list-of-investments/strategic-land.html

199 **Nearly all of it** Land Registry Corporate & Commercial data extracts for Legal & General companies. My full investigation into the location of Legal & General's land bank is online at https://whoownsengland.org/2018/02/04/how-pension-funds-are-land-banking-in-the-green-belt/

199 **submitting proposals** Savills, 'Luton Strategic Employment Gateway: Proposals by Legal & General', August 2012, http://www.slipend.co.uk/home/sites/default/files/LGLuton-Employment%20Gateway_FINAL_07%2008%2012_lr.pdf

200 **a small but crucial** 'Ransom strips in the UK', 1 September 2015, http://www.rics.org/uk/knowledge/glossary/ransom-strips/

200 **there will sometimes** Neil O'Brien MP, 'Green, pleasant and affordable: Why we need a new approach to supply and demand to solve Britain's housing problem', June 2018, http://www.ukonward.com/wp-content/uploads/2018/06/220618-Green-Pleasant.-Affordable-Web-ready.pdf

201 **as much as 30,000 acres** Analysis of the subsidiary companies that share the same address as Taylor Wimpey's head office and same Person of Significant Control, using Land Registry data on corporate land areas obtained by Christian Eriksson.

201 **whether housebuilders** Pete Jeffreys, 'Land banking: what's the story? (part 1)', Shelter blog, 14 December 2016, http://blog.shelter.org.uk/2016/12/land-banking-whats-the-story-part-1/

201 **failed to keep pace** Daniel Bentley, 'Planning approvals vs housebuilding activity, 2006–2015', briefing note, August 2016, http://www.civitas.org.uk/content/files/Planning-approvals-vs-housebuilding-activity.pdf

201 **I cannot find** MHCLG, 'Independent review of build out: draft analysis' ('The Letwin Review'), 25 June 2018, https://www.gov.uk/government/publications/independent-review-of-build-out-draft-analysis

201 **map the land** See Anna Powell-Smith's map of land owned by housebuilders at http://housebuilders.whoownsengland.org/

202 **review remit** Tweet by Neal Hudson (@resi_analyst), 23 June 2018, https://twitter.com/resi_analyst/status/1010628884696530944

202 **A group of private** Isabelle Fraser, 'The modern-day barons: inside the murky underbelly of land promotion', *Telegraph*, 5 August 2017.

202   90 per cent success rate http://www.gladmanland.co.uk/

202   never built a home Molior for Mayor of London, 'Barriers to Housing Delivery – Update', July 2014, https://www.london.gov.uk/sites/default/files/gla_migrate_files_destination/Barriers%20to%20Housing%20Delivery%20Update%20Report%20-%20July%202014_0.pdf

8 A PROPERTY-OWNING DEMOCRACY?

205   Our concern is Margaret Thatcher, Speech to Conservative Party Conference, 17 October 1981, Thatcher Archive: CCOPR 786/81.

205   no single piece Michael Heseltine, House of Commons debate on the Housing Bill (Second Reading), 15 January 1980, Hansard vol. 976 cc1443–575, https://api.parliament.uk/historic-hansard/commons/1980/jan/15/housing-bill

205   a million council homes Office for National Statistics (ONS), 'UK Perspectives 2016: Housing and home ownership in the UK', 25 May 2016, https://www.ons.gov.uk/peoplepopulationandcommunity/housing/articles/ukperspectives2016housingandhomeownershipintheuk/2016-05-25.

206   enabled millions more Richard Disney and Guannan Luo, 'The Right to Buy public housing in Britain: A welfare analysis', *Journal of Housing Economics*, Vol. 35 (March 2017), pp. 51–68. See also Hilary Osborne, 'Home ownership in England at lowest level in 30 years as housing crisis grows', *Guardian*, 2 August 2016.

206   Skelton argued Noel Skelton MP, 'Private Property: A Unionist Ideal', *Spectator*, 3 May 1924, p. 6, http://archive.spectator.co.uk/article/3rd-may-1924/6/private-property-a-unionist. For more on the history of the idea of a 'property-owning democracy', see Matthew Francis, 'Who invented the British dream of a "property-owning democracy"?, 26 July 2017, http://www.democraticaudit.com/2017/07/26/who-invented-the-british-dream-of-a-property-owning-democracy/

206   200,000 new houses Alastair Parvin, 'A Right to Build' (2011), p. 10, https://issuu.com/alastairparvin/docs/2011_07_06_arighttobuild.

207   price of an average home Ibid.

207   lowest level of housebuilding ONS, 'UK Perspectives 2016: Housing and home ownership in the UK', 25 May 2016, https://www.ons.gov.uk/peoplepopulationandcommunity/housing/articles/ukperspectives2016housingandhomeownershipintheuk/2016-05-25

207   END OF THE James Burton, 'End of the home owning dream', *Daily Mail*, 20 February 2018.

207   just 27 per cent Richard Partington, 'Home ownership among young adults has "collapsed", study finds', *Guardian*, 16 February 2018.

207   300,000 new homes BBC News, 'Budget 2017: Plans to build 300,000 homes a year', 19 November 2017, http://www.bbc.co.uk/news/business-42043084

207   14.3 million homeowners MHCLG English Housing Survey 2015–16 (2 March 2017), https://www.gov.uk/government/statistics/english-housing-survey-2015-to-2016-headline-report

207   about 9.6 per cent ONS, '2011 Census: Characteristics of Built-Up Areas', 28 June 2013, https://www.ons.gov.uk/peoplepopulationandcommunity/housing/

articles/characteristicsofbuiltupareas/2013-06-28. The ONS state that 1.4 million hectares – 3,459,475 acres, 9.6% of England and Wales – comprised built-up areas in 2011.

208   just 1.1 per cent UK National Ecosystem Assessment (UKNEA), 2011, p. 368: http://uknea.unep-wcmc.org/LinkClick.aspx?fileticket=u60Ugtegc28%3d& tabid=82. Alasdair Rae at Sheffield University, who has also investigated this issue, calculates that buildings in England take up 2 per cent of the land area (though this includes many non-residential buildings); see Alasdair Rae, 'Buildings of Great Britain', 19 September 2017, http://www.statsmapsnpix. com/2017/09/buildings-of-great-britain.html.

208   LET THE GRAB BEGIN *Scottish Daily Mail*, 24 January 2003.

209   Wyndham Land Act Fergus Campbell, 'Irish popular politics and the making of the Wyndham Land Act, 1901–1903', *Historical Journal* 45: 4 (2002), pp. 755–73.

209   over half a million BBC News, 'Communities in Scotland own more than 500,000 acres of land', 8 December 2017, http://www.bbc.co.uk/news/uk-scotland-highlands-islands-42280124

210   I took my spade Gerrard Winstanley, *A Watch-Word to the City of London and the Armie* (1649), reproduced in Christopher Hill (ed.), *Winstanley: 'The Law of Freedom' and Other Writings* (Maurice Temple Smith, 1972), p. 128.

211   Seeing the common people Gerrard Winstanley, 'Letter to Lord Fairfax', 8 December 1649, cited in Siobhan Brownlie, *Memory and Myths of the Norman Conquest* (The Boydell Press, 2013), p. 115.

211   the ownership of which John Gurney, '"Furious divells?" The Diggers and Their Opponents', in Andrew Bradstock (ed.), *Winstanley and the Diggers, 1649–1999* (Frank Cass & Co., 2000), p. 82.

212   It is part of 'St George's Hill', *Spectator*, 16 December 1911, http://archive.spectator. co.uk/article/16th-december-1911/10/st-georges-hill

212   the Beatles bought houses Toby Keel, 'Inside the mansion where John Lennon lived at the height of Beatles fame', *Country Life*, 15 November 2017. Ringo Starr also once lived there in a property called Sunny Heights.

212   Britain's Beverly Hills Harry Wallop, 'Elmbridge, Surrey: Life can be taxing in Britain's Beverly Hills', *Telegraph*, 20 May 2013.

213   value of £282 million http://www.private-eye.co.uk/registry. See also my blog, 'Who owns St George's Hill, birthplace of the Diggers?', 10 September 2017, https:// whoownsengland.org/2017/09/10/who-owns-st-georges-hill-birthplace-of-the-diggers/

213   one acre of land St George's Hill Residents' Association planning guidelines, revised April 2013, http://www.knightfrank.co.uk/resources/residential/insights/ esher/knight-frank-st-georges-hill-planning-guidelines-revised-april-2013-(r1).pdf

214   The nurseries of beggars J. Thirsk and J.P. Cooper (eds), *Seventeenth-Century Economic Documents* (Oxford University Press, 1972), p. 107; cited in Hill, *The World Turned Upside Down*, p. 50.

214   The poor increase Pseudomismus, *Considerations concerning Common Fields and Enclosure* (1665); cited in Hill, *The World Turned Upside Down*, p. 52.

214   They inclose all Thomas Moore, *Utopia* (1516), Book 1.

214   27–30 per cent Gregory Clark and Anthony Clark, 'Common Rights to Land in

England, 1475–1839', *The Journal of Economic History* 61: 4 (December 2001), pp. 1009–36.

214 Parliament passed Acts 'Enclosing the land', https://www.parliament.uk/about/living-heritage/transformingsociety/towncountry/landscape/overview/enclosingland/

214 just 5.2 per cent John Aitchison, Karl Crowther, Martin Ashby & Louise Redgrave, 'The Common Lands of England: A Biological Survey', Rural Survey Research Unit at University of Wales, Aberystwyth, for the Department of the Environment, Transport and the Regions, 1997, http://bromyarddowns.co.uk/media/1687/1997-common-lands-biological-survey.pdf, p. 10.

215 120 workmen Jan Marsh, *Back to the Land: The pastoral impulse in Victorian England from 1880 to 1914* (Quartet Books, 1982), p. 44.

215 7,000 registered commons Aitchison et al., 'The Common Lands of England'; 'The Commons Lands of Great Britain', http://www.foundationforcommonland.org.uk/the-commons-lands-of-great-britain

215 24,000 acres of commons 'Common land and village greens', https://www.surreycc.gov.uk/environment-housing-and-planning/enforcement-and-regulations/land/common-land-and-village-greens.

215 Three of the largest For a discussion of some of the complexities around common land registration and the New Forest, see the website of the New Forest Verderers (commoners), http://www.verderers.org.uk/rights.html

215 A fascinating survey https://data.gov.uk/dataset/05c61ecc-efa9-4b7f-8fe6-9911afb44e1a/database-of-registered-common-land-in-england – see spreadsheet labelled 'Commons register England, 2000', from which I have drawn the examples cited, including that of Worms Heath common at Tandridge in Surrey, part-owned by the Worms Heath Gravel Company.

215 appears to have been Aitchison et al., 'The Common Lands of England'.

216 This slander Garrett Hardin, 'The Tragedy of the Commons', *Science* 162: 3859 (13 December 1968), pp. 1243–8. One of the many critiques of Hardin's 'tragedy of the commons' is Simon Fairlie, 'A Short History of Enclosure in Britain', *The Land* 7 (Summer 2009), http://www.thelandmagazine.org.uk/articles/short-history-enclosure-britain

216 Piecemaster of Atherstone The commons officials listed here all appear in the ownership column in the Common Register of England (2000), https://data.gov.uk/dataset/05c61ecc-efa9-4b7f-8fe6-9911afb44e1a/database-of-registered-common-land-in-england.

216 Elinor Ostrom A useful introduction to Ostrom's work is Wyn Grant, 'Elinor Ostrom's work on Governing The Commons: An Appreciation', LSE Review of Books (17 June 2012), http://blogs.lse.ac.uk/lsereviewofbooks/2012/06/17/elinor-ostroms-work-on-governing-the-commons-an-appreciation/, which includes many links to Ostrom's books and journal articles.

218 an older, wiser way For a longer discussion of this interpretation, see Ronald W. Cooley, 'Kent and Primogeniture in "King Lear"', *Studies in English Literature, 1500–1900* 48: 2 (Spring 2008), pp. 327–48.

218 *gavelkind* R.J. Smith, 'The Swanscombe Legend and the Historiography of

Kentish Gavelkind', in Richard Utz and Tom Shippey (eds), *Medievalism in the Modern World: Essays in Honour of Leslie J. Workman* (Turnhout: Brepols, 1998), pp. 85–103.

219   The custom of the *gavelkind* N. Neilson, 'Custom and the Common Law in Kent', *Harvard Law Review* 38: 4 (February 1925), pp. 482–98.

219   This subdivision of land D.B. Grigg, 'Small and Large Farms in England and Wales: Their Size and Distribution', *Geography* 48: 3 (July 1963), pp. 268–79.

219   Wat Tyler . . . Jack Cade McLynn, *The Road Not Taken*, pp. 14, 71–2.

220   I think that no person Paul Foot, *The Vote* (Penguin, 2005), p. 29.

220   there may be a law Ibid., p. 30.

220   'Great' Reform Act 'The Reform Act 1832', https://www.parliament.uk/about/living-heritage/evolutionofparliament/houseofcommons/reformacts/overview/reformact1832/

220   a mere 8 per cent Foot, *The Vote*, p. 70

220   detach the discontented Francis Jeffrey, Lord Advocate, quoted in Foot, *The Vote*, p. 71.

221   enfranchise more and more McLynn, *The Road Not Taken*, p. 322.

221   the widespread and deep P. Searby, 'Great Dodford and the Later History of the Chartist Land Scheme', *Agricultural History Review* 16: 1 (1968), pp. 32–45.

221   A parliamentary select committee 'Dodford and the Chartist Land Plan', https://www.parliament.uk/about/living-heritage/transformingsociety/electionsvoting/chartists/case-study/the-right-to-vote/the-chartists-and-birmingham/dodford-and-the-chartist-land-plan/

221   legitimate aspirations McLynn, *The Road Not Taken*, p. 329.

221   Over 300 'land societies' Malcolm Chase, 'Out of Radicalism: The Mid-Victorian Freehold Land Movement', *English Historical Review* 106: 419 (April 1991), pp. 319–45.

222   Longton Freehold Land Society For maps showing the land bought by the society, see http://www.thepotteries.org/maps/trentham_parish_n.htm.

222   the cost of a single pint 'The Freehold Franchise', *Reformer's Almanac* (1849), p. 64, cited in Chase, 'Out of Radicalism'.

222   citadel of privilege Quoted in Chase, 'Out of Radicalism'.

222   extended the right to vote Chase, 'Out of Radicalism'

222   I am in favour Cited in Douglas, *Land, People & Politics*, p. 18.

223   cited by Theresa May Lewis Goodall, 'Who was Theresa May's political hero Joseph Chamberlain?', BBC *Newsnight* blog, 15 August 2016, http://www.bbc.co.uk/news/uk-politics-37053114

223   Besides the creation Joseph Chamberlain, *The Radical Programme* (1885), p. 66, cited in Douglas, *Land, People & Politics*, p. 49.

224   Allotments undoubtedly Colin Ward and David Crouch, *The Allotment: Its Landscape and Culture* (Faber & Faber, 1988), p. 270.

224   For many of us Ward and Crouch, *Allotments*, p. 156.

224   almost 1.5 million Statistics cited in the Departmental Committee of Inquiry into Allotments ('The Thorpe Report') (October 1969), pp. 47–50. After the First World War, the number of allotment plots stood at 1,330,000 in 1920; during the Second, the number peaked in 1942 at 1,451,888.

224   A Steve Bell cartoon Steve Bell's *If...* cartoon strip, 'Jedi Jeremy Corbyn gets down to earth', *Guardian*, 25 January 2016.

225   The 1908 Allotments Act For more on the complex legislation governing allotments, see this summary: https://www2.canterbury.gov.uk/media/892659/The-Law-and-allotments-summary-Appendix-28.pdf; the House of Commons Library's briefing on allotments, 21 March 2012, http://researchbriefings.parliament.uk/ResearchBriefing/Summary/SN00887#fullreport; National Society of Allotment and Leisure Gardeners' webpage on the history of allotments, https://www.nsalg.org.uk/allotment-info/brief-history-of-allotments/

225   90,000 people https://www.nsalg.org.uk/allotment-info/brief-history-of-allotments/; NSALG allotment waiting lists survey 2013, http://www.transition-townwestkirby.org.uk/files/ttwk_nsalg_survey_2013.pdf

225   Over 100,000 acres Departmental Committee of Inquiry into Allotments.

225   just 31,000 acres Author's analysis, using the Ordnance Survey Greenspace dataset, released July 2017. Measuring the area of the polygons in the dataset reveals that golf courses comprise around 310,000 acres across the UK, while allotments take up just 33,300 acres. For England alone, the figure for allotments is 31,712 acres: my thanks to Alasdair Rae at the University of Sheffield for his help in arriving at this number.

225   ten times more land Ian Johnston, 'Golf courses cover 10 times more land than allotments – and get £550,000 in farming subsidies', *Independent*, 21 July 2017.

225   average age today is sixty DEFRA, 'Agriculture in the United Kingdom 2017', May 2018, https://assets.publishing.service.gov.uk/government/uploads/system/uploads/attachment_data/file/712317/AUK-2017-31may18.pdf

225   The smallholding movement Susanna Wade Martins, 'Smallholdings in Norfolk, 1890–1950: a social and farming experiment', *Agricultural History Review* 54:2 (2006) pp. 304–30.

226   426,695 ... 215,155 Analysis by the author of various government datasets – including DEFRA annual smallholdings reports, the Curry Review 2008, the Northfield Inquiry 1979 and others – detailed in full at https://whoownsengland.org/2018/06/08/how-the-extent-of-county-farms-has-halved-in-40-years/.

226   Without council farms Quoted in David Thame, 'Shrinking opportunities for council farms', *Farmers Weekly*, 25 June 2009.

226   It's a beautiful farm BBC Radio 4 *On Your Farm*, 'Last Days of the Farm', 19 November 2017, https://www.bbc.co.uk/programmes/b09fjhzo

227   Glasgow Rent Strike BBC News, 'Statue of rent strikes campaigner Mary Barbour unveiled', 8 March 2018, https://www.bbc.co.uk/news/av/uk-scotland-glasgow-west-43338204/statue-of-rent-strikes-campaigner-mary-barbour-unveiled

227   In this context John Boughton, *Municipal Dream: The Rise and Fall of Council Housing* (Verso, 2018), p. 34.

227   It was unthinkable Ibid., p. 39.

227   Progressive-controlled Battersea David Rosenberg's *Rebel Footprints: A Guide to Uncovering London's Radical History* (Pluto Press, 2015) includes a great walk around Battersea taking in its Edwardian-era council estates, with road names like 'Freedom Street' and 'Reform Street'.

227   The Boundary Estate Description from Boughton, *Municipal Dream*, p. 8.

228   machines for living in Le Corbusier, *Towards a New Architecture* (1927).

228   swung sharply to the left See Paul Addison, *The Road to 1945: British Politics and the Second World War* (Pimlico, 1994).

228   800,000 council homes Boughton, *Municipal Dream*, p. 105.

228   National Housing Service Lynsey Hanley, 'An NHS for housing', *Guardian*, 14 February 2007.

228   even in those immediate Baroness Lee of Asheridge, House of Lords debate on Wealth Tax proposal and historic houses, 26 June 1974, Hansard vol. 352, col. 1511, https://api.parliament.uk/historic-hansard/lords/1974/jun/26/wealth-tax-proposal-and-historic-houses-1.

228   Some within Labour Blatchford was the utopian socialist founder of the Clarion Cycling Club, whose book *Merrie England* (1893) sold an astonishing two million copies – a testament to the popularity of its ideas, which were as much a form of early environmentalism as they were socialist. The 1918 Labour manifesto declared that 'land nationalisation is a vital necessity; the land is the people's and must be developed so as to afford a high standard of life'. See http://labourmanifesto.com/1918/1918-labour-manifesto.shtml

229   Let those who now hold Henry George, *Progress and Poverty* (1879), ch. 32.

229   the 1941 Uthwatt Report A useful overview of the report's main recommendations is a briefing by legal firm Mills & Reeve, 9 August 2010: https://www.mills-reeve.com/files/Publication/b9a8fa0d-730e-41fe-bca3-70eec7eb047f/Presentation/PublicationAttachment/c813a1c2-5a71-43e1-a537-758be697ce6f/The_Uthwatt_Report_Jul_10.pdf.

229   The reputable builder Minister of Town and Country Planning Lewis Silkin MP, House of Commons debate on the Town and Country Planning bill, 29 January 1947, Hansard vol. 432 col. 984, https://api.parliament.uk/historic-hansard/commons/1947/jan/29/town-and-country-planning-bill

230   repeal the charge See Daniel Bentley, *The Land Question: Fixing the dysfunction at the root of the housing crisis* (Civitas, 2017), pp. 42–3.

230   For 11 years Bentley, *The Land Question*, pp. 44–5.

230   229,000 council homes Boughton, *Municipal Dream*, p. 105.

230   LAND OWNERS GET Cited in Bentley, *The Land Question*, p. 44.

231   more than fivefold Richard Partington, 'Landowners reap benefits of soaring British land prices', *Guardian*, 5 December 2017.

231   Labour's shadow housing minister Robert Booth, 'Labour plans to make land-owners sell to state for fraction of value', *Guardian*, 1 February 2018.

231   deeply sinister Tweet by Liz Truss MP, 2 February 2018: https://twitter.com/trussliz/status/959346122790768640

231   more sensible Nick Boles MP has backed land value capture and reforming the 1961 Land Compensation Act in chapter 3 of his online book *Square Deal* (February 2018), http://www.squaredeal.org.uk/square-deal-for-housing/. Neil O'Brien MP similarly backs the reform of CPO rules to let councils acquire land cheaply, in a report for his think tank Onward, 'Green, Pleasant and Affordable: Why we need a new approach to supply and demand to solve Britain's housing problem',

June 2018, http://www.ukonward.com/new-policy-paper-green-pleasant-and-affordable-by-neil-obrien-mp/. Bim Afolami MP has called for a Permission Value Tax on landowners once planning permission is granted for developments: see his chapter in *New Blue: Ideas for a New Generation* (Centre for Policy Studies, May 2018), https://www.cps.org.uk/publications/new-blue-ideas-for-a-new-generation/.

231   Improving the ability Ryan-Collins, Lloyd and Macfarlane, *Rethinking the Economics of Land and Housing*, p. 197.

232   Number 10's housing adviser Catherine Neilan, 'Shelter policy head joins Number 10 as housing adviser', *City A.M.*, 2 May 2018, http://www.cityam.com/285114/shelter-policy-head-joins-number-10-housing-adviser

9 IN TRUST FOR TOMORROW

235   Even if we've never 'White Cliffs of Dover get writer-in-residence', *Telegraph*, 20 August 2012.

236   The *Daily Express* Serina Sandhu, 'Daily Express accused of editing White Cliffs of Dover front page to make cliffs look "whiter"', *inews*, 29March 2018, https://inews.co.uk/news/brexit/daily-express-brexit-white-cliffs-of-dover-front-page/

237   *Refugees Welcome* Global Justice Now press release, '"Refugees Welcome" projected on white cliffs of Dover ahead of far right march', 1 April 2016, http://www.globaljustice.org.uk/news/2016/apr/1/refugees-welcome-projected-white-cliffs-dover-ahead-far-right-march

237   614,000 acres Author's correspondence with National Trust data team, August 2018. National Trust land maps displayed as a map layer at http://map.whoowns england.org/, show a lower figure of 589,748 acres. Author's analysis of these maps shows that the Trust owns some 474,641 acres in England, with the remainder in Wales.

238   12 December 1894 Date of the signing of the Memorandum and Articles of Association for the National Trust, courtesy of the archives of the National Trust.

238   the need of quiet Gillian Darley, *Octavia Hill: A Life* (Constable, 1990), p. 310.

238   Any Commoner Jennifer Jenkins and Patrick James, *From Acorn to Oak Tree: The growth of the National Trust 1895–1994* (Macmillan, 1994), p. 3.

239   We see no reason *The Times* leading article, 17 November 1893, courtesy of the National Trust archives.

239   Why not nationalize B.L. Thompson, *Lake District and the National Trust* (Titus Wilson, 1946), p. 43.

239   granted inalienable status Author's correspondence with the National Trust's data team, who confirm that out of 614,000 acres of freehold land, some 562,000 acres have been declared inalienable, and that 'there will be other land which has been proposed inalienable, but for which the legal process may not yet have been completed'.

239   draw up such covenants The Law Commission, 'Conservation Covenants', report to Parliament No. 349, June 2014, https://www.lawcom.gov.uk/project/conservation-covenants/

239   for the first 40 Lydia Greeves, *Houses of the National Trust* (National Trust Books, 2008; revised edn 2017), p. 6.

240   At the trust's inaugural *The Times*, 17 July 1894. Courtesy of the National Trust archives.

241   imbuing it with reverence Jenkins and James, *From Acorn to Oak Tree*, p. 52.

241   presided over the most Ibid., p. 74.

241   Most of these [houses] Ibid., p. 79.

241   2.5 million unemployed James Denman and Paul McDonald, 'Unemployment statistics from 1881 to the present day', *Labour Market Trends*, 104: 15–18, 1 January 1996.

241   Why should the government Jenkins and James, *From Acorn to Oak Tree*, p. 80.

241   the scheme allowed landowners Ibid., ch. 4, *passim*.

242   James Lees-Milne The life and work of James Lees-Milne is attested to in his numerous diaries, and neatly summarised at http://www.jamesleesmilne.com/life.html.

242   to protect society George Monbiot, 'Britain's national parks are a farce: they're being run for a tiny minority', *Guardian*, 28 February 2018. Monbiot also heavily criticised the Trust during the years when he was involved in setting up The Land Is Ours (TLIO); see e.g. 'Whose Nation, Whose Trust?', *Guardian*, 27 September 1995, http://www.monbiot.com/1995/09/27/whose-nation-whose-trust/.

242   Put bluntly Jenkins and James, *From Acorn to Oak Tree*, p. 95.

242   Sir Charles Trevelyan is Ibid., p. 93. For more on the estates left to the National Trust by 'socialist aristocrats', see the National Trust centenary souvenir book (National Trust Books, 1995), p. 34.

242   Sir Richard Acland For more on Sir Richard Acland, a Christian socialist who went on to help set up CND, see Meredith Veldman, *Fantasy, the Bomb, and the Greening of Britain: Romantic protest, 1945–1980* (Cambridge University Press, 1994), pp. 164–8.

243   beauty for all The Labour Party, 'A nation without poverty: Labour's plans for organising a prosperous Britain', 1935.

243   an example of Hugh Dalton, *Practical Socialism for Britain* (Routledge, 1936).

243   you can spend as much James Lees-Milne, *Midway on the Waves* (Faber & Faber, 1985), p. 35.

243   the Trust acquired Giles Worsley, 'National Trust to take over city slums', *Telegraph*, 17 October 2001, https://www.telegraph.co.uk/finance/property/4814628/National-Trust-to-take-over-city-slums.html.

244   its now vast membership The National Trust's membership reached 5 million in September 2017: https://www.nationaltrust.org.uk/projects/5-million-members-how-we-got-here.

244   110,000 acres The Lake District National Park is 583,747 acres, according to the Lake District National Park Authority's website: http://www.lakedistrict. gov.uk/learning/factsandfigures. Measuring GIS maps of land owned by the National Trust within the Lake District NP gives an area of 110,124 acres. This is around 18 per cent of the Lake District. According to the Edwardes Report, a government review of National Parks in 1990, the National Trust then owned

24 per cent of the Lake District National Park Area; it's possible boundaries have changed slightly since then, or that some of the Trust's land has been sold.

244   'unfavourable' condition Lake District National Park Partnership's Nomination Dossier for the Lakes obtaining World Heritage Site status (2016), p. 535, Table 4.6, 'Condition of biodiversity', which shows just 24.6 per cent of SSSIs to be in 'favourable' condition; the other 75.4 per cent are in varying degrees of 'unfavourable' condition, from 'unfavourable recovering' to outright decline. Online at: http://www.lakedistrict.gov.uk/__data/assets/pdf_file/0012/729696/4.0-State-of-Conservation-and-factors-affecting-the-Property.pdf

245   Changes, and rules of Taste William Wordsworth, *A Guide through the District of the Lakes in the North of England: with a description of the scenery, etc., for the use of tourists and residents* (1835), ch. 3.

245   A *Punch* cartoon *Punch*, 5 February 1876, p. 34: https://punch.photoshelter.com/image/I00001V7Kz6dMPsI.

245   overspread with wood . . . Republic of shepherds Wordsworth, *A Guide through the District of the Lakes*, pp. 38, 57.

245   they will be nothing Cited in Jenkins and James, *From Acorn to Oak Tree*, pp. 59–60.

246   Overgrazing is a key factor Miles King, 'Sheepwrecked or a World Heritage Site? Thoughts on the Lake District', *A New Nature Blog*, 22 May 2017, https://anewnatureblog.wordpress.com/2017/05/22/sheepwrecked-or-a-world-heritage-site-thoughts-on-the-lake-district/

246   Come to the Fake EarthFirst!, *Do or Die: Voices from the Ecological Resistance* 10 (2003), p. 61.

246   degenerated into George Monbiot, 'The Lake District as a world heritage site? What a disaster that would be', *Guardian*, 9 May 2017.

247   People ask me Rory Stewart MP, video posted on Twitter ahead of a debate with authors George Monbiot and Mark Cocker, 9 July 2018, https://twitter.com/rorystewartuk/status/1016286082890166272?s=11

247   James Rebanks' bestseller James Rebanks, *The Shepherd's Life* (Penguin, 2016).

247   cultural landscape See the Lake District National Park Partnership's Nomination Dossier for World Heritage Site status (2016): http://www.lakedistrict.gov.uk/__data/assets/pdf_file/0005/729671/1.0-Exec-Summary-and-Identification-of-the-Property.pdf

247   one of England's best Professor Alasdair Driver, post on Twitter, 5 July 2017, https://twitter.com/AliDriverUK/status/1014904126336008195

247   reforest parts of Thorneythwaite See https://www.nationaltrust.org.uk/borrowdale-and-derwent-water/features/thorneythwaite-borrowdale-in-the-lake-district.

247   betrayal of Beatrix Potter's Geoffrey Levy, 'National Trust's VERY PC boss – and the betrayal of Beatrix Potter's Lake District legacy: Locals' fury as charity's Whitehall mandarin is accused of "mafia tactics" in Borrowdale land grab', *Daily Mail*, 21 November 2016

248   ten national parks Technically there are nine English National Park Authorities;

the Broads Authority is a distinct entity with different powers. However, in 2015, it rebranded as the Broads National Park.

248   Ninety-five per cent Ron Edwards, National Parks Review Panel, 'Fit for the Future' ('The Edwards Report') (Countryside Commission, 1990). Table 4.5.1 shows land ownership in national parks. In some cases this has changed slightly in the intervening years, but not substantially.

248   the privately owned half 57 per cent of Northumberland National Park is owned by private landowners: see Northumberland NPA, Management Plan (3rd review), 'A secure future for the land of the far horizons', 2003, p. 9, https://www.northumberlandnationalpark.org.uk/wp-content/uploads/2017/06/nationalpark managementplan2.pdf.

248   Or take the South Downs For more on land ownership within the South Downs National Park, see 'Who owns the South Downs?', 16 February 2018, https://whoownsengland.org/2018/02/16/who-owns-the-south-downs/

248   Exmoor National Park Exmoor is one of the few NPAs to publish a map of major landowners within its boundaries: see p. 2 of this (undated) briefing: http://www.exmoor-nationalpark.gov.uk/learning?a=122272. See also Adrian Dangar, 'When the law has its clause into you', *Telegraph*, 2 August 2003, https://www.telegraph.co.uk/finance/property/3315663/When-the-law-has-its-clause-into-you.html; League Against Cruel Sports webpage, 'Our Sanctuaries', https://www.league.org.uk/sanctuaries.

249   Sir Sebastian Anstruther Louise Gray, 'Britain's newest national park threatened by aristocrat's quarry plan', *Telegraph*, 5 June 2010.

249   the intensive management State of Nature Partnership, *State of Nature 2016*, https://www.rspb.org.uk/globalassets/downloads/documents/conservation-projects/state-of-nature/state-of-nature-uk-report-2016.pdf, p. 18.

249   97 per cent *State of Nature 2016*, p. 21.

249   Half of all farmland birds Claire Marshall, 'Farmland birds show rapid decline', BBC News, 23 October 2014, https://www.bbc.co.uk/news/science-environment-29728558.

250   a ranking system https://www.iucn.org/theme/protected-areas/about/protected-area-categories.

250   the only way to enjoy Bernard Rothman, *The 1932 Kinder Trespass* (Willow Publishing, 1982), p. 11.

250   lungs of the industrial north Eric Allison, 'The Kinder Scout trespass: 80 years on', *Guardian*, 17 April 2012.

250   the most successful Ibid. For more on the Kinder trespass, see Marion Shoard, *A Right to Roam* (Oxford University Press, 1999), pp. 180–2.

251   popular writer S.P.B. Mais see '"All the ways of life" by S.P.B. Mais', *Spectator*, 15 October 1937, http://archive.spectator.co.uk/article/15th-october-1937/40/all-the-ways-of-life-by-s-p-b-mais. On the broader inter-war 'cult of the great outdoors' and its various fascinating back-to-the-land movements, see Frank Trentmann, 'Civilisation and its Discontents: English Neo-Romanticism and the Transformation of Anti-Modernism in Twentieth-Century Western Culture', *Journal of Contemporary History* 29: 4 (October 1994), pp. 583–625.

251   one of the most spectacular Shoard, *A Right to Roam*, pp. 189–90.

252   Forbidden Britain Day see Kate Ashbrook, 'Fifteen years on', 30 November 2015, http://www.ramblers.org.uk/news/blogs/2015/november/fifteen-years-on.aspx.

252   People have fought Cited in Shoard, *A Right to Roam*, p. 284.

252   just 10 per cent Shoard, 'Into the woods'.

252   so much less than Scotland The wide-ranging right to roam provisions of the 2003 Land Reform (Scotland) Act are summarised by the Scottish Rights of Way and Access Society at https://www.scotways.com/faq/law-on-statutory-access-rights.

252   Sandford Principle see http://www.nationalparks.gov.uk/students/whatisana-tionalpark/aimsandpurposesofnationalparks/sandfordprinciple

253   99 per cent of fenland Michael McCarthy, 'Restoring the glory of waterworld', *Independent*, 29 June 2005.

253   it is only on land Peter Marren, *Nature Conservation* (HarperCollins, 2002), p. 107.

253   the survival or otherwise Richard Perry, *Wildlife in Britain and Ireland* (Croom Helm, 1978); cited in David Evans, *A History of Nature Conservation in Britain* (Routledge, 2nd edn 1997), p. 32.

254   a list of 284 E. Lewis and A. Cormack, 'The Rothschild List: 1915–2015 – A review 100 years on' (The Wildlife Trusts, 2015), https://www.wildlifetrusts.org/sites/default/files/2018-04/Rothschild%27s%20List%20100%20Years%20On.pdf

254   an enthusiastic supporter Jenkins and James, *From Acorn to Oak Tree*, pp. 36–7.

254   was for many years Marren, *Nature Conservation*, p. 63.

255   2,300 nature reserves https://www.wildlifetrusts.org/wildlife-and-wild-places/protecting-wildlife-sites/nature-reserves. It's unclear exactly how much land is owned freehold by the Wildlife Trusts, as opposed to being simply leased or managed by them. They state 98,500 hectares, i.e. 243,400 acres: I suspect most of this is leased from other landowners.

255   332,812 acres Analysis of GIS mapping data of RSPB reserves, published online at https://www.rspb.org.uk/our-work/conservation/conservation-and-sustainability/mapping-and-gis/. Unfortunately, it's not possible to tell from the RSPB's dataset which reserves are owned freehold and which are leases.

255   many a pleasant down Marren, *Nature Conservation*, pp. 109–10.

255   struggled to acquire John Sheail, 'Nature Reserves, National Parks, and Post-war Reconstruction, in Britain', *Environmental Conservation* 11: 1 (Spring 1984), pp. 29–34. Sheail states that the aspirations of the early conservation movement to acquire land were 'beyond the resources of the voluntary bodies involved' and that 'only central Government could provide them on the scale needed'. The Government's initial solution of passing the buck onto the nascent planning system was constrained by 'the sanctity of property rights and the consequent need to compensate those adversely affected by planning'.

255   had been stifled Robert Lamb, *Promising the Earth* (Routledge, 1996), p. 110.

256   the Nature Conservancy For an overview of the creation and history of the Nature Conservancy and NNRs, see John Sheail, *Nature Conservation in Britain: The Formative Years* (The Stationery Office, 1998), especially p. 34.

256   233,267 acres Figure from Natural England webpages, 'National Nature Reserves in England', https://www.gov.uk/government/collections/national-nature-reserves-in-england. To determine the acreage of NNRs owned or leased by the Government (DEFRA's arms-length body Natural England, the successor to the Nature Conservancy), I analysed Government Property Finder maps of public sector property. The data did not make clear what proportion is either leasehold or freehold.

256   at least 300,000 kilometres Hugh Warwick, *Linescapes: Remapping and Reconnecting Britain's Fragmented Wildlife* (Vintage, 2017), p. 43.

257   cover of a book Charlie Pye-Smith and Chris Rose, *Crisis and Conservation: Conflict in the British Countryside* (Penguin, 1984).

257   a legal responsibility Lamb, *Promising the Earth*, p. 112.

257   rural landowners Pye-Smith and Rose, *Crisis and Conservation*, p. 15.

257   you are unlikely to find ... Sir Ralph Verney Marren, *Nature Conservation*, pp. 83–4.

258   zealots and minions Jeremy Purseglove, *Taming the Flood: Rivers, Wetlands and the Centuries-Old Battle Against Flooding* (William Collins; revised edn, 2015), pp. 305–7, which also includes a photo of the burning effigies. See also Marren, *Nature Conservation*, p. 89.

258   Kingsthorpe Field Marren, *Nature Conservation*, p. 92.

258   in his waders Lamb, *Promising the Earth*, p. 154.

259   little more than bribes Ibid., p. 113.

259   blatant profiteering Marren, *Nature Conservation*, p. 94.

260   The remaining pockets Warwick, *Linescapes*, p. 4.

260   46 million tonnes BEIS, '2016 UK Greenhouse Gas Emissions – Final Figures', 6 February 2018, https://assets.publishing.service.gov.uk/government/uploads/system/uploads/attachment_data/file/680473/2016_Final_Emissions_statistics.pdf, p. 27.

260   The Knepp Estate See https://www.rewildingbritain.org.uk/rewilding/rewild-ing-projects/knepp-estate

261   extension of the planning system Shoard, *This Land Is Our Land*, pp. 432–7; Sheail, *Nature Conservation in Britain*, p. 235.

261   local wildlife sites Miles King, 'A Pebble in the Pond: Opportunities for farming, food and nature after Brexit', People Need Nature (2016), http://peopleneednature.org.uk/public-realm-policy/pebble-in-the-pond/

262   a statutory scheme The Law Commission, 'Conservation Covenants'.

10 AN AGENDA FOR ENGLISH LAND REFORM

266   homeowners' share of England The UK National Ecosystem Assessment 2011, Chapter 10, p. 368, states that domestic buildings and gardens sum to 5.4 per cent of England's land area. See also Chapter 8, 'A Property-Owning Democracy?'

266   total area of land Dan and Peter Snow, *Whose Britain Is It Anyway?*

266   own around 30 per cent This estimate, explored in more detail in Chapter 4, is based on 1) Roy Perrott, *The Aristocrats*, 1967 (Weidenfeld and Nicolson); 2)

Dan and Peter Snow, BBC2, *Whose Britain Is It Anyway?*, 2006; and 3) the Country Land & Business Association, who have stated that their 36,000 members own a third of England & Wales: see the CLA, 'Environmental standards in farming: consultation response from the Country Land and Business Association', 27 May 2009, https://www.cla.org.uk/sites/default/files/A0938084%20Environ. Standards%20Resp.pdf. While the CLA's membership is clearly a larger segment of landowners than simply peers and baronets, it's likely to include many other members of the traditional landed gentry.

266 17 per cent DCLG, 'Fixing our broken housing market'.

268 25,000 landowners DEFRA, Structure of the agricultural industry in England and the UK at June 2017, https://www.gov.uk/government/statistical-data-sets/ structure-of-the-agricultural-industry-in-england-and-the-uk-at-june. Under the England heading, select 'results by type of farm' and within the spreadsheet select the tab named 'Farm sizes (area and holdings)'; see the columns for numbers of farms >=100ha and the total farmed area under farms of this size. Analysis of this data shows that 25,638 farm holdings cover 16.5 million acres, or 52% of England's land area. Taking farm holdings as a proxy for landowners means that considerably less than 1% of the population own half of England. See also discussion in Chapter 4, 'Old Money'.

269 post-geography Andrew Bounds, 'UK entering a "post-geography trading world"', says Liam Fox', *Financial Times*, 29 September 2016.

269 we devote 10 per cent See e.g. the geographer Alasdair Rae's analysis of CORINE land use data, covered in Mark Easton, 'How much of your area is built on?', BBC News, 9 November 2017, https://www.bbc.co.uk/news/uk-41901294. England's land use is given as 72.9 per cent farmland, 8.8 per cent built on, and 14.5 per cent natural, with 3.8 per cent green urban (so = 18.3 per cent natural + green urban). Caution should be taken with some of CORINE's categories, however; much of what is classified as 'natural' includes heavily grazed upland areas. Nor, of course, should farmland be construed as totally lacking in nature; many hedgerows and field margins are very species-rich.

270 £21,000 per square metre See Anna Powell-Smith's analysis of Land Registry price paid data, https://houseprices.anna.ps/

273 Scottish Land Commission See https://landcommission.gov.scot/

273 the *cadastre* An overview of the French cadastral system is given, in English, by the French government's General Tax Directorate at http://www.eurocadastre. org/pdf/gil.pdf.

273 Denmark See https://eng.gst.dk/danish-cadastre-office/.

273 The state of Montana see http://svc.mt.gov/msl/mtcadastral/.

273 New Zealand See https://data.linz.govt.nz/group/owner-data-controlled-access-group/. For more on how a public register of trusts could work, see Andres Knobel, 'The case for registering trusts – and how to do it', Tax Justice Network, 3 November 2016, https://www.taxjustice.net/wp-content/uploads/2013/04/ Registration-of-Trusts_AK.pdf. Indeed, there is already a Trust Register, but registration isn't compulsory, and it's only accessible by the police and tax authorities.

274 public register of options on land See Catherine Banks, 'The case for greater

land market transparency', November 2016, http://england.shelter.org.uk/professional_resources/policy_and_research/policy_library/policy_library_folder/briefing_the_case_for_greater_land_market_transparency. The government has even promised to look into doing this; see DCLG, 'Fixing our broken housing market', p. 24.

275 land prices have spiralled Office for National Statistics, 'The UK national balance sheet: 2017 estimates', 5 December 2017, https://www.ons.gov.uk/economy/nationalaccounts/uksectoraccounts/bulletins/nationalbalancesheet/2017estimates

276 land prices began their inexorable The best, most succinct account of this is in Bentley, The Land Question.

276 60,000 homes Mason, 'Over 11,000 homes have stood empty for at least 10 years, data shows', The dataset, obtained by the Liberal Democrats by surveying councils, also shows that 60,000 UK properties have stood empty for more than two years.

276 300 per cent council tax premium For more on taxes to halt vacant properties, see https://endemptyhomes.org/.

279 to the task of rescuing Shoard, This Land Is Our Land, p. 433.

280 100,000-signatory petition Adam Vaughan, 'MPs to debate ban on grouse shooting', Guardian, 7 September 2016; Mark Avery, 'The 'debate' – some first thoughts', 2 November 2016, https://markavery.info/2016/11/02/debate-thoughts/

280 designated wild areas Alasdair Driver, 'It's time to bite the bullet for nature in National Parks', 13 July 2018, https://www.cnp.org.uk/blog/it%E2%80%99s-time-bite-bullet-nature-national-parks

281 hundreds of places King, 'A Pebble in the Pond', p. 5.

282 The buildings and countryside Matthew Bell, 'To the manor born: the female aristocrats battling to inherit the title', Independent, 15 June 2013.

285 sponsored sale Author's correspondence with Gwyn Williams. The relevant provisions are contained in the Water Industry Act 1991, consolidating earlier provisions included in the Water Act 1989, s.152.

285 county farms estate For more on county farms, see 'How the extent of County Farms has halved in 40 years', 8 June 2018, https://whoownsengland.org/2018/06/08/how-the-extent-of-county-farms-has-halved-in-40-years/ See House of Commons Library briefing, 'Assets of community value', 28 April 2017, http://researchbriefings.parliament.uk/ResearchBriefing/Summary/SN06366#fullreport

287 Community right to buy see https://www.gov.scot/Topics/farmingrural/Rural/rural-land/right-to-buy/Community

287 The isle of Eigg See Alastair McIntosh, Soil and Soul: People versus Corporate Power (Aurum, 2001).

APPENDIX

297 Land area ONS, 'The Countries of the UK' [archived content from Jan 2016], http://webarchive.nationalarchives.gov.uk/20160108051201/http://www.ons.

gov.uk/ons/guide-method/geography/beginner-s-guide/administrative/the-countries-of-the-uk/index.html. I have converted the ONS' area figures from km to acres.

297   **Population figures** ONS, 'Population estimates for UK, England and Wales, Scotland and Northern Ireland: mid-2017', 28 June 2018, https://www.ons.gov.uk/releases/populationestimatesforukenglandandwalesscotlandandnorthernireland mid2017

298   **Forestry Commission** Author's analysis of Forestry Commission GIS maps of their UK freehold and leasehold land, https://www.forestry.gov.uk/datadownload. For this and all other spatial datasets cited below, I used GIS mapping software to extract acreages for English freehold land only.

298   **Ministry of Defence** UK and English freehold land area published by Ministry of Defence, 'National Statistics: MOD land holdings bulletin 2017', 17 July 2017, https://www.gov.uk/government/statistics/mod-land-holdings-bulletin-2017. (Converted hectares to acres.)

298   **Highways England** Acreage calculated by measuring GIS maps, 2017, https://data.gov.uk/dataset/d92af767-a3d8-4860-b7da-d5edf596f90e/highway-boundary.

298   **Network Rail** Acreage calculated by measuring GIS maps supplied to the author following a Freedom of Information request, June 2016.

298   **Other Whitehall departments** Analysis of Government Property Finder ePIMS spreadsheet extracts, August 2018, available for download at https://e-pims.cabinetoffice.gov.uk/government-property-finder/SearchForProperty AndLand.aspx. This database covers most Whitehall departments but excludes MOD military land, Forestry Commission sites, and land owned by Highways England and Network Rail (hence my separate entries for these). For some reason, it's not possible to download an extract of land and property just for England; so instead I followed a process of elimination – downloading the entire UK-wide spreadsheet of freehold land, then freehold extracts for Wales, Scotland and Northern Ireland, and subtracting these from the total area.

298   **Local authorities** Figure is for land owned by English and Welsh local authorities and county councils. Data from Land Registry Corporate and Commercial spreadsheet, June 2015. I then sorted out the councils into English and Welsh local authorities to derive a figure for England.

298   **Oxbridge colleges** Figure from Xavier Greenwood, 'Oxford and Cambridge university colleges own property worth £3.5bn', *Guardian*, 29 May 2018. Greenwood obtained this figure by submitting FOI requests to all Oxbridge colleges; he kindly shared the full dataset with me and confirmed that, based on colleges' responses, virtually all the land they own is in England, save for a handful of small farmsteads in Wales.

298   **The Crown Estate** Annual report 2015–16: https://www.thecrownestate.co.uk/media/1701/the-crown-estate-annual-report-and-accounts-2015-16.pdf. This comprises 'landward' acres, which means it omits areas of foreshore and estuarial riverbeds. (A separate body, Crown Estate Scotland, manages Crown land in Scotland.) I submitted an FOI request to the Crown Estate to obtain a GIS map of their land, which is displayed at http://map.whoownsengland.org/.

298   **Duchy of Cornwall** Integrated annual report 2017–18, https://duchyofcornwall.

org/assets/pdf/DuchyOfCornwallIAR2018.pdf, p. 84 gives a total figure of 52,970 hectares (130,894 acres), and that 103 hectares (255 acres) of this is located in Wales: I have subtracted this from the total to give the English acreage.

298   Duchy of Lancaster Annual report and accounts for year ending 31March 2018, https://www.duchyoflancaster.co.uk/wp-content/uploads/2018/07/2018-DoL-Annual-Report-and-Accounts.pdf, which gives a figure for its total estate of 18,485 hectares (45,674 acres), and also states that the Duchy's only Welsh landholding, the Ogham Estate, is 1,645 hectares (4,064 acres).

298   Sandringham Estate According to www.sandringhamestate.co.uk, the estate totals 8,000 hectares (19,768 acres). Sandringham's official history states a round 20,000 acres; see Walch, *Sandringham*.

298   Church Commissioners Acreage figure from Ordnance Survey blog, 'Church Commissioners digitise mapping database', https://www.ordnancesurvey.co.uk/business-and-government/case-studies/church-commissioners-digitise-mapping-database.html.

298   Diocesan Boards Data from Land Registry Corporate and Commercial spreadsheet, June 2015. I searched the dataset for all entries for Diocesan Boards of Finance and added up the totals.

298   National Trust Figure for England and Wales obtained through correspondence with the National Trust's data team, August 2018. (The National Trust's website gives various total acreages ranging between 618,000 to 635,265 acres.) Author's analysis of National Trust GIS maps gives a slightly lower figure of 589,748 acres, for unknown reasons. Figure for the National Trust's English acreage derived by analysing these GIS maps, though this may slightly underplay the area it owns.

298   RSPB Analysis of GIS maps at https://www.rspb.org.uk/our-work/conservation/conservation-and-sustainability/mapping-and-gis.

298   Woodland Trust https://www.woodlandtrust.org.uk/about-us/what-we-do/. states that they own 26,000 hectares (64,000 acres) across the UK. Author's correspondence with Woodland Trust's GIS manager elicited a figure of 34,241 acres owned in England.

298   foreshore and estuarial riverbeds Total area derived as follows: 342,420 acres of foreshore and estuary are owned by the Crown Estate, calculated by measuring GIS maps of Crown Estate land and subtracting the landward acreage (336,000 acres) from the total. The Duchy of Lancaster owns 88,958 acres: see https://www.duchyoflancaster.co.uk/properties-and-estates/. The Duchy of Cornwall owns 114,000 acres, according to Cahill, *Who Owns Britain*, p. 84.

IMAGE CREDITS

Arundel Castle

Kingsway bomb shelter and telephone exchange

Forestry Commission pine plantation

A grouse moor in the Peak District

Nicholas van Hoogstraten's unfinished empty mansion in Uckfield, Sussex

Protesters battle for Greenham Common (*Sahm Doherty/The LIFE Images Collection/Getty Images*)

'Private – No Public Right of Way' sign

Protest outside empty Mayfair mansion

St George's Hill, birthplace of the Diggers

Queen's Chapel of the Savoy

Landfill site at Tilbury, Essex

White Cliffs of Dover

INDEX